Moral Limit and Possibility in World Politics

At what point can we concede that the realities of world politics require that moral principles be compromised, and how do we know when a real ethical limit has been reached? This volume gathers leading constructivist scholars to explore the issue of moral limit and possibility in global political dilemmas. The contributors examine pressing ethical challenges such as sanctions, humanitarian intervention, torture, the self-determination of indigenous peoples, immigration, and the debate about international criminal tribunals and amnesties in cases of atrocity. Their analyses entail theoretical and empirical claims about the conditions of possibility and limits of moral change in world politics, therefore providing insightful leverage on the ethical question of 'what ought we to do?' This is a valuable contribution to the growing field of normative theory in International Relations and will appeal to scholars and advanced students of international ethics and political theory.

RICHARD M. PRICE is Associate Professor in the Department of Political Science at the University of British Columbia. He is the author of *The Chemical Weapons Taboo* (1997) and the co-editor (with Mark W. Zacher) of *The United Nations and Global Security* (2004).

Cambridge Studies in International Relations: 107

Moral Limit and Possibility in World Politics

Cambridge Studies in International Relations is a joint initiative of Cambridge University Press and the British International Studies Association (BISA). The series will include a wide range of material, from undergraduate textbooks and surveys to research-based monographs and collaborative volumes. The aim of the series is to publish the best new scholarship in International Studies from Europe, North America and the rest of the world.

Series list continues after index

Moral Limit and Possibility in World Politics

Edited by
RICHARD M. PRICE

CAMBRIDGE
UNIVERSITY PRESS

CAMBRIDGE UNIVERSITY PRESS
Cambridge, New York, Melbourne, Madrid, Cape Town, Singapore, São Paulo, Delhi

Cambridge University Press
The Edinburgh Building, Cambridge CB2 8RU, UK

Published in the United States of America by Cambridge University Press, New York

www.cambridge.org
Information on this title: www.cambridge.org/9780521716208

First published 2008

Printed in the United Kingdom at the University Press, Cambridge

A catalogue record for this publication is available from the British Library

ISBN 978-0-521-88816-5 hardback
ISBN 978-0-521-71620-8 paperback

Contents

Contributors

Martha Finnemore, Professor, Department of Political Science, George Washington University.

Amy Gurowitz, Lecturer, Political Science Department and Peace and Conflict Studies Program, University of California, Berkeley.

Jonathan Havercroft, Assistant Professor, Department of Political Science, University of Oklahoma.

Marc Lynch, Associate Professor, Department of Political Science and Elliott School of International Affairs, George Washington University.

Richard Price, Associate Professor, Department of Political Science, University of British Columbia.

Christian Reus-Smit, Professor and Head, Department of International Relations, Research School of Pacific and Asian Studies, Australia National University.

Bahar Rumelili, Assistant Professor, Department of International Relations, Koç University, Istanbul, Turkey.

Kathryn Sikkink, Regents Professor and McKnight Distinguished University Professor, Department of Political Science, University of Minnesota.

Ann Towns, Assistant Professor, Department of Political Science, University of Delaware.

Preface

The intellectual trajectory from which this book grew owes much to my interactions and collaborations with fellow students, instructors and colleagues, and my own students over the years. The question of ethics in world politics has been my abiding intellectual interest since my master's degree at Carleton University, where I wrote a thesis on the ethics of strategic defences. Fen Hampson, an International Relations scholar, and Tom Darby, a political theorist, generously humoured my immature probings into a subject that didn't really fit in either discipline as commonly practised, particularly when I ventured astray from traditional moral philosophy and into interpretive approaches to ethics, the philosophy of technology and other terrain that was quite exotic for a subject traditionally under the ambit of strategic studies. As I look back upon that project, I see this volume in many ways as the logical and (hopefully) more mature outcome of that earlier, less self-conscious and more inchoate attempt to bridge philosophy, ethics and politics. Peter Katzenstein, Henry Shue and Judith Reppy subsequently lent their essential support to an interpretive and structural approach to understanding moral norms in world politics for my Ph.D. dissertation, later a book, which examined the chemical weapons taboo from a genealogical perspective. The move from interpretivism to constructivism, and later from structure to agency, occupied the next stage of my intellectual agenda, one that was particularly and powerfully influenced by my interactions with my fellow students at Cornell, colleagues encountered through Peter Katzenstein's Culture of National Security project and elsewhere, and colleagues and students at the University of Minnesota. Representatives from all of those intellectual communities are in this volume, though many of course could not be included within an already substantial book, which John Haslam of Cambridge University Press has been so generous in accommodating. But the absence of those colleagues and others from this volume is not because I have learned any less from them: Dan Thomas, Nina Tannenwald, Beth Kier,

ix

Michael Barnett, Alex Wendt, Thomas Risse, Emanuel Adler, Ward Thomas, Neta Crawford, Helen Kinsella, Rado Dimitrov, Kristin Willey, Nick Wheeler and Jeff Checkel to name a few, with sincere apologies to any I have neglected to mention. Often it was the flash inspired by a single comment from one such colleague that sparked core ideas for my own pursuit. My years at the University of Minnesota were the perfect sounding board for engaging the strengths and shortcomings of constructivism and critical theory in thinking about ethics, given the intellects of Kathryn Sikkink and Bud Duvall and the graduate students who sometimes felt pushed or pulled between mainstream International Relations, constructivism and critical theory, but who always came out the better because of it. This project grew directly out of those interactions, since I became convinced that the current incarnations of neither constructivism nor critical theory to date had satisfactorily responded to the pressing prescriptive questions of ethics. Namely, just what should we do? What is ethically justifiable if we are obviously not in a position to attain our highest ideals, which may spring from our most clever critiques of what others have actually been able to accomplish in the world? Both traditions of course have enormous potential to contribute in a more satisfactory and direct way to how we think about and answer ethical challenges in world politics, and this volume is a first attempt to lay out an architecture of what such a synthesis might entail. It is a genuinely collaborative book, to the extent that so many of the formulations or even precise sentences and paragraphs appearing in any given chapter may have come from another participant in the project that we decided to dispense with the courtesy of acknowledged sources with a footnoted 'thanks to so and so for this formulation' and instead issue this blanket acknowledgement that the individual chapters themselves typically bear no small imprint of the other collaborators.

This volume was supported by a Social Sciences and Humanities Research Council of Canada Aid to Research Workshops and Conferences in Canada grant, financial and administrative support from the Center of International Relations at the Liu Institute at the University of British Columbia, and matching financial support from the Department of Political Science, Faculty of Arts, and Vice President Research, all of the University of British Columbia. I am most grateful for the efficient research assistance of Alana Tiemessen and Scott Watson.

Sincere thanks to the reviewers of this volume, as engaging with their generous and challenging comments considerably improved this book. Thanks for the same reason to the participants at meetings where this project was presented – the University of Minnesota, University of Chicago, the Australian National University, the University of British Columbia, the University of Queensland, and the American Political Science Association Annual Meeting in Philadelphia.

Thanks to Jesse and Annelise for allowing pops/daddy to kick you off the computer so many times with such good cheer, to Lisa for putting up with the late nights spent at the keyboard, and to Nova for being such a good companion by my side as I typed.

Vancouver
May 18, 2007

1 | Moral limit and possibility in world politics

RICHARD PRICE

Introduction

At what point, if any, is one to reasonably concede that the 'realities' of world politics require compromise from cherished principles or moral ends, and that what has been achieved is ethically justified? How do we really know we have reached an ethical limit when we see one, or fallen short in ways that deserve the withholding of moral praise? Less abstractly, how might we seek to reconcile the cherished freedoms of liberal democracy with restrictions on immigration? Can war legitimately be waged in defence of human rights, and override competing moral claims to self-determination? Can the perpetuation of slaughter be risked by refusing amnesties to perpetrators of atrocities in order to enforce international criminal law? Is there any way to ethically navigate moral dilemmas such as the above, ones that seem to require choices between cosmopolitanism and communitarianism, or consequentialism and deontology, or the oft-competing demands between procedural and substantive justice?

As the history of ethics and international political theory attest, these are difficult enough questions for which to hope for some answer, not the least given traditions of thought like realism that deny the very existence of developments we could call ethically progressive change in world politics in the first place. But it becomes even more difficult still if a research programme that has itself led the charge in empirically documenting putative moral progress inherently problematises the very grounds upon which prima facie judgements of moral good are often made. How does one even approach the task of formulating robust answers to questions of ethics that can respond to charges of subjectivism and relativism when coming out of an intellectual tradition that suggests all such judgements and the complexes of intersubjective meanings that make them possible are themselves but time- and culture-bound constructions? Moreover, what if, due to the critical theoretical

1

insights underpinning social constructivism, constructivist analyses lead us to identify that what appear prima facie to be progressive initiatives are themselves revealed to come at the price of concomitant regress in other areas? What if, for instance, the price of extending a peaceful security community of democratic states is the 'othering' of outsiders? Or if domestic progress on gender issues was predicated upon political bargains that entailed setbacks in progressive immigration policy? What if transnational civil society's successful influence curtailing the use of landmines is bought at the price of simultaneously strengthening the surveillance and coercive powers of the state? Or if the bargains to establish an International Criminal Court (ICC) guard crucial elements of the prerogative of states as it forwards a paradigm of human security? How do we evaluate – and justify to victims and their families – amnesties given to perpetrators of atrocities, secured in order to stop ongoing slaughter? Or could they later not be rescinded in the name of justice?

Are there theoretical responses that can help us navigate through such ethical challenges that confront us in contemporary world politics? Talk of progress has long been the purview of liberal and critical theories of International Relations (IR), whose champions in different ways have laid claim to the moral high ground in pointing the ways to positive moral change. And yet both have been the targets of persistent charges of utopianism. Recent constructivist scholarship on the role of norms in international relations, I have argued elsewhere, has responded convincingly to such charges with careful empirical research that demonstrates the possibilities of moral change in world politics.[1] But while it has thus opened up convincing space for taking seriously the role of moral change in the study and practice of international relations, this literature for the most part has not offered its own normative or prescriptive defences of particular changes as good – such positions are often not explicitly articulated let alone rigorously defended.[2] Upon what basis are accounts of moral change, which are presumed to be desirable, to be accepted as in fact progressive? While the challenge of having to offer a convincing defence of the ethical desirability of norms like the abolition

---

[1] Richard Price, 'Transnational Civil Society and Advocacy in World Politics', *World Politics* 55:4 (2003), 579–606.

[2] See Nicholas Wheeler for a conspicuous exception: *Saving Strangers: Humanitarian Intervention in International Society* (Oxford: Oxford University Press, 2000).

of slavery or torture would not exactly keep too many constructivist scholars up at night, constructivist analyses do render many other cases potentially problematic as intimated above. Moreover, it is hardly the case that all self-designated constructivists agree on what is ethically right in a given situation, which problematises empirical claims of progressive change in world politics. Not all change is necessarily morally 'good', and neither is all behaviour that conforms with the international community's existing moral standards necessarily morally laudable – so what are the standards for evaluation, an externally derived set of moral standards, or ones dependent upon existing moral norms which constructivists take seriously as structuring the very ethical standards that are available to us to invoke for judgement? Rather than attempting to impose a singular definition for all the discipline of what counts as moral progress here in the introduction, the authors in this volume are rather inveighed to defend their usages of 'good' and 'progress' by being explicit concerning what they view as moral progress and from where it is derived, including to be as self-conscious as possible about how our/their own particular context may shape those very standards that they seek to employ. For the most part, the contributions of this volume share a humanitarian, cosmopolitan vein, though the relationship between constructivism and substantive theories of international relations is engaged in sections below and directly in the concluding chapter.

The evolution of criticisms of constructivist scholarship as well points to normative theorising as a next stage of the constructivist agenda. Much constructivist work was itself a response to scepticism that moral norms matter in world politics. While a few critics still seek to challenge that empirical claim, in the face of empirical scholarship demonstrating the explanatory value of moral norms, the centre of the debate moved to a challenge of how to explain why some norms matter in some places and not others,[3] and responses to that challenge have occupied much of the norms literature in recent years. The remaining avenue to challenge scholarship which touts moral change in world politics is that this agenda (and constructivism generally) has been beset by a normative bias in favour of 'good' norms that worked. While initially couched in

---

[3] Jeffrey Checkel, 'The Constructivist Turn in International Relations Theory', *World Politics* 50:2 (1998), 324–348.

methodological terms,[4] this challenge itself is only coherent with its own normative premise (namely, of what counts as 'good'). In order to respond to this criticism, scholars ultimately must turn to some form of normative defence, and how constructivism itself might help us to do so in a rigorous way is a central challenge taken up by this volume. To be sure, this challenge goes both ways: critics who make such charges can only make them intelligible on the basis of their own normative defences of what qualifies as good or undesirable norms, else the critique is simply incoherent. This has put the moral question front and centre, among additional reasons argued by Christian Reus-Smit in the next chapter. Not surprisingly, the more that constructivism has addressed the empirical, theoretical and methodological challenges of its critics, the more the sceptical critique has taken on an explicitly normative cast. In response to the plethora of scholarly works demonstrating the importance of norms and the role of transnational advocacy networks in world politics for such developments as the Landmines Convention, the rise of humanitarian intervention, and milestones in international criminal law including tribunals and the ICC, critics increasingly have been responding along the line that they simply don't agree that such norms are 'good'.[5] For all of these reasons, normative theorising is inescapable in making claims about possibilities of moral change in world politics, and thus central to practice and intellectual discourse in International Relations, even as professionally it has not been accorded pride of place in the American academy of International Relations which has been dominated by explanatory agendas that largely exclude normative theorising as the terrain of 'political theory', 'normative theory' or philosophy.[6]

[4] Paul Kowert and Jeffrey Legro, 'Norms, Identity and their Limits'. In Peter Katzenstein (ed.), *The Culture of National Security: Norms and Identity in World Politics* (New York, NY: Columbia University Press, 1996), 451–497.

[5] See, e.g., Kenneth Anderson, 'The Ottawa Convention Banning Landmines, the Role of International Non-Governmental Organizations, and the Idea of International Civil Society', *European Journal of International Relations* 11:1 (2000), 91–120.

[6] Surveying what are widely regarded as the top three journals in International Relations in North America – *International Organization, International Security* and *World Politics* – over the period 1990–2006, at most four articles could be identified that are arguably characterised as engaging in normative as opposed to primarily explanatory analysis. In contrast, International Relations scholarship in the UK has accorded a much more prominent place to normative theorising. Reus-Smit notes in his chapter, however, the normative turn in the work of Robert Keohane, one of the most prominent positive scholars of American International Relations.

While not expressed precisely in the above terms, the lack of pre-scriptive theorising issuing from the constructivist movement in the field of International Relations has not gone unnoticed in the literature. Mervyn Frost in particular has laid an important challenge in noting that critical and sociological approaches in International Relations have for the most part eschewed explicit ethical theorising in favour of descriptivism and explanation. As he puts it:

> the task of IR theory according to constitutive theorists is to reveal our global international social order to be a human construct within which are embedded certain values chosen by us and to show how this construct benefits some and oppresses others. This seems to be pre-eminently an exercise in ethical evaluation. It would seem to be self-evident that scholars (be they critical theorists, post-modern theorists, feminist IR scholars, constructivists, or structuration theorists) involved in such evaluative exercise must engage in serious ethical argument – argument about what is to count as oppression (as opposed to liberation), about what is to count as an emancipatory practice (as opposed to an enslaving one), about what would be fair in international relations, what just, and so on. However, in practice, constitutive theorists have done very little of this kind of theorizing. They do not for the most part tackle the question 'What would it be ethical to do in the circumstances?'[7]

Indeed, this is an astute observation and fair charge insofar as a chief motivation of some such constructivist work (at least I can speak for my own) precisely has been to open up space for moral progress in world politics by empirically documenting successes that give lie to the scep-tical position that the pursuit of moral progress in world politics is folly. That humanity is not simply and always condemned to the raw exercise of brute power is no small finding, since the consequences are of course unspeakably dire in an era of nuclear and other weapons of mass destruction if the sceptical thesis were correct. Nonetheless, this leaves unanswered – from constructivists, as of yet – the above challenge of normative defences of change in world politics, at least on Frost's terms, which are those of the traditions of ethical theory.

[7] Mervyn Frost, 'A Turn Not Taken: Ethics in IR at the Millennium', *Review of International Studies* 24 (1998), 127. As Neta Crawford has also noted, 'constructivists have little to say about what to do'. *Argument and Change in World Politics* (Cambridge: Cambridge University Press, 2002), 427.

Seen from the perspective of constructivists themselves, to take up this challenge may not simply translate into a charge for constructivists or others to engage in recognisably moral theorising of the type that might bring a Michael Walzer, Charles Beitz, Henry Shue or Peter Singer to mind. Indeed, a reasonable response could be that it is not to be expected that empirically oriented researchers should or even could become adequately accomplished moral philosophers. Rather, the challenge is whether constructivism has anything distinctive and valuable to offer in terms of normative theorising, in terms of the prescriptive dimension of political thought and practice, and thus to the practice of making decisions and judgements in world politics. That is to say, what does constructivism contribute to the prescriptive question posed for so long by political theorists, one so central to all politics: how are we to act? What exactly are the theoretical and practical implications of this constructivist opening up of moral space? Does constructivism itself have anything to offer towards normative theorising that can help resolve some of the evaluative dilemmas noted at the outset, and thus contribute in some capacity as moral guides to action? Or is its primary contribution simply to open a wider door for well-established ethical theories like utilitarianism, rights-based or deontological theories and the like to show their faces more fully and frequently in the scholarly field of International Relations, without challenging, modifying or contributing to those theories? What would constructivist contributions to normative theorising look like, if one were to integrate the insights of constructivism regarding the possibilities and limits of moral change? What advantages could it bring to existing normative theories and practice? In the next chapter, Christian Reus-Smit deals with some of these issues in the wider context of the purposes of International Relations scholarship and the development of the discipline, as well as making the case for a broader conception of ethics than the dominant mode of the deduction of principles. For now, it will suffice to state that the premise of this volume is that research programmes which have shown how moral norms arise and have an impact on world politics are well placed to help us answer the ethical question of 'what we should do'. *Since social constructivist analyses of the development and effects of moral norms entail theoretical and empirical claims about the conditions of possibility and limits of moral change in world politics, that agenda should provide insightful leverage on the ethical question of 'what to do' insofar as one accepts that a responsible answer depends not just on what one judges as right in the abstract, but also on what one may have some reasonable expectation of working, and thus prescribing as a course of action or judgement.*[8] That is, without denying altogether the essential role of idealism, an understanding of the limits and possibilities of moral change should provide additional rigorous grounds for ethics, particularly insofar as I argue in what follows that normative theory and ethical prescriptions cannot completely eschew their own empirical assumptions even as they rarely develop them as systematically as has constructivism. In this chapter I thus outline six major contributions of constructivism for theorising moral limit and possibility and addressing global ethical dilemmas that provide the framework for the substantive chapters which follow. They include: (1) attention to the relation between the ethical and empirical, including providing a way to help adjudicate the empirical bases of ethical positions; (2) recognition of the empirical importance of the debate between rationalist and constructivist accounts of agency and their relevance for normative theorising; which include (3) the identification of different kinds of hypocritical political practice which in turn imply different ethical evaluations of hypocrisy; (4) the illumination of neglected dimensions for ethics, including the identification of different kinds of dilemmas arising from a focus on the constitutive effects of norms; (5) the relevance of relations of co-constitution for thinking through issues of complicity and cooptation; and (6) a theoretical account of morality that avoids the tendency of philosophical approaches to ethics to sidestep questions of power, without falling prey to the shortcomings of post-structuralist ethics that do highlight power. Before outlining those contributions, I canvass how some of the major relevant works in the existing normative literature in International Relations have dealt with these issues in order to make readily apparent the value-added of constructivism, focusing in particular upon a few key recent works in contemporary critical and constitutive normative theory since they have addressed questions most directly similar to those posed here.

---

[8] Cognisant of the apparent contrast with Kant's criticism of what he termed the naturalist fallacy – that the 'ought' hinges upon the 'is' – I would note that Kant himself suggested that the demands of ethics stand independent of empirical likelihood but not to the point where ethics demands what is demonstrably impossible to fulfil. The position here seeks to excavate constructivism for help to answer the question of just how we know when we can say we've reached such conditions of possibility and impossibility.

Critical theory and normative theorizing in International Relations

Critical theory is a tradition in International Relations that has brought to the fore questions revolving around moral change and its limits. In response to the persistent charges of the utopianism of the critical theory tradition, Robert Cox notably acknowledged that while critical theory necessarily contains an element of utopianism, it is constrained by its sociological understanding of historical processes. As he argued:

> Critical theory allows for a normative choice in favour of a social and political order different from the prevailing order, but it limits the range of choice to alternative orders which are feasible transformations of the existing world. A principal objective of critical theory, therefore, is to clarify this range of possible alternatives. Critical theory thus contains an element of utopianism in the sense that it can represent a coherent picture of an alternative order, but its utopianism is constrained by its comprehension of historical processes. It must reject improbable alternatives just as it rejects the permanency of the existing order.[9]

Little concrete has been forthcoming, however, concerning how one would construct such a theoretical project or what it would look like, specifically in the sense of how one could tell a political and ethical possibility from an impossibility. Until recently, few explicit clues had been provided by critical International Relations theorists as to how to make these imperatives of the desirable and the possible mesh. Indeed, prominent critical theorists themselves have often been explicit that they do not seek to provide 'practical' ethics and solutions to substantive moral problems as that would be anathema to the critical theoretical project.[10] But how then would we know a justifiable ethical limit to change when we saw one, or recognise a possibility to be realised? How do we justify such limits and possibilities? This has been a particularly acute problem for critical theory, I would argue, since a number of

---

[9] Robert Cox, 'Social Forces, States, and World Orders: Beyond International Relations Theory'. In Robert Keohane (ed.), *Neorealism and its Critics* (New York, NY: Columbia University Press, 1986), 210.

[10] For a sympathetic overview of critical theory's contributions to ethics that provides a critical challenge to its reluctance to 'do ethics' in the applied sense, see Robyn Eckersley, 'The Ethics of Critical Theory'. In Duncan Snidal and Christian Reus-Smit (eds.), *Oxford Handbook of International Relations* (forthcoming).

recent initiatives like the landmines campaign of the 1990s that would prima facie appear to epitomise a morally progressive critical social movement were subjected to condemnation from some critically minded scholars in conversations within and outside the academy. This was most surprising not only to this scholar, nurtured in the varieties of critical theory, but perfectly bewildering to at least one government official deeply and very importantly involved in the campaign, and who himself had a critical IR theory background and self-identified with the 'progressive/critical' side of the political and academic spectrum. Similar encounters greeted the establishment of criminal tribunals for Yugoslavia and Rwanda (if here, then why not there?), and agreement on the International Criminal Court, championed by some as a great and unexpected victory for moral progress in world politics, chastised by others as merely a shield for great power guilt over having not acted to prevent genocide and ethnic cleansing in the first place. What actually existing or accomplished initiative, one might wonder, could possibly live up to the standards issuing from critical theory? Or is it indeed in a deep sense the essence of critical theory to provide moving and perhaps impossible standards, else the *raison d'être* of the critical project itself collapse? And what would we conclude of such a function of critical theory if it is so?

In the most forthright and systematic attempt to address some of these problems besetting critical theory, Andrew Linklater, in his magisterial work *The Transformation of Political Community*, has argued that the task of critical theory consists of a threefold agenda of ethics, sociology and praxeology. For Linklater, normative and sociological advances are incomplete without some reflection on practical possibilities. Boiled down to basic distinctions, his 'sociology' consists of the identification or explanation of the already immanent; his 'ethical' is the formulation of the not already immanent; and his 'praxeological' is guidance of how to realise the immanent. Concerning the last, he explains that 'praxeology is concerned with reflecting on the moral resources within existing social arrangements which political actors can harness for radical purposes'.[11] Linklater's praxeology seems to consist of teasing out the full implications of principles that have been but partly realised; that is, in identifying the moral capacity of already

---

[11] Andrew Linklater, *The Transformation of Political Community: Ethical Foundations of the Post-Westphalian Era* (Columbia, SC: University of South Carolina Press, 1998), 5.

existing potentials. His method, then, of arriving at the praxeological would seem to consist of identifying logical potentials of ideas immanent in society and following their logic. His procedure here, applied to developments such as how the language of citizenship provided its own dialectical development, does give us some leverage on the inherent power of ideas.

Schematically, Linklater's threefold typology of the critical project is a most fruitful architecture and impressive accomplishment. But this formulation does not escape long-standing suspicions of teleology in progressivist theories: how do we know when something is 'already immanent'? Linklater's formulation does not give us much insight into limits – there are plenty of contradictory and unrealised good ideals out there, others subject to backsliding, and so on. Neither does Linklater's account contain a theory of agency, nor of power. Thus it does not yet, in the final analysis, provide a clear bridge between the ethical and the immanent: how does the transition from the former to the latter occur? Despite his otherwise fruitful agenda, Linklater's formulation does not give us much of a sense of how these potentials are to be realised other than a progressivist mechanism of assumed evolution, thus undercutting this otherwise promising contribution to ethical theory when twinned with the absence of a sustained empirical analysis that could carry the argument.

The problem of power in turn presents difficulties for Linklater's ethics. Linklater's dialogic ethic requires that all participants 'stand back from authority structures and group loyalties' in which they are embedded, to willingly treat all other human subjects as equals, and to engage in dialogue problematising practices of privilege and subordination.[12] This move parallels in an important respect the move critical theorists themselves (among others) have found so implausible in Rawls' veil of ignorance, the thought experiment whereby the most reasonable responses to ethics are to be sought in the 'original position' whereby agents hypothesise what answers they would come up with if they did not know who they were, where they were from and what privileges of wealth and power they possessed. Just as the communitarian critique would have it, the procedural dimension of the ethic that Linklater proposes is strikingly at odds with the constructivist ontology underpinning most contemporary critical theory, including Linklater's

---

[12] Ibid. 87, 91.

own, which sees every agent and every moral position as unavoidably embedded in a historical and cultural context.

Linklater himself is of course not unaware of this potential paradox, disclosing that 'individuals cannot escape the moral language embedded in the social conventions which have previously constituted them as moral subjects ... [therefore] absolute foundations for the assessment of the merits of different cultures or historical epochs will necessarily elude them'.[13] A better expression of the social constructivist ontological position would be difficult to find. It does, however, seem deeply at odds with an ethic that requires what for the constructivist would seem to be the impossible. Namely, how to square the ethical shedding of the effects of power and identity inherent in actors necessarily being embedded in time and society and politics and culture, with an ontology whose premise is that such a move is in practice, if not intellectually, impossible?

The problem for Linklater's critical theory then, is that the more deeply true the critical ontological diagnosis of the human condition – the more socially constructed we are, the more language constructs our very agency – the less able we could ever hope to extract ourselves from the subtleties of its clutches, imbued as they always are with the tendrils of power relations. As an ethical ideal to strive for in the sense of a procedural rather than substantive ethic, this author finds much that is appealing indeed about discourse ethics; yet, it remains frustratingly elusive even on critical theorists' own ontological terms.

Here constructivist research methods can make a contribution to ethics when coupled with the self-reflexive epistemological underpinnings characteristic of many constructivists. If interventions in Kosovo or Iraq, for example, presented dilemmas for Western policy makers or scholars, they did so only for those with cosmopolitan sensibilities. But rather than simply ordain an ethical evaluation from a perspective one might defend on deontological or utilitarian grounds, constructivism would additionally encourage the empirical embodiment of a dialogic ethic to open up and buttress the grounds of such assessments. That is, as against exercises in ratiocination like Kant's categorical imperative or Rawls' thought experiment of the original position, communicative ethics of the sort championed by Habermas call for procedures of consensus through deliberation without coercion among all concerned

---

[13] Ibid. 64.

as the most promising path for justice. Some scholars, most notably those who have engaged in what has been called the 'ZIB debate',[14] have thus sought to investigate empirically the extent to which such practices are actually approximated in world politics. Thomas Risse has importantly responded to the empirical critique of idealism of the communicative action model – namely, the actual existence of situations characterised by actors who recognise each other as equals engaged in truth seeking towards consensus – by persuasively contending that 'the ideal speech situation is not meant as a statement about the empirical world or – even worse – some utopian ideal; instead it constitutes primarily a counterfactual presupposition' to be analysed for its influence in any given situation against other forms of action such as bargaining (as strategic action) and rhetoric which themselves are ideal types rarely uncontaminated by the other forms of action.[15] Risse concedes that his 'counterarguments to various objections raised against the possibility of an "ideal speech situation" in international affairs only help to some extent. The Habermasian condition of "equal access" to the discourse, for example, is simply not met in world politics'. Yet in empirical terms he is surely right that 'The real issue then is not whether power relations are absent in a discourse, but to what extent they can explain the argumentative outcome'.[16]

Deitelhoff and Müller for their part argue that while their systematic research attempt to discover instances of authentic persuasion suggests that it does occur in world politics, the project was 'unable to methodologically and empirically prove this assumption: it is a theoretical paradise that is empirically lost!'[17] Deitelhoff and Müller argue that this is so because one cannot adequately prove methodologically 'whether it was the better argument that carried the day, or other factors such as material power'.[18] While they thus abandoned the search for actor orientations (were actors really truth-seeking in the Habermasian sense or instrumentalist?), one could note that in the absence of convening or finding such an actual procedural ethic via the discovery of

---

[14] For the journal *Zeitschrift für Internationale Beziehungen*.
[15] Thomas Risse, '"Let's Argue!": Communicative Action in World Politics', *International Organization* 51 (2000), 17–18.
[16] Ibid. 18.
[17] Nicole Deitelhoff and Harald Müller, 'Theoretical Paradise – Empirically Lost? Arguing with Habermas', *Review of International Studies* 31 (2005), 177.
[18] Ibid.

intentions, other alternatives might be useful. For example, scholars could examine a dilemma empirically and ask, say in the case of an intervention: how did it look not just from the perspective of potential intervenors, which is the common ethical referent for debates over Kosovo, for example, but how did it look from the perspective of those who were the targets of outside intervention, and indeed all concerned? What is the position of the marginalised and those of diverse political theoretical persuasions in any given dilemma? How broadly acceptable are given responses to dilemmas? Constructivist research methods, as Deitelhoff and Müller show, can provide an empirical complement and indeed analogue to dialogical ethical theory; in this volume several authors take a related tack by pointing to an assessment of how the actual range of political possibilities are arrayed. As argued by Kathryn Sikkink in this volume, for example, an ethic upholding human rights norms is powerful precisely because such a moral position is not merely the ethical ideal of thinkers of a particular persuasion. Rather, human rights have been produced as consequential social facts through intensive negotiation (not to mention practice) among the vast majority of the world's states and numerous non-state actors for decades, finding champions among the privileged and marginalised alike. Jonathan Havercroft raises the dilemmas of indigenous governance as they appear not just to Western academics but to indigenous peoples themselves, which serves to identify how they inform or fail to inform dominant responses to question of indigenous self-determination. He argues that empirical examination reveals there are resources in indigenous traditions, contemporary international law and the political theory and practices underpinning modern sovereign states that can serve as common ground for just resolutions of the question of self-determination. These issues takes us to the first key contribution of constructivism to normative theorising, which is its explicit and particular attention to the relation between the empirical and the ethical.

The relation of the empirical to the ethical

Drawing more from continental traditions of ethics, Mervyn Frost has made perhaps the most sustained case to develop an ethical theory of world politics via working through the relationship between the normative and empirical in constructing a constitutive theory of international relations, which of course by the very name would seem to offer a project most compatible with a constructivist contribution to normative theorising. In his important book, Frost deftly shows how any explanation of international relations inescapably involves substantive normative theory.[19] He convincingly illustrates how even a preliminary description of, let alone explanation for, situations such as the conflict in the former Yugoslavia requires rather sophisticated normative judgements by social scientists, such as what counts as a national liberation struggle as opposed to terrorists, or a protection racket run by a warlord. Frost's main criticism of the mainstream of International Relations, and even much of critical theory, is that it eschews ethical theorising, and presupposes the ability to provide objectively correct descriptions or explanations even as Frost argues such exercises cannot escape normative theorising in the process. This is a persuasive argument in the end, even if his own analysis of critical and post-modern theory in the book is too underdeveloped to bear the full weight of all his charges.

However plausible Frost's case for the inevitability of normative theory for even empirical claims in International Relations, Frost's own constitutive theory, in turn, ultimately and ironically rises or falls depending upon the plausibility of his own *empirical* claims about the existence and content of what he terms 'settled' international norms that constitute the terrain of ethical possibility. To criticise realism Frost argues that no account of international relations is coherent without acknowledging the role of rules and norms, and that might and right 'are not conceptually and practically distinct in the way they need to be' to maintain the position that might prevails over right insofar as 'power always exists within a practice which is partially constituted by certain normative ideas'.[20] This critique of amoralism thus requires Frost to identify the constitutive social norms of world politics; Frost, however, does not himself engage in a lengthy empirical analysis and defence of those constitutive norms of the international system – as have constructivists, pitting them directly against alternative explanations – nor does he draw upon such work to robustly buttress his claims. Rather he for the most part simply posits them, confident it would seem that they are uncontroversial enough as to be unlikely to provide the resources to

---

[19] Mervyn Frost, *Ethics in International Relations: A Constitutive Theory* (Cambridge: Cambridge University Press, 1996), 35–39.
[20] Ibid. 60, 62–63.

undo his constitutive theory. To be fair, such an analysis would take him too far afield from his most central purposes, and thus is asking much within the single volume just as it may be asking too much to ask constructivists to provide ethical defences of the norms they document. And yet, the lack of adequate empirical defence of the contested nature of what he takes to be the empirical ground leaves his theory with much more of a conservative flavour than clearly is his intent. At this level, this is not an insuperable difficulty for Frost's position in my view, insofar as his theory is analytically neutral in principle to dominant forms of political community, thus leaving room for the rise of alternative forms and institutions other than the state. More importantly, however, the result in the end is that it does not give us much leverage in analysing the limits or possibilities of moral change. Consider, in particular, how Frost's theory and its applications might have looked had he systematically utilised Linklater's threefold agenda of critical theory to analyse immanent possibilities in the international system, and incorporated the findings of constructivist empirical research to underscore the changes in state sovereignty, the state system and its regulative and constitutive norms. Failing to do so weakens his analysis of central moral dilemmas such as that involved in his case study on intervention in Bosnia. Here he contended that 'From a moral point of view the task of outsiders in a dispute like the Bosnian one is to provide a dynamic framework within which the people may constitute themselves as citizens in a state or states'.[21] While he is probably wise indeed in arguing that at the end of the day the necessary relationships in such situations are best established by the actors themselves, he skirts the central ethical question that faced the international community to the point of begging it: what if outside force, indeed war, is judged to be needed to establish the 'framework conditions within which the institutions of reciprocal recognition may grow'?[22] Similarly, while Frost provides incisive refinements on our understanding of the importance of the practice of state recognition given his Hegelian theory of mutual recognition, he does not fully answer the pressing normative question that regularly faces politicians squarely in the face: what *should* be the criteria in terms of which states recognise one another? Are contemporary practices adequate? Must sovereignty change? Can it? How would we reach such assessment in

---

[21] Ibid. 209.   [22] Ibid. 211.

the absence of the help of sustained analysis of changes in the practice of sovereignty such as constructivism has engaged in and debated explicitly with other approaches?[23]

In short, while empirical research and International Relations theory may not be able to escape normative theorising, neither, I would contend, can normative theorising escape some degree of empirical descriptivism altogether – a side of the equation that Frost and many other works of normative IR theory don't systematically examine, thus limiting normative IR theory from offering all it otherwise could for the questions that animate this project about moral limit and possibility. This leaves normative IR theories like Frost's (and many others which make parallel moves) in a bind. Acceptance of Frost's constitutive theory requires that one agrees with the descriptive list of norms he proposes as 'settled' norms of world politics, which in turn is even less guaranteed on Frost's own terms since in Frost's view description depends upon the normative premises the analyst brings to the table. Frost argues that 'there is no objective way of choosing between paradigms'.[24] His invocation of a strong interpretivist epistemology obscures the degree to which normative claims do in fact depend in various ways upon empirical assumptions or claims about the world nonetheless, even if they cannot be established as objectively true in a positivist sense. Yet, no criteria are spelt out to defend those empirical elements – they are either arbitrary or simply reduced to purely ethical claims. Thus Frost's ethical theory is doubly weakened by not drawing upon empirical work to give a convincing account of his 'settled norms' – they are simply posited. In some respects it is a most sensible and indeed clever positing to be sure – by running everything through the state Frost insulates his position from the most obvious line of attack from realism for one, a tack Wendt has notably taken in his version of social constructivism.[25] Charles Beitz, in contrast, attempts to harness the ontological grounds of interdependence (as opposed to Frost's statism) as grounds for a cosmopolitan theory, to cite but one

[23] On the changing nature of sovereignty and international systems, see Christian Reus-Smit, *The Moral Purpose of the State* (Princeton, NJ: Princeton University Press, 1999).
[24] Frost, *Ethics*, 24.
[25] Alexander Wendt, *Social Theory of International Politics* (Cambridge: Cambridge University Press, 2000).

of a large number of alternative international ethical positions under-pinned by rival empirical grounds.[26]

Similarly, Steven Lee, in his profound tome dissecting our moral condition in the nuclear era and prescribing our moral choices with regard to nuclear weapons, has argued for the analytic utility and practical/ethical importance of a principle of 'tolerable divergence'.[27] By this he means that what moral norms prescribe should not diverge too greatly from what prudential norms prescribe, an eminently plausible formulation. Lee's normative theory revolves around the empirical claim that moral norms are unlikely to survive if adherence to them requires too great a sacrifice of prudential ends. This is exactly the kind of claim where the constructivist project of accounting for the existence, origins and durability of international norms is essential.

It is here, then, where the kind of empirical validation practised by constructivists could help adjudicate between ethical accounts, at least forestalling premature descent into an endless relativist circle of inter-pretation without hope of discrimination.[28] Constructivist scholars have often made claims about the (contingent) validity of interpreta-tions or explanations with a relative rather than absolute epistemologi-cal practice, established in good part by demonstrating the inadequacy of alternative accounts. Constructivist scholarship has thereby provided us with ways to unpack the dichotomy between relativism and positi-vism, establishing an epistemological halfway house by way of the practice of thoroughly adjudicating between alternative accounts to remove error where accounts in fact directly compete with one another (that is, in cases where the question is the same and both answers cannot be correct at the same time), or showing how putative rival explanations may in fact complement one another for a more holistic account. This produces a measure of plausibility to the empirical claims implicit in ethical theorising at least one degree removed from an unestablished

---

[26] Charles Beitz, *Political Theory and International Relations* (Princeton, NJ: Princeton University Press, 1999).

[27] Steven Lee, *Morality, Prudence and Nuclear Weapons* (Cambridge: Cambridge University Press, 1993), 21.

[28] For a complementary analysis which seeks to outline how to evaluate normative arguments by standard social science methods such as ability to explain or predict, see Jack Snyder, '"Is" and "Ought": Evaluating Empirical Aspects of Normative Research'. In Colin Elman and Miriam Fendius Elman (eds.), *Progress in International Relations Theory: Appraising the Field* (Cambridge, MA: MIT Press, 2003), 349–377.

basis of incommensurable ethics – and scholarship as pure politics – and instead offers contingent claims that can at least identify errors if not establish timeless objective truths. The contention here is that it is these kinds of close empirical analyses and the epistemological status of the claims characteristic of constructivist approaches to International Relations that can fill in some of the gaps in the otherwise fruitful beginnings by scholars such as Frost, Linklater and Lee in charting out assessments of moral limit and possibility in world politics, particularly for those interested in putting truth ahead of politics, as far as one is able, rather than the reverse. In addition to its other proclaimed bridge-building capacities, then, constructivism offers a way to think through the normative–empirical gap, thereby offering an avenue for grounding ethical claims in an additionally rigorous way.[29]

The method of closely weighing alternatives against one another, characteristic of many constructivist accounts, points as well to the importance of alternatives that did not happen when considering moral possibility. This intimate relation between empirical explanation and normative possibility thus counsels close attention not just to the empirical grounds underpinning normative positions, but specifically to the counterfactual grounds invoked or, more often, implied but not explicitly established, in claims about possibility. Such considerations are engaged throughout the chapters of this volume, with Sikkink's chapter in particular revolving around a careful identification of the different kinds of counterfactuals that often underlie ethical claims and a systematic dissection of their implications.

This study is not the first to proclaim the need to attend to empirical realities and ethical ideals in formulating a viable ethics for acute dilemmas in world politics. To cite but one recent contribution, Matthew J. Gibney, in his splendidly careful *The Ethics and Politics of Asylum*, seeks to avoid the 'practical irrelevance' that follows from ignoring the legitimate difficulties and dilemmas politicians face; thus, his 'aim is to derive prescriptions for state action that emerge from a process of reasoning in which the results of ethical theorizing are modified by an empirical account of the possibilities actually available

---

[29] On constructivism's bridge-building capacities see Emanuel Adler, 'Seizing the Middle Ground: Constructivism in World Politics', *European Journal of International Relations* 3:3 (1997), 319–363.

to states'.[30] This project shares this spirit entirely, though seeks to lay out more systematically elements of a practical ethic identified by constructivism that need to be considered, such as the constitutive effects of discourse and policy upon immigrants, as examined by Towns and Gurowitz. Moreover, as we are reminded above, constructivist theorising reminds us that it isn't simply a case of deriving ideal normative theory then subjecting it to the restraints of empirical reality, as if either could be done in isolation from the other rather than the two being integrally related as will be developed in this volume. Christian Reus-Smit dissects this relation in greater detail in his chapter which follows, which further paves the way for the substantive analyses that follow.

Before proceeding, a few words on terminology may be in order. Mindful of the traditions and indeed vociferous debates distinguishing between the terms ethics, morality and normative, these terms are employed relatively interchangeably, and simply, really, all to denote a wrestling with the prescriptive question regarding right conduct: what ought we to do? In deciding what is the right thing to do, we typically seek to enlist the aid of answers to supporting questions, such as 'can we do it?', and 'how do we know?', and the spirit of this project is to include explicitly such components as essential parts of the terrain of 'what is right'. The relation of these considerations and thus the contributions of various traditions of scholarship for global ethics are carefully dissected at much more length in Christian Reus-Smit's chapter that follows this introduction.

By constructivism I refer to a tradition of social and political thought that sees the world as not just consisting of material forces but of ideational social phenomena through which we interpret the material and construct our societies. Constructivism emphasises that such ideas are not just individually held, but occur in the form of intersubjective structures that form the broader social context out of which individual ideas emerge; thus, ideas and communities can be studied as social facts, as against the individualist ontology of rationalist theories. Within the subfield of International Relations in the discipline of political science – that is, given the theoretical contenders against which constructivism has been poised most often (realism and rationalism) – this has meant the importance of stressing that the interests of states are inadequately

---

[30] Matthew J. Gibney, *The Ethics and Politics of Asylum* (Cambridge: Cambridge University Press, 2004), 17, 19.

understood as invariably consisting of material interests (maximizing wealth and military power), but rather are shaped by norms and identities that give those interests value and meaning.[31]

Rationalism, constructivism and agency

For some critics, the approach taken by many constructivist IR scholars of taking on mainstream International Relations approaches like realism and rationalism on their own turf has been to artificially privilege those dominant approaches while distorting the contributions of critical contenders. On the other hand, one outcome of constructivism's engagement with rationalism in International Relations would seem to be the conclusion typical of many a sharp theoretical contention in social and political thought – both have something right. It would seem just as impossible to deny that some agents at least some of the time act as they see it in moral terms, as it is to deny that there are actors who act in resolutely instrumental ways (whether pursuing a relatively straightforward conception of maximising their self-interests defined as material power, or acting instrumentally upon more thickly socially constructed interests), with negligible capacity or willingness to learn or redefine interests or identities in the light of engagement with others.[32] As Risse has convincingly argued:

> one should not forget that the various modes of social action – strategic behavior, norm-guided behavior, and argumentative/discursive behavior – represent ideal types that rarely occur in pure form in reality. We often act both strategically and discursively – that is, we use arguments to convince somebody else that our demands are justified – and by doing so we follow norms enabling our interaction in the first place (language rules, for example). As a result, the empirical question to be asked is not whether actors behave strategically or in an argumentative mode, but which mode captures more of the action in a given situation.[33]

---

[31] See, among many others, Martha Finnemore, *National Interests in International Society* (Ithaca, NY: Cornell University Press, 1996); Katzenstein, *The Culture of National Security*; Wendt, *Social Theory*.
[32] See Finnemore, *National Interests*, for clear use of these distinctions.
[33] Risse, "'Let's Argue!'", 18.

Indeed, a major finding of Deitelhoff and Müller's study was that pure 'bargaining' (strategic action, which is based on fixed preferences and uses threats and promises of reward to coordinate actions) was the exception, and that 'arguing' (which presumes open preferences) was ubiquitous in international negotiations.[34] What is the implication of this latest 'great debate' between rationalism and constructivism in International Relations for normative theorising? Profound, I would contend.

A problem in many approaches to ethics is that there is little satisfactory engagement with the problem of whether and how to deal ethically with ruthlessly instrumental actors. As encountered above, a most powerful and prominent strain of contemporary theories of justice and ethics comes from the critical theory tradition, and in particular the influential work of Jürgen Habermas and those who have extended and applied his agenda to International Relations. The Habermasian project raises three major issues of concern for this research agenda: first, the relationship of the empirical to the normative for assessing moral limit and possibility discussed in the previous section; second, questions of agency that will be addressed here; and third, the role of power, to be addressed further in a section below.

In the Habermasian account of discourse ethics, the most plausible path to norms that are valid – that is, just and ethical – is if they are attained through a process of unforced truth-seeking dialogue among all agents affected by the norm, and accepted with their consent and agreement; that is, the product of rational consensus. Shapcott interprets Habermas to be claiming further that the rules of discourse ethics are universal regardless of the self-understanding of any agent; a slightly different reading of the passage cited by Shapcott is that anyone who accepts discourse ethics presupposes the rules are valid. In any case, although Shapcott and I may take different paths, we arrive at a similar point, which is the observation that in a Habermasian ethic those who do not accept 'the universal and necessary communicative presuppositions of argumentative speech' are excluded from consideration.[35] This Shapcott finds troubling for it circumscribes the inclusiveness of a dialogic encounter and thus compromises its ethical appeal in accommodating

---

[34] Deitelhoff and Müller, 'Theoretical Paradise', 170–171.
[35] Jürgen Habermas, *Moral Consciousness and Communicative Action*, 86, cited from Richard Shapcott, *Justice, Community, and Dialogue in International Relations* (Cambridge: Cambridge University Press, 2000), 114.

diversity and difference. My critique comes at the same issue but from more of an empirical bent, namely the observation above of the pervasiveness in world politics of practices and their enactors embodying both the logics of consequences and logics of appropriateness. What do we do in a situation – indeed, in a world – confronted constantly with agents who do not approach a negotiation or a crisis with the characteristics of the ethical encounter entailed in a dialogic ethic? With actors who do not see themselves as equal, who have no intent to enter the encounter open to learn, to be persuaded, to change their views of others and themselves, but who fully intend to bring their power to bear on the situation to realise their interests, which may well be defined by material interests, or parochial culture and traditions rather than a self-conscious awareness of their contingency and historical situatedness? With a hegemonic state, for example, which reportedly objected to even make a commitment to *engage in dialogue* over global climate change in negotiations in 2005? Does this mean that engagement with such actors is simply consigned outside the ethical realm, that decisions reached through political compromises with archetypal strategic actors would by definition be unjust, ruled out a priori as inherently unable to carry redeemable potential? If we were to concede that many, even most, perhaps virtually all, important political situations will contain elements of such strategic practices and instrumental actors, is the realm of the ethical thereby confined to the scraps? Is the effect to consign strategic action and instrumental actors to the realm of immorality, that which must fall short, and would this not be an impoverished political ethic serving less as a positive ideal and more to confirm a deep contemporary cynicism of politics – and politicians – as inherently disreputable? Or, on the contrary, would not a workable political ethic be one that confronts the everyday rather than define it as outside its jurisdiction? To use a practical political example: what is the valid conclusion to draw of the Reagan administration's conclusion of the INF (Intermediate Nuclear Forces) agreement with Gorbachev, achieved despite its initial proposal by the USA as a cynical gambit believed so outlandish as to be sure to be rejected, by agents including a chief interlocutor who would seem difficult to qualify a priori as 'post-conventional' agents in the Habermasian sense?[36] Indeed, most any international treaty

---

[36] As Shapcott questions, 'how does a universal postconventional theory of justice include those who do not share the same self understanding, that is, who are not,

dealing with subjects like human rights or war would seem to be a mix of the brutal bargaining of national interests sprinkled if not always enveloped with other, including humanitarian, considerations.

Constructivist accounts of moral agency are not necessarily to be taken to be claiming that moral entrepreneurs act 'irrationally', nor that members of transnational advocacy networks do not also act instrumentally in pursuit of their ethical goals.[37] Rather, constructivist empirical findings suggest that it is not only communicative dialogue that may be justifiable in a workable global humanitarian ethic, but indeed forms of counterinstrumental action. To date, what that might mean has not yet been well developed. Deitelhoff and Müller simply note the failure of even reasonably approximating ideal speech situations in world politics; that 'Once challenges occur, "normal" communication is hampered and needs to be suspended. Actors can either accept the breakdown of communication or they might decide to make an effort to rebuild agreement at a higher discursive level'.[38] Their empirical findings very importantly point the way to several strategies to contribute to the latter; namely the role of institutions and publicity in creating common life worlds and fostering approximations of ideal speech situations, as well as the importance of cultivating the reputational legitimacy and authority of the interlocutor in a given situation. Thus, without disagreeing with the desirability of the Habermasian answer to the question of 'what to do' – namely, seek truth towards a consensus – this volume points to the necessity to elaborate upon what additional ethically justifiable strategies might be available rather than resting with 'suspension' or attempting to reconstruct the elusive ideal speech situation in its absence. This volume thus seeks to push constructivist ethics beyond the limits of the important Habermasian contributions while including elements of it, most notably in the chapters by Marc Lynch and Jonathan Havercroft.

An implication of the empirical engagement of constructivism with rationalism then, is that the only pathway for a viable ethics lies not in positing how to respond as if myopically instrumental agents did not exist or were not who they were, nor with smuggling in a hidden

in Habermas' terms, part of the discourse of modernity?' *Justice, Community, and Dialogue*, 123.

[37] Martha Finnemore and Kathryn Sikkink, 'International Norm Dynamics and Political Change', *International Organization* 52:4 (1998), 887–917.

[38] Deitelhoff and Müller, 'Theoretical Paradise', 168.

premise hopeful of reforming unreconstructed instrumental actors. Such tacks would themselves ironically constitute forms of exclusion, something antithetical to the core of dialogic ethics itself. And indeed, such approaches would be a manifestly inadequate way to think of how to deal with actors like those who have animated the George W. Bush administration with their coming to power in 2001, a regime whose most powerful members would seem to exemplify – hardly uniquely, though prominently – the instrumental monological actor par excellence, impervious to learning and redefining their interests and identities in the light of dialogue and engagement (not to mention evidence), instead constantly deploying every conceivable means at their disposal to reinforce the pursuit of their already decided-upon goals. And all this from a position embraced explicitly as one of dominance, not equality. How else do we conceptualise of policies conceived and pursued with the conviction that what is good for the USA is good for the rest of the world?[39] That the world is either 'with us or against us' in Bush's oft-repeated phrase? Or of the view, in the words of John Bolton, the Bush administration's ambassador to the United Nations (UN), that 'There is no United Nations. There is an international community that occasionally can be led by the only real power left in the world, that is the United States, when it suits our interests, and when we can get others to go along.'[40] Such actors' approach to international interaction embodies the antithesis of Linklater's characterisation of genuine dialogue as 'not a trial of strength between adversaries who are hell-bent on converting others to their cause; it only exists when human beings accept that there is no a priori certainty about who will learn from whom and when'.[41] The ethical problem, then, is whether and how to deal morally with the existence of such instrumental actors pursuing their interests when the laudable procedural discursive ethic is unavailable. What will not do, then, to set the sights for constructivist contributions to ethics, is a conclusion to a moral dilemma whereby the author sighs, '*if* only government such and such had not been so obstinate in insisting upon maximizing its power/pursuing its narrow

---

[39] As put by Condoleezza Rice in 2000, who was shortly thereafter to become Bush's National Security Advisor, and then Secretary of State in 2005, in 'Campaign 2000: Promoting the National Interest', *Foreign Affairs* 79:1 (2000).

[40] John Bolton, 'In His Own Words', video clip. Accessed April 12, 2005; www.truthout.org/multimedia.htm.

[41] Linklater, *Transformation*, 92.

interests'. Rather, the chapters in this volume engage as a central challenge and necessary component of global ethics the question of 'what to do' when faced with instrumental actors relentlessly pursuing their interests.

If rational actor assumptions are taken to imply that *all* actors act in narrowly instrumental ways *all the time*, the proposition is simply false. More challenging for International Relations theory and ethics, however, is the 'bad apple' thesis: do not instrumentalist power-seeking agents force others to engage them on their own terms lest they be taken advantage of, even perish in extremis? Constructivism points to several responses. First, Wendt's argument about the tipping points when cultures of friendship, rivalry or enmity come to be seen by actors as constituting properties of the system as a whole rather than particular agents is most salient here.[42] The implication is that there is no one single static system of friendship or enmity in world politics, but fluid and cross-cutting subcultures, meaning there is scope for moral practice. That is, it is one thing to say that engaging with a particular actor in a given situation precludes a dialogic ethic, and quite another to contend that the system as a whole precludes such moral action. Concomitantly, however, practices engaging with such strategic actors do have constitutive effects, the cumulative effect of which determines whether the cultural system tips from cultures of amity or enmity. It is thus not simply the morality of a particular act per se that is highlighted by constructivism, but its constitutive effects on the social structures of world politics. This is brought out powerfully in this volume's analyses of the effects of hypocrisy on sanctions and immigration policies and on legitimacy more generally in world politics, and marks a core contribution of this agenda.[43]

Constructivism and hypocrisy

One of the contributions of constructivism for normative International Relations theory is an unpacking of the concept of hypocrisy, a concept that has lurked in the background of normative theory and that is

---

[42] Wendt, *Social Theory*, 264.
[43] There are some formal parallels with rule-utilitarianism here, which counsels as the best path to morality choosing to act according to the rules whose observance would have the best overall consequences.

ubiquitous in criticisms of political practice in global politics. The overwhelming connotation of the very term is one of moral condemnation,
even as hypocrisy seems to be used in a number of senses: that it is
wrong to say you are doing something for one reason that appears
morally good when it is really for another; that it is wrong to do something regarded as morally desirable in one situation but then not uphold
it in another (that is, it is wrong to be morally inconsistent in the
application of principles like protecting human rights); or that it is
wrong to hold another to standards that one does not meet oneself.

The theme of hypocrisy resonates throughout ethical literature in
International Relations. Michael Walzer ultimately defended the relevance of morality as a topic for his scholarly attention in his courageous
Just and Unjust Wars by paraphrasing La Rouchefocauld's aphorism
that 'hypocrisy is the tribute that vice pays to virtue'; that is, we would
only have hypocrisy and be able to identify it if morality did figure in
our political world in some less than trivial sense. Thus for Walzer, one
of the objectives of *Just and Unjust Wars*, as he put it, *was to expose
hypocrisy*,[44] the reason being that where there is hypocrisy there is
moral knowledge that can expose it as such.[45] For an undertaking
centred upon expounding upon the present structure of the moral
world and the stability of the practical judgements we make[46] in order
to study the social patterns of our moral judgements,[47] that indeed is an
appropriate and insightful technique. But while doing so is justified for
his task, this move simultaneously risks taking for granted the stability
of those structures, and in thereby positing hypocrisy as the necessary
antipode of morality provides little avenue for assessing possibilities of
critical moral change in world politics. This is not to criticize Walzer
insofar as this was simply not his purpose, but it is to note that his
approach to moral theory in world politics does not provide us with a
lever to think through the particular challenges of moral limit and
possibility identified for this volume.

In immigration policy, for example, what do we think of a situation
in which there are toughly worded legal restrictions against illegal
immigrants that are nonetheless weakly applied in practice? While
such 'hypocrisy' by the very naming as such is generally seen as

---

[44] Michael Walzer, *Just and Unjust Wars: A Moral Argument with Historical
Illustrations* (New York, NY: Basic Books, 2000), xxviii.
[45] Ibid. 19.   [46] Ibid. xxviii, 19.   [47] Ibid. 45.

condemnable, could this not be a desirable form of hypocrisy from a humanitarian point of view at least in the short term, perhaps provided that longer-term resolutions are simultaneously sought? Or take recent debates about torture, where it seems to be assumed by some commentators that hypocrisy above all is to be avoided.[48] That is, governments ought not put themselves in a position of proclaiming that torture can never be condoned while even in the rarest of 'ticking bomb' occasions its agents may engage in practices that may at the least blur the boundary between stressful interrogation and torture. But are we really to accept that such a painful resolution of this dilemma must be less desirable than legitimising torture (and all that would entail) on the rationale of avoiding the sin of hypocrisy? And how has hypocrisy come to be seen as so important that to avoid it one should actually counsel legitimising the torture of human beings?[49]

To take another prominent contemporary manifestation of these issues, few arenas of world politics are as rife with accusations of hypocrisy as that of intervention, and few events in the last decade received as much global attention as the US-led war against Iraq launched in 2003. In the run-up to that war, one of the justifications offered by proponents of the war was the human rights opportunity to remove a dictator of a repressive regime responsible for horrendous atrocities. This presented the human rights community with a serious dilemma, and indeed it produced divisive splits within the liberal/left side of the political spectrum. Some members of the human rights intellectual community like Michael Ignatieff supported the war on

---

[48] For the logic of an argument for 'torture warrants' on this basis see Alan Dershowitz, 'A Choice Among Evils', *Globe and Mail*, March 5, 2003. Accessed March 5, 2003; www.theglobeandmail.com/servlet/ArticleNews/TPPrint/LAC/20030305/CODERSH/. . .3/7/2003.

[49] Part of the answer here seems to lie in the empirical assumption that torture is going to occur anyway, so we should at least try to regulate it. But this completely fails to acknowledge that even if torture was legalised it is not at all empirically certain that this would eliminate the occurrence of non-sanctioned torture, though this position advocating the legalisation of torture silently relies upon the counterfactual that it would. Charged by Sikkink's injunction in her chapter to make explicit the counterfactuals that underpin normative arguments, the alternative counterfactual appears at least if not more likely – namely, that non-sanctioned torture would still go on, and indeed would in all likelihood become if anything more prevalent given the dramatically altered moral landscape permitting torture.

the basis of anticipated human rights benefits even while recognising
that the war was being prosecuted primarily for other reasons:

> What tipped me in favor of taking these risks was the belief that
> Hussein ran an especially odious regime and that war offered the only
> real chance of overthrowing him. This was a somewhat opportunistic
> case for war, since I knew that the administration did not see freeing
> Iraq from tyranny as anything but a secondary objective ... if good
> results had to wait for good intentions, we would have to wait forever.

Without disavowing the noble motives – of protecting Iraqis from
further atrocities from the Saddam Hussein regime – Ignatieff later as
much as conceded the mistake in this approach:

> So I supported an administration whose intentions I didn't trust,
> believing that the consequences would repay the gamble. Now I
> realize that intentions do shape consequences. An administration
> that cared more genuinely about human rights would have under-
> stood that you can't have human rights without order and that you
> can't have order once victory is won if planning for an invasion is
> divorced from planning for an occupation.[50]

The quandary faced by the human rights community in this case was
telling. For years, critics of the injection of human rights in foreign
policy from the sceptical left and the realist right have made that claim
that human rights norms cannot possibly really matter since they are
applied so inconsistently. Noam Chomsky notably among numerous
others has frequently objected that if human rights matter so much
for Western governments (say, in Kosovo), then why didn't it provoke
responses in places like Turkey, Colombia, Tibet or Chechnya?
Attentive to the relation between the empirical and normative, one
could in the first instance point out the glaring logical fallacy in this
empirical argument: simply because one consideration – human rights –
did not trump all other factors as an explanation in every case does not
mean it could not have prevailed in any one particular case. This is,
simply, an empirical matter, and requires careful empirical research to
carry the critical suggestion that such humanitarian concerns could

[50] Michael Ignatieff, 'The Year of Living Dangerously', *New York Times Magazine*
March 14, 2004. Accessed June 2, 2006; www.ksg.harvard.edu/news/opeds/
2004/ignatieff_year_dangerously_nyt_031404.htm.

never really be consequential motives for any intervention, a position constructivists have successfully rebutted.[51] Instead, as Sikkink alerts us to in her chapter, counterfactuals typically do all the heavy lifting in such arguments; moreover, there are numerous different types of counterfactuals whose usage needs to be considered with the utmost care, as Sikkink pursues in detail. The more normative response of human rights advocates would point out that there is nothing wrong with inconsistency insofar as it is unreasonable to require that human rights be applied in some mindless 'all or nothing' fashion – as if one must fanatically either pursue a consistent human rights agenda in every case including where it is sure to be utterly ineffective or even backfire, or not pursue human rights at all even in cases where prospects for positive change appear very strong.[52] Politically, however, such moral opportunism still raises the political liability of hypocrisy discussed above, since such charges do seem to often tap a sensitive public vein (Chomsky's books, after all, sell extremely well). Is there a way to defend against the charge of hypocrisy in such situations that is not, well, mere hypocrisy as commonly impugned?

Hypocrisy figures importantly in constructivist accounts as a mechanism on the road to compliance with norms, such as the literature which stresses the ultimate impact of holding governments to account even if they only rhetorically – that is, hypocritically – profess adherence to human rights norms.[53] Yet as Marc Lynch argues in his chapter, while rhetorical entrapment can offer real tactical benefits, it also threatens to evacuate the power of moral argument by undercutting the power of legitimacy altogether. While hypocrisy may thus be invited at the earliest of stages in the spread of international norms, it is a double-edged sword. A constructivist contribution here, then, is grounded in the first instance in taking the legitimacy effects of moral

---

[51] See Martha Finnemore, *The Purpose of Intervention: Changing Beliefs about the Use of Force* (Ithaca, NY and London: Cornell University Press, 2004); and Wheeler, *Saving Strangers*.

[52] Chris Brown, 'Selective Humanitarianism: In Defence of Inconsistency'. In D. Chatterjee and D. Scheid (eds.), *Ethics and Foreign Intervention* (Cambridge: Cambridge University Press, 2003), 31–50.

[53] Daniel Thomas, *The Helsinki Effect: International Norms, Human Rights, and the Demise of Communism* (Princeton, NJ: Princeton University Press, 2001); Thomas Risse, Stephen Roppe and Kathryn Sikkink, *The Power of Human Rights: International Norms and Domestic Change* (Cambridge: Cambridge University Press, 1999).

language seriously (which some prominent theories in International Relations do not), thus positioning the analyst well to uncover the nuances of progressive and regressive effects of even strategically moral uses of morality including hypocrisy.

A focus on hypocrisy arises as well from the basic structurationist ontological insight that grounds constructivism, which tells us that what may be constraining social structures at one historical juncture or cultural space may not be so at another. The ethical corollary – if international normative theory is to really take constructivist ontology seriously – is the possibility that one may morally justify a given course of action in a particular context, but then judge an alternative course of action morally justifiable in another place, or that same situation at a later time when structural conditions of possibility may have changed. Thus, might it not be mere hypocrisy (nor unjustified duplicity) but morally defensible to defend the granting of amnesties to the perpetrators of atrocities in an ongoing conflict to put a halt to the terror, and then justify the later withdrawal of that amnesty when the threat of a resumption of civil war had receded? Would not the structural conditions have changed so much that a moral assessment of genuine possibilities and limits of international criminal justice must itself be altered?[54] And if so, what, if any, are the differences of such considerations from a realist ethic of prudence which conceives of political ethics as 'the art of the possible', or even a ruthlessly opportunistic Machiavellianism?[55]

A constructivist analysis of the possibilities of normative action in world politics thus opens up ways in which situations typically castigated as mere hypocrisy may at least in principle be subject to more moral defence than the contemporary connotation of the term suggests. Yet, at the same time, a constructivist worry would be that too transparent and pervasive an application of such an approach might fatally undercut the social structures which underpin the practices of making and accepting such commitments altogether, something most constructivists would be loath to sacrifice given their findings on the importance of legitimacy for just and stable social orders. In short, a

---

[54] Conversely, Jack Snyder is correct to note that careful attention to empirical context might reveal that 'unsuccessful attempts to apply the norm to areas where it is unworkable would tend to undermine adherence to the norm in areas where it might otherwise have held firmly'. '"Is" and "Ought"', 369.

[55] The relation of the contributions of this project to the ethical stance of realism will be assessed in the conclusion.

constructivist ethic might evaluate such practices according to their effects upon the legitimacy of norm carriers, and upon the structural power of moral legitimacy itself. This would distinguish constructivist approaches to ethics from those realist approaches which discount the role of social legitimacy and norms. It is thus that hypocrisy garners attention across a range of chapters in this volume, most systematically in Marc Lynch's chapter on hypocrisy and sanctions and Amy Gurowitz's chapter on immigration, but it also figures as part of the background in the human rights themes engaged in the chapters on indigenous self-determination by Havercroft, intervention by Finnemore and international criminal tribunals by Sikkink.

Dilemmas and the constitutive effects of norms

A fourth contribution of constructivism to normative theory is, at first blush, to complicate the moral calculus – which of course might not seem like an advance at all – in the sense of identifying previously underappreciated regress which may accompany progress or which may even be the condition of possibility that accompanies moral change. This occurs through the identification of social conflict revolving around concerns such as ethics, legitimacy and identity that may be overlooked by other theoretical traditions but are taken seriously by constructivism. But after identifying additional kinds of moral consequences that follow from a focus on the constitutive properties of social practices, constructivism can help clear the waters it has muddied itself by identifying the structure of different kinds of moral problems and working through their implications for ethical limit and possibility.

A contribution of constructivism for normative theory inheres in the focus on the constitutive and not just restraining effects of norms on agents and identities, the contention that structures do not merely constrain already existing agents who have pre-given interests, but also constitute those very agents and their interests themselves. In International Relations, Alexander Wendt has provided the most thorough theoretical treatment of this phenomenon, but as Bahar Rumelili has noted, Wendt's account, like the security communities and democratic peace literatures, downplays a dark side of the constitutive processes of identity and interest formation. Wendt outlines the mix of Hobbesian, Lockean and Kantian cultures of anarchy that co-exist in contemporary world politics, arguing that we live predominantly in a

Lockean culture of tolerance, moving towards Kantian cultures of peace as contended by theorists of the liberal democratic peace. But what if the very condition of possibility of establishing a peaceful regional security community like the European Union or liberal democratic peace – within which the thought of inter-state war fades to insignificance – is the exclusion and othering of outsiders and all that such processes may imply? As Bahar Rumelili has argued, 'the discourses on the promotion of democracy and human rights are inevitably productive of two identity categories, a morally superior identity of democratic juxtaposed to the inferior identity of non-(or less) democratic',[56] thereby 'constructing the very differences that transformation would ostensibly eliminate'.[57] Similarly, Helen Kinsella shows that while contemporary analysts focus on the salutary effects of just war doctrines which place the protection of innocent civilians as paramount, neglected is her finding that such protections were granted at the price of excluding and producing a category of outsiders – heretics and infidels – which in turn justified some forms of slaughter and the Crusades.[58]

The additional dilemma raised by constructivist analysis then is: *what do we make of moral change whose own condition of possibility seems to involve the production of the very (unjust) phenomena that are supposed to be overcome?* More positively, the achievement of constitutive analysis here is to make us more aware of and sensitive to the consequences of recursive relations of structures and agents, as well as the link between identity construction and normative development, processes that have tended to fall outside the lenses of traditional moral theories like utilitarianism, Kantian deontology and rights-based theories, Rawlsian contractualism and so on, which have tended to black-box sociological descriptions or explanations of identity formation at least as they have appeared in their International Relations incarnations.

---

[56] Bahar Rumelili, 'Producing Collective Identity and Interacting with Difference: The Security Implications of Community-Building in Europe and Southeast Asia' (Ph.D. dissertation, University of Minnesota, 2002), 49.

[57] Roxanne Lynn Doty, *Imperial Encounters* (Minneapolis, MN, University of Minnesota Press, 1996), 136, quoted in Rumelili, *Producing Collective Identity and Interacting with Difference*, 49.

[58] Helen Kinsella, 'The Image Before the Weapons: The Genealogy of the "Civilian" in International Law and Politics' (Ph.D. dissertation, University of Minnesota, 2003).

Communitarian and identity-based political theory is conspicuously different on this score, of course, yet in turn such projects tend to struggle with the difficulty of how to deal with transcommunity morality such as international norms. Without wading into that enormous literature and its debates here, I will confine myself to noting that a constructivist focus on the exclusionary practices that accompany the securing of community identities (which in turn are at the base of any moral construction) are the subject of work in this volume by Amy Gurowitz, Ann Towns and Bahar Rumelili. The latter two engage the question of whether such practices of identity formation are inherently exclusionary (as seems to be the implication of post-structuralist accounts of identity that are predicated on difference and othering) and necessarily ethically noxious. They further identify in particular contexts how the undesirable features of identify formation (such as exclusion) may be avoidable, subject to amelioration or even morally beneficial, thus identifying a spectrum of otherwise elided considerations for moral judgement and practice by unpacking the ethics of 'othering'. As Sikkink and Rumelili note in their chapters, moral judgement itself at some point involves othering, so simply condemning 'othering' wherever it occurs does not get us very far ethically. Thus, this volume sets out to examine different forms of 'othering', an important mechanism in constructivist explanations for community building or lack thereof, and to evaluate their moral implications.

A contribution of the constructivist analyses in the chapters that follow, then, is the illumination of moral dimensions that arise from a focus on the constitutive properties involved in the development of new international norms (including that is, of even putatively progressive moral change in world politics). This project then pushes that analytical strategy further into normative theory, asking us to consider what we make of practices that at once contain elements of progressive change that are not to be summarily discounted – such as the protections of innocents in warfare, or peaceful relations among the powerful industrialised democracies – yet at the same time are predicated upon or produce the conditions of possibility for other forms of exclusion, inequality, repression or violence. Such an analytical awareness bears the potential of pre-emptively designing policies more sensitive to a multidimensional ethical sensibility and building in protections for the novel moral challenges raised by attempts to deal with previous problems.

The chapters in this volume thus seek to make explicit the additional and often painful ethical dimensions arising from the mutually constitutive construction of structures and agents. This includes reconstruction of the ethical worlds of the agents involved themselves.[59] In exposing them, however, the point is not to engage in post-facto condemnation with 20/20 hindsight, nor leave such critical analysis hanging in ethical limbo – rather the spirit is to put such constitutive empirical insights to work for a forward-looking ethic. That ethic may be one that regards the moral value of political practices as always a project in process, for which final moral judgement is virtually never available, insofar as instances of moral change may only admit ethical justification that takes into account the social structures such change is predicated upon and productive of, as well as the agents it empowers or excludes. Take, for instance, Peter Andreas' insightful research demonstrating that the popular tool of international sanctions – conceived of by many as a way of avoiding the tragic violence of war – may in fact have had the effect of entrenching corruption and criminalised black-market economies in target states, thus actually contributing to their pariah status.[60] Rather than conclude from such work that the enactors of sanctions are thereby to be condemned post facto for negative consequences, an approach informed by the above considerations might counsel forbearance by the international community in demanding fealty to standards of battling corruption and criminal justice to the extent that the very same community produced the conditions for the flowering of such pathologies in the first place, and the instantiation of these additional criteria for continued pariah status after the original pathology had subsided. Indeed it might counsel active support in granting exceptions and providing exceptional assistance rather than applying a one-size-fits-all universal standard and engaging in punishment for failure to live up to the standards one had a hand in constituting.

Complicity and co-optation in moral change

Attention to the constitutive nature of social and political relations as identified above can cut several ways. It can make what prima facie

---

[59] Thanks to Michael Barnett for pointing this out.
[60] Peter Andreas, 'The Clandestine Political Economy of War and Peace in Bosnia', *International Studies Quarterly* 48:1 (2004), 29–52.

might seem like an unproblematically progressive development appear much less so upon further analysis by underscoring new sources of exclusion or repression or violence opened up by new social structures. This is one sense in which this project responds to the criticism that constructivists have to date mostly studied the origins and operation of 'happy' international norms (such as the abolition of slavery) rather than 'bad' norms (such as, say, slavery itself) – constructivists themselves are particularly well placed to identify some of the morally undesirable implications of erstwhile progressive developments. This includes identification of complicity of the progressive with the oppressive. But this agenda also points towards the progressive potential in social structures that critical theorists have condemned for their repressive effects or potential. Thus, to take an example of the former, I would contend that the effort to ban anti-personnel (AP) landmines represents a progressive intervention in world politics insofar as its primary objective has been to protect the lives and limbs of innocent human beings wherever they live. This stands against conservative claims of statist or military imperatives that reject civil society infringements upon the security requirements of the state, or the critical legal argument that just war concepts promote rather than restrain warfare and thus that initiatives based upon those categories have been co-opted into the war convention that legitimates warfare.[61] Contrary to the latter, I find that the landmines ban has in some – though not all – respects crucially depended upon just war categories for its realisation, and with progressive results. Without the powerful connection made to the well-established if oft-violated just war norm of discrimination – that is, the argument that AP mines are inherently indiscriminate – the taboo against any use of anti-personnel landmines would not have been widely accepted by states, if at all.

This points to a potential disagreement between some variants of critical theory and constructivism on the question of ethics.[62] Reliance on existing social structures such as just war norms for critical change

---

[61] For the former, see Anderson, 'The Ottawa Convention Banning Landmines', 91–120. The latter the author has heard charged numerous times by critical IR scholars.

[62] For a defence of the compatibility between constructivism and critical theory, see Richard Price and Christian Reus-Smit, 'Dangerous Liaisons? Critical International Theory and Constructivism', *European Journal of International Relations* 4:3 (1998), 259–294.

should come as no surprise to constructivist International Relations theorists who take discourse, structure, culture, norms and institutions seriously. For if such phenomena are to have any significance we would expect that they could not simply be jettisoned at every conscious and instrumental whim, and that efforts, for example, to instantiate a new paradigm of human security (that places the security requirements of individuals before states) could not start anew from whole cloth. And yet, the insistence of some critical theorists amounts uncomfortably close to just that, lest critical change be tainted with undue complicity with previous social structures beset by forms of domination. Norms of warfare, notably, have been excoriated by critical theorists as ineffective at best and complicit in state violence at worst. Jochnick and Normand do not recoil from charging that 'despite noble rhetoric to the contrary, the laws of war have been formulated deliberately to privilege military necessity at the cost of humanitarian values. As a result, the laws of war have facilitated rather than restrained wartime violence. Through law, violence has been legitimated.'[63]

These claims about the violence-legitimising function of laws of war are not altogether without any foundation. But it is precisely the dilemma of how to judge such double-sided developments that this volume seeks to address rather than rest with one-sided theoretical critique that is all too often quickly refuted by careful empirical work. The general argument has some appeal insofar as it is grounded upon a brutal correlation: the twentieth century witnessed the flourishing of elaborate laws and codes of war, and yet it was the bloodiest century of warfare in history. In one sense, then, critics of just war norms importantly underscore that these norms do suffer from often severe inadequacies in actually and always restraining the character of contemporary large-scale violence. But: *compared to what?* We need to note that there are difficulties with the one-sided critique of these claims, not the least the lack of consideration of counterfactual scenarios and ethical consideration of the implications of so many cases to the contrary. To cite but one obvious but very telling example, what on earth would the destruction visited upon Iraq in the Gulf War of 1991 have looked like (the source of the just war criticisms of Jochnick and Normand as well as David Campbell among others) in the absence of

---

[63] Chris af Jochnick and Roger Normand, 'The Legitimation of Violence: A Critical History of the Laws of War', *Harvard International Law Journal* 35:1 (1994), 50.

norms which constrained the blatant targeting of civilians enough to prevent any bombing of Iraqi cities after the bombing of a Baghdad air-raid shelter, let alone the obliteration of Iraq with nuclear weapons? In her chapter, Kathryn Sikkink dissects meticulously the sources and moral perils of confining one's analysis to a counterfactual that is based upon an implicit 'comparison to the ideal'.

While the empirics of war at once give some support to critiques of just war norms while also belying them in particular instances, over-looked in this critique is the fact that since World War II, most civilian deaths have not been the result of state to state violence, which we call war, but rather civil conflicts. A key question that arises then, is whether the structure of laws and rules of warfare written for state to state warfare can adequately transform and respond to the changing nature of contemporary warfare. Given that the International Criminal Court embodies the norms of the just war tradition, even as it introduces what I would term a revolutionary paradigm of individual criminal respon-sibility into the traditional sovereignty-based paradigm of state respon-sibility, the ICC by implication would seem to be a prime subject for indictment on the above critical theoretical grounds. This raises several questions. Are these norms subject to the same criticisms as just war concepts? Are they best understood as merely statist creations in origin and effect, carrying with them the presumption of protecting statist (read: militarist) imperatives, and great power ones at that? Or are those imperatives changing in an adequately progressive sense? These are some of the background considerations for analyses such as Kathryn Sikkink's chapter on criminal tribunals and their critics; here she takes on the conservative critique that such tribunals are too idealistic, but also the critical theoretical critique that such efforts fall short of the ideal. Her retort is that the ICC is not the ideal, national prosecution is, and that it is those who don't adequately acknowledge that the new social reality includes global justice norms institutionalised in a variety of ways that risk being idealists. Similarly, the critical theoretical stance is sceptical that attempts to develop new norms of humanitarian inter-vention are anything but new guises for Western domination, one of several elements that inform the dilemmas of humanitarian interven-tions addressed by Martha Finnemore in her chapter.

Critical international theorists and critical legal scholars would seem to expect little more of such new norms than their complicity in the service of the military imperatives of dominant states, at the expense of humanity and justice towards the vulnerable. Alternatively, one might argue that in part these criminal norms necessarily build upon those very just war norms whose utter rejection and displacement is called for by their critics, and in fact those very just war norms form the very conditions of possibility of progressive developments in how the world deals with crimes of war. It is in this vein that in his analysis of indigenous self-determination, Jonathan Havercroft argues that 'the involvement of so many groups representing indigenous peoples' at the UN forum for a declaration on indigenous self-determination 'is significant insofar as it means that for most indigenous peoples, the system of international law that facilitated their oppression does have resources that can be positively harnessed'.

In this sense, a key argument here is that the normative ground of a critical theoretical perspective (at least for a good number of its practitioners) betrays its constructivist ontological underpinnings by not taking social structures seriously enough. Pushed too far, this ultimately results in a critical theory that seems inadequate to recognise progress short of wholesale revolution. This effectively leaves it stranded between irrelevance or ethical paralysis since the demand seems to be for some ethical *tabula rasa* that bans all forms of even complicity in violence, domination or exclusion, without in turn engendering new forms (yet such forms of injustice are seen as inherent in all social relations and political communities).

This ontological–ethical tension derives from several sources. First is the relentless critical tendency to engage in the unmasking of each and every political practice as being inevitably complicit in forms of domination, an alleged tendency of the likes of Foucault and Derrida seized upon by their critics, and also present in the works of International Relations scholars like Ashley, Walker and Campbell who have 'gained inspiration from the critical themes of continental philosophy',[64] as well as theorists more in the neo-Marxian tradition of critical political economy. This relentless identification of every new social formation as yet another form of domination, since relations of domination can never be eliminated (having dispensed with the teleology of Marx), seems no less applicable towards those developments that would seem to have a prima facie case for being progressive and hence ethically praiseworthy.

---

[64] David Campbell, *Writing Security* (Minneapolis, MN: University of Minnesota Press, revised edition, 1998), 216.

To the extent that this is so leaves theorists so inclined in something of a bind. Since there must be some hidden agenda of complicity with domination in every political practice – for power is everywhere – the analytical imperative leads such theorists to too quickly look past – let alone analyse ethically – progressive change for what it is where it occurs. It is almost as if progressive developments that have been achieved, because they have become reality, cannot be sufficient praised as ideal, because their very realisation then resets the ethical bar of possibility. To be sure, this might be more a matter of analytical focus insofar as the practice of such scholars is typically to identify hidden forms of exclusion and domination to prepare the way for further expanding the realms of autonomy and freedom and respect for diversity and difference.[65] And yet, there is a risk of disjuncture between the ontology of the diagnosis and practice of critique as response:

> Exposing the inconsistencies between the normative, rhetorical, and practical performances of global capitalism has no preventive or transformative capacity. The forces of power have proven to be immune to such exposure; revelations have had no serous political consequences; moral indignation has had a very limited reach.
>
> . . .
>
> Expecting effects from revealing the inconsistencies between the rhetorical and practical would imply that the global structures of power are erected on different principles than they really are; that paradoxes, pain, unnecessary deaths of men, women, and children mean something; and that the system can be shocked or shamed into generosity and solidarity. It would mean that one is appealing to a sense of justice that does not rule our world.[66]

In the process, an effect of this neglect is a perpetual ratcheting up of ever more stringent litmus tests that political action seems to almost always necessarily fail to meet, since the goalposts are constantly being moved else the critical enterprise have nothing to critique, and since

---

[65] See Jim George and David Campbell, 'Patterns of Dissent and the Celebration of Difference: Critical Social Theory and International Relations', *International Studies Quarterly* 34 (1990), 269–293.

[66] Radmila Nakarada, 'The Uncertain Reach of Critical Theory'. In Paul Wapner and Lester Edwin J. Ruiz (eds.), *Principled World Politics: The Challenge of Normative International Relations* (Lanham, MD: Rowman and Littlefield, 2000), 68.

some form of domination is never precluded. In one sense the ontological underpinnings of this position are entirely consistent with constructivism; one calls something progressive moral change if it represents a moral improvement upon the current social and political constellation, so in that sense the present – and the standards of ethics situated in the present – always form something of a contingent historical–cultural baseline from which change is judged. As such, this may not be a position that constructivist-informed international ethics can dispense with even as it cannot realise it either. Sensitivity to the fact that ethical standards applied in any given case may not be those embraced by all others, or that those that are widely accepted may nonetheless be interpreted quite differently in disparate cultural contexts, is a constructivist tenet that must therefore pervade the analyses called for by this volume.

Another source of the critical paradox identified above issues from the reticence of many such theorists to engage in explicit ethical theorising, at least of a form obviously recognisable as such and applicable towards justifying action or alternative courses. This tendency is born of the post-Enlightenment sensitivity to the pitfalls and potential terror of such totalising narratives of modernity, and a conviction that it is modernity's very urge to provide universals that is the root of the problem. One result of this scepticism about moral philosophy has been a critical project that might leave us as sceptical about the ontological possibility of meaningful and progressive change as the hard-bitten realist agenda of International Relations theory; indeed, there are no small affinities between the Marxian, post-structuralist and realist traditions regarding their scepticism about the role of morality in world politics given the prominence of power in their analyses.

The result (often if not necessarily) is a backward-looking tack that frequently characterises critical theoretical arguments. Thus, while constructivist and other scholars have shown just war norms to have had meaningful effects in restraining death and atrocity that would otherwise have taken place, Jochnick and Normand level stinging criticisms that 'the basic fact that nations purport to respect the rule of law helps protect the entire structure of war-making from more fundamental challenges'.[67] Yet the alternatives are not stated, and remain mysterious, pointing perhaps to an implied banning of all war itself as the only acceptable moral action in dealing with war, a proposal that has been

[67] Jochnick and Normand, 'The Legitimation of Violence', 58.

the only alternative this author has heard on the issue by critical scholars, and one that is rather ripe for the critical theorists' own sceptical scalpel among just a few others. The main point here is not to discourage such criticism, which is indispensable, but to point out nonetheless that critical accounts which do not in fact offer constructive alternatives in the aftermath of critique ironically lend themselves to being complicit in conservative agendas opposing erstwhile progressive change in world politics. In short, this volume seeks to leverage the constructivist agenda of empirically explaining how moral progress has occurred for the critical project of plausible moral alternatives to deal with global dilemmas.

Constructivism offers a way out of the potential critical trap by taking the prevalence of power seriously without precluding the possibility of meaningful progressive moral change nonetheless. It does so by recognising that complicity in previous social structures is inherent in social change whether regressive, reformist or even those that are revolutionary, that varieties of co-optation of some agents of change to forms of domination is likely common or perhaps even pervasive rather than the exception for political action that amounts to more than self-sacrifice and defeat. Thus this volume enjoins the careful identification of such elements of power, co-optation and complicity carefully in the context of constituting and reconstituting social and political constellations, analysing and assessing them without reflexively casting upon them the shadow that the mere and very identification of complicity renders the developments of which they are a part irrecoverably problematic by association in ethical terms.[68] Thus, Havercroft's analysis revolves around the insight that 'indigenous peoples face just the kind of dilemma around which the contributions to this volume revolve, namely whether a critical rejection of the existing system is required to avoid co-optation, or self-determination as an element of that sovereign system can be harnessed to progressive purposes'. Moving from the constitutive effects of structure to agency, Rumelili argues that the critical element of constructivism for ethics requires it to 'recognise the complicity of the self in the construction' of the others upon whom it may depend for the creation of peaceful security communities like

---

[68] The critical theorist might respond that such a position would evacuate any revolutionary potential from constructivism (thanks to Adriana Sinclair for pointing that out). This is an important issue addressed in the conclusion to the volume.

the European Union or states that populate a zone of liberal democratic peace.

While thus attentive to the use of 'complicity' as a short cut that forestalls more careful unpacking and assessment of ethical substitutes, this volume hardly denies that the charge may indeed carry decisive weight. But what indeed constitutes ethically justifiable pragmatism, or conversely what constitutes a 'sell-out' – and by what metrics would we tell? The above section on hypocrisy highlighted the effects of strategic behaviour on the legitimacy of moral structures, which gives us one metric on this issue. In addition, we must consider the effects of compromise and pragmatism on agency – that is, on the legitimacy and moral status of norm entrepreneurs themselves. As Michael Barnett points out:

> The ICRC's [International Committee of the Red Cross] stance during the Holocaust, where it stuck to its principles of 'speak no evil', meant that it helped to reproduce the silence as the Jews were exterminated. The ICRC might be able to justly claim that there was little else that it could do in the situation, which might be true, but others might also note that this compromise undermined its ethical position. The UN during the Rwandan genocide might have been acting pragmatically, because it could know with certainty that no intervention would take place. But others suggest that this act of pragmatism compromised its very ethical soul.[69]

Research has shown the indispensable role of moral entrepreneurs for the origins and effectiveness of international norms – in this light, the question is: if they don't stick to principle when it may be needed most, who will? And can moral norms under severe duress survive to live another day without agents occasionally engaging in sacrifice to uphold their moral authority, which research shows is such a key asset? On the other hand, at what point would such sacrifice fatally undercut the political relevance and thus the very agency of such actors?[70] Just because we can ask a question does not mean there must be an answer

---

[69] Michael Barnett, correspondence.

[70] Thus, Barnett considers the position of some in the UN that attempting an intervention in Rwanda was morally wrong insofar as the most likely outcome would have been a fatal discrediting of the UN such that it would not be available for future cases when it could have a salutary effect. See his wrenching account in *Eyewitness to a Genocide* (Ithaca, NY: Cornell University Press, 2002).

to it, and this volume does not presume there is some universal answer that matches the level of abstraction of this formulation. But the authors in the chapters that follow are enjoined to take up this challenge, and to do so by carefully contextualised assessments of the ethics of pragmatism and limit in their particular domains.

Power and dialogic ethics

A final contribution of constructivism to normative theorising in world politics extends the importance of power broached above. In attending to the power of ideas and norms, recent constructivist scholarship in International Relations provides a way to avoid a liability of previous generations of liberal- and critical-minded scholarship, not to mention the traditional criticism of philosophy by political scientists, by eschewing the undue divorce of ethics from power. Jürgen Habermas' discourse ethics has of course been one of the most influential contributions to ethics in the last half-century, and his approach has been put to a number of adaptations in International Relations as we have already seen.[71] But as I have argued above, there remain important respects in which the critique of utopianism still haunts approaches like his which assess ethical outcomes by the force of the better argument between interlocutors divested of the dialogically corrupting accoutrements of power, since such situations would seem to be empirically rare if not indeed theoretically impossible for some versions of constructivism. Must one then simply condemn all situations tainted by any form of power? One approach, eminently sensible, is to underscore that the ethical task for International Relations flowing from a Habermasian approach to justice is not to try to find the ideal types and weigh events against them: 'You don't confirm or disaffirm the ideal type. You use it as a standard to measure the closeness or remoteness of empirical phenomena to it; this comparison then generates the question of which circumstances help to explain the different distances from the ideal type.'[72] This approach, followed by Risse as well, is eminently sensible in adjudicating the theoretical debate between rationalism and constructivism as an empirical issue of what each accounts for in the

---

[71] In addition to others already engaged, see also Crawford, *Argument and Change in World Politics*, chapter 9.
[72] Deitelhoff and Müller, 'Theoretical Paradise', 178.

explanation of a given situation.[73] However, in harnessing Habermas'
approach for empirical purposes of explanation, it does not give us
guidelines concerning how much or what forms of intrusions of power
might be ethically defensible.

Alternatively, Ann Towns in this volume alerts us to the simultaneously homogenising and stratifying effects of norms, dissecting them
to identify those elements she regards as unwarranted. She shows how
the discourse on gender equality of the past decade in Sweden, regularly
held as a model for the world, in fact 'has become constitutive of ethnic
difference and inequality in Sweden, defining gender equality as
"Swedish culture" and setting it apart from "immigrant/non-Western
culture"'. What constructivism contributes to normative theorising
becomes clear: 'One needs to be able to ethically justify and take
responsibility for, rather than plead ignorance to, the deleterious effects
of approaching gender equality in such a way.'

Bahar Rumelili comparably demonstrates the exclusionary effects of
the production of collective identities, even ones that have otherwise morally praiseworthy effects. Highlighting forms of power, she argues that
ignoring the role outsiders play in the formation of collective identities

> silences the relations of power and domination in the interaction of
> security communities with outsiders, by reducing it to a voluntaristic
> process where outsiders fulfill certain conditions and the community
> institution admits those states that validate its identity. Such an
> understanding disregards the authority of the community institution
> to define and shape the dominant discourses that ascribe identity and
> difference, its power to include and exclude and thereby bestow or
> inflict on the outsider states both the material and the symbolic
> benefits and costs of inclusion and exclusion, its ability to construct
> the outsiders as morally inferior and as potentially threatening, and
> thereby authorise certain forms of behaviour towards them.

These analyses remove as an ontological premise the divide between
morality and power, a move common to many of the contributors, but
without thereby evacuating the relevance of ethics. In doing so, constructivism addresses the traditional 'so what?' question often asked of
philosophical approaches to ethics which may deduce a desirable moral
principle of action without a satisfying analysis of how it may be

[73] Risse, '"Let's Argue!"', 14–18.

plausibly put into practice. Kathryn Sikkink is puzzled why the ethics producing human rights norms aren't more obviously recognised as a powerful force in human affairs (in IR theory at least) since presumably just about everyone would prefer not to be tortured than to be tortured. To cast aspersions of idealism towards their embodiments such as international criminal tribunals ironically substitutes an ethical argument for the empirical fact that such tribunals and the denial of amnesties for war crimes are becoming such prevalent social facts – that is, reality. By analysing the different and intimate relations between ethics and power, then, a normative theory informed by a constructivist ontology is from the outset inoculated from what has been at the heart of most critiques of moral theory in world politics in their various forms – idealism in the form of the divorce of morality from power as such – since particular kinds of moralities are here understood as forms of power insofar as they irreducibly involve empowerment and disempowerment. As Rumelili puts it, 'the practices of external differentiation that are necessarily implicated in community-building are not a price to be paid for progress but an essential mechanism that guarantees the ever-contested nature of identities in international relations'.

This is a crucial contribution of constructivism since it simultaneously provides a response to two critiques that could emerge from the Habermasian and Foucauldian poles of contemporary political and social theory. On the one hand, the accounts of ethics and politics in thinkers like Habermas or Linklater privilege those outcomes that issue from deliberation, argument and consensus, 'the force of the better argument' as free as possible from what they see as the distorting influences of power. Without denying the appeal of this ethical ideal, one could still note that constructivist analyses have demonstrated that ethically progressive change has been attained in other ways, and indeed that confirmation of the Habermasian ideal may be methodologically and empirically next to impossible.[74] This suggests that the Habermasian account may not provide the only viable account of a

---

[74] Deitelhoff and Müller, 'Theoretical Paradise', 170–171, state 'our research design failed, at least in part. While we found important arguing instances, our assumption that arguing as a mode of communication involved a truth-seeking actor-orientation was not confirmed ... We demonstrated the importance especially of moral and ethical argumentation. However, arguing could not be isolated empirically from bargaining.'

cosmopolitan global ethic, and indeed may be in danger of providing a largely unworkable account of politics.

On the other hand, and as alluded to above, another vein of critically minded scholars like Richard Ashley, Jim George and David Campbell among numerous others have insisted on placing power front and centre in their analyses of world politics, while contending against the mainstream of explanatory positivism that International Relations is all about ethics. Campbell in particular has centrally engaged the question of ethics, taking up the challenge that 'radical' interpretivists cannot provide a workable ethics. A more earnest engagement with ethics in international relations is not to be found; to date, however, it is difficult to claim that the fruits of such labours have succeeded in providing workable responses to the kinds of questions of ethical judgement and decision being posed here that are also meaningfully distinct from the morality produced by the liberal, Enlightenment or modern thought that is the target of their criticism. This is due to several reasons.

The first is that these kinds of questions often are simply not directly engaged given the different critical tasks taken up by scholars. David Campbell's subtle and informed deconstruction of the conflict in Bosnia attempts to show how 'the settled norms of international society – in particular the idea that the national community requires the nexus of demarcated territory and fixed identity – were not only insufficient to enable a response to the Bosnian war, they were complicit in and necessary for the conduct of the war itself'.[75] The vast bulk of his analysis is descriptivist in Frost's sense, though on the premise that deconstructive thought is a necessary prerequisite for historical and political progress, a term, notably, from which he does not recoil.[76] But in the end he does recoil from addressing in a straightforward way the kinds of ethical dilemmas that, I would argue, genuinely arose in that case and were put at some point to various practitioners, dilemmas that have since arisen in other contexts. Namely: is war to be waged in defence of humanitarian principles, and if so, what kind of war could possibly be so waged? Could it be said that air strikes genuinely seemed to be the only non-suicidal political possibility for Western politicians, and if so, what then? While Campbell does go so far as to criticise the air

---

[75] David Campbell, *National Deconstruction: Violence, Identity and Justice in Bosnia* (Minneapolis, MN: University of Minnesota Press, 1998), 13.
[76] Ibid. 14.

strikes in Bosnia in an insightful way, he follows this by stating 'this is *not* to suggest that large-scale military intervention should have been undertaken'[77] – leaving it at that.

Some scholars eschew the provision of ethics as conventionally understood since they diagnose the very urge to do so as lying at the heart of the problem of contemporary ethics and politics.[78] Others, however, recognising that not answering the question does not in the end answer it, and granting that such questions are indeed important ones which it might be appropriate for scholars to address, have taken initial steps to take the question of ethics – in the sense of having to make decisions and/or judge – more to heart. Perhaps not dissimilar to this effort to extract the utility of the sociological programme of constructivism for ethics, Campbell in his later work follows more explicitly the conventional question of ethics – what to do – left mostly unanswered in his earlier work. He has drawn upon the work of Levinas to posit not a theory of ethics akin to the universalising injunctions à la Kant's categorical imperative or Rawls' difference principle, but rather an ethical relation in which responsibility to the other is the basis for reflection.[79] For Campbell as for Levinas, being is a radically interdependent condition made possible only because of my responsibility to the other, thus incurring an obligation to other.[80] This formulation, however, even as one can grant the social core of identity, is deeply problematic as a basis for ethics insofar as it ultimately delegates one's own ethical responsibility to the other without providing any grounds for distinguishing when that other is morally reprehensible and not deserving of such moral consideration as opposed to ontological recognition. Campbell himself is forthright enough to acknowledge this: 'We may still be dissatisfied with the prospect that Derrida's account cannot rule out forever perverse calculations and unjust laws. But to aspire to such a

---

[77] Ibid. 226.
[78] Richard Ashley, 'The Achievements of Post-Structuralism'. In Steve Smith, Ken Booth and Marysia Zalewski (eds.), *International Theory: Positivism and Beyond* (New York, NY: Cambridge University Press, 1996), 240–253.
[79] David Campbell and Michael J. Shapiro, 'Introduction: From Ethical Theory to the Ethical Relation'. In David Campbell and Michael J. Shapiro (eds.), *Moral Spaces: Rethinking Ethics and World Politics* (Minneapolis, MN: University of Minnesota Press, 1999), x.
[80] David Campbell, 'The Deterritorialization of Responsibility: Levinas, Derrida, and Ethics After the End of Philosophy'. In Campbell and Shapiro, *Moral Spaces*, 32–35.

guarantee would be to wish for the demise of politics, for it would install a new technology.'[81] Thus, despite Campbell's earnest wrestling with the ethical question front and centre, we are returned in the end back to the original problem of this project if the solution is to privilege the diverse struggles of politics over the homogenising domination of the good.[82] Rumelili reorients the ethical compass somewhat here by similarly noting that 'The normative implications of the claim that identity is complicit in the production of others as different are profound', though she uses it to point out 'that the moral responsibility for being different does not fall squarely on the other; the self is simultaneously responsible for perceiving and representing the other's differences in a certain way'. She thus proposes ethical criteria for different forms of othering, marking a significant constructivist contribution to normative theorising.

In short, while interpretivist scholars like Campbell have placed power central in their analyses of ethics, they have not squared the circle with normative theory to date in a way that provides anything like a satisfactory guide to practical ethical questions of the type with which this chapter began: what ought the practitioner or citizen do? How does one know that one is in a situation calling for action within ethical limits not of one's own design nor that one approves of?

In their eschewing the label and allegedly the logic of constructivism, sometimes very pointedly as in the case of Campbell, I would contend that strong interpretivist approaches have missed the ways that constructivism may help to offer ways out of what has become something of a normative trap for critical or interpretivist theories in world politics. Campbell himself has launched a harsh critique of constructivism as failing to take the radical insights of critical social theory to their logical conclusions.[83] But in his enthusiasm to sharply distinguish his own work as not constructivist,[84] he has overlooked the fact that he has

---

[81] Ibid. 51.

[82] Nor does the vague call for a Derridean cultivation of 'new gestures' which aim to 'encompass' rather than resolve contradictory demands as counselled by Zehfuss get us there, unless those new practices are actually articulated (as is approximated in Gibney, *The Ethics and Politics of Asylum*, for instance); Maja Zehfuss, *Constructivism in International Relations* (Cambridge: Cambridge University Press, 2002), 258.

[83] Campbell, *Writing Security*, Epilogue.

[84] For an effort to engage in dialogue between critical theorists and constructivists that argues Campbell is constructivist in important senses of the term, see Price and Reus-Smit, 'Dangerous Liaisons?'.

lumped a diverse range of scholars into one category of constructivism, accusing them all of the sins he identifies in but a very few that he takes as exemplary of the genre. This is rather an odd sin for a scholar given to complain that the very use of labels like post-modernism has served not to accurately describe the work of a group of thinkers but rather to cultivate a negative disposition, since the effect of his treatment of constructivism is indeed precisely that.[85] This is unfortunate, since many constructivists have no small sympathies to critical elements of work like Campbell's and take very seriously the resulting insights. More importantly for this project, however, the lack of direct engagement with the logic of constitutive claims made by social constructivists in favour of a strategy of dismissal of all such efforts as explanatory and causal (and thus misdirected in Campbell's view), deprives critical theorists of a crucial lever upon which to make plausible claims about ethical possibility and limit apt to have some political resonance. The disavowal of the empirical and all explanation does not provide this position with the resources to engage questions of possibility inherent in the ethical.

Yet, self-consciously eschewing as they do the language and logic of causal claims as impossible,[86] self-professed interpretive accounts nonetheless routinely invoke verbs such as 'legitimise', 'facilitate', 'mask', 'reveal' and so on to account for the workings of discourses, bringing in empirical explanation through the interpretivist door. However, the grander the claims being made on behalf of civilisational structures such as modernity, the liberal project, imperialism, globalisation, the end of history, nihilism and the like, the more the social scientists' Scylla of overdetermination and Charybdis of variation creep in. While a typical constructivist formulation is to claim to account for conditions of possibility (as opposed to causality), the most trenchant contributions of constructivism specifically seek to attend to these difficulties by explicitly addressing the nexus between claims of possibility and those of actuality or (constitutive) causation, and doing so by taking into account both agency and structure and their recursive effects upon one another. The chapters that follow attempt to do so, and thereby seek to discern the possibilities and constraints – structural and agent-oriented – of critical interventions in world politics. To preview but one startling finding in this volume along these lines, Ann Towns discovers

---

[85] Campbell, *Writing Security*, 212.   [86] Campbell, *Writing Security*.

that while they have dominated the political debate, 'no clear line can be drawn between "Swedes" and "immigrants" as cultural categories' when analysing gender equality, and thus "there is no necessary trade-off between multiculturalism and gender equality as conceptualised in Sweden'.

As such, one can see how many of the contributors to this volume recoil from the lengths to which post-modern critics of constructivism such as Zehfuss push the contention that any positing of a 'reality' out there that is taken to impose limits on political action is nothing but 'an *unfounded* violence', a closure of thought 'based on *nothing* but a prior decision'.[87] This strong interpretivist position is unobjectionable inso-far as any positing of limitations and opportunities entailed in 'the present' is itself an interpretation, an interjection in the production of social reality, and thus Zehfuss and Campbell are surely right to make us suspicious of any invocation of 'political realities' as a pre-given limit. And yet, at the same time it is not difficult to appreciate the merit in empirical claims like Towns' above, or the claim that the rise in asylum claims in Germany by 8,000 percent from 1980 to 1993 presented politicians with a pressing new political reality, one that politicians did not have to deal with in, say, 1973 when some 5,595 asylum claims were made, compared to the 438,000 in 1992, a number which repre-sented two-thirds of all claims made in Western Europe that year.[88] This is so even if those numbers were themselves the products of prior political decisions, as Zehfuss reminds us, and even if the very subject of the 'refugee' is itself politically constructed, for it still presented itself to politicians as a social fact given its widespread acceptance among target populations and indeed asylum applicants themselves. That 'nothing' referred to by Zehfuss thus becomes a something, the accu-mulation of social practices and decisions that, however arbitrarily grounded, constitute an existence beyond the ability of one person's interpretation to change.

The notion of political crisis in this context emerges as a particularly salient ingredient for a constructivist ethic. Invocation of a situation of 'crisis' is a powerful device to invoke as a limit on political and ethical possibility. Yet the social constructivist would ask: just how do we define what comes to constitute a genuine crisis? And crisis for whom

---

[87] Zehfuss, *Constructivism in International Relations*, 197, my emphasis.
[88] Gibney, *The Ethics and Politics of Asylum*, 3, 86, 97.

or for what? What is it reasonable to ask of politicians to risk in dilemmas such as that which faced Western policy makers over Kosovo in 1999? Are politicians to do what is otherwise deemed 'right' – intervene militarily in situations of mass atrocity, say, or expand accommodations provided to refugees – even if strongly opposed by their own domestic public opinion or in the face of stark resistance among allies, and even if the result is the risk or actual loss of political power? Zehfuss rightly underscores that while it is common to hear in such dire dilemmas that one 'had no choice', the very claim that no choice was available is not solely a reflection of an unalterable and objective outside reality so much as a political contextualisation of actions,[89] a political construction, I would add, that of necessity includes normative judgements about what is acceptable to be sacrificed as Mervyn Frost's position would hold.

'Crisis' thus emerges as a particularly salient concept for thinking about moral limit and possibility, particularly since scholars have identified moments of perceived crisis as crucial catalysts for ideational and political change.[90] And yet, definitions of just what constitutes a crisis are as varied as theoretical perspectives in International Relations. What counts as a domestic or international political crisis is by no means given, even in the case of something like the Cuban Missile Crisis that is widely taken as a quintessential crisis.[91] For post-structural theorists, sovereignty (not to mention all the rest of our taken-for-granted foundations) is always already in crisis, the 'crisis of representation of modern subjectivity'. From a Marxian perspective, the global economy is always already in crisis. For Malthusians and contemporary environmentalists alike, it is the global ecological system that has been and now is at a precipice. And so on.

The upshot is that we require a theoretically self-conscious unpacking of the social construction of the relevant thresholds that animate crucial

[89] Zehfuss, *Constructivism in International Relations*, 256.
[90] See, e.g., Peter Haas, 'Introduction: Epistemic Communities and International Policy Coordination', *International Organization* 46:1 (1992), 1–35. Thanks to Adriana Sinclair for pointing out that a focus on addressing moral dilemmas conceived as acute 'crises' carries inherently conservative potential insofar as it distracts attention from the everyday agonies of poverty and the like that do not pose threats to dominant structures such as capitalism.
[91] Jutta Weldes, *Constructing National Interests: The United States and the Cuban Missile Crisis* (Minneapolis, MN: University of Minnesota Press, 1999).

questions of ethics – namely, what political or personal cost and risks can ethics demand, and what situations qualify as the kinds of crisis that demand such sacrifices? Was a putative crisis in part of one's own making or perceived as such in the context of one's own political benefit? Careful and self-conscious empirical investigation of the social construction of choice, and of crisis as a trigger for political action (or inaction) is necessary to contextualise what is at stake in a given situation.

The task for a constructivist contribution to ethics that follows, in short, is to unpack and identify the sources and different kinds of moral dilemmas. As the tragic realist view of politics among others reminds us, there simply may be genuine dilemmas not subject to ethically satisfying resolution, and this is the situation that Martha Finnemore tries to navigate through in her chapter on the dilemma between self-determination and humanitarian intervention. Constructivists stand at varying points along a continuum in their willingness to grant the existence of immutable material realities, from Wendt's 'rump' materialism to a post-structuralist denial of any political reality that could be said to exist outside of discursive practices. Putative dilemmas, however, may be revealed to be the product of the contestation of social practices amenable to long-term transcendence if not immediate resolution, and whose irresolvable character evaporates upon further analysis. Thus the power of Towns' demonstration that while gains in gender equality in Sweden were achieved by defining gender equality as 'Swedish' culture and setting it apart from 'immigrant/non-Western' culture, the key to gender equality does not have to be found in culture conceptualised this way, and thus a politician is not forced to choose as if in a genuine and immutable moral dilemma.

It is here, I would argue, that constructivism's structurally contextualised empirical analyses of the possibilities of change and the limits imposed by social structures become indispensable for normative theorising. It is to the substantive analyses of moral dilemmas in world politics along the dimensions identified in this chapter that the rest of this volume now turns, though not before Christian Reus-Smit orients the place of the constructivist normative agenda in the larger traditions of International Relations scholarship and philosophy in the next chapter to finally set the table for the chapters that follow.

2 | Constructivism and the structure of ethical reasoning

CHRISTIAN REUS-SMIT

Why should we study international relations? What ought to be the purposes of this field of study? Is it sufficient to be a group of scholars animated by nothing more than our idiosyncratic intellectual curiosities? Or does 'science for science's sake' constitute a compelling rationale for our endeavours? Are there deeper purposes than these that should, or perhaps do, animate our research, teaching and public engagement? And if there are such purposes, what are their implications for how we imagine International Relations (IR) as a field of inquiry, and for how we go about our scholarly pursuits?

In the following pages I make the case for one possible answer to these questions, that International Relations ought to be concerned first and foremost (though not exclusively) with the praxeological question of 'how should we act?' that animates this volume. It should confront directly, and unashamedly, the most challenging issues of human action in a globalising world, a world characterised by political convergence and division, cultural homogenisation and diversification, economic growth and persistent inequality, and the transformation of organised violence. It is a purpose rooted in the origins of our field, one that its early architects took as axiomatic, one that E. H. Carr saw as the mark of a 'mature science' of International Relations. It is also a purpose still animating the field, though in a subterranean fashion, as much forgotten as denied.

I begin by excavating Carr's vision of a mature science of international politics, a science in which 'sound political thought' would be based on 'elements of both utopia and realism'. I then examine the field's gradual contraction away from such a vision. In a mutually reinforcing double move, positivists have sought the ideal of a purely empirical (or positive) theory of international relations, while international ethicists have succumbed all too often to the lure of empirically unencumbered philosophy. The net result is a field with a depleted capacity to speak to problems of human action in contemporary world politics. If we wish to rectify this situation, we have little choice other than to place ethical reasoning at the heart of our scholarly endeavours. But as much as this contradicts the positivist search for purely empirical theory, it also demands a more expansive, holistic conception of ethical reasoning than is common. The third part of the chapter takes up the central task of developing such a holistic conception, arguing that ethical reasoning is only partly about the logical formulation of principles of action; that it necessarily, and integrally, entails questions normally considered the province of empirical enquiry. In the fourth part of the chapter, I draw out the contributions that constructivism can make to ethical reasoning by relating six dimensions of such reasoning to the six contributions identified by Richard Price in the previous chapter.

A 'mature science' of international politics

Carr's critique of utopianism is usually taken as his signature contribution to the emerging discipline of International Relations. Challenging the naive faith that liberal internationalists placed in human reason, he held that it was simply 'untrue that if men reason rightly about international politics they will also act rightly, or that right reasoning about one's own or one's nation's interests is the road to an international paradise'.[1] Most scholars have assumed from this that Carr himself was a quintessential realist, as he so vigorously contrasted this perspective with utopianism. Legro and Moravcsik provide one of the most recent of these characterizations,[2] but critically inclined scholars have also squeezed Carr into the same pigeonhole.[3]

   Yet Carr's position was more sophisticated than this, and his challenge to the fledgling discipline of IR more demanding. Utopianism was the mark of an immature science, an initial stage 'in which the element of wish or purpose is overwhelmingly strong, and the inclination to analyse facts or means weak or non-existent'.[4] But unalloyed realism was equally bankrupt. Carr was adamant that we 'cannot ultimately find a resting place in pure realism; realism, though logically

[1] E. H. Carr, *The Twenty Years' Crisis* (New York, NY: Harper and Row, 1939), 40.
[2] Jeffrey Legro and Andrew Moravcsik, 'Is Anybody Still a Realist?' *International Security* 24:2 (1999), 5–55.
[3] Jim George, *Discourses of World Politics* (Boulder, CO: Lynne Rienner, 1994), 77–80.
[4] Carr, *The Twenty Years' Crisis*, 5.

overwhelming, does not provide us with the springs of action which are necessary even to the pursuit of thought'.[5] This was true for Carr in two senses: intellectual and political. In *What is History?*, Carr made it clear there was no such thing as objectively studying the 'facts'. The very act of historical interpretation is structured by the purposes and values of the historian. 'The facts only speak when the historian calls on them: it is he who decides to which facts to give the floor, and in what order or context . . . a fact is like a sack – it won't stand up till you've put something in it'.[6] Politically, Carr argued that 'consistent realism breaks down because it fails to provide any ground for purposive or meaningful action'.[7] This, ultimately, is the crux of his position in *The Twenty Years' Crisis*. Utopianism may be a naive (and hence dangerous) guide to political action, but 'consistent realism' is no guide at all. Not only is it impossible to identify or interpret 'the facts' of the world objectively, the facts alone can never tell us how we should act in this world – only our purposes can tell us this, and these derive from the subjective realm of values and beliefs.

Contrary to the standard interpretation, Carr concluded that 'any sound political thought must be based on elements of both utopia and reality'.[8] By 'sound political thought', Carr clearly meant thought capable of informing political action. Not political action in the narrow sense of policy guidance, but in the broad sense of action directed toward reconstituting the international order. Carr imagined a 'science of international politics' that would help foster international peace and economic justice through a rigorous combination of empirical and normative inquiry, difficult as he recognised this to be. Neither unqualified utopianism nor untempered realism could sustain such a science; the former was immature, the latter sterile. Carr not only thought that political engagement was a mark of sound political thought (and a mature science of international politics), he saw such thought as itself a form of political action. Just as Carr believed that political thought must combine empirical and normative inquiry, he held that 'Political action must be based on a co-ordination of morality and power'. 'The illusion that priority can be given to power and that morality will follow, is just as dangerous as the illusion that priority can be given to

---

[5] Ibid. 89. [6] E. H. Carr, *What is History?* (Harmondsworth: Penguin, 1961), 11.
[7] Carr, *The Twenty Years' Crisis*, 92. [8] Ibid. 93.

moral authority and that power will follow.'[9] Carr's call for a science of international politics that engages the empirical and the normative is thus inextricably linked to his belief that effective political action is mindful of both power and morality.

Echoes of Carr's exhortation for International Relations scholarship to engage the empirical and the normative can still be heard, and not all emanate from the critical margins of the field. Calls from these margins have of course been strong. For Robert Cox, critical theory was all about the formulation of 'realistic utopias' – it 'contains an element of utopianism in the sense that it can represent a coherent picture of an alternative order, but its utopianism is constrained by its comprehension of historical processes'.[10] Andrew Linklater elaborated this idea when he argued that critical theory ought to combine sociological, normative and praxeological forms of inquiry. Closer to the core of the field, the English School has long sought to bridge empirical and normative inquiry, evident in the long-standing debate between pluralists and solidarists over the relationship between order and justice. The most recent call for a science of international relations that Carr would recognise has come, interestingly, from Robert Keohane. In his 2004 Presidential Address to the American Political Science Association, Keohane argued that 'Political science as a profession should accept the challenge of discovering how well-structured institutions could enable the *world* to have a "new birth of freedom"'. To meet this challenge, political science – and International Relations in particular – had to engage in both empirical and normative enquiry, in explorations of the 'real' and the 'ideal'.[11]

---

[9] Ibid. 98.
[10] Robert W. Cox, 'Social Forces, States, and World Orders', in Robert O. Keohane (ed.), *Neorealism and Its Critics* (New York, NY: Columbia University Press, 1983), 210.
[11] Robert O. Keohane, 'Governance in a Partially Globalized World', *American Political Science Review* 95:1 (2001), 1. Keohane's work has since been marked by a sustained attempt to engage the empirical and the normative. See Allen Buchanan and Robert O. Keohane, 'The Preventive Use of Force: A Cosmopolitan Institutional Proposal', *Ethics and International Affairs* 18:1 (2004), 1–22; Allen Buchanan and Robert O. Keohane, 'The Legitimacy of Global Governance Institutions', *Ethics & International Affairs* 20:4 (2006), 405–437; and J. L. Holzgrefe and Robert O. Keohane (eds.), *Humanitarian Intervention: Ethical, Legal, and Political Dilemmas* (Cambridge: Cambridge University Press, 2003).

What unites this diverse group of scholars is a commitment to International Relations as a field of practical inquiry, a field animated by the question of how we should act in a violent and unequal world. Their answers vary widely. For some the commitment to human emancipation looms large; for some the cosmopolitan renovation of international institutions is the goal; and for some the preservation of international society's most fundamental norms is the priority. But for all of them the question of how we should act animates their inquiries, and as soon as they embrace this practical intent – intent beyond analysis for analysis' sake – they are compelled to bring empirical inquiry into dialogue with normative reflection. It is difficult to see how embracing this praxeological question could lead us anywhere else. Pure empirical analysis or positive theory can never, in and of itself, tell us how we *should* act, as it can never tell us our purposes. And purely normative, philosophical enquiry can tell us nothing about the parameters of action, about the constraints and opportunities provided by the context – material and non-material – in which we seek to act. The purely empirical guide to action is as mythological and naive as the purely philosophical. Ironically, this is lost on those who most vigorously uphold policy engagement as the sole measure of legitimate scholarship in International Relations. Normally of strong realist predilections, these scholars trumpet empirical analysis over theory, and eschew the philosophical pretensions of normative inquiry altogether, failing to realise what Carr saw, that the practical impulse (of which policy engagement is one form) demands both empirical and normative inquiry.

The contraction of the field

Carr held that sciences evolve progressively through a series of dialectical phases. Their initial, immature phase is generally utopian, characterised by a dominance of purpose over understanding, will over capacity. This provokes a realist backlash in which an obsession with 'the facts' smothers concern for purposes. It is the equally impoverished nature of these early stages of inquiry – the naivety of the former and the sterility of the latter – that Carr believed ultimately spurs the development of mature science. *The Twenty Years' Crisis* was a critique of the utopian phase in the study of international politics, and a call for greater realism. But ultimately it was an exhortation for the field to move beyond realism to a more mature mode of inquiry, one that occupies the difficult terrain between the *is* and the *ought*. The best one can say is that the study of international politics has not yet reached the age of maturity, as Carr understood it. The worst is that the field, at least as defined by the mainstream (particularly within the United States), has contracted, moving from the more eclectic scholarship of classical realists and liberals to a situation in which the terrain between the empirical and the normative has been all but evacuated by most scholars, at least as a desired destination.

For classical realists, determining the scope of moral action in an international system characterised by competition and insecurity was an essential component of international inquiry. Hans Morgenthau famously denied that states ought to be bound by universal, cosmopolitan values in their dealings with one another. But this was not because he thought morality had no place in international relations. It was because he believed states were bound by a different kind of moral obligation, the obligation to engage in successful political action, 'itself inspired by the moral principle of national survival'.[12] Universal values might still be pursued, but a state's primary obligation to protect the national interest demands that such values 'be filtered through the concrete circumstances of time and place'.[13] Raymond Aron deployed a similar logic when upholding the 'morality of prudence' (by which he meant something closer to 'wisdom'), a value defended by Morgenthau as well. States could not deny the 'morality of struggle', a morality grounded in the need for national survival in a world where 'war remains the final sanction'.[14] Nor could they deny the 'morality of law', as international law offered some prospect of a norm-governed order. But these moralities would always be in tension, and the morality of prudence offered the only way to navigate between them. Placing himself firmly on the terrain between the empirical and the normative, Aron concluded that the 'morality of prudence, the best on both the level of facts and that of values, does not resolve the antinomies of

---

[12] Hans J. Morgenthau, *Politics Among Nations: The Struggle for Power and Peace* (New York, NY: McGraw Hill, sixth edition 1985), 12.

[13] Morgenthau, *Politics Among Nations*.

[14] Raymond Aron, *Peace and War: A Theory of International Relations* (London: Weidenfeld and Nicolson, 1966), 609.

strategic–diplomatic conduct, but it does attempt to find in each case the most acceptable compromise'.[15]

Classical liberals were criticised by Morgenthau, Aron and others for naively believing that liberal political values could tame the competitive dynamics of international politics. But just as the classical realists had not eschewed moral reasoning, the classical liberals had not eschewed engagement with the 'facts', as they saw them. Norman Angell is now best known as Carr's great nemesis, the hapless liberal whose unqualified utopianism helped fuel the twenty years' crisis. But Angell's conception of sound political thought and action was not dissimilar to Carr's. 'It seems fatally easy', he wrote, 'to secure either one of two kinds of action: that of the "practical man" who limits his energies to securing a policy which will perfect the machinery of war, and disregard anything else; or that of the pacifist, who, persuaded of the brutality or immorality of war, just leaves it at that, implying that national defence is no concern of his. What is needed', he concluded, 'is the type of activity which will include both halves of the problem . . . To concentrate on either half to the exclusion of the other half is to render the whole problem insoluble.'[16] What distinguished Angell from the likes of Carr, Morgenthau and Aron was not his purported disregard of political reality, but his different conception of what that political reality was, and how it constrained or enabled moral action in world politics. For realists, the balance of material power was the critical reality, but for Angell it was a prevailing set of ideas, ideas which held that the best way to enrich a state was through warfare. Not only were these ideas demonstrably false, he contended, they could also be changed, a proposition vindicated by the subsequent rise of the trading state.[17] Classical realists and liberals thus differed in their understandings of the political dynamics driving international politics, and this conditioned their differing conceptions of the realm of moral possibility. But it was taken for granted by both that international inquiry had to engage the *is* and the *ought*, as this engagement was essential to a practical discourse.

---

[15] Aron, *Peace and War*.
[16] Norman Angell, *The Great Illusion 1933* (New York, NY: G. P. Putnam's Sons, 1933), 327–328.
[17] Richard Rosecrance, *The Rise of the Trading State* (New York, NY: Basic Books, 1987).

The story of the field's development over the past half-century has been told in any number of ways, the most common being the narrative of three 'great debates': realism versus idealism, classicism versus behaviouralism, and positivism versus post-positivism. The critical divide, however, that separates the field as Carr, Morgenthau and Aron imagined it from mainstream approaches today is epistemological. Both Carr and Morgenthau thought that they were engaged in a scientific project, and they cast their visions for the field in terms of its development as a 'science'. Their understandings of 'science' differed in important ways, with Morgenthau exhibiting much greater faith in the possibility of identifying objective laws of interstate relations. Yet their conceptions of a science of international relations clearly had room for normative reflection. As we have seen, Carr was adamant that such a science had to combine empirical and ethical inquiry, and Morgenthau insisted that realism was 'aware of the moral significance of political action'.[18] This contrasts markedly with the conception of science embraced by scholars in the mainstream of the field today. The scientific study of international relations is now conceived as a purely empirical enterprise, concerned exclusively with facts not values. Not only are the scientist's values to be quarantined from the process of inquiry, but ethical inquiry is considered out of court.

The contrast between Carr's vision of a science of international relations and Kenneth Waltz's could not be starker. In advancing his 'theory of international politics', Waltz distinguishes between 'philosophic interpretation' and 'theoretical explanation'.[19] The former encompasses normative reflection, while the latter is concerned with the more delineated task of explaining empirical regularities, or laws. Waltz's project falls into the second of these categories. Distancing himself from 'traditional political theory', which he associates with philosophic interpretation, he draws tight fences around his preferred model of a purely explanatory theory of international politics. His definition of what a theory is excludes any form of moral or ethical inquiry, placing such things outside the study of international relations, either in the political theory subfield of political science or in the entirely different discipline of philosophy. Waltz insists that the 'urge to explain

---

[18] Morgenthau, *Politics Among Nations*, 12.
[19] Kenneth Waltz, *Theory of International Politics* (New York, NY: Random House, 1979), 6.

is not born of idle curiosity alone. It is produced also by the desire to control, or at least to know if control is possible, rather than merely to predict'.[20] In other words, a purely explanatory theory is justified not merely as 'science for science's sake' but for its practical consequences, for its ability to enhance 'control'. Carr would have argued, of course, that these practical consequences are illusory, that a purely explanatory theory is radically insufficient. There is nothing within such a theory that can tell us the purposes of control, or even if control is desirable. What do we wish to control? Why do we want such control? And what means of control are acceptable, as opposed to merely possible? Only normative reflection can answer these questions, and without such reflection control has no purpose.

I have argued elsewhere that Waltz's greatest impact on the field may not have come from his substantive realist theory, but from the model of theory and social science he advances.[21] Within the (largely American) mainstream, the positivist criteria he defines have become the measure of legitimate theoretical inquiry and scholarly endeavour, defining the terms of debate and rules of the game. Perhaps the clearest example of this is the way in which liberalism has been redefined as a positive social scientific theory. Liberalism has long been the quintessential political theory, a theory that identifies both the verities of political life as well as its ethical precepts. But over the past three decades liberal international theory has contracted into a largely explanatory project. Robert Keohane has always been sensitive to the normative dimensions of his work, especially his own commitment to enhancing institutional co-operation.[22] Until recently, however, this element of his work was carefully quarantined, obscured by his primary emphasis on the development of a positive theory of international institutional development.[23] This recasting of liberal theory as a purely explanatory project has been taken to the extreme by Andrew Moravcsik, who not only distances himself from Keohane's neo-liberal institutionalism (which he denies is truly liberal), but explicitly seeks to purge liberal

[20] Waltz, *Theory of International Politics*.
[21] Christian Reus-Smit, 'The Strange Death of Liberal International Theory', *European Journal of International Law* 12:3 (2001), 582.
[22] Robert O. Keohane, *After Hegemony: Cooperation and Discord in the World Political Economy* (Princeton, NJ: Princeton University Press, 1984), 10–11.
[23] Robert O. Keohane, *International Institutions and State Power* (Boulder, CO: Westview Press, 1989), 174.

theory of its normativity. To date, he claims, critics have been able to dismiss liberal theory 'as a normative, even utopian, ideology', something that has greatly impoverished debate within the discipline. The solution, according to Moravcsik, is not to defend liberal theory's normative position, but to reformulate it 'in a nonideological and non-utopian form appropriate to empirical social science'.[24]

The tendency of contemporary realist and liberal scholars to eschew normative inquiry is mirrored in the equally strong tendency of students of international ethics to avoid systematic empirical inquiry, and together these tendencies have constituted a double movement vacating the terrain between the empirical and the normative. There is a general preference among scholars of international ethics for a form of philosophical inquiry characterised, first and foremost, by logical reasoning from first principles. Empirical propositions about human nature, society and human action are invoked to define the realm of moral possibility, but these are almost always ad hoc rather than systematic. This is most apparent in neo-Kantian writings, but equally so in the work of moral sceptics. The former invoke the fact of international interdependence to warrant the need for global principles of justice, while the latter make categorical claims about the lack of communal bonds beyond the state to deny the need for such principles. In both cases, an unreflective dilettantism characterises engagement with the empirical. 'Facts' are chosen selectively to undergird the preferred line of moral reasoning, and often voluminous amounts of relevant empirical research and theory are ignored. In this respect, many writings on international ethics treat the empirical in the same way that classical liberal theorists treated the state of nature, where primitive anthropologies (imaginings of 'native Americans', for example) were used to define the human capacity for moral action.

One might respond that these examples of the double movement away from the terrain between empirical and normative inquiry are not representative of the broad tenor of the scholarship in the field, as critical theorists, post-structuralists, feminists and sectors of the English School have all sought to occupy this terrain in one way or another. Nothing here denies this point. Each of these approaches rejects the pull toward purely empirical or purely normative inquiry evident above, and

---

[24] Andrew Moravcsik, 'Taking Preferences Seriously: A Liberal Theory of International Politics', *International Organization* 51 (1997), 513.

some even question orthodox conceptions of the empirical and the normative altogether. Yet, whatever the virtues of this scholarship (and they are multiple), none of it has managed to colonise or engage the American mainstream of the field, something that is central to the self-identities of these diverse projects. Moreover, the mainstream's failure to engage explanatory and ethical inquiry is central to the critique levelled by these approaches, and my claims here will appear hardly novel to these scholars. The crucial point is that mainstream International Relations scholarship now exhibits a profound vacuum, one in which the field's core paradigms, and the scholars who labour under their banners, have nothing of a scholarly nature to say about ethics. Where are the realists today who demonstrate any serious interest in the 'moral significance of political action'? And with a few notable exceptions, where are the liberal International Relations scholars whose ethical reflection extends beyond the simple and enticing proposition that democracies don't fight each other and therefore spreading democracy is a paramount value? Even those IR scholars who work on human rights, and whose work evinces a strong liberal ethic, tend to focus on the empirics of human rights promotion, not the ethics.[25] In general, scholars who do confront issues of international ethics tend to be located either outside the field in political theory or philosophy, or they are found in the critical approaches of the sort discussed above.[26]

Arguing that contemporary International Relations scholars generally eschew self-conscious, systematic and sustained ethical reflection is not the same as arguing that their work evinces no normativity. To the contrary, even those most ardently committed to International Relations as a positive social science make normative propositions, and in almost all cases these propositions play a vital role in their theoretical schemas. The priority realists give to the values of order and stability is perhaps the most notable example of this, as is their emphasis on the national interest, the defence of which is as much an ethical project as

[25] A notable exception here is Jack Donnelly.
[26] A recent *Foreign Policy* survey of International Relations scholars provides evidence of this. A list of the field's most influential scholars includes no specialists on international ethics, and none of the most celebrated ethicists of International Relations – such as Michael Walzer, Henry Shue or Thomas Pogge. See Daniel Maliniak, Amy Oakes, Susan Peterson and Michael J. Tierney, 'Inside the Ivory Tower: TRIP Survey of International Relations Faculty in the United States and Canada', *Foreign Policy*, March/April 2007.

the pursuit of distributive justice. Without these values the realist account of rational state action under anarchy would be at best incomplete, at worst nonsensical. As would be their often heard laments about irrational state conduct, conduct that undermines rather than furthers those values of order, stability and the national interest. Similar things can be said for just about any positive theory of international relations one chooses. For instance, although it was underdeveloped in his earlier work, Keohane was at least explicit about the values of improving 'political amity and economic welfare' that animated his development of neo-liberal institutionalism.[27]

Why does contemporary International Relations scholarship – with all its commitment to purely explanatory inquiry – still evince such lurking normativity? The answer lies in the persistent and pervasive character of International Relations as a practical discourse. This chapter argues that our work ought to be animated by the central praxeological question of 'how should we act', and that taking this question seriously requires that we occupy, in a systematic and self-conscious fashion, the difficult terrain between the *is* and the *ought*. The irony is that the field is already structured by this question, though largely in a hidden and unacknowledged form. Consciously or subconsciously, it animates what we study and the conclusions we reach. Realists, liberals, Marxists, constructivists, critical theorists and post-modernists alike, it stands as a common motive, despite our epistemological, ontological and methodological differences. It fuels our most heated debates, and influences our scholarly alliance formations. It lies behind our differences on 'real world' political issues, and our arguments about the appropriate role of the academy in engaging such issues. It is the hidden hand of this praxeological question that pushes even the most positivistic of our colleagues in the normative realm. For as Carr understood, the question of how we should act demands not only an understanding of context, material and non-material, but also of purposes and ends. The problem is that there is now a disjuncture between the persistent and pervasive character of International Relations as a practical discourse and the prevailing model of science which defines ethical inquiry into purposes and ends as beyond the pale. The net result, we should not be surprised, is the impoverishment of the field's capacity to speak to the most urgent issues of human action in contemporary world politics.

[27] Keohane, *After Hegemony*, 10.

A holistic conception of ethical reasoning

Behind the marginalisation of normative inquiry in International Relations lies a widespread misconception about the nature of ethical reasoning. For both International Relations scholars and political philosophers, ethical reasoning is generally conceived as the logical deduction of ethical principles, as the reasoned formulation of precepts governing right conduct. This is most strikingly apparent in how scholars have defined 'international political theory' and 'normative international relations theory'. In his classic work, *Political Theory and International Relations*, Charles Beitz provides a quintessential articulation. The purpose of the political theorist, he writes, 'is to formulate and examine alternative principles and to illuminate the reasons why some are more persuasive than others'.[28] A more recent formulation is provided by Molly Cochran in her excellent *Normative Theory and International Relations*: '[N]ormative IR theory takes as its subject matter the criteria of ethical judgement in world politics and seeks shared principles for extended moral inclusion and social reconstruction in international practice.'[29] Further evidence of how ethical reasoning is generally conceived narrowly in terms of the logical deduction of ethical principles can be found in a new website devoted to 'international political theory' which explicitly gives 'less prominence to those kinds of International Relations theory which proceed by way of social theoretic explanation or which focus on the epistemological status of claims in empirical international relations research'.[30]

When International Relations scholars place normative inquiry in a separate scholarly universe – in the realm of political theory or philosophy – they are working with this narrow conception of what constitutes ethical reasoning. And because students of international ethics have themselves internalised this understanding, they too contribute to the ongoing bifurcation of studies of international relations. Profound differences separate students of international ethics, fuelling the well-honed debates between cosmopolitans and communitarians, deontologists and consequentialists, and Kantians, Grotians and

---

[28] Charles Beitz, *Political Theory and International Relations* (Princeton, NJ: Princeton University Press, 1979), 5.
[29] Molly Cochran. *Normative Theory in International Relations: A Pragmatic Approach* (Cambridge: Cambridge University Press, 1999), 2.
[30] See www.international-political-theory.net.

Hobbesians. But underneath these differences lies an unstated consensus as to the narrowly defined nature of ethical reasoning, and this unstated yet powerful consensus reinforces the divide between scientists and ethicists, but this time from the other direction.

The notion that ethical reasoning is confined to the logical deduction of ethical principles is questionable, however. Let us consider two situations in which members of international and world society been asked to exercise ethical reasoning. The first concerns the repeated phenomenon of genocide or ethnic cleansing. In responding to such atrocities, it is immediately apparent that members, individually or collectively, must address at least two questions: what obligations if any do we have to address such phenomena? And, if we do have obligations of some kind, what if anything should we, or can we, do to fulfil our obligations? The second situation concerns the persistent problem of global poverty. Again, members confront a similar array of questions: are we under any obligations to address the problem? And, if we are, how should we act to fulfil these obligations, if we have any capacity to act at all? Clearly, deducing relevant ethical principles is part of addressing these questions. Weighing competing ethical principles is one element of determining our obligations, and even if we decided that legal, as opposed to ethical, principles will dictate our obligations, observing the law is itself an ethical principle. Equally clearly, however, deducing relevant ethical principles is not all that these chains of questions require. Buried within them are issues of diagnosis (what is the nature of the problem?), identity (to whom does the pronoun 'we' refer?) and capacity (what do we have the power to do?), to name but a few. More than this, there is no good reason why this spectrum of issues and questions should not be treated as integral to ethical reasoning. To begin with, defining the 'we' that is to act is an ethical (as well as a sociological and political) choice, as is designating the resources that 'we' would be willing to deploy in fulfilling our obligations. In addition to this, the issues and questions raised above are often, if not always, mutually dependent. How actors define the 'we' often determines how they rank competing ethical principles, and how they define an issue can mandate or preclude the application of particular ethical principles.

In the world of actual actors responding to actual issues, ethical reasoning is thus never confined to the logical deduction of principles of right conduct, as if we were all Rawlsian individuals deducing principles behind a veil of ignorance. Ethical reasoning, as a human practice integral to (and constitutive of) social life, is necessarily multi-faceted, encompassing philosophical, sociological and outright political forms of reflection and debate. To help systematise this expanded conception, it is useful to differentiate six of these forms that, in the world of practising human agents, structure ethical reasoning:

(1) *Idiography.* As we seen, ethical reasoning necessarily involves the definition of the moral agent invested with obligations. Saying that 'I' or 'we' have obligations, or denying that this is the case, requires the logically prior definition of 'I' or 'we'. Because obligations can be both burdensome and empowering, the definition of who holds them is intensely political. At times actors embrace obligations because this licenses action; at other times they shun them to avoid action. The classic example of this process is how states and peoples define the 'national we', a process that is almost always about delimiting the scope of moral obligations to others. In such cases, actors engage in the frequently paired processes of identity construction and inclusion and exclusion. The same kinds of idio-graphic reflection and debate occur with respect to rights as well as obligations.

(2) *Diagnosis.* When actors consider how they ought to respond to issues such as genocide and global poverty they go through a process of issue or problem definition. This is in part an empirical process, a process of mapping the contours of a particular phenom-enon. But as with any process of mapping, this is as much an exercise in social construction as collating the 'facts'. How we name a phenomenon has much to with how we define our obliga-tions. Recall the unedifying refusal of leading Western powers to call the Rwandan genocide a genocide. Mapping and naming occur in tandem with a third diagnostic process, that of moral evaluation. Historically, similar phenomena have attracted radically different moral evaluations. The expulsion of the Jews from Spain in 1492 provoked no moral outrage from the powers of the day, but today it would be called ethnic cleansing and labelled a crime against humanity.[31]

---

[31] See Heather Rae, *State Identities and the Homogenization of Peoples* (Cambridge: Cambridge University Press, 2002).

(3) *Consequences.* A distinction is often drawn between deontological and consequentialist ethical theories, the former articulating abstract moral principles against which conduct ought to be judged, the latter contending that conduct ought to be judged in relation to its consequences. In reality, consequentialist thinking enters most if not all ethical reasoning. Debates about the ethics of humanitarian intervention, for instance, often hinge on whether intervention will do more harm than good. As with capacities, it is tempting to think of consequences in highly objective terms, as though serious consideration of the 'facts' and scrutiny of all imaginable scenarios will reveal *the* consequences of particular actions. But because the relevant 'facts' are selected and interpreted by observers, and because scenarios are just that, scenarios, consequential thinking is always an act of imagination, a point Kathryn Sikkink dissects in greater detail in her chapter's discussion of the use of counterfactuals in ethical and empirical claims. Actors socially construct consequences in the same way at they construct risk; in fact the two are closely related. Culture, belief and history are all implicated in structuring this component of ethical reasoning.

(4) *Principle.* In addition to the idiographic and diagnostic elements of ethical reasoning, there is also the deliberative element, that element which most closely approximates the reasoned formulation of ethical principles. When considering how to respond to issues such as genocide and global poverty, actors do seek and invoke principles to guide their conduct, and these run the entire gamut from the most other-regarding to the most self-interested. I use the term 'deliberation' purposefully here. Deliberation refers to both 'weighing in the mind' and to 'discussion of reasons for or against'.[32] In other words, it is both an internal act of reason, and a public act of argument and debate. In the process of ethical reasoning, both of these are present. Actors weigh in their minds competing ethical principles, and they argue about these principles publicly. The philosophical project of logically deducing ethical principles contributes to this dimension of ethical reasoning. Philosophers are themselves actors weighing competing ethical principles, and so too are they participants in public discourse. Moreover, other actors deliberate philosophically when they reason about principles

---

[32] *Concise Oxford English Dictionary.*

of conduct and argue about their merits; even if their thinking is less systematic and professionalised.

(5) *Context*. When actors engage in ethical reasoning they do so within concrete social and historical circumstances, and these circumstances are critical in defining what they see as the realm of moral possibility. All ethical arguments assume that there are limits to moral action; in fact, the idea of moral limits is essential to ethical reasoning. If there were no such limits, ethical conduct would be the uncontroversial norm, and we would have no need for ethical reasoning. How actors define the limits to moral action is thus crucial, and prevailing social and historical contexts play an important role in such definitions. We can see this at work in existing perspectives on international ethics. Realist scepticism about the possibility of a cosmopolitan transformation of world politics is based, first, on their emphasis on the material reality of an international system divided into territorially demarcated sovereign states, and second, on their view that this system is characterised by continuity not change. If we see the system of sovereign states as a social institution, however, and we are sensitive to its relative historical novelty, then we will, perforce, define the realm of moral possibility differently. We see from this that perceptions of social context matter in ethical reasoning. 'Rump' material factors may well dictate a range of feasible options, but how actors understand these will be at least as important, as will be the spectrum of non-material factors they engage, such as national cultural forms or the prevailing institutional architecture of society.

(6) *Capacity*. Much of what has been said about context also applies to capacity. When actors engage in ethical reasoning they negotiate the relationship between their obligations and their capacities. A Timorese citizen might well acknowledge that all peoples have a moral obligation to prevent genocide when it occurs, but at the same time argue that the Timorese people lack the capacity to fulfil this obligation in all but the most limited of circumstances. On the surface, capacity is often treated as objective facts – you either have them or you don't, and this constitutes an unproblematic constraint or enabling factor. But capacities are almost always interpreted through the lenses of self-image and social perception. Sometimes actors mistakenly or deliberately inflate or underestimate their capacities, and they do this to others' capacities as well.

Furthermore, while capacities might be finite, they are often fungible, and decisions about whether one has the capacity to fulfil an obligation almost always depend on whether fulfilling that obligation falls within one's hierarchy of interests, which is itself constituted by self-image and social perception. Important here too is the fact that changes in technology shift the realm of ethical possibility. In an era without rapid international communications and travel, coming to the aid of earthquake victims halfway around the world did not exist as a moral problem or opportunity. The very fact that it is possible today, along with so many other realms of action, only exists as a moral possibility due to changes wrought by technology.

Each of these six elements – idiography, diagnosis, consequences, principle, context and capacities – plays a vital role in the human practice of ethical reasoning. One could argue that the term 'ethics' is appropriately applied only to (4), the process of principle deliberation. But if one takes one's cue from how really existing people reason ethically, it is unclear how this process could be disentangled from the other five. And if this is true, why would we wish to confine our conception of ethical reasoning within such narrow confines?

The contribution of constructivism

Preceding sections have advanced three key propositions: (1) that International Relations scholarship ought to confront, in a systematic rather than unreflective fashion, the praxeological question, 'how should we act?'; (2) that the field's capacity to do this has diminished with its heightened emphasis on empirical enquiry and positive theory, and the attendant quarantining of such inquiry from normative reflection; and (3) that the resulting separation of the study of international relations from international political theory derives in large measure from the widespread assumption that ethical reasoning consists solely in the logical deduction of moral principles, an assumption inconsistent with the nature of ethical reasoning as a concrete human practice. If these propositions are compelling, then we face two imperatives, both of which point in the same direction – confronting the praxeological question of how we should act demands that we bring empirical and normative enquiry into dialogue, and the holistic nature of ethical reasoning makes purely normative reflection radically insufficient.

Whether we come at the issue from a praxeological starting point, or from a concern with ethical reasoning, the implication is the same – some way must be found to engage the empirical and the normative.

This challenge of engagement is faced by all of the major theories of international relations, and by the various strands of international political theory as well. Realism that does not interrogate its animating values, such as stability, order and the national interest, is realism without the intellectual resources to confront the question of how we should act in the contemporary global order. It is also realism that asks us to accept these values at face value, not on the basis of sustained argument – argument that would have to be normative in nature. The same can be said of positivistic versions of other grand paradigms, such as liberalism and Marxism. Interestingly, it can also be said of radically anti-positivistic perspectives, such as post-modernism. Post-modernism that does not interrogate its empirical assumptions and normative commitments has nothing more to say about how we should act than desiccated realism. A post-modern critic might respond that addressing the question of how we should act is antithetical to the post-modern position, but this cannot be true, as their recommended strategies of relentless critique and deconstruction are forms of human action, no more or less. They might also respond that interrogating empirical assumptions and normative commitments is integral to the post-modern approach, but that post-modern interrogation avers normative pre-scription and rejects, epistemologically, the very notion of empirical enquiry. This is belied, however, by the prominence of values such as diversity and multiplicity which play such an important role in the post-modern narrative, and also by the plethora of empirical propositions that punctuate post-modern writings on international relations.

My concern here, however, is with constructivism and the challenge of engagement. Central to the constructivist project is a concern with the politics of norms, with the social construction of intersubjective ideas of rightful membership and action, and with the multiple ways that such ideas condition political outcomes. Constructivists have made an art out of tracing how social and legal norms – and the ethical and moral precepts they instantiate – frame the realm of political action, conditioning actors' self-identities, interests and preferred strategies. In doing so they have confronted head on two sacred cows of traditional International Relations scholarship: the idea that ethics and morals play no role in world politics (or that what passes as ethical is simply the interests of the powerful); and the notion that international politics is simply a 'realm of recurrence and repetition'. Despite these contributions, however, constructivists have been repeatedly criticised for having no normative theory, for spending all of their time exploring the politics of norms while neglecting altogether the norms of politics. Constructivists are political sociologists, no more and no less, and in restricting themselves to the terrain of empirical inquiry – interpretive or otherwise – they are said to reproduce the general tendencies of the field.

Trends in the constructivist scholarship over the past decade appear to vindicate such claims. Early articulations of constructivism located it within a broad family of critical theories, a family that includes postmodernists, neo-Marxists, feminists and others. This was partly because constructivists share with these perspectives an ontological 'concern with how world politics is "socially constructed," which involves two basic claims: that the fundamental structures of international politics are social rather than strictly material (a claim opposed to materialism), and that these structures shape actors' identities and interests, rather than just their behaviour (a claim opposed to rationalism)'.[33] But it was also because constructivists shared with these approaches a normative commitment to bettering the human condition. Alexander Wendt argued explicitly that the reason constructivists focus on the possibility of change in world affairs is that if such change '*is* possible, then it would be irresponsible to pursue policies that perpetrate destructive old orders, especially if we care about the well-being of future generations'.[34]

Ted Hopf has usefully distinguished between 'critical' and 'conventional' constructivisms, arguing that as 'constructivism creates theoretical and epistemological distance between itself and its origins in critical theory, it becomes "conventional" constructivism'.[35] If we focus on constructivism's contribution to expanding our understanding of the social construction of world politics, its proximity to the critical project remains close, even essential. But if we turn to its normative contribution – to constructivists' self-conscious endeavours to contribute to ethical reasoning – a gulf between constructivism and critical

---

[33] Alexander Wendt, 'Constructing International Politics', *International Security* 20:1 (1995), 71.

[34] Ibid. 80.

[35] Ted Hopf, 'The Promise of Constructivism in International Relations Theory', *International Security* 23:1 (1998), 181.

theory has opened. This is partly evident in the changing self-identification of many constructivists. Most constructivists no longer identify themselves or constructivism with the broad family of critical theories; reflecting, as much as anything else, a discomfort with the normative overtones of the very term 'critical'. It is also evident, however, in the general failure of constructivists to forge links, within their own work or collaboratively, between their sociological explorations of change in world affairs and other, more philosophical, dimensions of ethical reasoning. This volume seeks to launch an agenda to forge just these links. Like all theories of international relations, constructivism betrays a lurking set of (largely liberal) ethical commitments. But when constructivists have been criticised for this, a criticism that usually takes the form of 'constructivists only study good norms', to date they have responded largely by asserting their scientific credentials, not by defending the values that animate their work. Constructivists remain a diverse band of scholars, but the ambition of many constructivists, particularly in the American mainstream, appears little different from Moravcsik's ambition for liberalism, to reformulate it 'in a nonideological and nonutopian form appropriate for empirical social science'.[36]

As with all theories, though, this retreat into purely empirical inquiry or positive theory comes at the cost of a diminished capacity to address our central praxeological question of how should we act. David Dessler argues that constructivism has enormous potential to 'contribute directly to debates over meaning and purpose in international political life'.[37] For him, this potential is best realised if constructivists develop 'reconstructive explanations that reveal the development and impact of norms and identities *in their particularity*', an approach distinct from the development of 'covering-law theory'.[38] If we adopt the holistic conception of ethical reasoning advanced earlier, this kind of reconstructive inquiry has a clear contribution to make, especially in the areas of idiography, diagnosis, context and capacity. The problem is that Dessler imagines that constructivism can contribute to debates over meaning and purpose in international life as a purely positivist theory. He fails to recognise that empirical inquiry and positive theory are

---

[36] Moravcsik, 'Taking Preferences Seriously,' 514.
[37] David Dessler, 'Constructivism within a Positivist Social Science', *Review of International Studies* 25 (1999), 136.
[38] Dessler, 'Constructivism within a Positivist Social Science'.

radically insufficient when addressing questions of meaning and purpose. 'Reconstructive explanations' can tell us the meanings or purposes that animated actors in particular contexts, but alone they cannot tell us what such meanings and purposes ought to be. If Dessler genuinely believes that constructivism's most enduring contribution will come from its 'social relevance', as he argues, then telling us what kind of empirical inquiry and theorising is most appropriate to the task is only one step in the right direction. What Dessler misses is that the real issue is not where constructivism fits within a positivist social science, but what contribution it has to make to ethical reasoning, broadly construed.

So what contribution can constructivism make to ethical reasoning about world politics? In a 1998 article, Richard Price and I advocated a division of labour within an overarching emancipatory research agenda.[39] The agenda was provided by Linklater, who argues that the study of international relations ought to be centrally concerned with issues of inclusion and exclusion in world politics. The pursuit of this agenda, Linklater contends, requires three forms of inquiry: normative, sociological and praxeological. Price and I argued that constructivism was ideally placed to undertake the second of these forms of inquiry, as constructivists had already done more than any other group to push 'the analysis of the normative foundations of the sovereign international order and the sociology of moral community to the forefront of the discipline'.[40] Our assumption was that this sociological work of constructivists would, at some point in time, be brought into dialogue with the normative inquiries of political philosophers and political theorists, a dialogue that would ultimately inform an emancipatory praxeology.

The limitations of this approach are now apparent. To begin with, it buys into the conventional, narrow conception of ethical reasoning. The overarching, emancipatory framework is normative, in the sense that it is animated by a concern with reducing practices of exclusion in world politics. But it is not a conception of ethical reasoning per se. For Linklater, the practice of ethical reasoning is located in the 'normative' pillar of his three-pronged research strategy, alongside the sociological

[39] Richard Price and Christian Reus-Smit, 'Dangerous Liaisons? Critical International Theory and Constructivism', *European Journal of International Relations* 4:3 (1998), 259–294.
[40] Ibid. 285.

and praxeological pillars. The sociological inquiry Price and I imagined constructivists undertaking is meant to engage with ethical reasoning, but it is not conceived as part of such reasoning. Second, the assumption that the sociological work of constructivists would be brought into dialogue with the deliberation of principles of conduct has proven overly optimistic. Examples of constructivists linking their sociological inquiries with such deliberation are scarce, as are instances of constructivists joining forces with political theorists and philosophers.[41] The division of labour approach not only misconstrues the nature of ethical reasoning, therefore, confining it to the partial task of principled deliberation, it also overestimates the willingness of constructivists to self-consciously and systematically locate what they are doing within a broader normative project, whatever they might decide that to be.

The holistic conception of ethical reasoning outlined above recommends a more ambitious contribution for constructivism, a contribution this volume is designed to push forward. Its ambition stems in part from the change in self-identity it demands of constructivists, a change that has two faces. On the one hand, it requires constructivists to locate their sociological inquiries within a broader frame of ethical reasoning. This is partly because these inquiries are already linked to undisclosed and unjustified normative commitments, but most importantly because placing their sociological inquiries within such a frame is essential if constructivists are to contribute in any meaningful way to public discourse about how we should act. On the other hand, it prompts constructivists to be more self-assertive about the integral role sociological insights play in ethical reasoning and thus their value of their own contribution. It also arms them with a powerful response to the chauvinism of many self-styled international political theorists; a response that insists that the logical deliberation of principles of conduct no more amounts to ethical reasoning than pure sociological inquiry.

Part of constructivists making such an identity change is being clear about exactly what insights of their sociological work can contribute to ethical reasoning. Here it is useful to situate the insights identified by Price in the previous chapter within the six dimensions of ethical reasoning outlined above. Table 2.1 plots these against one another, illustrating the critical contribution constructivism can make to the practice of

---

[41] A notable exception to this general trend is Robyn Eckersley, *The Green State: Rethinking Democracy and Sovereignty* (Cambridge MA: MIT Press, 2004).

Table 2.1. *Constructivism and the structure of ethical reasoning*

Dimensions of ethical reasoning	(1) Idiography	(2) Diagnosis	(3) Consequences	(4) Principle	(5) Context	(6) Capacity
Contributions of constructivism						
(1) Empirical–normative gap	How are identities being constituted and how is this affecting perceived moral obligations?					
(2) Agency		Are principal actors driven by a logic of consequences or appropriateness, and what strategies of ethically justifiable change are available?				

(3) Hypocrisy	What roles does hypocrisy play in shaping outcomes?
(4) Moral dilemmas	When will the pursuit of one principle compromise another, and what strategies can mitigate such conflicts?
(5) Complicity and co-optation	What is the transformative potential of existing social structures?
(6) Power	How does the relation between power and legitimacy affect the capacities of different actors to bring about normative change?

reasoning ethically about world politics. For each dimension of ethical reasoning, the table identifies a key question (against one of Price's contributions) that constructivists have a demonstrated track record in answering. I have matched dimensions of ethical reasoning against constructivist contributions randomly, simply matching the next dimension on the table against the next contribution, only then identifying a relevant question that constructivists are well placed to answer. In all likelihood, however, all of Price's constructivist contributions will be relevant to all of my dimensions of ethical reasoning.

Before proceeding, two clarifications are needed. First, in suggesting that constructivism has analytical resources that can be fruitfully conscripted in an enlarged process of ethical reasoning, I am not suggesting that it contains within it substantive, quasi-universal answers to the question 'how should we act?' This praxeological question is asked in diverse circumstances, and my claim is simply that constructivism offers conceptual and analytical tools that can aid the process of ethical reasoning in such circumstances. Second, I am not making the chauvinistic claim that constructivism alone has resources that can assist ethical reasoning about problems in world politics. Constructivism's insights into the conditions under which norms, principles and values shape actors' identities and interests, and in turn political outcomes, are clearly of some importance, but asserting this is not to deny the value of insights generated by other theoretical or analytical perspectives.

Turning to Table 2.1, and starting with the idiographic dimension of ethical reasoning, we see that constructivism's insights into the empirical–normative divide include answers to the crucial, yet largely unscrutinised, questions of how our own and others' social identities are being constituted and how this conditions perceived moral obligations, questions that receive prominent attention in the following chapters. Similarly, if we take the diagnostic aspect of ethical reasoning, we see that constructivism's understanding of human agency can help us determine whether the principal actors in a moral crisis are driven by logics of consequences or appropriateness, and more importantly, what strategies can best affect ethically justifiable change in such a context. Constructivism can also enhance our understanding of the consequences of our moral choices in multiple ways, from detailing the conditions under which actions create normative precedents to explaining the conditions of a hegemon's moral authority. Constructivist insights into the consequences of hypocrisy are particularly valuable here. Hypocrisy is generally seen as cause for moral sanction, but as constructivists have shown, it can also perform positive social functions, enabling the medium- to long-term achievement of seemingly incompatible goods, such as ending a conflict and ultimately punishing those criminally culpable for its instigation and prosecution.

When we come to the 'principled' dimension of ethical reasoning, one might expect that constructivism will have less to offer. But deliberation on contending principles of right conduct almost always involves assessments of the moral, as well as material, costs of pursuing one principle over another. As the chapters by Finnemore and Towns in this volume demonstrate, constructivism is a powerful tool for elucidating the clash of first principles that attends many moral choices. The contextual dimension of ethical reasoning is where one would expect constructivism to have most to offer. And as Price has elaborated, an important element of this is constructivism's insights into the transformative potential of social structures. Nowhere is this more apparent than in constructivism's contributions to our understanding of the nature of sovereignty, which turns out to a variable, practically constituted institution (not a categorical empirical fact), whose moral implications and dilemmas are examined by Finnemore and Havercroft in this volume. Finally, with regard to the 'capacity' dimension of ethical reasoning, it is the value of the constructivist conception of power that stands out. In contrast to the more recent variants of realism, constructivism offers a nuanced, variegated conception of power which highlights the critical importance of legitimacy and social communication, a conception that sensitises us to the transformative capacity of materially weak social actors and the attendant limitations of materially well-endowed ones.

Adopting an expanded conception of ethical reasoning, and identifying the points at which constructivism can contribute, has important implications for the one sociological approach to international relations that has long engaged ethical questions, namely the English School. I have argued elsewhere that a distinguishing characteristic of this approach is its explicit and sustained concern for the nature and limits of moral action in world politics, a concern evident in its interrogation of the vexed relationship between order and justice.[42]

---

[42] Christian Reus-Smit, 'Imagining Society: Constructivism and the English School', *British Journal of Politics and International Relations* 4:3 (2002), 490.

Over time the English School's engagement with ethical questions has polarised into a debate between 'pluralists' and 'solidarists'. The former see international society as a 'practical association', a social aggregation of states that have different purposes but who can nonetheless agree on certain practical rules of co-existence. Because these rules sustain order among states, pluralists see their preservation as a cardinal value, even if this means accepting social injustice.[43] Solidarists, in contrast, see international society as a 'purposive association', an association made up of states who can share common purposes and recognise institutional rules and norms that facilitate more than co-existence. For solidarists, injustice is generally seen as corrosive of order, and they see development of cosmopolitan norms as justified qualifications of rules of co-existence.[44]

In essence, this is a debate between two different views of the limits of moral action in world politics; one that sees the scope for moral action as tightly circumscribed, the other that sees genuine opportunities for moral progress. Yet these positions are built on sets of assumptions that are seldom interrogated, let alone defended in any systematic fashion. Behind the pluralist position lie assumptions about the nature and constitution of state interests, about international society as a social formation, about the sources of order and its relation to rules of co-existence, and about the empirical relationship between the preservation of order and the politics of justice. Similarly, the solidarist position is predicated on assumptions about the capacity of states to develop other regarding interests, about international society's connections with the wider world society and about the political sociology of expanding or contracting moral community.[45] It is also unclear which of the solidarist propositions about the scope of moral action are normative and which are empirical. Is international society a purposive association, or is it desirable that it become so?

---

[43] See Terry Nardin, *Law, Morality, and Relations of* States (Princeton, NJ: Princeton University Press, 1983); James Mayall, *World Politics: Progress and Its Limits* (Cambridge: Polity Press, 2000); and Robert Jackson, *The Global Covenant: Human Conduct in a World of States* (Oxford: Oxford University Press, 2000).

[44] See Andrew Linklater, *The Transformation of Political Community* (Cambridge: Polity Press, 1998).

[45] For a particularly rigorous engagement with these issues, see Nicholas J. Wheeler, *Saving Strangers: Humanitarian Intervention in International Society* (Oxford: Oxford University Press, 2000).

The holistic conception of ethical reasoning advanced above offers a framework for either placing these views of the limits of moral action on more conceptual and empirical foundations or moving beyond them altogether. Furthermore, showing how constructivism can contribute to thinking through each dimension makes available analytical resources previously untapped by the English School. The English School has been at the forefront of empirically informed ethical reflection on international relations, but constructivism may now offer resources that can push such reflection to a new level. In this respect, the ideas outlined in this volume complement moves within the English School itself to break out of its established intellectual rituals, one of which is unnecessarily dichotomised debate between pluralists and solidarists.[46]

Conclusion

At the outset of this chapter, I argued that the field of international relations ought to be more squarely focused on the praxeological question of how we should act in a complex global order, the central question animating this volume. My position is not a totalising or homogenising one; many scholars may well conclude that there are other purposes that ought to animate our work, such as personal satisfaction or science for science's sake. Much of our work is, however, animated by an unacknowledged and unsystematic concern with informing action, and this is as true of post-modernists advocating relentless critique and deconstruction as it is of realists doing 'policy relevant research'. A consequence of this being unacknowledged and unsystematic, though, is that a disjuncture has been allowed to emerge between this hidden purpose and the prevailing model of science which defines ethical inquiry into purposes and ends as out of court. The field has contracted away from the classical vision of IR as a science that explores both the *is* and the *ought*, seriously corroding our capacity to speak to pressing issues of human action. If we take this seriously as an end of scholarship, then we have no choice other than to re-engage the empirical and the normative. My argument is more ambitious than this,

---

[46] See Barry Buzan, *From International Society to World Society* (Cambridge: Cambridge University Press, 2004); and Richard Little and John Williams (eds.), *The Anarchical Society in a Globalized World* (London: Palgrave, 2006).

though. I have argued that we need to adopt a more holistic conception of ethical reasoning, a conception that encompasses six modes of reflection, of which only the third is concerned with the deliberation of principles of right conduct. One virtue of this conception is that it provides us with a framework to demonstrate the critical role that constructivism can play in ethical reasoning about world politics, a role hitherto dismissed by critics. In elucidating this role, I have drawn strong links between my conception of ethical reasoning and the contributions of constructivism identified by Price in the previous chapter. The following chapters explore these contributions in greater detail.

3 | The role of consequences, comparison and counterfactuals in constructivist ethical thought

KATHRYN SIKKINK

First let me plead guilty to one of the charges that Price aims at constructivists.[1] Although I believe that some of my work has demonstrated the possibilities of moral change in world politics, I have not explicitly articulated a normative or prescriptive position of particular changes as good. And this is the case despite the fact that my students and my colleagues get irritated when I (not infrequently) bristle with moral indignation. The story of why I and other constructivists have not engaged in normative theory is complicated. I don't claim to fully understand it and I don't want to dwell on it here, but just mention a few possible explanations. When I started working on human rights in the late 1980s, the choice of topic alone was a sufficiently normative signal that I felt obliged to spend the rest of my time demonstrating that I was being rigorous in my theory and method. Perhaps I believed that my normative argument was implicit and the discerning reader would know where I stood. Maybe Frost is correct and even constructivists have concealed our ethical stances under a disguise of (our own kind of) scientific objectivity?[2] After over twenty years of doing serious empirical research to document key trends in world politics, I'm still annoyed at being categorised in a recent article by Jack Snyder and Leslie Vinjamuri among those 'idealists' who don't understand the 'political realities' of world politics.[3] It is not the 'idealist' charge that irritates, but the notion that we don't understand political developments in the world.

[1] I wish to thank Richard Price, Robert Keohane, Michael Barnett, Raymond Duvall, Ann Towns and Henry Shue, as well as participants in the Vancouver workshop and participants in the Political Theory Colloquium at the University of Minnesota for their helpful comments on earlier drafts of this paper.

[2] Mervyn Frost, 'A Turn Not Taken: Ethics in IR at the Millennium', *Review of International Studies* 24 (1998), 119.
[3] Jack Snyder and Leslie Vinjamuri, 'Trials and Errors: Principle and Pragmatism in Strategies of International Justice', *International Security* 28:3 (2003/04), 5–44.

But I also think that the options for normative theorising that I perceived as open to me failed to capture the essence of my enterprise. In other words, the options for normative theorising often seemed to ask me to leave my empirical hat at the door, and since my empirical research was just as dear to me as my ethics, I refused. As long as the appeals to address ethics essentially said 'stop being a researcher and become a moral philosopher', it wasn't very attractive to me.[4] Some scholars, like Andrew Linklater, Charles Beitz or Henry Shue, can combine the two roles.[5] Personally, I have neither the training nor the inclination to engage in abstract moral philosophy. It is only now, with a different kind of push from Richard Price, and a few years of teaching a course on International Ethics and Global Citizenship under my belt, that I feel able to begin to find an approach to normative theorising that combines my ethical concerns and my empirical commitments. Relatively few scholars of international relations offer any genuine guidance about how to chart this particular path.[6]

Despite the divide in ethical theorising between deontological and consequentialist traditions, I believe that when we begin to combine ethical and empirical inquiry, deontological and consequentialist concerns are intimately linked.[7] One reason why constructivists have focused so clearly on careful empirical research is that I suspect we believe (at least implicitly) that often we need to know something about the empirical consequences of some norms in order to judge their ethical desirability. Here I suggest an interactive approach where

[4] This is essentially what Frost says, when he asks us to start addressing the 'classic questions of political ethics: such as "in what would a just order consist?" "What is freedom, what forms of political authority are just?"'. 'A Turn Not Taken', 129.

[5] Andrew Linklater, *The Transformation of Political Community: Ethical Foundation of the Post-Westphalian Era* (Columbia, SC: University of South Carolina Press, 1998); Charles Beitz, *Political Theory and International Relations* (Princeton, NJ: Princeton University Press, 1979); Henry Shue, *Basic Rights* (Princeton, NJ: Princeton University Press, second edition 1996).

[6] See however, Matthew Gibney, *The Ethics and Politics of Asylum: Liberal Democracy and the Response to Refugees* (Cambridge: Cambridge University Press, 2004); Michael Barnett, *Eyewitness to Genocide: The United Nations and Rwanda* (Ithaca, NY: Cornell University Press, 2002); Joseph Nye, *Nuclear Ethics* (New York, NY: Free Press, 1986); J. L. Holzgrefe and Robert O. Keohane (eds.), *Humanitarian Intervention: Ethical, Legal, and Political Dilemmas* (Cambridge: Cambridge University Press, 2003).

[7] Similar points have been made by Nye, *Nuclear Ethics*, and J. L. Holzgrefe, 'The Humanitarian Intervention Debate'. In Holzgrefe and Keohane, *Humanitarian Intervention*, 50–51.

we begin with ethical commitments that may guide the choice of a research topic *and* the results of research may in turn shape future ethical judgement. My discussion will look at related questions of consequences, comparison and counterfactuals to try to offer some insights for normative thinking from the realm of empirical constructivism. I will illustrate my arguments with reference to two current human rights debates: the debate over the US use of torture and the debate over the impact of the increasing use of global human rights trials, both of which have been the focus of my current research.[8]

Some of the most important intellectual disagreements I have had with very diverse individuals in my lifetime were so deeply felt exactly because they were simultaneously ethical and empirical. But I was often unable even to identify this and to explain cogently how I combined ethical judgement with the results of my empirical research to arrive at strongly held positions. This essay attempts a clarification. I suggest that disagreements are often not the product of different principles we begin with but of different empirical evaluations of consequences. If this is the case, our ethical debates could be more fruitful if we were clear about the research and reasoning processes through which we arrive at our evaluations of consequences.

Principles and consequences

One distinctive contribution of any empirically oriented researcher to ethical thought is to realise and emphasise that ethical judgement requires both choices of principles and evaluation of consequences in terms of those principles. In other words, to answer the question 'what to do?' we need to ask not just 'what is right?' but also 'what may work?' to bring about outcomes consistent with my principles.[9] For example, in the case of human rights trials, it is not enough to ask 'is it right or good to hold human rights trials?' I also want to know what impact human rights trials have on actually protecting human rights. The answer to the

---

[8] Kathryn Sikkink, 'U.S. Compliance with International Human Rights Law'. Paper prepared for the annual conference of the International Studies Association, March 2005, Honolulu, Hawaii; Kathryn Sikkink and Carrie Booth Walling, 'The Impact of Human Rights Trials in Latin America', *Journal of Peace Research* 44:4 (2007), 427–445.

[9] I am indebted to Richard Price for this particular formulation.

second question 'what impact do human rights trials have?' could affect the answer to the first question, 'is it right or good to hold human rights trials?' Discerning and evaluating consequences is an inherently comparative and empirical enterprise, and thus empirically grounded scholars can make an important contribution. I heartily agree with Price's argument that normative theorising cannot escape some degree of empirical description. Constructivists and other empirically oriented scholars of world politics can contribute to thinking, researching and writing clearly about consequences and then link this work on consequences to thoughtful normative judgement. This research on consequences doesn't have to be about causality, it could also be a constitutive theorising or about conditions of possibility, but it needs to be explicit and precise in order to be persuasive.

In order to weigh consequences, we must first have specified what principles we intend to use to evaluate which consequences are most valued and beneficial. I propose to start with international human rights principles. Thus, when I consider consequences, my question will be: what are the consequences for human rights, as defined in current human rights law?[10] Amartya Sen provides a model of such an effort to link a rights-based approach with a concern for consequences in his 'goal rights system'. To make a normative evaluation, Sen proposed both to include rights in the goals themselves (deontological criteria) and to evaluate outcomes based on which rights are fulfilled and not fulfilled (consequentialist criteria).[11] His approach is different from a classic utilitarian approach, which is interested in overall welfare and does not privilege the actual protection of rights, as opposed to other welfare goals. Sen thus overcomes one of the main criticisms of utilitarianism – 'that it cannot take rights seriously enough'.[12] He refers to this as a rights–consequence system, because the fulfilment of rights is the major goal of the system. It is not a fully consequentialist system, but one that blends rights goals and concern with rights fulfilment. Sen in turn uses this approach as the basis of his 'capabilities approach to

---

[10] Here I clearly part paths with utilitarians and most consequentialists who have a welfarist rather than a rights-based approach to evaluating consequences.

[11] Amartya Sen, 'Rights and Agency'. In Samuel Scheffler (ed.), *Consequentialism and Its Critics* (Oxford: Oxford University Press, 1988), 187–223.

[12] William H. Shaw, *Contemporary Ethics: Taking Account of Utilitarianism* (Oxford: Blackwell Publishers, 1999), 185.

development', an approach that has also been articulated, in a slightly different way, by Martha Nussbaum.[13]

I share with Sen and Nussbaum the idea of combining rights-based principles with an evaluation of the fulfilment of rights as a starting point for my normative theorising. But both Sen and Nussbaum begin as if the world were a *tabula rasa* on which they could construct the set of principles of their choice. As much as I generally admire the work of Sen and Nussbaum, I have always been puzzled about why they believe that they must start from scratch in inventing their central list of rights or capabilities. Nussbaum says almost as an aside that 'capabilities as I conceive them have a very close relationship to human rights, as understood in contemporary international discussions'.[14] Sen, in his early discussion of his promising goal rights system, seems to disregard existing human rights law, although he refers to human rights more directly in his later work.[15]

To the empirically oriented researcher, however, it may seem illusory to act as though the modern world wasn't dense with existing norms and laws, and to pretend that we could design the ideal code we could imagine. If our starting point is a 'rights–consequence system', I prefer to start with existing human rights principles embodied in international human rights law, especially the International Covenant on Civil and Political Rights (ICCPR) and the International Covenant on Economic, Social and Cultural Rights (ICESCR). When one set of human rights principles come into conflict with another, I prioritise the non-derogable rights of the ICCPR, especially the right to life and freedom from slavery and torture. The non-derogable rights will also be those principles that I hold absolutely without regard to any information about consequences. Thus, in my rights–consequence system, there will be a small handful of rights that will not be subject to any consideration of consequences or effectiveness. I justify the priority on the non-derogable rights in a couple of ways. First, the non-derogable rights clause comes as close as I can find to expressing a genuine international consensus about what rights are most important. The international community, when drafting one of its central human rights documents, decided that

---

[13] Martha C. Nussbaum, *Woman and Human Development: The Capabilities Approach* (Cambridge: Cambridge University Press, 2000).
[14] Ibid. 97.
[15] See, for example, Amartya Sen, 'Freedoms and Needs', *The New Republic* January 10/17, 1994, 31–38.

there were a small handful of rights that could not be put aside under any circumstance. This seems like a good starting place for normative argument. Starting with actually existing international norms drafted through exhaustive debate and consultation among many states has the virtue of being less ethnocentric than having the analyst substitute her own normative criteria.

Other colleagues will say that this starting place is also the crystal-lisation of power relations from centuries of legal developments. That is without doubt the case. But recent close studies of the drafting processes of the Universal Declaration of Human Rights, the ICCPR and the ICESCR reveal that delegates from countries representing diverse cul-tural, political and theological positions debated virtually every phrase in these documents in hundreds of consultations and meetings.[16] Secondly, by their ratification of the ICCPR, including its non-derogable rights clause, and the ICESCR, an even wider range of countries has expressed their support for these principles and norms. So, today, over 150 countries have signalled their support for these norms by the voluntary ratification of the ICCPR and the ICESCR, including over forty-five African countries, which were the single largest group not present at the drafting stage, since most were still colonies at that time. Finally, thousands of non-governmental human rights organisations representing citizens from around the world have also debated and embraced these norms.

From a procedural point of view, the deliberative processes that went into the construction of these international human rights norms were more voluntary and more participatory than many other international processes. I do not claim that the drafting of these conventions took place under the conditions of an ideal speech act or that this is a concrete empirical and international analogue to a dialogic ethic. But because of the procedures through which these norms were developed, they pro-vide a more legitimate source of general principles than any I or any

---

[16] See Johannes Morsink, *The Universal Declaration of Human Rights: Origins, Drafting and Intent* (Philadelphia, PA: University of Pennsylvania Press, 1999); Mary Ann Glendon, *A World Made New: Eleanor Roosevelt and the Universal Declaration of Human Rights* (New York, NY: Random House, 2001); Paul Gordon Lauren, *The Evolution of Human Rights: Visions Seen* (Philadelphia, PA: University of Pittsburgh Press, 1998); Mary Ann Glendon, 'The Forgotten Crucible: The Latin American Influence on the Universal Human Rights Idea', *Harvard Human Rights Journal* 16 (2003), 27–39.

other individual or group of researchers could invent. In the current political climate, it would be difficult to organise any equally participatory process of drafting new human rights norms, nor could we be certain that the result would be as strong. Thus there are both procedural and pragmatic grounds for using principles in existing human rights law as a benchmark against which to measure consequences. As Jack Donnelly has argued, there is now an 'overlapping international political consensus' around the norms of the core human rights treaties. He clarifies that this is an 'overlapping (rather than complete) and political (rather than moral or religious) consensus'.[17] Nussbaum uses the same term, overlapping consensus, drawn from Rawls, to characterise her list of central human capabilities.[18]

In the introductory chapter, Price asks us to define and defend our understanding of progress in international relations. Following the discussion above, I define as progress an improvement in the enjoyment of any of the human rights listed in international human rights law as compared to an earlier period if such improvement does not cause a commensurate regress in other rights or in other places. I will be particularly attentive to sustained improvement of the non-derogable rights. This definition is consistent, I believe, with the ethical intent of the authors who drafted human rights law and those states and non-governmental organisations that later embraced it. It is thus my own definition and an attempt to capture the ethical world of the actors involved. This definition requires us to consult empirical research to make ethical judgements, as we must be able to have some measure of the enjoyment of rights, and know what changes have occurred from one period to another.

We could inquire further about the sources of this international consensus around certain human rights. I am always tempted to make more foundational claims for these norms. I believe that nothing does greater and more long-lasting harm to people than when other people intentionally and directly inflict bodily harm on them. The bonds of trust on which human communities are founded are sundered most completely by the direct and intentional inflicting of pain and suffering of one human on another. Research on post-traumatic stress, for

---

[17] Jack Donnelly, *Universal Human Rights in Theory and Practice* (Ithaca, NY: Cornell University Press, second edition, 2003), 40.
[18] Nussbaum, *Woman and Human Development*, 5.

example, shows that human-induced traumas from torture or child abuse are more severe and more difficult to recover from than trauma produced by accidents or natural disasters. I personally believe that this small core of basic rights is intrinsically appealing to many individuals. It is perfectly acceptable for political scientists (including constructivists) to suggest that all humans have an innate drive for power or wealth. But to suggest that many humans intrinsically find certain human rights ideas appealing is somehow more questionable. Yet it does not strike me as particularly odd to suggest that almost everyone would prefer to be alive than dead, free than imprisoned, secure than tortured, fed than hungry. Core human rights norms have resonated so profoundly in the world in part because of this intrinsic appeal. It is surprising to watch how quickly humans, even those embedded in cultural scenarios that tell them otherwise, come to believe that they are entitled to something better.

Nevertheless, my argument does not rest, nor depend, on such foundational claims. It is sufficient for our purposes that many states, groups and individuals, through an extended process of international negotiation, mutually arrived upon a set of international human rights norms and that since that time, virtually all of these states and many more have further endorsed such norms through the voluntary ratification of the relevant treaties. This overlapping international political consensus is then the starting point for my discussion of evaluation of consequences.

The problem with starting with the overlapping political consensus of existing human rights law as a basis for ethical judgement is that it would appear to exclude new human rights norms in the process of emergence. I can take this position comfortably in 2006, writing in an atmosphere dense with international human rights norms, but what would one have written in 1941 before these norms were established?[19] I believe that empirical researchers writing about ethics will want to situate themselves in a particular historical context. If I were writing in 1941, I would have to write something completely different, but likewise, I should not write in 2006 as if I were in 1941. But the deeper point is that in our current period there are many new norms in the process of emergence. How do we appreciate this transformational process of the emergence of new norms? Much of my empirical research has focused

---

[19] I am indebted to Raymond Duvall for raising this specific question and the broader concern.

on the emergence of new norms, and I believe that this will continue to be an avenue for promising new research. As an analyst, I have argued that the primary way that normative change has happened is through the advocacy of norm entrepreneurs.[20]

The purpose of choosing existing human rights law as a starting point for ethical analysis is not to exclude or denigrate movements proposing new norms. But I would treat new norms as ethically and empirically distinct from existing norms because they do not yet represent any international consensus. Ethically, they represent a proposal for normative change by one group that has not yet been broadly endorsed. The challenge for any norm entrepreneur, as they know all too well, is to seek to persuade other actors to create an international consensus. Empirically, the dynamics of new norms are different from those of well-established norms.[21] To treat an emergent norm as if it were hard law is an empirical mistake. Emergent norms have different properties, provoke different responses, impose different obligations and require different kinds of work on the part of advocates.

The most complicated ethical and political dilemmas in international politics involve cases where some of these basic human rights norms come into conflict with one another or with other core norms and values of the international system. For example, debates over humanitarian intervention are so difficult in part because one has to weigh the possibility of preventing genocide or mass human rights violations against other key norms against war and intervention, as Finnemore analyses in her chapter. Many of these ethical debates cannot be resolved with reference to empirical research. But other debates that appear to be intractable debates over conflicts of principles are actually debates over different predictions about consequences. Such debates can be addressed fruitfully, although rarely resolved, with reference to empirical research about consequences.

The most attractive version of consequentialism for the empirically minded researcher is 'rule consequentialism'. Consequentialism is usually divided between its act and rule variants: act consequentialism holds that the consequentialist criterion is to be applied directly to

---

[20] Margaret Keck and Kathryn Sikkink, *Activists beyond Borders* (Ithaca, NY: Cornell University Press, 1998).

[21] Martha Finnemore and Kathryn Sikkink, 'International Norm Dynamics and Political Change', *International Organization* 52:4 (1998), 887–917.

particular acts, while rule consequentialism applies to general rules or principles. People should comply with rules if their general observance will produce the best consequences, even if in a particular circumstance such a rule might not lead to the best consequence.[22] So, a rule-consequentialist, when wondering about the morality of some conduct, asks, 'what would the consequences be if everyone felt free to do that?'[23] To illustrate the difference with regard to the case of torture, act-consequentialism would ask about the consequences of torturing a particular individual and base a decision on those. Rule consequentialism would ask instead, what would be the consequences if all countries felt free to torture? In turn, some rule-consequentialists distinguish between primary and secondary rules, which may be related to the distinction I am making here between non-derogable rights and other rights.[24] As we can see, rule-consequentialism narrows the distance between consequentialist and agent-centred approaches, as both focus on the need for codes or principles.

Evaluating consequences

The huge philosophical debate about consequentialism and the closely related school of utilitarianism has not hinged on what would seem to be the glaring issue for any empirical researcher. How can we know with any confidence about consequences? A large body of (consequentialist) normative thought is based on the notion that morality depends on what we can reasonably expect to happen. But most philosophers aren't in the business of trying to find out what we can reasonably expect to happen.[25] The task is left to empirical researchers to fill the gap. But having filled the gap, we then need to reconnect our conclusions back to their normative implications.

In both cases discussed in this chapter, that of the debate over the use of torture by the US government and the issues of human rights trials,

---

[22] Shaw, *Contemporary Ethics*.
[23] Brad Hooker, *Ideal Code, Real World: A Rule-consequentialist Theory of Morality* (Oxford: Clarendon Press, 2000).
[24] Shaw, *Contemporary Ethics*.
[25] For example, Shaw argues that 'most expected outcome utilitarians' think about consequences as 'calculated by a reasonable and well informed agent based on the available evidence'; *Contemporary Ethics*, 30. This description sounds like a reference to an empirical researcher.

the empirical question of what we can reasonably expect to happen has important ethical implications. In a recent article on human rights and war crimes trials, Jack Snyder and Leslie Vinjamuri suggest that under certain circumstances such trials can lead to more atrocities, sustain conflict and undermine democracy.[26] If they are correct about what we can reasonably expect from human rights trials, a consequentialist reading would say that countries *should not* carry out such trials. If, to the contrary, as Carrie Booth Walling and I have argued, there is little empirical support for the argument that trials lead to more atrocities, sustain conflict or undermine democracy, the normative equation is different.[27]

This may help clarify why for me careful empirical research using the best tools at our disposal is not just a professional obligation, but also an ethical one. Exactly because the ethical and normative questions are so important, and because, from my point of view at least, most ethical judgements require some knowledge about reasonable expectations about consequences, good research is necessary for ethical judgement.

This then takes us to the question that Price poses in his introductory chapter. What should we do if 'constructivist analyses lead us to identify that what appear prima facie to be progressive initiatives are themselves revealed to come at the price of concomitant regress in other areas'? Constructivist analysis that points to ethically progressive change in world politics *and* constructivist analysis that problematises such progress by talking about concomitant regress in other areas is research about consequences. It is mainly historical and comparative research that tries to identify the consequences of key changes and continuities in world politics. As such, this knowledge of consequences should permit both normative judgement about the past and guidance for action in the future. Because such historical research is the best guide we have for what we can reasonably expect in the future, it must go one step further than simply pointing to progress and/or regress. Research about consequences needs to try to evaluate the relative importance and weight of such progress and regress. It is not enough simply to say that there are both costs and benefits of different changes. In order to make an ethical judgement about action in the future, we need to have an idea of the

[26] Snyder and Vinjamuri, 'Trials and Errors'.
[27] Sikkink and Walling, 'The Impact of Human Rights Trials in Latin America'.

relative balance of the different consequences, or the conditions under which certain benefits or costs will be more likely.

Trials and consequences

Let me illustrate some of these arguments with examples from current research on international, foreign and domestic human rights trials. Ellen Lutz and I have argued that since the 1980s there has been a dramatic new trend: states throughout the world are beginning to hold individuals, including heads of state, accountable for past human rights violations. We have labelled this trend as 'the justice cascade'.[28] The question that concerns us here is: given that such trials are occurring with considerable frequency, what impact or consequences do they have? Snyder and Vinjamuri argue that the consequences can be dangerous because states that pursue justice for past human rights abuses may destabilise their societies and sustain conflict. Therefore, these scholars advise that amnesties are more effective at ending atrocities than trials.[29]

These are empirical claims. To address them, Carrie Booth Walling, Hunjoon Kim and I created a new data set of the main transitional justice mechanisms: truth commissions and domestic, foreign and international trials for past human rights violations. This new data both definitively demonstrates the existence of the justice cascade and allows us to explore empirical questions about the impact of trials.[30] Our initial research indicates that human rights trials do not make the human rights situation worse, and in some situations human rights trials are associated with an improvement in the human rights situation.

A purely deontological approach might say that providing justice for victims of human rights violations and accountability for perpetrators is such an important principle that countries should proceed with trials

[28]   Ellen Lutz and Kathryn Sikkink, 'The Justice Cascade: The Evolution and Impact of Foreign Human Rights Trials in Latin America', *Chicago Journal of International Law* 2:1 (2001), 1–34.
[29]   Snyder and Vinjamuri, 'Trials and Errors'; see also Stephen Krasner, 'After Wartime Atrocities Politics Can Do More Than the Courts', *International Herald Tribune* January 16, 2001.
[30]   Sikkink and Walling, 'The Impact of Human Rights Trials in Latin America'; Hunjoon Kim and Kathryn Sikkink, 'Do Human Rights Trials Make A Difference?' Paper presented at the American Political Science Association Annual Meeting, Chicago, August 28 – September 2, 2007.

regardless of the consequences. While I understand and respect that ethical argument, I'm not willing to make it myself. I agree that providing justice and accountability are worthy goals that should be pursued. But accountability for past human rights violations does not form part of the core 'non-derogable rights' of the human rights regimes. At best, there is an emerging norm that states have an obligation or duty to punish individuals who carry out mass atrocities,[31] but this is not yet a clear rule of international human rights law. In this case, I believe that knowledge of expected consequences is important for helping make hard ethical choices.

This is not just a simple question of whether trials are good or bad. Empirical research can also help us understand under what conditions human rights trials could improve human rights and under what conditions they might make them worse. So, for example, Snyder and Vinjamuri look at thirty-four cases of civil wars. They provide evidence that that in some civil war situations an immediate demand for trials could undermine peace negotiations and thus sustain conflict and that amnesties in these situations could lead to conflict resolution. This involves an ethical trade-off: peace vs. justice and accountability.

Because previous quantitative empirical research shows that civil war is closely correlated with human rights violations,[32] it may be an ethically justifiable trade-off to offer amnesties in order to secure peace settlements. But Snyder and Vinjamuri don't limit themselves to generalising about civil war cases but instead make broad and sweeping statements about the impact of human rights trials.

Since Snyder and Vinjamuri derive important moral, theoretical and policy implications from their research, their failure to be more careful about the generalisations they make calls into question their ethical judgements. I believe it is premature to draw ethical implications from this work until there is further empirical verification of their findings. Carrie Booth Walling and I have to date also only focused on a subset of cases with human rights trials – those in Latin America. Thus, we cannot

---

[31] Juan Mendez, 'In Defense of Transitional Justice'. In A. James McAdams (ed.), *Transitional Justice and Rule of Law in New Democracies* (Notre Dame, IN: University of Notre Dame Press, 1997), 5.

[32] See, for example, Stephen Poe, C. Neal Tate and Linda Camp Keith, 'Repression of Human Rights to Personal Integrity Revisited: A Global Cross-National Study Covering the Years 1976–1993', *International Studies Quarterly* 43:2 (1999), 291–313.

yet make generalisations to the entire universe of cases and must consider the possibility that there is some form of Latin American 'exceptionalism' that makes human rights trials have a more positive effect in Latin America than elsewhere.

This is one way in which principled based arguments and consequentialist arguments might be combined. Particularly in cases where important and valued principles are at stake, the presumption should be in favour of the principle, and only very substantial and well-established evidence against the principle would be sufficient to lead us to call it into question. So, for example, the principle of accountability for past human rights violations is sufficiently well established that in order to suspend it, we would want to see very persuasive research that it is counterproductive. If, however, very persuasive future research actually confirms the Snyder and Vinjamuri hypothesis that trials lead to more atrocities, I would re-evaluate my ethical support for human rights trials.

Weighing consequences

Resolving empirical questions about consequences is important for making normative judgements about desirable policies. It is not only a question of determining which policies are good and bad, but rather specifying the conditions under which different policies can lead to better or worse outcomes. To go back to Price's questions, I believe that constructivists who raise questions of progress and regress in world politics not only need to evaluate the progressive versus the regressive outcomes of policies, but also try to specify more carefully the conditions under which a more progressive or less progressive outcome is likely.

Much important work by critical constructivists has focused exactly on the unanticipated consequences of acts and policies. Ann Towns, in her contribution to this volume, for example, has alerted us that one of the consequences of gender equal discourses and policies in Sweden has been to further stigmatise and marginalise immigrant populations. But rather than rejecting gender equality struggles as a result, she then goes on to incorporate these exclusionary effects 'in the moral calculus guiding action'.[33]

---

[33] Ann Towns, this volume.

Such a weighing of consequences is neither easy nor straightforward. It often involves counterfactual arguments about the past, and also may imply some kind of prediction about the future, or what some people have called a 'future counterfactual'.[34] Since predictions about the future can be notoriously uncertain, individuals can differ in their claims about consequences, and such differences are difficult to resolve. Good predictions about the future rely on the best research about the past. Even with careful intentions, predictions will be inaccurate because the very nature of the social world makes possible the unanticipated, as humans learn and change their world. It could be that any constructivist would be so distrustful of prediction that they dismiss any effort at consequentialist normative theorising. Indeed, one important contribution of constructivism has been demonstrating exactly how some change that was seen as 'unimaginable' previously could become a new norm in the present.

But I want to argue that we can't avoid some kind of efforts to understand the future. Robert Cox (quoted in Price's introductory essay) discusses normative choice, but would limit 'the range of choice to alternative orders which are feasible transformations of the existing world'. But how do we know what is feasible? I would argue we know what is feasible from the research about how change has occurred in the past. In other words, like the language or not, we know what is feasible by making 'predictions' about the future based on our best research on the past. Call it 'prediction' or a future counterfactual, or call it our best hunches about what could happen, I will argue that we can't eschew completely consequentialist theorising because discussions of consequences are ubiquitous in political life.

I place this emphasis on the importance of consequences fully aware that we are on dangerous ground. Consequentialist ethical arguments are more suspect because they lend themselves, I believe, to more manipulation. Counterfactual arguments are often open to manipulation because people can propose far-fetched or improbable future counterfactuals, and they are difficult to oppose because it is just my counterfactual against yours. I will argue that this is exactly what is

---

[34] Steve Weber, 'Counterfactuals: Past and Future'. In Philip Tetlock and Aaron Belkin (eds.), *Counterfactual Thought Experiments in World Politics: Logical, Methodological, and Psychological Perspectives* (Princeton, NJ: Princeton University Press, 1996), 268–288.

happening with the US government justification for the use of torture. Bush administration officials posed an improbable but frightening counterfactual – 'if we don't torture, we will suffer another terrorist attack' – and thus gained support for their policy.

Joseph Nye has similarly pointed to the dangers of consequentialism in his discussion of nuclear ethics. 'Once the ends justify the means, the dangers of slipping into a morality of convenience greatly increase. To calculate all the consequences of one's actions is impossible, and when the calculation is fuzzy, abuse is possible ... And given human proclivities to weight choices in our own favor and the difficulties of being sure of consequences of complex activities, impartiality may be easily lost in the absence of rules.' Despite these misgivings, Nye still concluded that a nuclear ethics had to include consideration of motives, means and consequences.[35]

To cede the ground of discussing consequences hampers one's ability to participate in political discussions, including normative and ethical ones. So, for example, we could respond to the US government's consequentialist justification of torture with a purely deontological argument by saying that it is always wrong to torture, regardless of the consequences. But that would grant the plausibility in the argument about the consequences of torture. I would prefer that we both stress principles *and* engage in the most rigorous debate possible about consequences. So, how do we go about weighing consequences? I will argue that there are four particularly prominent forms of reasoning often used to evaluate consequences: (1) mental simulations of counterfactual worlds; (2) pure counterfactuals; (3) comparison to the ideal; and (4) empirical comparisons. I will discuss each of these forms of reasoning below.

Four kinds of reasoning commonly used to evaluate consequences

Mental simulations of counterfactual worlds
In their discussion of five types of counterfactuals, Tetlock and Belkin highlight one type that is most relevant to normative theorising. They call it the 'mental simulation of counterfactual worlds' and point out that 'asking people to imagine and work through the detailed

[35] Nye, *Nuclear Ethics*, 19.

implications of hypothetical worlds is a powerful educational and rhetorical tool'. In particular, such simulations can 'reveal double standards in moral judgments', and 'unwanted biases such as the certainty of hindsight'.[36] I would suggest that such mental simulations are pervasive in philosophical thought and they are not just important for revealing double standards, but for clarifying normative thought more generally. Rawls used the veil of ignorance as such a mental simulation. Onora O'Neill used the hypothetical of the lifeboat to discuss the responsibility to avoid unjustifiable deaths in famine.[37]

Counterfactual mental simulations are useful tools as long as we accept them for what they are – made up scenarios that don't correspond necessarily to anything in the real world. The danger comes when people turn the counterfactual simulation into a consequentialist causal story about the world. Here is where careful attention to the best possible empirical research is crucial to counteract far-fetched and dangerous counterfactuals.

So, for example, the Bush administration has engaged in this kind of counterfactuals with regard to torture. The entire ticking time bomb scenario is a type of counterfactual morality tale often used by philosophers to help people think through difficult ethical trade-offs and the logic of our reasoning. The tale goes that there is a ticking time bomb somewhere, and the government has arrested a person who knows about it. If we torture him he will tell us where the bomb is, which allows us to save the lives of thousands of people. Given this scenario, most people will choose torture. If we accept the notion of this kind of counterfactual as helping clarify inconsistencies in moral rules, its 'lesson' is that we don't believe in a complete prohibition of torture, because there is a scenario where we would justify it. The problem with the ticking time bomb scenario is that it has been converted from a hypothetical scenario that may be useful to help us clarify our ethical positions and difficult trade-offs, to an actual description of the world and to a justification of policies that have alarming ethical implications. It is proposed as an empirical description of the world. There really is a ticking bomb, and we really have the person who knows about it, and if

---

[36] Tetlock and Belkin, *Counterfactual Thought Experiments in World Politics*, 13–14.
[37] Onora O'Neill, 'Lifeboat Earth'. In Charles Beitz *et al.* (eds.), *International Ethics* (Princeton, NJ: Princeton University Press, 1985), 265.

we don't torture him thousands of people will die. This is then used to justify the actual use of torture. Once some kind of ethical 'permission' for torture has been given in the abstract and limited case of the ticking time bomb, once we accept that the prohibition of torture is not absolute, this is then taken as a more blanket permission for the use of torture.

As a description of the world, this scenario is deeply misleading. Interrogators will tell you that they rarely if ever encounter an actual ticking time bomb scenario in their work. Instead of the clean hypothetical of the torture of one (guilty) person against the lives of thousands of (innocent) people, you have a much more difficult scenario of the torture of hundreds (?) of innocent (?) people without even being certain that there is a bomb, or if we could discover it and dismantle it and save lives.

Prior to 9/11, the commonplace belief in the United States was that torture was wrong and that the United States would never use or condone torture. After 9/11, a few people began to question this belief, but initially they seemed at the margins, or testing the waters. By 2004/2005 however, there was a very substantial opinion in the United States that although most forms of torture may be wrong, it may be necessary and desirable to use some forms of 'torture lite' or cruel, inhuman or degrading treatment to gather information and to keep America safe in this new situation of a war on terror. These arguments are not being made just by conservative commentators, but by some respected members of the liberal intellectual establishment.[38] Almost all the arguments start with the ticking time bomb scenario and then move quickly to the premise that torture is indeed 'effective'. Rarely do these commentators provide adequate evidence for this premise that torture actually works. Recent cases have shown the risks of relying on information extracted from torture.[39] The most revealing case is that of Ibn al-Shaykh al-Libi, who provided the testimony about ties between Iraq and al-Qa'ida used by the Bush administration as one of its justifications for the Iraq war. Libi later recanted, saying that he had fabricated the information to

---

[38] See the debate, for example, in Sanford Levinson, *Torture: A Collection* (Oxford: Oxford University Press, 2004).

[39] See, for example, 'The Costs of Outsourcing Interrogation: A Canadian Muslim's Long Ordeal in Syria', *New York Times* May 29, 2005; 'German Held in Afghan Jail Files Lawsuit: Mistaken Identity is Basis of Claim', *New York Times* December 7, 2005, A16.

escape torture in Egypt, where he had been sent by the United States as part of the policy of 'extraordinary rendition' of high-level suspects to other countries for interrogation purposes.[40] Even some US interrogators have come forward to argue that they did not get useful information through harsh interrogation.[41] Yet the entire argument for torture rests on the premise of effectiveness.

The movement from interesting counterfactual mental simulation to actual description of the world that in turn justifies a policy that goes way beyond the antecedent conditions of the mental simulation is a sleight of hand with pernicious human results. I believe it is very dangerous to go from a hypothetical tool of this sort to a policy recommendation for the real world. Instead, we would prefer to base our policy recommendations on careful empirical research about what has actually happened in the world. Nevertheless, counterfactual arguments of some sort may be difficult to avoid.

Pure counterfactuals

A second kind of argument often used both in discussions of torture and in discussions of human rights trials is what we could call the pure counterfactual. Counterfactuals are subjunctive conditions statements (i.e. they take the form, if x then y would have ...) in which the first part of the statement is not true. The argument about the effectiveness of torture often takes this form of a counterfactual argument. That is, the argument is that the situation with torture is better than it would have been if torture had not been used. The policy makers say, 'believe me, worse things would have happened had we not tortured'. Counterfactual arguments are very common in the policy world, and they are common in social science as well. But they are a particularly tricky kind of argument and they need to be handled with care. Because for every counterfactual that says, we are now safer because we have tortured, we can compose a plausible counterfactual that says we are not safer because of torture. It is one person's view of what might have happened compared to another person's view of what might have happened. Counterfactual arguments can never be proven or established definitively. Nevertheless, this does not mean that all

---

[40] 'Iraq War Intelligence Linked to Coercion', *International Herald Tribune* December 9, 2005.
[41] Anthony Lagouranis, 'Tortured Logic', *New York Times* February 28, 2006.

counterfactuals are equal, and we need to use the best evidence at our disposal to try to distinguish more plausible from less plausible counterfactuals.

To deal with counterfactual causal statements about torture, for example, we need to look at evidence. If we look for historical evidence of real-world examples of ticking time bombs, we find very few. Joseph Lelyveld, in a *New York Times Magazine* article where he interviewed many Israeli security agents, says that despite the long use of harsh punishment in Israel, he could get only one specific case where torture actually stopped a ticking time bomb.[42] But counterfactuals about torture are often particularly troubling counterfactuals, because policy makers may also say that for national security reasons, they can't produce the evidence to prove their statement because it is classified. When 'evidence' is produced for torture's effectiveness, it is almost always provided by a person who has carried out torture or authorised it. In other words, since torture is a crime, the 'evidence' for the effectiveness of torture is provided by the person who has committed the crime of torture. Such a person has a strong self-interest in convincing themselves and the audience of the necessity of torture. If they wish to live with themselves and justify their behaviour to others, they must convince all of us that torture was effective. So, we have a counterfactual situation, where the evidence we are using to weigh whether or not torture was effective is being provided by someone who has committed a crime and has strong legal and psychological reasons for justifying it. No serious researcher would accept evidence in these circumstances.

In addition to asking for evidence of effectiveness, we expect that a good causal consequentialist argument needs to do a more complete accounting of costs and benefits This may sound callous, but policy makers are already doing a cost–benefit analysis of torture. If they are going to do it, at a minimum, one should insist that the costs are fully accounted for in both a cosmopolitan and long-range sense. In the case of torture we need to weigh the (possible, yet unknown) benefits of saving lives against the known costs of torture to individuals. There is a very extensive literature on the human costs of torture; we know it extends beyond the victim to the victim's family, and from the first

---

[42] Joseph Lelyveld, 'Interrogating Ourselves', *New York Times Magazine* June 12, 2005, 36.

generation into future generations. Finally, we need to calculate the legitimacy costs and the propaganda costs of the use of torture. How much harm to the US reputation in the world have the photos of Abu Grahib done? We can't know these costs precisely, but any more long-term understanding of consequences must take them into account. In other words, it is not enough to chart out benefits, but we also need to try to weigh the costs against the benefits.

Because of the notorious trickiness of this kind of consequentialism, ethical reasoning has preferred the deontological: do not torture. In that particular case, I agree. I believe that there should be some basic deontological principles so that we don't have to reopen the ethical debate about the consequences at every point. Do not torture is one of those basic deontological principles. It is also a basic legal principle in domestic and international law. But I'm also convinced that the justification for torture uses very bad consequentialist reasoning, and it is not wise to grant anyone the empirical claim that torture is actually effective. We should answer both that torture is wrong, and that its effectiveness is unproven, and based on the most flimsy evidence.

In response to Price's question of what to do when faced with instrumental actors relentlessly pursuing their interests, one way is to realise that they are frequently providing implausible consequentialist accounts, and it is important to dispute both the principles, the causal logics and the cost–benefit consequentialist analysis. This approach is all the more important if we accept that some of the instrumental actors (and many of their supporters and followers) actually believe the implausible counterfactuals. The obligation of researchers is to be just as relentless in questioning implausible accounts and proposing more plausible ones, realising that we can never be fully persuasive, not only because the instrumental actors are immune to facts but also because we are always going to be working in the range of one counterfactual vs another.

But aside from these perverse forms of manipulation of consequentialist arguments, there is also what we might call well-intentioned disagreement about plausible consequences. I agree with Price that virtually all normative claims depend in various ways upon empirical assumptions or claims about the world. What I would add to this is that the great bulk of them depend on counterfactual claims about this world.

Differences among well-intentioned people (as opposed to differences with relentlessly instrumental actors) often have to do with not clarifying the nature of our ethical and empirical reasoning. I suggest that people are engaged in different kinds of reasoning and thus talking past one another. One common disagreement may result from what I would call the unstated but implied counterfactual.

I would argue that 'conditions of possibility' arguments sometimes take the form of an unstated counterfactual. That is, conditions of possibility arguments involve empirical statements about what actually exists and how it became possible. But they also imply or suggest that other outcomes were at one point possible and eventually became less possible. Such arguments serve one purpose of a counterfactual, and that is to 'call attention to what could have happened, thereby locating what did happen in the context of a range of possibilities that might . . . have taken place instead'.[43] Tetlock and Belkin argue the alternative to an open counterfactual model is often a concealed counterfactual model.[44] In a concealed model, the reader is aware that the author thinks that other outcomes were both possible and desirable, but must infer the preferred alternatives from the critique of what did happen, rather than read them stated clearly with both their 'possibility' and 'desirability' defended. In this sense, I would find it useful in a critical constructivist account, in addition to critiquing what did happen, if the analysts would spell out clearly the desired alternative.

Comparison to the ideal

Yet another important difference is between what some scholars call 'ideal theory' and 'non-ideal' theory, that is, the difference between theorising about the ethical ideal vs. theorising about what is possible for governments or individuals to do in a non-ideal world.[45] I prefer to think about this distinction as the difference between 'comparison to the ideal' – a comparison of what actually happened to what should have happened in an ideal world – and empirical comparison. The world of 'ideal theory', following Linklater, might be further divided between that which is 'already immanent' and that which is not already immanent.[46] However, as Price suggests in his introductory chapter,

---

[43] Tetlock and Belkin, *Counterfactual Thought Experiments in World Politics*, 15.
[44] Ibid. 4.   [45] See, for example, Gibney, *The Ethics and Politics of Asylum.*
[46] Linklater, *The Transformation of Political Community.*

clearer guidelines will be needed for how to identify and distinguish what is already immanent from other comparisons to the ideal.

Let me illustrate these with reference to the issue of human rights trials. First, comparison to the ideal can be explicit or implicit. The implicit comparison to the ideal is very common in discussions of human rights trials. So, for example, many people have discussed the flaws in the international trials of the International Criminal Tribunal for the Former Yugoslavia (ICTY) in terms of its failure to actually arrest the most senior suspected war criminals, or for its wrong-headed efforts at even-handedness, or because by giving Milosevic the chance to represent himself, the Tribunal gave him yet another opportunity to traumatise his victims, this time when they testified against him. Because these flaws offend the sensibilities of those committed to justice, they make an argument that it would have been better to have no trials at all than to have the flawed trials of the ICTY.

This is not a counterfactual argument about what would have happened in the former Yugoslavia without the ICTY. They are not saying that the countries of the former Yugoslavia would have held more or better trials on their own. Nor are they saying that Yugoslavia, or Croatia or Kosovo would have been better off in terms of human rights, or democracy or conflict without the ICTY.

Nor is it an empirical comparison to other comparable trials or to other countries. They are usually not saying, for example, that the Nuremberg trials or the Rwanda trials are better than the ICTY trials, and thus should serve as a model. It is a comparison to an ideal of what international trials should be. And if the actually existing trials do not live up to that ideal, the belief is or the implication is that it would be better not to hold them at all.

This kind of reasoning is not only the province of idealists, but I would argue, is actually very present in critical constructivist thought and even in some realist or liberal thought. For example, Gary Bass, in his book on international war crimes tribunals, explains tribunals as something the countries of the West designed to assuage their guilt at not doing anything to intervene and stop human rights violations in countries like the former Yugoslavia or Rwanda. This is an example of comparison to an ideal. The ideal is that wealthy states should intervene to stop human rights violations in other states. When they fail to do so, we hold them up against this ideal and find them wanting. When they do something else (set up war crimes tribunals, in this case) it is again measured against the ideal (preventing the human rights violations in the first place) and found wanting, and thus dismissed as flawed.[47]

This is an important form of ethical reasoning. We need to keep the ability to hold our actual practices up to our ideals, and constantly measure where they fall short. Such reasoning is a powerful pressure for change in the international system. It is one of the main tools that advocacy groups use in the world. But, it is also very important to be careful how we use this form of the ideal comparison and to distinguish it very clearly from empirical comparison and counterfactual reasoning. First, comparison to the ideal should be explicit rather than implicit. The author should clarify that the practice or institution in question is being compared not to an empirical example in the world, but to a set of ideals of what such a practice or institution should look like.

Many arguments about inconsistency or hypocrisy are also comparisons to an ideal of perfect political consistency. Why do we get trials in the case of the former Yugoslavia but not in the case of war crimes by US officials in Iraq? This is a valuable ideal comparison. In an ideal world, we would have greater consistency and that could include war crimes tribunals of US policy makers. But it does not follow that the ICTY is thus not historical progress just because we don't have full consistency. In other words, some of our differences exist because we do not distinguish when we are engaged in comparison against the ideal, or ideal theory, and when we are engaged in empirical comparison or counterfactual reasoning.

Empirical comparisons

The comparison of practices or institutions not to the ideal but to other current or historical practices can lead to rather different evaluations.[48] So, for example, an evaluation of the ICTY that uses empirical comparisons to other international tribunals might arrive at different conclusions. For example, I would argue that the ICTY is an example of a 'successful' international war crimes tribunal, in the sense that it

---

[47] Gary Bass, *Stay the Hand of Vengeance: The Politics of War Crimes Tribunals* (Princeton, NJ: Princeton University Press, 2000).

[48] In his work on poverty, Thomas Pogge proposes various kinds of empirical comparisons and empirical baselines as a way to evaluate the impact of the international order on domestic poverty; Thomas W. Pogge, '"Assisting" the Global Poor'. In Deen K. Chatterjee (ed.), *The Ethics of Assistance: Morality and the Distant Needy* (Cambridge: Cambridge University Press, 2004), 273–277.

actually indicted, tried and convicted criminals using due process, something that had not happened since Nuremberg. Instead of holding the ICTY up against an ideal of how international justice might look, I compare it to other cases in the past and the present. How often in the past did powerful states act to punish human rights violations in countries where they were not the victors in war? Never? If they now do it in the case of ICTY and the International Criminal Tribunal for Rwanda (ICTR), that makes something new in the area of accountability for past human rights violations. This looks to me like significant historical change of a progressive kind, given the definition of progress I used earlier in the chapter. I would argue that with the ICTY there is more accountability for past crimes in the former Yugoslavia than there would have been without the ICTY (a counterfactual argument) and that with all its shortcomings, the ICTY is still an improvement in some ways on previous international trials (e.g. less an application of victors' justice than at Nuremberg, fewer immense delays with their attendant violations of the rights of defendants than at the ICTR). Even weighing some of the negative consequences, I still find the overall balance positive, compared to what would have happened without the ICTY. This is not to say that we should forget the problems, or be naive about our expectations for the future. But, neither should we let our ideals interfere with the actual documentation of change in the system.

Let me give another example using domestic human rights trials in Latin America. Carrie Booth Walling and I use various kinds of empirical comparisons to address the issue of the consequences of human rights trials in the region. We compare the human rights situation in individual countries before and after trials to see if we can discern the impact of trials on human rights. We compare countries without trials to countries that had trials to gain further insight into the effects of trials. Finally, we compare those countries that had a greater number of trials to those countries that had fewer trials. Using these empirical comparisons, we find that there is no empirical evidence that human rights trials worsen human rights, democracy or conflict in Latin America, and that in fourteen of our seventeen cases, the human rights situation improved in countries that used trials.[49] Such empirical evidence can then be used to craft ethical arguments in favour of human

[49] Sikkink and Walling, 'The Impact of Human Rights Trials in Latin America'.

rights trials, arguments that are attentive both to principles of justice and to consequences of actual trials.

Ethical arguments of these different types are ubiquitous and necessary. But because they are also slippery, we also need to be very careful and precise about how we go about using them. I would recommend that first we distinguish very carefully between the comparison to ideals and historical empirical comparison. I believe that many critical constructivist accounts rely on the comparison to the ideal or to the conditions of possibility counterfactual argument. In almost every critical constructivist work there is an implicit ideal ethical argument. This argument is implicit because it is rarely clearly stated, but it is found in the nature of the critique. So, for example, in her discussion of US human rights policy, Roxanne Doty critiques a human rights policy carried out by actors who use it for their own self-aggrandisement and to denigrate others.[50] The implicit ideal this presents is a human rights policy that is not used for denigration or surveillance or othering those it criticises or conversely, of elevating those who advocate it. What would be examples of such a policy? The book does not provide examples. We do not know if examples exist in the world. So the implicit comparison is a comparison to an ideal – a never fully stated ideal, but one present in the critique of what is wrong with the policies discussed.

Nicolas Guilhot makes a similar argument; the promotion of democracy and human rights, he claims, are increasingly used in order to extend the power they were meant to limit. He examines how progressive movements for democracy and human rights have become hegemonic because they 'systematically managed to integrate emancipatory and progressive forces in the construction of imperial policies'.[51] But the book does not offer any alternative political scenario. Guilhot admits that the book 'does not provide answers to these dilemmas. At most, its only ambition is to highlight them, in the hope that a proper understanding constitutes a first step toward the invention of new courses of action.'[52] Ethically, Guilhot believes that the democratic critique of democracy is sufficient. But if critique is to open space for new courses of action, as Guilhot wishes, some hint at what those new courses look like would be useful.

---

[50] Roxanne Doty, *Imperial Encounters: The Politics of Representation in North–South Relations* (Minneapolis, MN: University of Minnesota Press, 1996).

[51] Nicolas Guilhot, *The Democracy Makers: Human Rights and International Order* (New York, NY: Columbia University Press, 2005), 222–224.

[52] Ibid. 14.

This kind of critique has a crucial role to play in pointing to hypocrisy (as Price highlights in the introduction to this volume). It could also serve as a catalyst for policy change in the direction of policy that would include less surveillance or less co-optation of human rights discourse. But it is unlikely to serve as a catalyst for new action or policy change unless it ventures something more than pure critique, unless it risks a political or ethical proposal. Without that, it potentially has the impact of delegitimising any human rights policy without suggesting any alternative. Any policy to promote human rights or democracy is shown to be deeply flawed or even pernicious. The ethical effect is to remove normative support from existing policies without producing any alternatives. This is similar to what Price means when he says that 'critical accounts which do not in fact offer constructive alternatives in the aftermath of critique ironically lend themselves to being complicit with the conservative agendas opposing erstwhile progressive change in world politics'.

Neither Doty nor Guilhot, for example, contrast human rights policies or democracy promotion policies to previous policies that I would suggest were more pernicious – such as national security ideology and support for authoritarian regimes in the Third World. By presenting no contrasts, the critique would appear to say that there is no ethical or political difference between a policy that supports coups and funds repressive military regimes and a policy that critiques coups and cuts military aid to repressive regimes. These policies would appear to be ethically indistinguishable. Doty and Guilhot give me no ethical criteria to distinguish among the policies of the Nixon/Kissinger administration, the Carter administration and current Bush administration policy.

Because the comparison is an implicit ideal, never an empirical real-world example, the critique is very telling and can delegitimise the critiqued policy. But nothing is put in its place. It puts the analyst in an ethically comfortable position, but by not proposing any explicit comparison, it demobilises the reader. We learn what to oppose, to critique, but we don't learn explicitly what to support in its stead. The result can be political paralysis.

There is a long tradition in political theory of such critique, but theorists more often propose alternatives.[53] I believe critical constructivists have often unstated ideals for the international system. Because of

---

[53] See, for example, Peter Singer, 'Famine, Affluence, and Morality'. In Beitz *et al.*, *International Ethics*, 247–261.

the prevalence of the critique of 'othering' it would seem that the main principle defended is that of equality and non-discrimination, both among individuals and among states. Critical constructivists at least implicitly often seem to be especially concerned about advocating the principle of the equality of states when invoking the concept of hierarchy as a key critical focus.

One problem with a tradition that places such emphasis on equality in action and in language is that is renders other judgement problematic. Almost any ethical judgement leads to a conclusion that some actions by some states or individuals are worthy of praise or of condemnation. If you praise or you condemn, critical constructivists seem to suggest, you inevitably rank or other in some form. But I do not know how it is possible to engage in ethical judgement without some kind of praise or condemnation. Equality is certainly a valuable goal, but is state equality the priority goal that trumps all others? And must our commitment to equality make all attempts at ethical judgement suspect?

In the process of research and writing as well, I believe that the scholar must both critique and inspire.[54] This is similar to what Price calls for when he says that we need to put constitutive empirical insights to work for a forward-looking ethic. For critical theorists to remind us of the dark side of many apparently benevolent policies is a necessary antidote against naivety, hubris or self-congratulatory smugness. Likewise, there are historical moments when there is nothing but critique and resistance. Gadflies are always necessary in these smug times. But I believe that we need to make judgements and take action. Judgement implies an ability to evaluate, to weigh, to make a decision in matters affecting action.

Smart students, for example, will read our work, and wonder – what should we do? Should we hold more war crimes tribunals? How can the US government promote democracy and human rights? How do the laws of war need to be reformulated? Those of us doing empirical research will want to draw on our principles and our research to try to provide answers to these questions.

Judgement is a result of a combination of the premises and commitments we begin with and the empirical research results about the consequences of action. I believe that the best ethical judgement requires the best empirical research we can do using all the research tools at our

---

[54] I thank Susan Bickford for this insight.

disposal. This will ensure that we render judgement keeping in mind the limits and possibilities of the real world of politics. The research will often involve difficult counterfactuals and different kinds of comparisons. Well-intentioned researchers will disagree about results. We can improve our discussions by being more explicit about our processes of ethical reasoning and by relating our research findings more explicitly to their normative implications. This volume is one important step in that direction.

4 | Sovereignty, recognition and indigenous peoples

JONATHAN HAVERCROFT

Scholars of international relations have long studied the importance of the central institution of sovereignty, and how the practices and rules of mutual recognition have shaped the identities, interests and behaviours of states and constituted the international system itself. And yet, normative questions about what constitutes a just form of recognition in international politics have largely been pushed aside. Is it just, for instance, that only sovereign states are fully recognised under international law? Which actors should or should not be recognised in global politics and international law? How are different groups and agents mis-recognised or unrecognised? What are the consequences of such mis-recognition or non-recognition? And what can be done to promote more just forms of recognition?

In this chapter I propose to answer these questions as they apply to the particular case of indigenous peoples in world politics.[1] The same system of international law that has promoted norms of sovereignty and human rights has also been complicit in European processes of conquest and colonialism. These processes have meant that only certain actors – the sovereign states of Europe and states that were recognised as sovereign over time by the original members of this exclusive club – have full recognition under international law. The self-governing political communities of indigenous peoples have never been incorporated or recognised in this system, even though they were self-governing prior to first contact and in most instances – despite overwhelming pressure from settler societies – these peoples have maintained a form of self-government down to this day.

---

[1] By the term 'indigenous person' I am referring to the descendants of original occupants of territories now controlled by settler states. It is a socially constructed category that has been in common use since the 1980s. For a discussion of the history of the social construction of this identity see Ronald Niezen, *The Origins of Indigenism: Human Rights and the Politics of Identity* (Berkeley, CA: University of California Press, 2003), chapter 1.

Recent debates on the recognition of indigenous peoples under both domestic and international law have focused on whether or not and how a right to self-determination applies to indigenous peoples.[2] Paul Keal and James Anaya, working from an international perspective, have argued persuasively that a right of self-determination for indigenous peoples under international law would constitute a just form of recognition.[3] The *Declaration on the Rights of Indigenous Peoples*, which was adopted by the United Nations (UN) General Assembly on September 13, 2007 includes two articles that recognise the right of indigenous peoples to self-determination. These articles were the source of considerable controversy between indigenous peoples who argued that a Declaration without this right was a non-starter and the governments of settler states such as Canada, New Zealand, Australia and the USA who felt that the inclusion of such a right would threaten their territorial integrity and sovereignty.[4] Within the themes of this volume,

[2] There is an emerging literature on indigenous peoples within the field of International Relations. For an account of indigenous transnational activism see Allison Brysk, *From Tribal Village to Global Village: Indian Rights and International Relations in Latin America* (Stanford, CA: Stanford University Press, 2000). For two studies by anthropologists on the relationship between the international system and indigenous peoples see Niezen, *The Origins of Indigenism*; Richard Perry, *From Time Immemorial: Indigenous Peoples and the State System* (Austin, TX: University of Texas Press, 1996). For normative arguments that question the exclusion of indigenous peoples from participation in the international system see Franke Wilmer, *The Indigenous Voice in World Politics* (Newbury Park, CA: Sage, 1993); Paul Keal, *European Conquest and the Rights of Indigenous Peoples: The Moral Backwardness of International Society* (Cambridge: Cambridge University Press, 2003). For an examination of the complications that arise in using the term 'indigenous' in international law see Benedict Kingsbury, '"Indigenous Peoples" in International Law: A Constructivist Approach to the Asian Controversy', *The American Journal of International Law* 92 (1998), 414–457. For a critique of these attempts by IR scholars to create a space of inclusivity for indigenous peoples within the discipline of International Relations see Karena Shaw, 'Indigeneity and the International', *Millennium: Journal of International Studies* 31:1 (2002), 55–81.

[3] Keal, *European Conquest and the Rights of Indigenous Peoples*; James Anaya, *Indigenous Peoples in International Law* (Oxford: Oxford University Press, 1996).

[4] The final UN Assembly resolution on the *Declaration* passed with a vote of 143 in favour, 4 opposed and 11 abstentions. The four opposing states were Australia, Canada, the USA and New Zealand. 'United Nations; Indigenous Rights Declaration Approved', *The New York Times*, September 14, 2007. For Canada's objections to this declaration see 'Statement by Ambassador Paul Meyer, head of delegation, Working Group on the Draft Declaration on the Rights of Indigenous

debates over the recognition of the indigenous right to self-determination raise the question: does self-determination constitute a moral limit? To date, scholars who have tackled this question have done so from the perspective of 'ideal theory', arguing what a just form of recognition might be. Conversely, critics of the recognition of an indigenous right to self-determination, such as Alan Cairns and Tom Flanagan as well as the governments of New Zealand, the United States and Australia, have argued that the recognition of such a right is politically impossible as it would quickly fragment the world into a whole set of micro-states.[5] Furthermore, the realities of international law development mean that states, and only states, can create and ratify an international legal instrument that would protect the right of indigenous peoples to self-determination. This means that indigenous peoples have very little formal power in the development of international law that affects them directly. These power differentials represent obvious political obstacles that make the recognition of indigenous rights and particularly the right of self-determination very difficult if not impossible to recognise in international politics.

Therefore, these struggles over the recognition of an indigenous right to self-determination represent both an ideal and a hard case for constructivist analysis. It is an ideal case because it involves transnational actors with very little material power drawing upon and developing international norms to socialise states in such a way as to alter their

Peoples to the 1st Session of the Human Rights Council', Geneva, Switzerland, June 29, 2006; www.dfait-maeci.gc.ca/canada_un/geneva/HRC_June29_06-en. asp. Accessed July 9, 2006. For the objections of Australia, New Zealand and the United States see, 'WGDD: Self-Determination Proposal of Australia, New Zealand, and the United States of America'; http://www.unpo.org/article.php? id=3367; accessed October 10, 2007.

5 Both Cairns and Flanagan are writing from the perspective of Canadian constitutional law. Flanagan argues that any recognition of indigenous peoples as self-governing is destructive to both the Canadian state and indigenous peoples. See Tom Flanagan, *First Nations? Second Thoughts* (Montreal and Kingston: McGill-Queen's University Press, 2000), especially chapter 4, for an argument that the doctrine of *terra nullius* means indigenous peoples have no right to self-government under international law. Alan Cairns takes a more moderate approach in arguing that recognising a full-blown right of self-government for indigenous peoples would lead to the disintegration of the Canadian state. Instead, Cairns argues that indigenous peoples should be recognised as 'citizens-plus'. That is, they should be treated as full citizens of Canada with extra entitlements to preserve their indigeneity. See Alan C. Cairns, *Citizens Plus: Aboriginal Peoples and the Canadian State* (Vancouver, BC: University of British Columbia Press, 2000).

behaviour and perhaps even their identities (to a post-colonial state) and their interests (to see that it actually *is* in the interests of settler societies to recognise the right of indigenous peoples to self-determination). This chapter uses a constructivist approach to analyse the practical obstacles to the normative ideals put forward by scholars such as Keal, Anaya, Alfred, Corntassel, Tully and Young, including indigenous activists.[6] Through a discursive analysis of debates at the United Nations Working Group on the *Draft Declaration on the Rights of Indigenous Peoples*, I analyse the arguments put forward by indigenous peoples for adoption of the right of self-determination as well as arguments raised by settler states against adopting this declaration. On the normative level I conclude that non-recognition of an unqualified right of self-determination of indigenous peoples is hypocritical because such a right has already been extended to all other 'peoples' under international law. As an alternative, I propose that the norm of consent could form the basis of a just recognition of indigenous peoples under international law. A constructivist approach enables us to see that consent is not simply an ideal principle but that it has several interesting political features and ethical implications, namely: it is a common ground for indigenous peoples and settler societies; and second, consent represents *a real limit on political possibility.*

Recognition

In constructivist approaches to International Relations (IR) the concept of recognition does a lot of the theoretical work. If, as constructivists argue, an actor's interests and behaviours are shaped by the ways in which they have internalised a given identity, both the actor and those whom the actor is interacting with in a given context must *recognise* the

---

[6] Keal, *European Conquest and the Rights of Indigenous Peoples*; Anaya, *Indigenous Peoples in International Law*; Taiaiake Alfred, *Peace, Power, and Righteousness: An Indigenous Manifesto* (Oxford: Oxford University Press, 1999); James Tully, *Strange Multiplicity: Constitutionalism in an Age of Diversity* (Cambridge: Cambridge University Press, 1995); Jeff Corntassel, 'Towards a New Partnership? Indigenous Mobilization and Co-optation during the First UN Indigenous Decade (1995–2004)', *Human Rights Quarterly* 29:1 (2007); Iris Marion Young, 'Hybrid Democracy: Iroquois Federalism and the Post-Colonial Project'. In Duncan Ivison, Paul Patton and Will Saunders (eds.), *Political Theory and the Rights of Indigenous Peoples* (Cambridge: Cambridge University Press, 2001), 237–258.

actor as having a given identity in order for the actions to have any meaning. As Wendt has argued, 'identities and their corresponding interests are learned and then reinforced by how actors are treated by significant others'.[7] Actors, according to the social interactionist theory of identity formation, will come to see themselves as they think the others with which they interact perceive them. How each actor recognises the other actor will affect how the actors behave towards each other. Consequently, much of the explanatory power of constructivist theories of international politics rests on analyses of how states recognise themselves (e.g. as good states that abide by international norms) and how they recognise other states (e.g. as enemies, friends and rivals).[8]

As most constructivist analyses are primarily concerned with understanding and explaining phenomena in world politics, constructivist research has tended to focus on analysing how states recognise themselves and each other. If constructivists wish to develop a normative dimension to their work that parallels the empirical studies of how states adopt norms, then an important line of inquiry must be into what is a just form of recognition in international politics.[9]

---

[7] Alexander Wendt, *Social Theory of International Politics* (Cambridge: Cambridge University Press, 2000), 327.

[8] Martha Finnemore, 'Constructing Norms of Humanitarian Intervention'. In Peter J. Katzenstein (ed.), *The Culture of National Security: Norms and Identity in World Politics* (New York, NY: Columbia University Press, 1996); Martha Finnemore and Kathryn Sikkink, 'International Norm Dynamics and Political Change', *International Organization* 52:4 (1998); Ronald L. Jepperson, Alexander Wendt and Peter J. Katzenstein, 'Norms, Identity, and Culture in National Security'. In Katzenstein, *The Culture of National Security*; Margaret E. Keck and Kathryn Sikkink, *Activists Beyond Borders: Advocacy Networks in International Politics* (Ithaca, NY: Cornell University Press, 1998); Richard Price and Nina Tannenwald, 'Norms and Deterrence: The Nuclear and Chemical Weapons Taboo'. In Katzenstein, *The Culture of National Security*; Thomas Risse and Kathryn Sikkink, 'The Socialization of International Human Rights Norms into Domestic Practices: Introduction'. In Thomas Risse, Stephen C. Ropp and Kathryn Sikkink (eds.), *The Power of Human Rights: International Norms and Domestic Change* (Cambridge: Cambridge University Press, 1999); Nicholas J. Wheeler, *Saving Strangers: Humanitarian Interventions in International Society* (Oxford: Oxford University Press, 2000).

[9] While not explicitly constructivist in orientation, Mervyn Frost's constitutive approach to international ethics does make the process of mutual recognition a cornerstone of his normative theory. Indeed, central to Frost's theory is the principle that both states and the international community 'are constituted by people mutually recognizing one another as reciprocally bound by a certain set of

Whereas the normative aspects of recognition have not been thoroughly examined by constructivist scholars, the normative dimensions of recognition have been a primary concern of political theorists. Over the last fifteen years there has been significant work done on the concept of recognition and its applicability in contemporary multicultural societies.[10] While the details of the recognition literature need not detain us here, there are three key insights from this debate that are particularly salient for normative work on the concept of recognition in International Relations. First, scholars of recognition agree that 'difference-blind' approaches to domestic laws can lead to mis-recognition or non-recognition of marginalised groups within a society.[11] While difference-blind approaches are commendable for their promotion of universal standards that treat all individuals equally, advocates of the politics of recognition have argued that many injustices can result from such difference-blind approaches. First, difference blind approaches can require minority groups to renounce essential aspects of their customary ways of life if they wish to participate fully in the dominant culture.[12] Second, mis-recognition can lead historically oppressed and marginalised groups to engage in forms of self-hatred, thereby denying these groups the ability to participate fully in a society.[13] Third, various forms of non-recognition can lead entire groups of people to be excluded from society and may enable practices of oppression and domination to be used against minority groups.[14]

One way of turning the empirical discussion of recognition in International Relations towards a normative enquiry is to inquire into the justness of historical cases of non-recognition or mis-recognition. The particular case of non-recognition and mis-recognition in international

rules'; Mervyn Frost, *Ethics in International Relations: A Constitutive Theory* (Cambridge: Cambridge University Press, 1996), 60.

[10] Will Kymlicka, *Finding Our Way: Rethinking Ethnocultural Relations in Canada* (Oxford: Oxford University Press, 1998); Will Kymlicka, *Multicultural Citizenship* (Oxford: Oxford University Press, 1995); Charles Taylor, 'The Politics of Recognition'. In Amy Gutmann (ed.), *Multiculturalism* (Princeton, NJ: Princeton University Press, 1994); James Tully, 'The Struggles of Indigenous Peoples for and of Freedom'. In Ivison *et al.*, *Political Theory and the Rights of Indigenous Peoples*; Iris Marion Young, *Inclusion and Democracy* (Oxford: Oxford University Press, 2000).

[11] Iris Marion Young, *Justice and the Politics of Difference* (Princeton, NJ: Princeton University Press, 1990).

[12] Kymlicka, *Multicultural Citizenship*, chapter. 1.

[13] Taylor, 'The Politics of Recognition', 25–6.   [14] Ibid. 27.

politics that I will address in this chapter concerns the status of indigenous peoples with respect to international law. Indigenous peoples have occupied an ambivalent place in the history of global politics. A large part of this ambivalence is due to the fact that European colonisers have repeatedly mis-recognised indigenous populations in order to facilitate imperial expansion. A second cause of this mis-recognition is due to the fact that many indigenous understandings of politics and intercommunity relations could not easily be translated into European conceptions of international law. Consequently, indigenous peoples were never fully recognised as nations within the society of states. This meant that indigenous peoples were often left at the mercy of the sovereign states that had colonised their ancestral lands.

In the last three decades there has been an increased recognition of indigenous peoples under international law. In large part, the positive developments with respect to indigenous peoples were the result of activism on the part of indigenous peoples.[15] The two most significant advances have been the 1989 International Labour Organisation (ILO) *Convention on Indigenous and Tribal Peoples* and the 1994 UN *Draft Declaration on the Rights of Indigenous Peoples* (hereafter referred to as the *Draft Declaration*).[16]

While the ILO *Convention on Indigenous and Tribal Peoples* is significant as the first international legal document to formally recognise the rights of indigenous peoples, most of the recent focus of indigenous activists has been on the United Nations' *Draft Declaration*. In March 1995 the UN Commission on Human Rights created an inter-sessional working group to review the *Draft Declaration* (hereafter referred to as the WGDD). Unlike the working group that had drafted the initial declaration, this inter-sessional working group was composed of member states, which could 'in principle ... veto an objectionable

---

[15] For the recent history of these indigenous NGO movements see Brysk, *From Tribal Village to Global Village*; Niezen, *The Origins of Indigenism*.

[16] A slightly revised text of the *Draft Declaration on the Rights of Indigenous Peoples* was ratified in September 2007 as the *Declaration on the Rights of Indigenous Peoples*, just as this volume was headed to press. As most of this chapter focuses on the debate surrounding the development of the *Draft Declaration* and there are differences between these two texts, unless otherwise noted, the term *Draft Declaration* refers to the text originally adopted in 1994 by the United Nations Working Group on Indigenous Populations.

element of the draft'.[17] While normally non-governmental organisation (NGO) groups are not permitted to submit formal proposals at draft sessions, the chair of the inter-sessional working group, José Urutia, granted indigenous NGOs procedural equality with member states.[18]

The first meeting of the WGDD established a precedent for full participation of indigenous NGOs and adopted the working group on indigenous populations draft as its starting point.[19] The meeting also made it clear that many states had strong objections to significant portions of the *Draft Declaration*. In fact, 'Of the forty-three substantive articles of the draft on which governments took explicit positions, only two met with no objections at all'.[20] In the ten years since this initial meeting, the working group has met annually to review the *Draft Declaration* and hear proposals from member states and indigenous NGOs to review the draft. In June 2006 the *Draft Declaration* was approved by the UN Human Rights Council and forwarded to the UN General Assembly for ratification in September 2007.

What are the consequences of mis-recognition?

While these recent developments in the status of indigenous peoples under international law show some promise, as we shall see below a large part of the debate in the WGDD involved exactly how to recognise indigenous peoples. Before examining this debate in greater detail, I will first evaluate what have been the consequences of this history of mis-recognition and non-recognition of indigenous peoples under international law. Above I outlined three effects on oppressed groups that political theorists have argued occur to groups that are mis-recognised within a society: compelling groups to renounce essential parts of their customary ways of life; the creation of self-hatred within oppressed groups because they are led to believe that their ways of life are inferior to those of the dominant culture; and exclusion from full participation within the dominant culture on the basis of cultural differences of the oppressed groups. The mis-recognition of indigenous peoples under international law has led to two of the effects identified by theorists of

---

[17] Russel Lawrence Barsh, 'Indigenous Peoples and the UN Commission on Human Rights: A Case of the Immovable Object and the Irresistible Force', *Human Rights Quarterly* 18:4 (1996), 783.
[18] Ibid. 786. [19] Ibid. 806. [20] Ibid. 804.

the politics of recognition – compelling indigenous peoples to renounce essential parts of their ways of life, and denying indigenous peoples full participation in the dominant culture. While a strong case can be – and has been – made that the mis-recognition of indigenous peoples under international law has also promoted self-hatred within indigenous communities, I will not address that issue here as in order to make such a case it would involve engaging in detailed research that is beyond the scope of this project.

First, many of the historical instruments of international law had as their explicit purpose the destruction of indigenous cultures. For instance, in his sixteenth-century lectures on the status of the 'Indians' under international law, Francisco de Vitoria argued that the Spanish could impose a government on the indigenous peoples of the Americas in order to 'improve' the culture of the indigenous peoples.[21] This argument was clearly premised on a mis-recognition of indigenous culture. Implicit with any language of cultural improvement is the belief that the culture of the coloniser should serve as the measure of the culture of the colonised. Throughout the history of indigenous peoples under international law, European culture has served as the yardstick against which all other cultures of indigenous peoples were measured. Indigenous cultures that are most similar to European cultures – such as the Cherokee nation in the case of Chief Justice Marshall US Supreme Court's decision – were granted greater recognition under international law.[22] When indigenous cultures were seen as dissimilar to the cultures of the colonisers, this mis-recognition led directly to policies that called for the assimilation or 'improvement' of indigenous cultures. Regardless of the techniques used in the specific cases, the aim of all of these policies was to forcibly change the culture of an indigenous people so as to make their culture recognisable by destroying those aspects of the culture that were significantly different from the culture of the settler society.

Second, these policies have led to a double exclusion of indigenous peoples from the dominant culture. First, indigenous peoples have been excluded from full participation within settler societies. There has been

---

[21] Francisco de Vitoria, *De Indis Et Ivre Belli Relectiones*, translated by J. Bate (Washington, DC: Carnegie Institute of Washington, 1917).
[22] Cherokee Nation v. Georgia, 30 1 (1831).

a long history around the globe of genocide, destruction of culture, seizure of indigenous land and confinement of indigenous peoples to small reservations. Many of the explicit policies of states in the nineteenth and twentieth centuries such as the 'Trusteeship Doctrine' and explicit policies of assimilationism were aimed at preventing indigenous peoples from having any meaningful form of participation in the political and cultural life of settler societies.[23]

The second way in which indigenous peoples have been excluded from the dominant culture is through their exclusion as members of international society. As we saw in the previous section, indigenous peoples did not have any status under international law until the development of the Trusteeship Doctrine, and when that doctrine was implemented indigenous peoples were placed completely at the mercy of the governments of settler states. This exclusion continues today, with the fact that indigenous peoples have no formal say in the development of international legal instruments – such as the *Declaration* – that affect them directly. Although the WGDD did permit indigenous NGOs to make submissions and comment on various proposals surrounding the *Declaration*, no indigenous group had the ability to vote on the *Draft Declaration*. Consequently, only the governments of sovereign nation states – most of which are settler societies – had the final say on the form of the *Declaration*. In effect, while indigenous peoples now are permitted to discuss international legal documents that might affect them – an improvement from previous eras where such documents were developed without any input at all – indigenous peoples are still denied any real power in terms of shaping these documents. This, I contend, is manifestly unjust whether one proceeds from a procedural/ discourse ethic approach following Habermas, a more agonistic theory of justice such as advanced by Tully or from Frost's constitutive theory of international ethics. From a Habermasian perspective the denial of indigenous participation in the shaping of the *Draft Declaration* is a clear violation of his famous discourse principle: 'Just those action norms are valid to which all possibly affected persons could agree as

---

[23] The Trusteeship Doctrine was used by countries such as Great Britain, the USA, Canada and Brazil to place indigenous populations under direct government control with the aims of socially 'reengineering their cultural and social patterns in line with the European conception of civilized behavior', Anaya, *Indigenous Peoples in International Law*, 24.

participants in rational discourse.'[24] Because indigenous peoples are
excluded from substantive participation in the development of the
Declaration they have a priori been excluded from even having the
ability to consent to norms that affect them through rational discourse.
A more agonistic approach to justice argues that in cases of cultural
recognition, such as the indigenous struggles for recognition under
consideration here, the concrete particularity of specific groups makes
universal consensus on questions of justice extremely difficult if not
impossible. Habermas' discourse principle has been criticised by agonistic theorists of justice for universalising a European Masculine norm
of discourse. Nevertheless, agonistic theorists of recognition and justice
such as Tully have argued that constitutional arrangements[25] are just
only so long as they are 'an intercultural dialogue in which the culturally
diverse sovereign citizens of contemporary societies negotiate agreements on their forms of association over time in accordance with the
three conventions of mutual recognition, consent and cultural continuity'.[26] The systemic and continuous exclusion of indigenous peoples
from participating in the development of international law on the rights
of indigenous peoples, then, violates all four aspects of Tully's criteria
for a just constitutional order: the *Declaration* is not part of a genuine
intercultural dialogue, it is not based on mutual recognition as states
refuse to recognise first nations as equal partners, it is being imposed
without the consent of indigenous peoples and it is imposing an
order that disrupts the cultural continuity of indigenous traditions of
self-governance. From the perspective of Frost's constitutive theory of
international ethics, it is wrong for a group to exercise its right to self-
determination if it involves subjugating other peoples in the process.[27]
The *Declaration*'s legitimacy hinges on its recognition as just by all
parties governed by its norms. So long as indigenous peoples are
excluded from being equal partners in the negotiation of the *Draft*

---

[24] Jürgen Habermas, *Between Facts and Norms: Contributions to a Discourse Theory of Law and Democracy*, translated by William Rehg (Cambridge, MA: MIT Press, 1999), 107.
[25] Tully's use of the term constitutional arrangement is far broader than the constitution of a particular state. By the term constitution, Tully means an ongoing form of dialogue between all members of a society whereby the members come to agreement on the ways in which they will associate with each other; see Tully, *Strange Multiplicity*, chapter 2.
[26] Ibid. 30.   [27] Frost, *Ethics in International Relations*, 210.

Declaration then the adoption of the *Declaration* is, according to Frost's reasoning, a form of subjugation rather than a practice of freedom for indigenous peoples.

While there are significant differences between the discourse ethics approach, the constitutive approach and the agonistic approach, what is worth noting is that when considered from any of these perspectives, international law with respect to the rights of indigenous peoples – including the *Declaration* – is manifestly unjust because it fails to recognise indigenous peoples as full participants in the development of international laws that directly affect them and international law has repeatedly been imposed on indigenous peoples without their consent. In the final section I will return to this issue of the input indigenous peoples have in the development of the *Declaration*, to consider how indigenous peoples can be accorded greater recognition under international law and what strategies may be available to indigenous activists and their allies in order to alter state behaviour so that such recognition might be possible. Before I do that, however, I must first address the issue of how indigenous peoples should be recognised under international law through a careful examination of recent debates at the WGDD over the concept of 'self-determination' in the *Draft Declaration* which led to the final *Declaration*.

How should indigenous peoples be recognised under international law?

The WGDD met for over eleven years before deciding on a final draft of a *Declaration of the Rights of Indigenous Peoples*. Much of the resistance by states to adopting the *Draft Declaration* focused on the concept of self-determination. Article 3 of the *Draft Declaration* states 'Indigenous Peoples have the right of self-determination. By virtue of this right they freely determine their political status and freely pursue their economic, social and cultural development.' Many groups representing indigenous peoples at the WGDD defended leaving Article 3 of the *Draft Declaration* untouched because it provides a just form of recognition for indigenous peoples under international law. Some indigenous activists and scholars have expressed reservations about indigenous peoples seeking recognition for a right of self-determination through the United Nations. The primary concern is that settler states may use the UN process as a means to blunt the indigenous right to self-determination

and to co-opt indigenous groups, representing a classic concern emble-
matic for this volume regarding the balance between moral possibility
and co-optation.[28] Nevertheless, the involvement of so many groups
representing indigenous peoples at the WGDD is significant insofar as it
means that for most indigenous peoples, the system of international law
that facilitated their oppression does have resources that can be positively
harnessed. This means that the rejection of the system of international law
given its constitution by states as sovereign agents need not be the only or
even the appropriate strategy. Self-determination as provided for in
Article 3 can provide the basis for just recognition in two ways. First, it
recognises indigenous peoples as distinct peoples, with their own forms of
government, languages, histories and cultures. Second, this Article recognises that as peoples, indigenous nations have a right to self-determination
under international law. Indigenous peoples have championed the concept of self-determination as the means by which they can achieve just
recognition under international law. Meanwhile, the governments of
many states have objected to an unqualified right of self-determination
being included in the *Draft Declaration*.

One of the fears of the states participating in the *Draft Declaration*
was that recognising an indigenous right to self-determination may
foster a new wave of separatism and irredentism. For instance, during
the first session of the Working Group on the Draft Declaration, Chile
argued that the principle of self-determination should be rephrased as
'internal self-determination', which would recognise a:

> space within which indigenous peoples can freely determine their
> forms of development, [including] the preservation of their cultures,
> languages, customs, and traditions, in the context and framework of
> the States in which indigenous peoples live.[29]

Other states, including the USA, the Netherlands, Finland and the
Ukraine, supported qualifying the right of self-determination of indigenous peoples with language that would make this right internal to states
and ultimately subordinate to the legal structures of states. The governments of France and Japan rejected outright the recognition of even an

---

[28] For arguments along these lines see Corntassel, 'Towards a New Partnership?'.
[29] Cited in Barsh, 'Indigenous Peoples and the UN Commission on Human
Rights', 797.

internal right of self-determination.[30] Other states, including Australia, Canada, New Zealand, Nicaragua, Fiji, Denmark and Norway, all opposed the insertion of qualifying language at the initial session on the Draft Declaration in 1995 on the grounds that qualifying a right to self-determination would 'undermine the principle of equality of all people, and dissipate the credibility of the declaration among indigenous peoples'.[31] In fact, the government of Australia went so far as to declare:

> Australia considers that self-determination encompasses the continuing right of peoples to decide how they shall be governed, the right to participate fully in the political process and the right of distinct peoples within a State to participate in decisions on, and to administer, their own affairs.[32]

From a normative perspective, a complete rejection of an indigenous right to self-determination would be the height of hypocrisy. The right of self-determination is a right that *all peoples* already have under several human rights documents. As such, an attempt to water down the right to self-determination for indigenous peoples would mean that this right would apply to all peoples *except* indigenous peoples. There are two possible political rationalisations for watering down an indigenous right to self-determination. The first rationalisation, most often made by governments of states, is that an unqualified right to self-determination could lead to a new wave of separatist movements around the world, thereby promoting greater instability in world politics. The second rationalisation is that watering down the right to self-determination may serve as a strategic stepping-stone for greater protection of indigenous rights under international law in the long term.

States most often cited the first rationalisation in their arguments against adopting the *Draft Declaration*. Since 1995, much of the debate within the WGDD has hinged on what form, if any, the right of indigenous peoples to self-determination should take. These debates

---

[30] Ibid. 800.
[31] Ibid. 798. It is important to note that changes in government in states participating in the WGDD have led to changes in that state's official policy with respect to the draft declaration. For instance the change in Australia from a Labour Party government to a more conservative Liberal Party government has led to a withdrawal of Australia's support for an unqualified right to self-determination in the *Draft Declaration*.
[32] Cited in Barsh, 'Indigenous Peoples and the UN Commission on Human Rights'.

came to a head at the January 2006 meeting of the WGDD, where the delegates debated two possible compromises. The first compromise, spearheaded by Norway, called for Article 3 in the Draft Declaration – the article that deals directly with self-determination – to be left intact, and for limits on the right of self-determination to be built into other articles in the Draft Declaration. The alternative proposal, spearheaded by the United States, Australia and New Zealand called for qualifying language to be included in Article 3. Representatives of these states expressed concern that 'Article 3 of the Declaration cannot be a note by note repetition of the common Article 1 [of both the International Covenant on Civil and Political Rights and the International Covenant on Economic, Social and Cultural Rights]'.[33] While the statement by these three states criticised the Article in terms of its 'ambiguity', the concern expressed by these states on the right of self-determination was that this Article might permit secession or independence for indigenous groups. In their statement before the WGDD, the representatives of these three states argued that indigenous peoples 'are saying they want the freedom to exercise the right without any clear or agreed understanding being articulated in the declaration itself'.[34] In addition to objections that the right of self-determination could lead to secession by indigenous peoples, some states have expressed concern that recognising the right of self-determination – a collective right – might end up trumping individual rights.

The response by indigenous groups to this proposal was overwhelmingly negative. A November 2005 submission to the WGDD by thirty-six Indigenous NGOs objected to introducing language into the *Draft Declaration* that would set specific limits on the right of self-determination. One of the arguments that the indigenous NGOs have made against altering the Draft Declaration is that such manoeuvres would represent a form of hypocrisy on the part of states. Whereas many other human rights documents – including the *Covenant on Civil and Political Rights* and the *Covenant on Economic, Social, and Cultural Rights* – have used virtually identical language with respect to broad human rights, the indigenous NGO intervention argued of the proposal to qualify language on self-determination that 'These double

---

[33] 'WGDD: Self-Determination Proposal of Australia, New Zealand, and the United States of America'.
[34] Ibid.

standards on Indigenous peoples' human rights would be highly dis-criminatory'.[35] The point the indigenous NGOs are making is that in all other international human rights declarations the collective right of self-determination is an unqualified right. To qualify the right to self-determination in the *Declaration* would effectively mean that all peoples except indigenous peoples would have an unqualified right to self-determination. Furthermore, it rests on the assumption that indigen-ous peoples should recognise the right to self-determination of states without states reciprocally recognising the right to self-determination of indigenous peoples.

As several of the other chapters in this volume have demonstrated, one of the ways to detect when a moral limit has been reached politically is through the act of hypocrisy. In demonstrating the double standard of qualifying a right of self-determination only for indigenous peoples, but leaving it unqualified in cases of indigenous peoples, indigenous peoples are drawing the attention of states to a moral limit in world politics. Exposing hypocrisy is one means of unearthing the ways in which moral knowledge is productive in world politics. The constructivist analyses of hypocrisy in this volume, however, have pointed to some counterintui-tive normative insights.[36] The response from states such as the USA, New Zealand and Australia is that an outright recognition of the right to self-determination in the case of indigenous peoples may not be politically practical as it could open the door to secessionist movements and the creation of thousands of micro-states. In terms of the issues addressed in this volume, then, the debate at the WGDD over the language of self-determination is a classic example of a clash between moral limit – a universal application of the right to self-determination – and political possibility – the fear that recognising this right in the

[35] UN Document, 'General Provision of the Draft *Declaration on the Rights of Indigenous Peoples*', 31.
[36] See especially Marc Lynch (this volume) for his argument that while the moral use of hypocrisy did create a normative consensus on sanctions it left the reputations of many international actors and institutions damaged. The use of the 'hypocrisy game' by indigenous actors may also be able to generate support for the Declaration beyond its declaratory value, particularly if states such as Canada, New Zealand, Australia and the USA are invested in being perceived by the international community as supporting human rights initiatives such as the Declaration. These states are particularly vulnerable to charges of hypocrisy from states that have been targeted in the past for human rights abuses by the governments of Canada, Australia, New Zealand and the USA.

context of indigenous peoples may lead to a proliferation of micro-states.

Does this argument about the practical obstacles to recognising an unqualified right of self-determination justify the refusal by states to adopt the *Declaration*? I would argue that at the heart of this putative dilemma is the belief that self-determination must always take the form of an independent sovereign state. James Anaya, however, has pointed out that there is a confusion between the substantive aspects of self-determination and the remedial aspects.[37] While groups seeking sovereign statehood have often invoked the right of self-determination, there are two parts to this right being invoked. First, groups are arguing that their right of self-determination is being denied by the state against which the claim is being made through denial of participation in political processes, lack of representation and the imposition of policies upon a group without the consent of the group. Second, if a state denies a group's right of self-determination in these ways, then the group can seek remedies for these wrongs. The most common of the remedies for a violation of a right of self-determination during the twentieth century was for oppressed groups to form their own sovereign states. There is, however, no logical reason why this must be the only, or even the predominant means by which a denial of a group's right to self-determination can be remedied. If states amend their practices towards indigenous populations so that policies that affect indigenous peoples are not imposed upon them without their consent, then a state would no longer be in violation of a people's right to self-determination. Therefore it is at least theoretically possible for states to recognise a right of self-determination for indigenous peoples without fears that it would necessarily lead to secession by these groups. Indeed, apart from mass delusion, it would be difficult to explain how 143 states adopted the *Declaration* if its formulation provided such an obvious step to the dismemberment of contemporary nation-states.

In fact, if we turn to how indigenous peoples actually articulate this right to self-determination, we see that it is often the case that they do not understand it as necessarily leading to state sovereignty. One reason for this is that indigenous groups often argue that the concept of sovereignty is a Western concept, and thus understanding the indigenous right of self-determination in terms of state sovereignty ironically is

[37] Anaya, *Indigenous Peoples in International Law*, 80–85.

as best inappropriate and at worst a form of imperialist co-optation itself. While indigenous groups are not necessarily seeking sovereign statehood, they still see the right of self-determination as a means of exercising control over their own lives without interference from the governments of settler societies. For instance, Taiaiake Alfred has argued that:

[S]overeignty is an exclusionary concept rooted in an adversarial and coercive Western notion of power. Indigenous peoples can never match the awesome coercive force of the state; so long as sovereignty remains the goal of indigenous politics, therefore Native communities will occupy a dependent and reactionary position relative to the state. Acceptance of 'Aboriginal rights' in the context of state sovereignty represents the culmination of white society's efforts to assimilate indigenous peoples.[38]

In rejecting sovereignty, Alfred is not arguing that an indigenous right to self-determination can take place within existing sovereign states. Instead, Alfred is calling for the rejection of the very idea of organising the world in terms of sovereign states. Alfred equates sovereignty with coercive, hierarchical political authority that exerts power over particular territories and populations. This very way of thinking about political power is inimical to most indigenous political philosophies 'that honor the autonomy of individual conscience, non-coercive authority, and the deep interconnection between human beings and other elements of creation'.[39] When self-determination is rephrased in Alfred's terms, it makes it clear that the primary concern of states such as the USA, Australia and New Zealand, that indigenous peoples will use the right of self-determination *for sovereign states*, is misplaced. However, Alfred makes it just as clear that the alternative models for 'internal self-determination' or 'domestic autonomy' in which indigenous peoples would govern themselves within and subordinate to the governments of sovereign states are just as problematic:

By allowing indigenous peoples a small measure of self-administration, and by foregoing a small portion of the money derived from the exploitation of indigenous nations' lands, the state has created incentives for integration into its own sovereignty framework. Those communities that cooperate are the beneficiaries of a patronizing

[38] Alfred, *Peace, Power, and Righteousness*, 59. [39] Ibid. 60.

false altruism that sees indigenous peoples as the anachronistic rem-
nants of nations, the descendents of once independent people who by
a combination of tenacity and luck have managed to survive and
must now be protected as minorities.[40]

That is, indigenous peoples face just the kind of dilemma around which
the contributions of this volume revolve, namely whether a critical rejection of the existing system is required to avoid co-optation, or whether
self-determination as an element of that sovereign system can be harnessed to progressive purposes (here not defined as 'progressive' in
Western terms but often as a return to *traditional* practices).[41] To recognise indigenous peoples only as minorities within states would be
problematic for two reasons. First, it would continue the practice of
colonisation that instruments such as the *Declaration* are trying to put
an end to. To reduce indigenous peoples to minorities within states would
imply that indigenous groups had consented to become a part of a state,
which is rarely the case. To require that indigenous peoples become self-
governing minorities within states would only perpetuate the colonial
myths of settler societies and deny indigenous rights of self-determination.
If indigenous peoples have not consented to be governed by a state, then
to compel them to be a minority within a state – whether or not they are
granted the right to 'internal self-determination' – would be a denial of
their right to self-determination. Second, it would deny indigenous
peoples a say in the most important aspect of their self-determination –
the very way in which they exercise the right to self-determination.

The reason the recognition of an unqualified right of self-determination
for indigenous peoples represents a moral limit is that this right of self-
determination would give first nations around the world the ability to
consent to or reject political arrangements between themselves and
settler societies. A norm of consent has the potential to form the basis
of a just recognition of indigenous peoples under international law. The
idea of consent has a long history in both indigenous and settler societies. Within European history the norm of consent can be traced back to

---

[40] Ibid.
[41] In this sense progress is measured against the criterion of consent outlined
below. So what makes this change progressive is not the return to tradition per
se but the fact that indigenous peoples are consulted and consent to the norms
that govern them as opposed to the status quo in which settler societies impose
a way of life on indigenous peoples without their consent.

the ancient Roman law '*quod omnes tangit ab omnibus comprobetur*' (what touches all should be agreed to by all). This norm of consent 'applies to any form of constitutional association, ensuring that a constitution or an amendment to it rests on the consent of the people, or the representatives of the people who are touched by it'.[42] This norm applies just as much to the international constitutional order as it does to the domestic constitutional orders of states. We see the principle operate in the development of treaty-based international law, which requires a state to consent to an international treaty before that treaty can govern the state's behaviour. Similarly, the norm of consent has a long-standing tradition in indigenous legal and constitutional theory and practice.[43] As such, the norm of consent could form the basis for an overlapping consensus between the two communities on how to proceed with the development of indigenous rights under international law. A constructivist approach, however, enables us to see that consent is not simply an ideal principle; it has several interesting political features and ethical implications. First, it is a common ground for indigenous peoples and settler societies. Both European theories of democracy and indigenous practices of governance recognise consent as a constitutive feature of governing. As such, in addition to being a common norm, consent has rhetorical power in debates between both sides. Imposing deals without consent would be hypocritical for settler societies. However, this norm of consent also addresses one of the concerns raised by the governments of settler states opposed to recognising an indigenous right of self-determination. For instance, the government of Canada has argued that Article 10 of the *Declaration*, which prohibits the relocation of indigenous peoples without their free prior and informed consent, is tantamount to giving indigenous peoples a veto. However, implicit in

---

[42] Tully, *Strange Multiplicity*, 123.
[43] Tracing out the various permutations the norm of consent takes in the thousands of different indigenous cultures of the world is beyond the scope of this chapter. One relevant example of its significance is the Iroquois *Gus-Wen-Tah*, Two Row Wampum treaty belt. According to Williams, 'the Iroquois would explain its basic underlying vision of law and peace between different peoples as follows: "We shall each travel the river together, side by side, but in our own boat. Neither of us will steer the other's vessel"'; Robert A. Williams, *Linking Arms Together* (Oxford: Oxford University Press, 1997), 4. This idea of each nation travelling down a common river together, but each refraining from steering the other's boat, means that any actions taken by one nation that might affect the 'steering' of the other nation must be undertaken with the consent of both nations.

the norm of consent is that *all* who are affected by a law or a policy must consent to it in order to be valid. As such, the right to self-determination necessarily implies that indigenous peoples must also seek the consent of settler societies when implementing laws and policies that might affect them. All the norm of consent does is place a check on unilateral action by one party against others who may be affected by the action. While consent may make it more difficult for settler states to act unilaterally against indigenous peoples, this check is justified. It does not prevent either settler societies or indigenous peoples from pursuing policies in the interests of their communities. The norm of consent only requires that when such policies affect others, the consent of those affected is first sought and when the other parties have objections, those objections must be resolved through mutual dialogue and negotiation.

The second rationalisation for watering down the indigenous right to self-determination was that recognition of a qualified right of self-determination is all that is politically possible. This argument can take two guises. The first is the strategic argument that recognition of a qualified right of self-determination could be a strategic stepping-stone that indigenous peoples could later leverage into more full-blown recognition of their rights. Indeed, in much constructivist scholarship there is evidence that activists can later leverage strategic concessions by state actors in areas such as human rights in order to get greater compliance with international norms. One reason that a strategic concession in this case might have backfired on indigenous peoples is that it is a strategic concession over the principle itself as opposed to the implementation of the principle. If the *Draft Declaration* had qualified the language of self-determination, this would actually have weakened the standing of indigenous peoples, who could already point to an unqualified right of self-determination in other human rights instruments such as the *Universal Declaration of Human Rights*. However, a qualified language of self-determination in the *Declaration* would actually have given the rhetorical power to settler states to argue that indigenous peoples have less of a right to self-determination than other nationalities, and as such the state is justified in the unilateral imposition of policies on its indigenous populations.

A second line of objections about the political possibility of recognising an indigenous right to self-determination challenges the very possibility of a global political order encompassing self-governing indigenous communities. A sceptic may applaud the principles behind Alfred's call for rejecting the organisation of the world in a Westphalian state system, but the sceptic might also question how feasible a vision such as Alfred's might be given the realities of global power politics. Here is another location where constructivist research can offer a useful insight. Alfred's vision of a global political system in which indigenous communities can participate fully could operate as a useful guiding principle; it may well answer the question 'what is just?'. But empirically oriented constructivist research can supplement this argument with insights about 'what may work', and how activists can leverage short-term compromises of principles for greater long-term actualisations of these principles. In this case, I believe that a constructivist line of research tells us that the norm of consent is not only an ideal to be strived for; it also represents *a real limit on political possibility*. While imposing an order without consent is always possible for a powerful group in any interaction, such imposition is necessarily coercive. It creates a structure of domination that only provokes future resistance. The fact that there still are struggles for recognition by indigenous peoples 500 years after first contact with European cultures, demonstrates that the previous approaches to recognition were: (1) imposed on indigenous peoples without their consent; and (2) that these impositions have not ended resistance, in fact they have only intensified resistance. Ironically, the imposition of a solution by settler societies without the consent of indigenous peoples is the real idealism, whereas consent is what is politically possible. So long as political orders are imposed without consent there will be resistance.

What is to be done?

In order to achieve a just form of recognition for indigenous peoples in world politics some very radical changes to the basic structures of world politics will be required. The most immanent change that could have a significant impact on the recognition of indigenous peoples would be for the ratification and implementation of the Declaration on the Rights of Indigenous Peoples just adopted by the UN General Assembly in September 2007. The *Draft Declaration* was completed in 1994, but the General Assembly had failed to adopt this document until 2007. As I noted above, a particular site of contention was the language of self-determination within the *Draft Declaration*. The final text recognised the indigenous right to self-determination in the following way:

Article 3

Indigenous Peoples have the Right to Self-Determination. By virtue of that right they freely determine their political status and freely pursue their economic, social and cultural development.

Article 4

Indigenous peoples, in exercising their right to self-determination, have the right to autonomy or self-government in matters relating to their internal and local affairs, as well as ways and means for financing their autonomous functions.[44]

The introduction of Article 4 was a result of a compromise brokered by Norway to leave the right of self-determination unqualified within the charter, but to expand on how the right to self-determination should be exercised in later articles. The Declaration was approved on June 29, 2006 by the UN Human Rights Council in a vote of thirty states for, two states opposed, twelve abstentions and three absences and subsequently ratified in the General Assembly by a vote of 143 for, four states opposed and eleven abstentions.

One of the interesting developments in the UN Human Rights Council vote was the reversal on the part of the government of Canada. During the discussions on the *Draft Declaration* at the WGDD, the government of Canada had been a strong supporter of ratifying the Draft Declaration. However, when the Declaration was voted on at the Human Rights Council, Canada was one of only two countries (the other was Russia[45]) to vote against the Declaration. The

---

[44] UN Document, 'United Nations Declaration on the Rights of Indigenous Peoples' A/61//L.67, September 7, 2007, 4.

[45] Russia has two significant indigenous populations. The first is Siberia with a population around 200,000; the second group, the Udege, with a population of 20,000, lives in southeast Siberia. Both groups continue their traditional ways of life and self-government despite persecution and displacement by the former Soviet Union and current Russian governments. For more information see *Survival International*'s 'Tribal World'; http://survival-international.org/tribes. php. Accessed April 1, 2007. Russia chose to abstain from the UN General Assembly vote on adopting the *Declaration*. Speaking in explanation of their vote to the General Assembly, Ilya Rogachev, the delegate from the Russian Federation, stated that 'It was not a truly balanced document, in particular regarding land and natural resources or the procedures for compensations and redress.' For these comments see UN Document GA/10612 'General Assembly Adopts Declaration on Rights of Indigenous Peoples: "Major step forward" towards human rights for all, says President', September 13, 2007.

immediate reason for this reversal was the change of the party in power in Canada. When the Liberal Party formed the government in power (from 1993 until early 2006), the Canadian delegation at the UN had been – along with Norway and Denmark – a leader in pushing for the Draft Declaration's ratification. With the election of the Conservative Party, the government of Canada joined the USA, Australia and New Zealand as the strongest opponents of the Draft Declaration.[46] The government of Canada's primary reason for opposing ratification of the treaty was that the treaty supported indigenous 'claims to broad ownership over traditional territories even where rights to such territories were lawfully ceded by treaty'.[47] The government of Canada also expressed reservations about how the Declaration could give indigenous governments a veto over laws passed by other 'levels of government' in Canada. The governments of Australia, New Zealand and the United States also expressed reservations about the Draft Declaration at the time of the UN Human Rights Council vote, stating that 'separatist or minority groups with traditional connections to the territory where they live – across the globe – could exploit this declaration to claim the right to self-determination, including exclusive control of territorial resources'.[48]

The objection settler states have made to this treaty, then, comes from two areas. First, there is the concern that self-determination would give indigenous peoples control over the natural resources in a given territory, and as such self- determination would have an adverse effect on the economies of settler states. Second, there is a concern that the right to self-determination would give indigenous peoples the power to ignore or override the laws and policies of other levels of government within settler states. At its most extreme, this could lead to indigenous peoples separating from settler states and forming micro-states.

The real issue from the perspective of settler states then, is whether they can afford to pay the costs associated with these impositions. A sceptic might respond, yes, states have demonstrated time and again

---

[46] Interestingly, when both New Zealand and Australia were governed by left of centre parties in the early 1990s they had also been advocates of the ratification of the Draft Declaration. When both countries elected more conservative parties in the mid-1990s, the governments of Australia and New Zealand also reversed their policy with respect to the Draft Declaration. So, it seems that changes in domestic politics can lead to very dramatic changes in government policy with respect to this Draft Declaration.

[47] 'Statement by Ambassador Paul Meyer'.   [48] Ibid.

that they will bear the cost associated with imposition of rule on indigenous peoples, so these states must be getting more than the imposition costs them. This line of argument reduces the question of recognising a right of self-determination to an empirical one of a cost–benefit analysis, albeit one that may point a way out of the impasse. While it may appear at first glance that the cost of recognising an indigenous right to self-determination may be greater to settler states than non-recognition of this right, there is evidence that this is actually not the case. *The Royal Commission on Aboriginal Peoples* in 1996 hired an economist to look at the cost to Canadian society of the status quo. The conclusion was that it cost Canada $7.5 billion dollars annually (approximately one percent of the gross domestic product) in reduced government revenue and increased social spending on health care, social services, policing and remedial programmes.[49] These are just social costs, which don't include expensive court cases to correct past wrongs such as compensation to victims of past government wrongs such as the Residential Schools within Canada. Similar studies of the social and economic costs of government policies in other settler states could be reasonably expected to reveal similar costs in those states as well, though this is certainly a subject for further research that could impact upon the contingent claims made here. Furthermore there are economic costs to industry and businesses for unresolved land claims, court cases and potential boycotts of businesses that profit from resources extracted from disputed territories. Finally there are the political costs of continued imposition. Consider both the shame and tensions created within settler societies by road blockades protesting land claims, and political outrage over lack of access to potable water on reserves. Indigenous activists can leverage the media attention created by these activities to shame settler states into recognition of an indigenous right to self-determination by arguing to the international community that indigenous peoples would be more effective at addressing these issues than settler states have been to date.

A constructivist analysis can show us a clear set of tactics that activists could engage in to promote the implementation of the *Declaration on the*

---

[49] Royal Commission on Aboriginal Peoples, Canada, *Report of the Royal Commission on Aboriginal Peoples*, volume 5, 'Renewal: A Twenty Year Commitment' (Ottawa, ON: Minister of Supply and Services, Canada, 1996), 24. Thanks to James Tully for drawing my attention to this argument.

Rights of Indigenous Peoples, which tap the theoretical mechanisms of moral change from the persuasion of states to redefining their definitions of interests through more coercive techniques:

(1) Point out the hypocrisy of states extending the right of self-determination to all peoples except indigenous peoples.
(2) Use shame to point out the great social injustices indigenous people endure because of the status quo.
(3) Point out the cost of the status quo in real material terms through lost productivity and increased government spending.
(4) Raise the material cost through civil disobedience: road blockades, denial of access to disputed territories and organisation of global boycotts.

Until such time as states implement a right of self-determination for their indigenous populations this type of resistance will continue. While the *Declaration on the Rights of Indigenous Peoples* is merely a declaratory regime, the fact that this *Declaration* was adopted by such a wide majority of the General Assembly provides moral legitimacy to the recognition of indigenous rights. Just as other declaratory regimes have provided moral leverage for transnational activists in their human rights campaigns with states, the adoption of this *Declaration* by the United Nations should provide similar moral and political leverage to indigenous activists engaged in struggles with the governments of settler societies. The political task for indigenous activists is two-fold. First, indigenous activists and their allies should make clear to states that there is not simply a moral cost in non-recognition of the right to self-determination, but that this moral cost also has very clear material costs. Second, indigenous activists and their allies should develop (I would predict that they will) global campaigns aimed at raising the costs to states for their non-recognition of indigenous rights to self-government.

5 | Policy hypocrisy or political compromise? Assessing the morality of US policy toward undocumented migrants

AMY GUROWITZ

Introduction

Immigrant receiving countries like the USA frequently profess their desire to keep out undocumented migrants. They use strong rhetoric to convey this to those inside and outside the state, and they adopt policies aimed at doing so. Yet, many of these policies are either known to be deficient or are only selectively enforced. The USA for example 'cracks down' on undocumented migration with methods known to be generally unsuccessful in deterring migration, and all the while not addressing what is referred to by experts as the 'linchpin' of migration control: employer demand.

In short, many aspects of immigration policy, especially those policies directed at undocumented migrants, display a high degree of hypocrisy. How do we assess our policies directed at undocumented migration from a moral standpoint? Are our immigration policies, or our selective enforcement of them, by definition immoral because they are knowingly, even at times intentionally, designed to obscure – in this case most often to convince the public that something is being done to stop undocumented migration when in reality government actions are half-hearted and intended to appease many different audiences of which a generally restrictionist public is just one? Most of us would want to answer in the affirmative – the hypocrisy is by definition immoral. Furthermore, theorists of ethics looking at migration also tend to agree that our policies toward undocumented migrants are morally questionable. Specifically, both Joseph Carens and less obviously Michael Walzer, two of the most prominent theorists of ethics who have written most directly on this topic, and who disagree on most aspects of what constitutes ethical state policy with regard to migration, would likely find these approaches unethical, in part, though not entirely, because of their hypocrisy. In short, our common-sense morality in judging hypocrisy, and our most prominent guides through the ethics of the issue, would find deep problems with our current policies.

Yet politically the disconnect between official policy goals and implementation makes sense. Policy makers must balance employer and humanitarian demands with popular sentiment that is generally restrictionist. Hypocrisy, defined as 'the practice of professing beliefs . . . or virtues that one does not hold or possess' (*American Heritage Dictionary*), is not merely or simply a cynical approach, it allows for the balancing of different demands. Hypocrisy as used here can range from turning a blind eye in the face of evidence, to outright lying. Given the very real strictures faced by policy makers, what is the most moral policy? Put differently, given the politically viable alternatives – or as Richard Price puts it in the introduction to this volume, the art of the possible – are the hypocritical policies immoral? Should we, in short, ask what it is ethical to do *in these circumstances*, rather than abstract the question from political reality?

The approach I take here is similar to that taken by Matthew Gibney in his examination of liberal democratic state responsibility to refugees. Gibney argues that in looking at what responsibilities these states have, most people have argued from the standpoint of a moral ideal and in doing so have abstracted from both the character of modern states and from various aspects of the current political environment. He argues instead for an approach that can be applied in the non-ideal world. His purpose, and mine, is not to criticise the use of ideal theory in scrutinising deeply entrenched practices, but to argue that, in addition, we need other approaches to make demands of states as they exist here and now.[1]

To gain some traction on these questions (yet most specifically not to attempt to outline an ethical immigration policy in any grand sense) this chapter will focus on the US case. A focus on the USA is valuable to the extent that the USA is among the largest targets of immigration in the world. Thus, an improvement in US immigration policies would be no small gain. Many of the core issues concerning immigration raised here are not simply specific to the USA, though to be sure all the particularities concerning immigration in other parts of the world are

[1] Matthew J. Gibney, 'Liberal Democratic States and Responsibilities', *American Political Science Review* 93 (1999), 170.

beyond the scope of this chapter. But generic issues such as the hypocrisy facing those with liberal-democratic sensibilities travel well beyond just the US case.

This chapter thus proceeds as follows: I will first spell out current approaches to undocumented labour entering the USA, offering some historical context. There are many categories of non-citizens in the USA, including legal temporary workers, permanent residents and refugees. In this chapter I focus on undocumented migrants because not only are they the most controversial, it is policy toward them that represents the largest gap between policy and outcome, and arguably the highest degree of hypocrisy. I will then assess these policies from the perspective of Joseph Carens and Michael Walzer, two of our most thoughtful guides through the ethics of this issue area. While it is immediately clear that Carens would find our approaches wanting, at first glance it is less clear that Walzer would. However, I will argue that upon further analysis it becomes apparent that Walzer too would find our policies unethical. I will then argue that it is not politically possible at this time to arrive at either Walzer's or Carens' ideal ethical position. While our current policies raise serious moral questions, some of which I will argue are unacceptable, it is not clear what approach we should take given the absolute lack of consensus about our desire and need for migrant workers – in short given the political reality that US policy makers face. Taking seriously the political context here and now leads us to question our current approach from a perspective less demanding than those of Carens or Walzer and it is not immediately clear where we should turn. Drawing on constructivist insights about the power of language and normative structure in allowing us to see new avenues for action, I will argue that we should in fact condemn our current approach on moral grounds, not only from the ideal perspectives of Carens and Walzer but because, even given current political constraints, we can do better. I will essentially argue from a constructivist perspective that our current approach is immoral, but not because of its hypocrisy per se.

I conclude by arguing that while current proposals for reforming the system through legal temporary worker programmes are a far cry from the standards set by Carens and Walzer, and retain varying levels of wishful thinking such that one could argue that they are as hypocritical as our current policies, they are a better alternative. At a glance the reform proposals simply buy time and in a few years the USA will face the same situation. But constructivist theorising draws our attention to the importance of public, and especially power/official, discourse in shaping our thinking and shared expectations about migrants. By changing the tone of the debate, and seeking a system that more honestly matches our intended, if muddled, approach, we might open up space for further change in a direction more morally acceptable.

Throughout this discussion I will make the assumption, from a generally humanitarian perspective, that the welfare of migrant workers must play some role in our decision making, if for no other reason than that the USA has in fact let in large numbers of undocumented migrants and employed them. In other words, while I will not argue for precisely how to balance the interests of various actors in the USA and the interests of migrant workers, I will assume that some balance must be made. In this sense I am defining progress as movement towards a policy that better accounts for the welfare of migrants, while still balancing the interests of the receiving state. As I will conclude, this involves some form of legalisation of currently illegal migrants. I will also argue that one component of progress involves a move toward better congruity between our stated policy and outcomes with regard to low-wage migrant labour.

US approaches to undocumented migrants

Cornelius and Tsuda argue that in the area of immigration control most receiving countries of immigration experience a significant gap between their stated policy objectives and outcomes.[2] In the USA the most notable gap is between the stated goal of significantly reducing the flow of undocumented labour into the country and the reality of significant and growing numbers. Before discussing the specifics of the US case, it is important to understand the different possible explanations for the policy gap. First, some policies may have unintended consequences. For example, when the government steps up border control it contributes to longer stays by migrants who cannot cross back and forth as easily as they previously could. Migrants are often then joined by family, thus increasing the number of undocumented migrants in the country.

---

[2] Wayne A. Cornelius and Takeyuki Tsuda, 'Controlling Immigration: The Limits of Government Intervention'. In Wayne A. Cornelius, Philip L. Martin and James F. Hollifield (eds.), *Controlling Immigration* (Stanford, CA: Stanford University Press, 2004), 5.

Second, despite stated intentions, the USA has often developed watered-down policies to meet what has become in many countries a structural demand for labour or to appease interest groups opposing restrictionist legislation.[3] For example, governments might put policies in place to appease restrictionists while failing to give them teeth, or by allowing side-doors for entry, to fulfil labour demands.

Finally, many policies are simply not enforced, often because intentions differed from stated policies in the first place.[4] For example, employer sanctions are rarely enforced in the United States. Nor do government agencies consistently round up large numbers of undocumented migrants despite widespread knowledge of where they work (for example most of the agricultural fields in California). Through the following discussion of US immigration policy, it will become apparent that all of these causes of the gap between intentions and outcomes are relevant for the US case and that furthermore, each involves an element of hypocrisy.

Like many developed countries, the USA has a structural demand for low-wage migrant labour – much of it undocumented and much of it Mexican. The USA has had some level of undocumented migration for as long as such migration has been regulated. This migration has increased since the mid-1980s and has grown to an estimated ten million, with approximately 80 percent in the workforce and about three-fifths from Mexico.

While the topic of our demand for labour has gotten much attention in the past couple of decades, it is no newer than our history of turning a blind eye to it. For example, during the Bracero programme begun in 1942 to bring in Mexican labour to fuel the war effort, many undocumented migrants were either allowed in and taken directly to employers or were walked back across the border and allowed to re-enter legally. And from that time until today policy makers have known about and in various ways accepted growing numbers of undocumented migrants. One border area that illustrates our approach to undocumented migrants is an area referred to as the soccer field. The soccer field is on the US side of the border but was without fencing or demarcation separating the US from Mexico.[5] During the 1980s border agents frequently sat and watched Mexicans waiting for night to cross further into the USA. But

---

[3] Ibid. 9–11.   [4] Ibid. 14.
[5] Leo R. Chavez, *Shadowed Lives: Undocumented Immigrants in American Society* (New York, NY: Harcourt Brace Jovanovich College Publishers, 1998), 48.

they often were not apprehended as this was understood to be neutral territory.

There have of course been concerns about undocumented migrants in the past as there are today. For example, the 1950 'Operation Wetback' is probably the most well-known 'illegals panic' in which 3.8 million Mexicans were deported. And there has been media attention, though somewhat fleeting, given to undocumented migrants as early as the 1970s when the use of the term 'illegal' became the common term to refer to undocumented aliens.[6] But the consistent and intense focus on what was increasingly viewed as the crisis of undocumented migrants really began in the 1980s.

The 1986 Immigration Reform and Control Act (IRCA) was a response to increasing concern about undocumented migrants during the 1980s. IRCA was intended to be a carrot and stick approach. It created an amnesty programme for undocumented aliens who had been in the USA since before January 1, 1982. IRCA required that employers verify the status of all employees and made it illegal for them to knowingly employ an undocumented alien. In reality, employer sanctions were not enforced and verification of documents is a formality that places the burden on migrants to find documentation (usually through illegal intermediaries) because the employer just has to see a document, not know if it is real. It was clear from the beginning that the stick side of the equation was more like a thin twig. To cite just one example, it is well known that agricultural employers in the USA have been hiring undocumented aliens since World War II. The most effective way for Immigration and Naturalization Service (INS) agents to apprehend them once they have crossed the border is to conduct raids in the fields during harvest time. Yet due to pressure from congress people representing grower interests, the new law forbade INS agents from interfering with workers in the fields.

Following IRCA a number of groups became much more vocal in speaking out against various forms of immigration. The reasons were complex and included growing anxiety about immigration more generally (both the increasing numbers and the increasing diversity), a surge in the number of asylum seekers and economic recession. There was also at this time a developing narrative, in public discourse and

---

[6] Joseph Nevins, *Operation Gatekeeper: The Rise of the 'Illegal Alien' and the Making of the US–Mexico Boundary* (New York, NY: Routledge, 2002), 112.

among academics, that the state was losing control, or had lost control, of its borders.[7]

During the 1990s media attention became more intense, including high-profile cover stories. The *National Review*, the main voice of American conservatism that had generally not focused on immigration, now became more outspoken. Books such as *Alien Nation* and the *Bell Curve* focused national attention on migration and diversity.[8] Both political parties were, by the 1990s, solidly behind the idea that immigration was a problem in need of fixing and that cracking down on undocumented migration was necessary.

In response, in the summer of 1993 President Clinton announced aggressive new measures to combat illegal immigration. This previously somewhat sidelined issue now became very high profile with frequent visits to the border by the US Attorney General, the INS commissioner and the newly appointed 'Border Czar'.[9] In October 1993, Operation Hold the Line was put in place at the border in El Paso, Texas. Referred to as a deterrence-oriented deployment, INS agents were placed along the border in highly visible positions in an effort to deter border crossers. Apprehensions in the sector affected by Hold the Line dropped by 70 percent, though migrants weren't entering less, they were just entering elsewhere.

In October 1994, Operation Gatekeeper transformed the San Diego border from a fence to a heavily manned and armed barrier with high-tech equipment including infrared night vision scopes and ground sensors to spot potential undocumented migrants. As a result of these operations the INS became the fastest-growing federal agency as their budget nearly tripled and the number of border patrol agents in the southwest more than doubled between 1993 and 1999.[10] In addition, the amount of fencing or other barriers increased from nineteen to over forty-five miles.[11]

---

[7] Peter Andreas, *Border Games: Policing the US–Mexico Divide* (Ithaca, NY: Cornell University Press, 2000) makes this point persuasively.

[8] Richard J. Hernstein and Charles Murray, *Bell Curve: Intelligence and Class Structure in American Life* (New York: Free Press Paperbacks, 1996); Peter Brimlow, *Alien Nation: Common Sense About America's Immigration Disaster* (New York: Random House, 1995).

[9] Andreas, *Border Games*, 89.   [10] Ibid.   [11] Nevins, *Operation Gatekeeper*, 4.

Like Operation Hold the Line, Operation Gatekeeper was hailed as a huge success. But again, it did not reduce migration. Rather, migrants have just moved to less guarded, and more dangerous areas of the border. The effects have been perverse: dramatically increased border deaths, up over 500 percent at the California border between 1994 and 2000, and a booming industry in smuggling.[12] So, in what sense are the operations considered a success? Peter Andreas argues that policing of the border has less to do with deterrence than with managing the image of the border. In this sense he sees Gatekeeper as a success even if it does not deter migrants. It was a political success in that it appeased calls for greater control as evidenced by the fact that for close to a decade the issue died down significantly.[13] And, critically, Gatekeeper allowed for the continued flow of much-needed low-wage labour into the USA, albeit at a much higher cost to the migrant.

Following Gatekeeper, legislation and attempted legislation continued to target undocumented migrants. First, Proposition 187, California's 'Save our State Initiative', was driven by the idea that undocumented migrants are a tax drain. Proposition 187 passed 59–41 percent and, among other provisions, barred undocumented migrants from public education (kindergarten to university) and publicly paid non-emergency medical care and required authorities to verify the legal status of clients. A few weeks later a federal judge in Los Angeles barred enforcement of almost all provisions and in July 1999 Governor Davis and civil rights organisations reached a mediated agreement ending legal challenges to 187. Although it was not implemented, the passage of proposition 187 altered the political landscape and the terms of debate and sparked a larger movement nationwide.

Finally, the 1996 Illegal Immigration Reform and Immigrant Responsibility Act again doubled the number of US border patrol agents (but again without effectively preventing migrants from finding employment) and granted INS officials at the border authority to decide whether someone seeking asylum is legitimate (with seven days to appeal a negative decision). Today in 2007 the issue of control is front and centre yet again with wide agreement across the spectrum that we

---

[12] Wayne A. Cornelius, 'Death at the Border: Efficacy and Unintended Consequences of US Immigration Control Policy', *Population and Development Review* 27 (2001), 669.
[13] Andreas, *Border Games*, 9.

should 'do something' about undocumented immigration whether for reasons of fairness or security.

One way of looking at Gatekeeper and other control approaches is that as a country we are not really sure if we want to control the border, in large part because it is difficult to clearly identify the 'we'. On the one hand, business, including agribusiness, manufacturing and the service industry, want labour (not to mention the middle and upper classes who want nannies, maids, gardeners, etc.). And while most people are loath to actually argue that we should turn a blind eye to undocumented migrants, there is pressure from humanitarian groups, and more broadly our liberal humanitarian sentiments, to not get too draconian (most tend, for example, to look upon the Malaysian government's round-up of undocumented Filipina maids attending Sunday church services as a bit nasty). On the other hand, the public, encouraged by some political groups and media sources, call for control and express increasing concern about the very nature of illegality, downward pressure on wages, use of public services, etc. In short, it is unclear what the national interest on border control is.

Thus the government achieved what it wanted – the quieting of outcry and the supply of labour. This is not an argument about conspiracy theory. Rather it is an argument about government policy responding to pressures pushing and pulling in different directions with the result that policy makers are espousing policies that they have or should have every reason to believe will not work to meet their stated goals. And they maintain a focus on failed policies in the face of direct evidence of their failure to control immigration. The results are seemingly confused policies – ones that we know do not work to reduce numbers, but do, sometimes, work to appease publics. The most damning commentary on the US approach to control, an approach that focuses almost entirely on the border, comes from looking at employer sanctions. The US Commission on Immigration Reform has said that reducing the employment magnet is the linchpin of a strategy to reduce undocumented migration.[14] Similarly, a 1994 presidential report on immigration states that 'everyone agrees that the primary incentive for illegal immigration is employment. Work-place enforcement of labor standards and employer sanctions are the instruments for reducing that incentive'.[15]

[14] Quoted in Andreas, *Border Games*, 100–101.
[15] Quoted in Andreas, *Border Games*, 101.

Yet the USA has almost totally ineffective employer sanctions for hiring undocumented aliens and in 1996, just two years after Gatekeeper and at a high point of government self-congratulations on its success, only about 2 percent of the INS budget was devoted to sanction enforcement. While it is clear that there are practical problems with policies ostensibly designed to keep certain migrants out yet unsuccessful in doing so, it is less clear how to assess them morally. In the next section I look to leading ethical theorists of immigration for guidelines in assessing these policies.

The philosophical debate: Carens and Walzer

Joseph Carens and Michael Walzer have put forth the most clearly argued debate over the ethics of border control and the rights of non-citizens once they enter the country. It is therefore instructive to turn to these theorists as guides through the ethics of US policy toward undocumented migrants. Carens approaches the issue from a cosmo-politan standpoint, one that focuses on individual rights and universal-ism, while Walzer approaches it from what some have called a communitarian approach and others have referred to as a 'morality of states position'. For Walzer, communities have rights in and of them-selves, most notably the right to be self-determining. And, critically for this and many of his other arguments, state borders are presumptively the outer borders of community. For Walzer, obligations are not uni-versal but arise from a sense of community. Therefore we have member-ship obligations to other nationals of our state before those beyond our borders.

Walzer argues that it is up to the citizens of a country to decide who to admit and what the appropriate criteria for admission are.[16] We should make these decisions, according to Walzer's reasoning, in accordance with our own understanding of what membership means in our com-munity and of what sort of community we wish to have. The use of 'we' here is quite deliberate – for Walzer these are collective or communal decisions. To understand this claim, we have to understand Walzer's argument that without admission and exclusion control, there can be no communities of character, no historically stable associations where

---

[16] Michael Walzer, 'Membership'. In David Jacobson (ed.), *Immigration Reader* (Oxford: Blackwell Publishers, 1998), 342.

members have a special sense of their common life.[17] This distinctiveness of cultures and groups depends on closure.[18] And if distinctiveness is a value, which he believes most people would argue, then we need closure somewhere – and in our world that somewhere is with state borders. In short, Walzer argues, 'admission and exclusion are at the core of communal independence. They suggest the deepest meaning of self-determination' and self-determination is the value that Walzer seeks first and foremost to uphold.[19]

The right of states to exercise self-determination in deciding whom to let in is not without constraint. For example, Walzer argues for the obligation to help those in dire need and for the obligation that existing inhabitants not be expelled from territory when a state is formed. There are also constraints once the state, or community, has decided to let certain people in based on whatever criteria they choose – constraints directly relevant for our case. Walzer argues that while immigration decisions are political ones, naturalisation is entirely constrained.[20] Every new immigrant or refugee must have the opportunity of citizenship. His reasoning goes back to the principle of self-determination and the idea that no state can claim that it is self-determining its fate when decisions are being made by only some portion of those affected. This would, according to Walzer, be a form of tyranny.[21] His theory then is based on the right of closure, necessary for communities, and the obligation of political inclusiveness. Critically his argument extends to guest workers as well. They too must, under most circumstances, have the right to become citizens. In democracies, Walzer argues, citizens have a choice: they can bring in new workers and put them on the path to full membership (citizenship), or they can exclude them.[22]

Carens takes quite a different view, at least on the question of who should be let in. His cosmopolitan approach is based on the idea that state borders, while of great practical significance, may not have moral significance. And that therefore we as individuals, and our government, should assess our actions based on the idea that all people, regardless of citizenship, are of equal moral worth. When applying this to borders,

---

[17] Ibid. 362.   [18] Ibid. 349.   [19] Ibid. 362.   [20] Ibid.   [21] Ibid. 363.
[22] Ibid. 361. The one exception to this stark choice is to obtain political and civil rights for guest workers another way. For example, host countries could negotiate formal agreements with sending states setting out a list of rights similar to those that the migrants might fight for themselves if they had the ability to do so (Walzer, 'Membership', 360).

Carens argues that borders should be generally open – people should be free to leave their country of origin and settle in another (subject to the rules that citizens of that receiving country must abide by).[23] He argues that this applies most strongly to those from poorer countries coming to richer countries because, in his view, citizenship in Western liberal democracies is the modern equivalent of feudal privilege – an inherited status that greatly enhances one's life chances.[24] He also points out that freedom of movement, and the application of universal values, is central to our culture.[25] Therefore if we are making communal decisions based on our culture, we cannot make ones that run counter to it, as closing our borders does. Carens goes on to argue that, contrary to Walzer's concern, this would not lead to the absence of distinctions between communities. Different cities in the USA have very distinctive cultures despite the fact that there are no border restrictions between them.[26] And, Seattle, for example, has much more in common with Vancouver than with Little Rock.

Not surprisingly given his views on entry, Carens argues that those allowed to reside and work in a nation should be granted the right to become citizens following a brief passage of time (say five years) and some reasonable formalities (and cultural assimilation is not considered reasonable because it assumes that social membership may be defined in terms of social conformity). Children of residents should have the right to citizenship in their state of residence (as is the case in the USA).[27] Importantly, these moral claims do not derive from the terms under which they were admitted – it doesn't matter if they were undocumented or not, or their residency was tied to employment.[28] His reasoning is that to require integration beyond a brief residency period violates the principle of toleration and respect for diversity and calls into question the equal status of current citizens who differ from the majority.[29] Long-term residency without citizenship leads to unequal and disenfranchised members of the state.[30]

---

[23] Joseph H. Carens, 'Aliens and Citizens: The Case for Open Borders'. In Jacobson, *Immigration Reader*, 365.
[24] Ibid. 365–366.   [25] Ibid. 379.   [26] Ibid. 380.
[27] Joseph H. Carens, 'Membership and Morality: Admission to Citizenship in Liberal Democratic States'. In William Rogers Brubaker (ed.), *Immigration and the Politics of Citizenship in Europe and North America* (Lanham, MD: University Press of America, 1989), 31.
[28] Ibid. 33.   [29] Ibid. 40.   [30] Ibid. 36.

How can these approaches guide us in regard to undocumented migrants in the USA? The story of border control and undocumented migrants in the USA is a story about a state that is schizophrenic – that wants but doesn't want undocumented labour (one might argue that we want the labour but not the people). It seems clear that Americans – many of us – want them from an economic point of view. We collectively employ them on a widespread basis, we enjoy the goods that they produce at low cost to us, and, critically, we are not trying to get rid of them in ways that experts think work (most obviously with employer sanctions). I would argue that in a sense most Americans want them in other ways too. We want to be the kind of country that does not round up large number of migrants and ship them out. We even have qualms about denying certain rights to people within our borders regardless of the legality of their stay here as witnessed in the opposition to Proposition 187. In this sense any realistic policy proposal, even from more restrictionist politicians, must take into account the political reality that Americans on the whole may well not have the political, let alone the economic, stomach for either severely restricting low-wage migration or for expelling large numbers of undocumented migrants who are already here.

Yet, on the other hand, we don't want them. Public opinion polls, which I will return to, show consistent concern about what is viewed as the state's lack of ability to control the borders, about perceived crime, use of public services, etc. The 'we' who has such an insatiable demand for cheap labour from south of the border is the same 'we' complaining about it. How do we apply the two most prominent ethical approaches to migration to help us wade through this tension?

Presumably Carens would be displeased with this state of affairs. But since he argues for generally open borders and for no distinction in naturalisation rights between documented and undocumented migrants, the situation surrounding this particular case is somewhat beside the point. While not necessarily in the business of making policy recommendations, if Carens were to present his ideal policy for the USA it would allow for vastly more migration from Mexico to the USA and the almost unquestionable integration and naturalisation of those wishing to stay.

But while our border control policies run totally counter to what Carens sees as our obligations, they are at first glance in line with Walzer's idea that we have a right to decide who to let in. To reiterate,

Walzer argues that the community, in this case the state, has a right, even an obligation, to decide who to let in (subject to his exception for those in dire need). The community has the right to be self-determining. One might argue that the USA has exercised this right. The USA has clear laws about how many people and which categories of people are to be let in each year and we have border procedures, greatly enhanced in recent years, to keep out those who do not enter through these established mechanisms.

But what would Walzer make of a situation in which we do not make full use of the laws at our disposal? Arguably our eagerness to hire undocumented migrants, and the extremely weak enforcement of our existing laws, in short, our schizophrenia about border control, indicates that we do not in fact have a communal consensus on migration. It seems quite clear that for Walzer we cannot have our cake and eat it too. If we recall his argument that once migrants are allowed in they must be allowed to naturalise, it becomes even more clear that we cannot have a communal consensus that we want cheap labour that we keep illegal and don't integrate.

I have essentially been arguing, drawing on others, that our border control policies are in many ways a façade – one that would not meet Walzer's criteria for morally justifiable policies. Our policies focus on policing of the borders while allowing and in fact encouraging the hiring of migrants who can find a way around the barriers. This policy began in earnest during the 1990s and continues to be our focus today. Wayne Cornelius has recently stated that 'The fences themselves have simply diverted the flow . . . there is no evidence that fences per se has been an effective deterrent. They have helped to jack up smugglers' fees and forced crossings into more remote and dangerous spots.' Echoing Peter Andreas' point he goes on to state that fences 'are simply a symbolic show of force'.[31]

While it is widely recognised that our border control policies are ineffective, in some ways a façade, there has been neither the political will nor the economic desire to change our policies in favour of more effective enforcement. It is in this sense that the USA has muddled along by having our cake (cheap and flexible labour) and eating it too (not risking falling into the political or economic pitfalls involved in either

---

[31] Cited in John M. Broder, 'With Congress's Blessing, a Border Fence May Finally Push Through to the Sea', *New York Times* July 5, 2005, A8.

legalisation or real enforcement). The problem from a moral standpoint is that this means placing full responsibility for migrating on the part of undocumented migrants – full responsibility for something that we both allow and encourage. It requires a Janus-faced policy that essentially has one side saying 'come in' while the other side shouts 'we've lost control of the border' and 'we must keep the illegals out'.

Critical here is to stress the role of the state in this process. As Peter Andreas and others have so keenly pointed out, this is not, as is often portrayed, a case of an impotent state being overrun by migrants bursting through the gates. First, the idea that the state has lost control implies the questionable proposition that there was a golden age of control.[32] Second, states help create the migration that they are trying to control. When governments, like the US, push for economic globalisation, with its incumbent movements of goods, information and communication, they also create a world in which people can more easily move about. The more easily connections are made across borders, the more easily people can imagine crossing them (even if the physical crossing has gotten much more difficult and dangerous). It is for this reason that we end up with what was earlier referred to as the gap between our official goals and the results. It is not because the state keeps pushing to reach its goals and is not powerful enough to do so (though that is an open question). It is because the goal is unclear.

To sum up, Carens and Walzer present us with two options with regard to undocumented labour. These broad options could play out in different ways but might look something like the following: for Carens, we should allow migrants who want to come and work here to come. The category of undocumented or illegal would thus largely become obsolete and those migrants who wish to stay long term should be able to become US citizens. For Walzer our options are wide open. We could, theoretically, make a Carens-like decision; we could decide to close our borders to all but those in dire need (and most of the workers from Latin America probably won't qualify), or we could come up with something in between (letting in a certain number of migrant workers). Critically though, whoever we let in must have the option to gain citizenship if they stay. And, even more critically, what we must do is come to some sort of communal understanding. We must be able to defend our policy

---

[32] On this point see John Torpey, *The Invention of the Passport* (Cambridge: Cambridge University Press, 2000).

in terms of communal self-determination. What we cannot do is turn a clear lack of consensus into public policy and call it the self-determining will of the community. Carens and Walzer thus leave us with two options: essentially open borders or a communal consensus that can warrant the term self-determination. In what follows I will argue that neither of those is possible, and that therefore muddling through will continue. How we muddle through however, can be assessed in different ways.

Political reality

Why is it not politically possible, given current circumstances, to meet the moral demands of either Carens or Walzer? Turning first to Carens, while there are many reasons why dramatically opening the borders to legal migration from Mexico would not be politically feasible, including the potential economic impacts and the response from restrictionist politicians and think-tanks, one of the most obvious reasons involves public opinion. Depending on the poll and the phrasing of the question, approximately 50–70 percent of Americans polled have negative views about immigration. For example, a 2002 poll conducted by the Chicago Council on Foreign Relations indicates that 60 percent of the public regard the present level of immigration to be a critical threat to vital US interests.[33]

These polls are not picking up temporary blips. Historical research indicates that surges of anti-immigrant sentiment tend to follow sharp economic downturns. This has been due partly to the tendency of politicians and labour union leaders to blame foreign workers for unemployment and downward pressure on wages. But during the 1990s in the US anti-immigrant sentiment held in good times and bad. In California in the late 1990s when the economy outperformed the national economy, polling continued to show a negative view about immigrants – much of it implicitly or explicitly directed at Mexicans. This presents a bit of a puzzle because in the mid-1990s a majority in most polls rightly thought that immigrants mostly took jobs that natives did not want. Part of the reason for the consistency in negative opinion,

[33] Roy Beck and Steven A. Camarota, 'Elite vs. Public Opinion: An Examination of Divergent Views on Immigration', *Center for Immigration Studies Backgrounder* (December 2002), 1.

even during economic improvement, lies in the roots of opinion. While immigration debates tend to focus on economics, much restrictionist sentiment has its roots in cultural concerns. Analysts tend to find that rather than narrow economic self-interest, those polling negatively on immigration tended to be influenced by broader economic anxieties, ideology and affective orientations towards particular ethnic groups and to be concerned about language, the unity of the country and cultural fragmentation.[34] Critically, these cultural causes tend to be much more entrenched than those driven by economic self-interest.

Assessing the feasibility of any approach would also involve questioning whose interests would be served or injured by a policy that let much higher numbers of low-wage workers from Mexico migrate. From Carens' cosmopolitan perspective one would presumably look at people as a whole rather than American interests versus Mexican interests, or might potentially focus on the interests of the sending states. But many approaches, including Walzer's, would make an ethical argument for American policy serving the interests of Americans first. Most scholars argue that, as things stand now, migrant workers are on balance a benefit for the USA, even if some argue that the benefit is small. Among workers who should compete with low-wage migrants, those migrants can have the effect of displacing native workers and depressing wages but many argue that the nature of the US labour market is such that many of those workers move to find work elsewhere.[35]

In addition to employment issues, the other major question during the 1990s was whether or not migrants and their families pay more in taxes than they consume in services paid for by those taxes. More complicated is to 'measure' the cultural effects of migration, or the balance

[34] Jack Citrin, Donald P. Green, Christopher Muste and Cara Wong, 'Public Opinion Toward Immigration Reform: The Role of Economic Motivations', *The Journal of Politics* 59 (1997), 858–881; Joel S. Fetzer, 'Economic Self-interest or Cultural Marginality? Anti-immigration Sentiment and Nativist Political Movements in France, Germany and the USA', *Journal of Ethnic and Migration Studies* 26 (2000), 5–23; Wayne A. Cornelius, 'Ambivalent Reception', in Marcelo M. Suarez-Orozco and Mariela M. Paez (eds.), *Latinos: Remaking America* (Berkeley, CA: University of California Press, 2002). For the argument that these studies downplay economic factors too much see Alan Kessler, 'Immigration, Economic Insecurity, and the Ambivalent American Public', The Center for Comparative Immigration Studies Working Paper No. 41, September 2001.
[35] Philip L. Martin, 'The United States: The Continuing Immigration Debate'. In Cornelius *et al.*, *Controlling Immigration*, 71.

between the economic and the cultural effects. The purpose of this discussion is not to argue that large-scale low-wage migration is beneficial or not, but simply to point out that before we can argue that a Carens' style approach is the correct one, we would have to be clear about who we think should benefit from our immigration policies.

As discussed previously, Walzer's approach is more complicated. To meet his threshold for an ethical immigration policy we would need communal consensus. And, as I have argued, the consensus cannot be one that says we will have a policy that is essentially a façade and that allows us to have cheap labour while keeping it intentionally illegal. I have alluded to the different pressures on government in making immigration policy. I will discuss them in more detail to convey how hard anything resembling a consensus is to imagine.

Public opinion is certainly one important component on the restrictionist side. But public opinion also has to be shaped and conveyed. This has often happened when politicians, opportunistically or out of beliefs, play the immigration card as then Governor Pete Wilson did in his 1994 campaign for Proposition 187. It was in part these voices that were to be appeased by programmes like Operation Gatekeeper.

Yet there were others who were perfectly content to see Gatekeeper succeed politically while failing to keep out migrants, namely employers. Employers in many sectors hire migrants, documented or undocumented, for a number of reasons. Even as the economy evolves toward more knowledge-intensive businesses there is still demand for low-skilled workers. These jobs often not only pay poorly, they may involve dirty and dangerous work, they offer little or no advancement opportunity and are therefore often not attractive to many native-born workers. In addition, social networks often keep jobs being fed to particular communities and many employers prefer to hire through these networks.[36]

Demand for Mexican labour seems insatiable. It is not as affected by business cycles as classical economics would predict and we should expect demand to continue as service and agricultural sector jobs increase and automation possibilities are maxed-out. Furthermore, as the number of dual-income households increases, the demand for domestic labour rises. In short, as Cornelius argues, the structural

---

[36] Wayne A. Cornelius, 'The Structural Embeddedness of Demand for Mexican Immigrant Labor: New Evidence from California'. In Marcelo Suarez-Orozco (ed.), *Crossings* (Cambridge, MA: Harvard University Press, 1998), 125.

embeddedness of demand for Mexican labour means that small- and medium-sized businesses are likely to resist or evade efforts to reduce their access to immigrant labour.[37] It should also be pointed out that allied with employers against ambitious immigration restriction in general are ethnic and human rights organisations, free-market conservatives and rights-oriented liberals.[38]

Finally, in making the case for the absence of any sort of policy along the lines of communal self-determination, we have to bear in mind that there is a substantial gap in the USA between the American public and 'opinion leaders' on the issue of immigration – and the gap appears to be increasing. While 60 percent of the public in the previously cited Chicago Council on Foreign Relations survey argued that immigration is a threat to US vital interests, only 14 percent of the country's leadership agreed. And on the specific issue of illegal immigration, the public ranked it as the sixth biggest foreign policy problem while elites ranked it twenty-sixth. Beck and Camarota argue that 'there is no other foreign policy-related issue on which the American people and their leaders disagreed more profoundly than immigration'.[39]

The point is that it is hard to imagine, at least in the immediate to short term, a consensus that would result in a coherent policy. Does the USA commit to dramatically reducing undocumented labour by giving our border control policies real teeth with things like enforced employer sanctions, thus alienating the employer/civil rights side of the equation and suffering the economic consequences? Or should the government allow more legal migration with the chance of citizenship, alienating the concerned public side? Looking at migration policy from this perspective draws our attention to the tension between moral demands and democracy – more specifically the views of citizens in a democracy. Leaving the world of ideal theory for a moment, one might even argue that despite its hypocrisy our current approach is, if not desirable, not *entirely* negative given the political realities of immigration politics in the USA.[40] One reason for this conclusion might be that current policy

---

[37] Ibid. 140.
[38] Daniel J. Tichenor, 'Commentary'. In Cornelius *et al.*, *Controlling Immigration*, 92.
[39] Beck and Camarota, 'Elite vs. Public Opinion', 1.
[40] One exception to my argument that our current policies might represent something of a moral grey area involves the skyrocketing numbers of border deaths caused by migrants crossing the US–Mexico border at more and more

is essentially an approach worked out outside of public discourse and it is not easy to predict what the outcome of a public debate required to make significant changes would be. Guiraudon has documented in Europe that more progressive (in the sense of expanding rights) approaches to migrants tend to result from processes that take place outside the realm of major democratic debate – in large part because public opinion tends to view migration negatively.[41] In other words, one could argue that our current policies, however flawed, fill jobs and employ the otherwise potentially unemployed, *and* it is not clear what sort of policy would emerge from a truly open and democratic debate about undocumented migration. At a minimum, the evidence seems to run contrary to Carens' attempt to turn Walzer's communitarian argument against itself, insofar as the liberal-democratic culture he posits as likely to favour freedom of movement in fact has tended to produce political pressures for less, not more immigration. The point is that at a glance many people, especially those arguing from a more cosmopolitan standpoint with regard to immigration policy, are in favour of both the democratic process and progressive policies toward immigration, while it is not at all clear how compatible those are. In this sense, and as I will argue below, hypocritical policies may be preferential, from a humanitarian or cosmopolitan standpoint, to policies that force a choice in one direction or another, almost certainly to the detriment of the economy, or migrants, or both.

Illegal immigrants

I have thus far argued that neither Carens' nor Walzer's ideal approaches are politically feasible. We therefore, I argue, need another basis from which to critique our current policies. In short, what is morally preferable, or what moral demands should be made on the state, that are realistic enough in the here and now as to proffer a real prospect of genuine moral gain? This is a critical and not at all abstract question because currently, in both public opinion and in Washington, there is consensus on one thing: that the current system needs to be

dangerous locations. It seems to me that even the most imperfect policy must find a way to address this dire need.
[41] Virginie Guiraudon, 'The Evolution of the Rights of Non-Nationals in Western Europe: Different Explanatory Frameworks'. Paper presented at ECPR, Bordeaux, France, 1995.

fixed. But that is where agreement ends. Before turning to the current
policy debate and some of the proposed immigration reforms to assess
what it is most ethical to do under our current circumstances, I want to
draw attention to what I argue is the most problematic aspect of our
current policy approach: the result of widespread illegal status for
migrant workers. I will argue that this, rather than the hypocrisy of
our current policies, is the most critical aspect in need of reform and that
therefore the goal of any reform being debated should work towards
remedying illegal status. That is, a constructivist focus on the effects of
practices on constituting identities points us to address the production
of migrants as criminals rather than taking that identity as a given.

Illegality has a number of problems associated with it. Perhaps most
obvious from the perspective of the state, there are security problems.
Presumably we do want to know who is inside our borders and when.
From the perspective of the migrants themselves there are concerns
about workers' rights and, as already mentioned, there has been a
dramatically increased rate of death at the border. But there are more
subtle reasons that help highlight the problem of placing all the burden
of illegality on the migrants themselves. First, allowing a situation that
relies on undocumented labour gives, or perpetuates, the impression
that the state is unable to control its borders. This idea that no one is
minding the store is, as I have indicated, only partly true as it is not clear
that as a collective we want to mind the store. The perception, when
incomplete, is problematic. It is problematic first because the negative
sentiments about migration created by this fear of loss of control may,
and often do, spill over into negative sentiments about immigrants in
general regardless of illegality.

The idea that no one is minding the store also increases negative
perceptions of undocumented aliens, constructing them as criminals.
It is one thing to believe that there is some potential mutual and desired
benefit to be had from undocumented migration. It is quite another to
allow the perception to persist that the government is doing everything
it can to keep migrants out and those (devious, untrustworthy, possibly
criminal) people just keep coming anyway. While the idea of the undocumented migrant working in the USA as criminal is legally correct,
I have argued that since they are in many ways invited, it is morally
wrong. In addition, framing the issue of 'illegal' immigrants as being
about undocumented, poor, largely Mexican, migrants clearly ignores
whole other components of undocumented migration, particularly that

of student and tourist visa over-stayers who are most often from wealthy countries, not to mention the effects this framing has on immigration issues more generally. This issue draws our attention to the constitutive role of social structures, in this case law. If we as a society have constructed the undocumented migrant as a criminal, we, it seems, are faced with two choices: we can let them dissolve into society or we can arrest or deport them. As long as they are constituted as illegal and criminal, we cannot easily acknowledge the critical role that they play in the economy or our role in bringing them here.

Finally, the hypocrisy inherent in the misperception that no one is minding the store, or that it is being minded ineffectually, discredits and delegitimises the actors who are supposed to be in charge.[42] The popularity of the 'Minutemen' in some areas of the country may be due in part to the perception that they are filling a void in taking up a role that should be, but is not, fulfilled by the federal government.[43]

A second, related, reason why illegality is problematic is that it leads to discrimination, even hostility against undocumented migrants (the same ones we tacitly invite in and regularly hire) and often leads those migrants to stay in the shadows for fear of retribution. Again, being constituted as criminals has implications not only for how we the rest of society thinks of migrants, but how they must act themselves. This can, and often does, involve not seeking medical care, not making use of educational resources for children, not reporting crimes to authorities, and so on.

Third, as Nevins points out, labelling certain groups of migrants illegal stifles discussion: 'For many, there is no reason to debate policies that aim to stop "illegal" immigration, something that is simply wrong.'[44] As Gutierrez argues:

[F]or a growing proportion of the American public, the issues involved in the immigration controversy are fairly straightforward. Adhering to a view in which the issues of an immigrant's standing in American society and ability to fit into the American way of life should be

---

[42] See Marc Lynch in this volume on the costs of hypocrisy.
[43] Groups like this should serve as a warning to those who see such promise in civil society groups for progressive change at least as defined in cosmopolitan terms. This example shows that civil society activism can cut in many directions. I thank Dick Price for pointing this out.
[44] Nevins, *Operation Gatekeeper*, 147.

determined simply by ascertaining the individual's formal status before the law, many apparently believe that devising appropriate immigration policies should be a simple matter. For such individuals the question of who rightly should be considered a fully vested member of the American community is unambiguous: one is either legal or illegal, a citizen or an alien, and American or a foreigner. If one accepts this starkly bifurcated system of categorization, it follows that coming to basic decisions about who rightfully belongs to, and who must be excluded from, that community should be an easy matter.[45]

These problems with the conceptualisation of immigrants as illegal draw our attention to constructivist insights about the importance of language and normative structure. As Reus-Smit argues, normative structures shape actors' identities and interests through three mechanisms: imagination, communication and constraint.[46] The first two mechanisms are particularly relevant here. Normative structures, of which language is one part, shape what actors see as possible. They shape how we imagine possibilities for action. They also shape how we communicate. When we explain or justify actions, we usually do so with appeal to established norms. Currently the norm most commonly referenced in justifying action with regard to undocumented migration is the norm of 'control that which is illegal'. Normative structures also constrain action. As Gutierrez makes clear, for many no further conversation is necessary.

My argument is that until we can shift from a conceptualisation of undocumented migrants as illegal, our resources in fixing the current situation are limited – they are limited in what we can imagine and in what will make sense to a public primed, quite rationally, to assume that if it is illegal it should be gotten rid of. Lakoff and Ferguson drive the point home when they argue that 'linguistic expressions are anything but neutral. Each framing defines the problem in its own way, and hence constrains the solutions needed to address that problem.'[47] In short,

---

[45] David G. Gutierrez, *Walls and Mirrors: Mexican Americans, Mexican Immigrants, and the Politics of Ethnicity* (Berkeley, CA: University of California Press, 1995), 211. Quoted in Nevins, *Operation Gatekeeper*, 147.
[46] Christian Reus-Smit, 'Constructivism'. In Scott Burchill *et al.* (eds.), *Theories of International Relations* (Hampshire: Palgrave, second edition, 2001), 218.
[47] George Lakoff and Sam Ferguson, 'The Framing of Immigration'; www.rockridgeinstitute.org/research/rockridge/immigration.

language has power. To reiterate, the label of illegal is entirely correct from a legal standpoint. But it is practically and morally problematic in large part because, as I have shown, this is not a case of the state doing everything it can to deter undocumented migrants who, hell bent on breaking the law, burst in anyway. The very migrants kept illegal are the ones we have in many ways encouraged, or at least not discouraged, to come to fill our labour needs.[48]

What next?

At this writing various proposals to fix the immigration system with regard to undocumented migrants are floating around Washington. All proposals stress increased border enforcement. The key differences centre on whether, and if so how, they offer a path to legalisation for those who have been here illegally and whether they provide for some form of legal guest worker program.

What will happen in Washington remains to be seen. The question posed here is: what should be done? Using Carens' and Walzer's approaches as moral guidelines, but recognising the political impossibility of achieving their ends now, how should we proceed? Both Carens and Walzer would agree that, for those already established here, being put on a route to naturalisation is the solution. For those needed, Carens would argue for letting them in with the possibility of citizenship. Walzer would argue that our choices are either allowing them in with the possibility of citizenship, or keeping them out.

For those workers already here for a significant length of time, many with families, I see no solution given the policy hypocrisy that I have outlined, other than to allow them, given certain reasonable conditions, to eventually naturalise. In short, even given the political difficulties I see no solution other than the one demanded by Carens and Walzer: that they be put on a path to eventual citizenship. Given that 'amnesty' is now considered a dirty word for politicians, this is a tall order. Yet, I can see no alternative that, given our past policies, is morally acceptable. If the case were made that it was to be business as usual punctuated by

---

[48] One reviewer points out the useful distinction between responsibility that derives from our social positions, and responsibility that derives from our actions that have caused harm. Both forms of responsibility may be relevant here, though this aspect of the argument focuses on the latter.

occasional amnesties, it would certainly be political suicide to propose it. But if it is coupled with a more realistic policy going forward, it becomes potentially more palatable.

For those wishing to enter, and wanted for work, it seems quite likely that we are destined for some form of legal temporary worker programme. As I have argued, this would not meet the standards laid out by Walzer or Carens. But it holds some potential to be an improvement over our current situation in that it would provide needed workers with legal status and legal rights. Again, this would reconstitute them as rightful members, if temporary, of US society, and would open up space for new kinds of action on their part and new ways of viewing them on the part of current citizens. While temporary worker programmes tend, with good reason, to be thought of negatively, recall that the USA has 'skilled' temporary worker programmes that are relatively non-controversial. That said, legal temporary worker programmes are problematic for reasons that go beyond Walzer and Carens: they don't work as intended. Case after case in country after country tells us that large numbers of temporary workers do not stay temporary. They get settled and rooted in lives in their host states and they stay. Furthermore, because we know this, a change to expanded temporary worker programmes will maintain some level of hypocrisy – we will continue to espouse policies that we know to be flawed. We will essentially postpone another great debate over immigration policies when we find that many temporary workers have lapsed into illegal status (some proposed incentives might help).

However problematic, and to whatever extent they postpone parts of the debate about our national schizophrenia on low-wage migration to a future date, temporary worker programmes, if well structured, would be an improvement on our current situation. They could help legitimise the role of migrants in our economy in the eyes of many. The language of 'illegality' surrounding them, problematic from so many angles examined above, would be ameliorated. Temporary worker programmes would take a small step toward recognising that we are not in fact trying desperately to keep people out who, despite our best efforts, keep coming. The reason why this is important (leaving aside some important practical reasons) is that, as constructivists have so well demonstrated, ideas, frameworks and language matter. They shape what we see as possible and what is outside our purview. If we could get beyond the discussion of illegality and the storming of the gates, it is possible that official discourse embodied in law could go some ways toward reshaping our thinking and shared expectations about migrants. As I've argued, it is important in this sense to not underestimate the power of the term 'illegal' (and the corresponding power of the term 'legal'). Lutz and Sikkink argue that law has an important expressive function and that it formally restates social values and communicates norms.[49] By changing the tone of the debate, and seeking a system that more honestly matches our intended approach, we open up space for further change in a direction more morally acceptable.

Lynch argues that constructivists might embrace hypocrisy as a mechanism for positive change.[50] As constructivists have pointed out, many governments have been intentionally hypocritical in their approaches to human rights. For example, often governments sign onto human rights treaties or make pronouncements in support of human rights norms to quiet dissent or bow to pressure, but with no intention of complying. Yet often they become trapped by their own rhetoric and activists have an opening to call them on their hypocrisy and challenge them to live up to their pronouncements. I have argued that the dominance of illegality in the current debate has largely stifled this type of approach. It is very difficult for those wanting change in our policies to argue for rights of any sort for someone who is illegal. It is even hard to imagine a policy toward 'illegals' that does anything but punish them, ignore them or keep future ones out. I have argued that a switch to a temporary worker programme, with all of the evidence we have of their flaws, would still be a hypocritical move. Yet, if we were able to move toward a system in which the dominant conceptualisation of low-wage migrant labour was that of temporary worker (i.e. someone who contributes to the economy and is here because we want or need them) as opposed to that of illegal migrant (i.e. someone who is criminal and uninvited) we might find ourselves faced with the kind of hypocrisy embraced by many constructivists in that it would be a type of hypocrisy that could be used to push for further change, perhaps even more in a direction acceptable to Carens or Walzer.

In short, I am arguing from a constructivist approach that takes seriously the power of public policy to construct both our views of

---

[49] Ellen L. Lutz and Kathryn Sikkink, 'International Human Rights Law and Practice in Latin America', *International Organization* 54 (2000), 657.
[50] Lynch, this volume.

immigrants and therefore what is, from a public opinion and governmental perspective, practically possible. Our flawed policies matter, not only in their immediate effects but also in their impact on the possibilities for change. Even if we cannot meet the stringent demands of ethics theorists like Carens and Walzer, we must take account of and recognise the power of policy in constructing the political space in which future policies are developed.

6 | Lie to me: sanctions on Iraq, moral argument and the international politics of hypocrisy

MARC LYNCH

Buffy: 'Does it ever get easy?'
Giles: 'You mean life?'
Buffy: 'Yeah. Does it get easy?'
Giles: 'What do you want me to say?'
Buffy: 'Lie to me.'
Giles: 'Yes, it's terribly simple. The good guys are always stalwart and true, the bad guys are easily distinguished by their pointy horns or black hats, and, uh, we always defeat them and save the day. No one ever dies, and everybody lives happily ever after.'
Buffy: 'Liar.'

> *Buffy the Vampire Slayer*, episode 2.07 'Lie To Me', written by Joss Whedon

The sanctions on Iraq (1990–2003) posed an excruciating moral and strategic political dilemma. By the end of the decade it was clear to all that the sanctions caused immense human suffering, especially among the young, elderly and infirm, while doing little to unseat Saddam Hussein from power. For some, this reality created an urgent moral imperative to lift the sanctions immediately, at whatever cost. But given the absolute brutality of Saddam's regime, lifting the sanctions – and awarding the tyrant a significant political victory – seemed at best a problematic moral stance. Saddam bore some responsibility for the horrific effects of the sanctions, both in his refusal to comply fully with United Nations (UN) disarmament resolutions and in his cynical manipulation of the flow of humanitarian relief for his own domestic and foreign political ends. As UN Secretary General Kofi Annan eloquently summarised the situation in 2000: 'The humanitarian situation in Iraq posed a serious moral dilemma for the United Nations, which was in danger of losing the argument – if it had not already lost it – about who was responsible for the situation: Saddam Hussein or the

United Nations.'[1] The difficult moral decisions were compounded by perplexing strategic concerns. The sanctions succeeded in preventing Iraqi acquisition of weapons of mass destruction, and significantly weakened Iraqi military capabilities, but at the same time actually strengthened Saddam's domestic position, and by the late 1990s had evolved into a potent instrument of Iraqi foreign policy.[2]

Ethical analyses of the sanctions on Iraq have consumed mountains of paper, with investigations of whether they could be reconciled with just war tradition or international law or various schools of ethical theory.[3] Because sanctions are often presented as an 'ethical' or 'humane' alternative to war, they carry a particular moral burden which makes them an easy target for accusations of hypocrisy. Indeed Joy Gordon has denounced sanctions in general as 'simply a device of cruelty garbed up in self-righteousness'.[4] This chapter takes a different approach. Rather than assess the ethical standing of the sanctions regime, I ask whether constructivism can offer a unique perspective on the political significance of the moral arguments. I argue that the distinctively moral tone of the international argument about Iraq explains otherwise puzzling

---

[1] UN Press Release SC/6833, March 24, 2000.

[2] 'Duelfer Report' (Comprehensive Report of the Special Advisor to the DCI on Iraq's WMD), United States Central Intelligence Agency, September 30, 2004; www.cia.gov/cia/reports/iraq_wmd_2004/chap1.html; 'Volcker Report' (Independent Inquiry Committee into the United Nations Oil-for-Food Program), United Nations, 2005; George A. Lopez and David Cortright, 'Containing Iraq: Sanctions Worked', *Foreign Affairs* (July/August 2004); Andrew Mack and Asif Khan, 'The Efficacy of UN Sanctions', *Security Dialogue* 31:3 (2000), 219–232; John Mueller and Karl Mueller, 'Sanctions of Mass Destruction', *Foreign Affairs* 78:3 (1999), 43–53; Meghan O'Sullivan, *Shrewd Sanctions* (Washington, DC: Brookings Institution Press, 2002); David Cortright, 'A Hard Look at Iraq Sanctions', *The Nation* 3 (December 2001).

[3] I do not directly address the ethical implications of the sanctions, therefore, or offer my own normative account. For good examples of such analysis, see Joy Gordon, 'A Peaceful, Silent, Deadly Remedy: The Ethics of Sanctions', *Ethics and International Affairs* 13 (1999); David Cortright and George Lopez, 'Are Sanctions Just? The Problematic Case of Iraq', *Journal of International Affairs* 52:2 (1999), 735–755; Lori Fisler Damrosch, 'The Collective Enforcement of International Norms Through Economic Sanctions', *Ethics and International Affairs* 8 (1994); Anthony Arnove, 'Iraq Under Siege: Ten Years On', *Monthly Review* 52:7 (2000).

[4] Gordon, 'A Peaceful, Silent, Deadly Remedy'; also see Joy Gordon, 'When Intent Makes All the Difference in the World: Economic Sanctions on Iraq and the Accusation of Genocide', *Yale Human Rights and Development Law Journal* 5 (2002), 57–84.

outcomes: the empowering of an otherwise quite weak transnational activist network; the rhetorical entrapment of the United States and the UK into backing the creation of an unprecedented humanitarian relief programme within the sanctions regime ('Oil for Food'); the sudden collapse of compliance with the sanctions in the late 1990s; and ultimately the failure of the United States to win international backing for the invasion of Iraq in 2003.

Constructivism has generally viewed public moral argument as a vital force in international affairs.[5] More controversially, it has postulated a potentially positive role for hypocrisy in moral progress, a pragmatic embrace which contrasts sharply with the thundering exposure and denunciation of hypocrisy beloved of many critical polemicists on the right and the left, and with the indifference to hypocrisy typical of realist and rationalist International Relations theory. Key constructivist theories see hypocrisy as a crucial mechanism for slowly forcing compliance with norms, as great powers are first hectored into admitting the relevance of a norm, and then shamed into policy change by exposure of their failure to live up to their moral rhetoric. Such dynamics can be clearly seen in the case of Iraq, where anti-sanctions activists leveraged American and British moral rhetoric into the creation and periodic refinements of the Oil-for-Food Programme. By paying lip service to humanitarian norms and backing a humanitarian relief programme, the United States could maintain the containment of Iraq and deflect claims that sanctions were harming Iraqi innocents. For Iraq, blaming the UN for domestic problems at least partially of its own making allowed considerable domestic and regional gains even at the expense of its own people. And for the UN, a humanitarian relief programme within a sanctions regime facilitated the otherwise nigh-impossible reconciliation of intensely competing interests. Anti-sanctions activists who leveraged this array of often cynical moral argument into some morally progressive changes and real humanitarian relief, rarely fully grappled with the moral implications of their dealing (however tacitly and unsympathetically) with a brutal Baathist regime.

Moral argument about the Iraq sanctions generated a new normative environment, along with practical tools for more targeted sanctions, which virtually guarantee that no future multilateral sanctions regime

---

[5] Neta Crawford, *Argument and Change in World Politics* (Cambridge: Cambridge University Press, 2002).

will be allowed to have the catastrophic impact on civilians which afflicted Iraq. To the extent that this means that future international sanctions regimes will cause less useless suffering, this represents moral progress. But pervasive hypocrisy carries a cost which constructivists may not appreciate. Drawing on Habermas, I argue that hypocritical moral argument over time devastates the credibility of all moral argument, and erodes the legitimacy of almost all major actors and institutions. The expectation of hypocrisy renders meaningful dialogue nearly impossible, stripping away even the possibility of a normative consensus. The potentially beneficial contribution to moral progress offered by the leveraging of hypocrisy must therefore be weighed against the degenerative potential of a systemic loss of legitimacy.

In the case of Iraq, the costs of pervasive hypocrisy were profound. Loss of American credibility doomed the smart sanctions reforms to failure, while the loss of moral consensus contributed to the near collapse of compliance with the sanctions by 2000.[6] American support for the sanctions became a major facet of the Arab and Muslim set of grievances which arguably lay behind 9/11, while driving a wedge between the USA and its allies over Iraq which would return in the run-up to war in 2002–2003. When the United States presented itself as the liberator of the Iraqi people in 2003, invading Iraq for humanitarian reasons, much of the world – convinced of the leading American and British role in inflicting massive suffering on the Iraqi people over the course of a decade – simply could not credit such moral claims with a modicum of sincerity. Beyond its effects on America, pervasive hypocrisy harmed other actors and the system itself. For the United Nations, the Oil-for-Food scandals evolved into one of the worst crises of legitimacy in that institution's history. And many Arabs, who believed themselves to have been heroically defending the 'suffering Iraqi people' against the sanctions, were stunned by the hostility to them expressed by many Iraqis after the war.[7] While hypocrisy can strengthen norms, failure to act can cause a backlash. In the words of Max van der Stoel, the UN's Coordinator for Human Rights in Iraq, 'The first thing that Iraqis want is for officials in all countries of the world to stop expressing

[6] On the relationship between legitimacy and compliance, see Jeffrey T. Checkel, 'Why Comply? Social Learning and European Identity Change', *International Organization* 55:3 (2001), 553–588.
[7] Marc Lynch, *Voices of the New Arab Public* (New York, NY: Columbia University Press, 2006), chapter 6.

concern about their suffering and dedication to their well-being [without acting] . . . such self-consoling hypocrisy adds insult to injury'.[8]

The sanctions rested heavily upon a moral consensus, which offered unusual possibilities for an anti-sanctions movement highlighting humanitarian disaster combined with strategic failure. The anti-sanctions movement succeeded at harnessing moral outrage over the sanctions, and at consolidating this outrage into an institutionalised normative and policy change at the United Nations level. Sanctions critics were able to win widespread acceptance for their basic moral claim – that sanctions imposed by the United Nations should not inflict disproportionate harm on civilians – and developed a set of refined policy instruments allowing this normative stance to be realised in practice. Against this very important success – which constitutes a real example of moral progress in world politics – must be set the movement's failure at getting the sanctions lifted, the scandals which hit the UN over corruption in the Oil-for-Food Programme, and the enormous legitimacy gap which the sanctions crisis opened up between the United States/United Kingdom and much of the rest of the world.

This chapter uses the arguments over the sanctions on Iraq to explore the politics of hypocrisy and moral argument in an area of the highest strategic concern. It shows that an analysis which takes the moral language of norms seriously helps us uncover both the progressive and regressive effects of the strategic use of moral language. Constructivism can not only follow in its analysis both a logic of appropriateness and a logic of consequences, it can demonstrate the interaction of those logics in complex political environments in ways lost upon realist, rationalist and materialist analyses which don't take the effects of moral language seriously. This leaves IR theory better placed to weigh complex trade-offs through sustained attention to otherwise neglected or hidden dimensions of moral progress and regress.

Moral argument and hypocrisy in international affairs

Hypocrisy differs from deception in the nature of the misrepresentation. The hypocrite does not simply aim to deceive, she does so in such a way as to present herself in ways which will draw moral acclaim from a

---

[8] Quoted in *Mideast Mirror* 13, no. 214, November 5, 1999.

relevant audience. Hence, I define hypocrisy as an intentionally deceptive moral stance. Unlike lying (defined simply as intentional misrepresentation), hypocrisy always contains an explicitly moral edge. The
analysis of hypocrisy is necessarily two-faced: on the one hand, showing
how actors were in fact hypocritical in their rhetoric; on the other,
showing how actors played a distinctive 'hypocrisy' game, using
moral rhetoric, and demands that others live up to their own moral
rhetoric, for strategic advantage.[9]

The prevalence of hypocrisy requires no assumption of widespread ill
intent, nor should it necessarily be reflexively excoriated. In strategic
terms, hypocrisy often pays off in the short term. Moral claims, however
hypocritical, are especially useful for materially weak actors such as
non-governmental organisations (NGOs). What is more, it often plays a
useful social function, making co-existence and co-operation possible
even under conditions of extreme levels of disagreement. Indeed, Judith
Shklar concludes bluntly that 'liberal democracy can not afford public
sincerity. Honesties that humiliate and a stiff-necked refusal to compromise would ruin democratic civility in a political society in which people
have many serious differences of belief.'[10] Finally, particularly for constructivist theories, hypocrisy plays a key role in normative change, as
actors can be shamed into living up to their own hypocritical rhetoric.
Hypocrisy implies some level of public acceptance of a norm, after all:
however evil they might otherwise be, authoritarian regimes become
hypocrites only after they have signed human rights treaties. Taken too
far, radical scepticism can destroy any hope for progressive change.

The potentially progressive role of hypocrisy matters, because the
demands of international politics push rather inexorably towards
hypocrisy, particularly for great powers who espouse universal ideals
whose realisation exceeds their capabilities or conflicts with other
important interests. Stephen Krasner goes so far as to contend that

---

[9] Hypocrisy should be distinguished from Frank Schimmelfenig's closely related
conception of 'rhetorical action', defined as 'the strategic use of norm-based
arguments'. Schimmelfenig's interesting analysis of the use of community identity
and liberal internationalist norms to win arguments over EU expansion addresses
nothing inherently moral; Frank Schimmelfenig, 'The Community Trap: Liberal
Norms, Rhetorical Action, and the Eastern Enlargement of the European Union',
International Organization 55:1 (2001), 47–80.

[10] Judith Shklar, *Ordinary Vices* (Cambridge, MA: Harvard University Press,
1984), 78.

'organized hypocrisy is the normal state of affairs' in the international system.[11] International relations seems to be the epitome of what Judith Shklar described as 'the endemic and systematic character of public hypocrisy and its maze-like inescapability'.[12] This is particularly the case since moral rhetoric is so endemic, even in a system where moral action is allegedly rare. States tend to justify their policies in ethical rather than self-interested terms, despite the prevalence of realpolitik behaviour.[13] In Kenneth Thompson's incisive phrase, 'we claim more for the benevolence of our policies than they deserve and arouse the resentment of peoples already inclined to envy our power and wealth'.[14]

This pervasive hypocrisy does not greatly concern most realist or rationalist theorists. For realists, it is a commonplace that states will say anything to win, and international history is replete with the bald-faced lies of great powers cheerfully made for tactical reasons.[15] Since interests and power are always the real motivations for action, almost any appeal to moral or ethical standards is by definition hypocritical. Machiavelli famously concluded that 'the experience of our times shows those princes to have done well who have little regard for good faith'.[16] Moral rhetoric might be useful for mobilising power and support, but should never be taken at face value or, worse, taken seriously or believed by those invoking it. Only the most brazen acts of hypocrisy are even deemed worthy of notice – unless, of course, there is political advantage in their exposure.

Rationalist theories, dispensing with normative judgements, high-light the strategic dynamics of asymmetric information and strategic misrepresentation. Misrepresenting one's preferences offers strategic advantage, forcing all actors to assume that others will do so.[17] Credibility is problematic because 'states have incentives to lie', and

[11] Stephen D. Krasner, *Sovereignty: Organized Hypocrisy* (Princeton, NJ: Princeton University Press, 1999), 9.
[12] Shklar, *Ordinary Vices*, 6.
[13] Crawford, *Argument and Change in World Politics*.
[14] Kenneth W. Thompson, 'The Limits of Principle in International Politics', *Journal of Politics* 20 (1958), 437–467, quote at 447.
[15] John Mearsheimer, 'Lying in International Politics'. Paper presented to annual meeting of the American Political Science Association, September 2004.
[16] Frederick Bailey, *The Prevalence of Deceit* (Ithaca, NY: Cornell University Press, 1991), 65.
[17] James D. Fearon, 'Rationalist Explanations for War', *International Organization* 49 (1995), 379–414.

are 'opportunistic actors who will engage in "calculated efforts to mislead, distort, disguise, obfuscate, or otherwise confuse"'.[18] Indeed, deceit is taken to be so prevalent that talk is too cheap to matter, and only signals 'so costly that one would hesitate to send them if one were untrustworthy' can hope to satisfy others of one's sincerity.[19] The only consensus of concern is strategic – the outcome of self-interested rational bargaining – with moral consensus, or shared understandings, playing little role at all. While recent attempts at a rationalist–constructivist synthesis have begun to incorporate notions of argument, cheap talk and varying levels of 'common life-world', the focus is still on the effective communication of preferences and strategies rather than on moral argument or hypocrisy.[20]

Critical theorists have been more prone to focusing on hypocrisy, but in almost purely negative ways. For some, the exposure of the hypocrisy of American foreign policy is nearly an end unto itself.[21] During the Kosovo campaign, Edward Said argued that 'the first duty is to demystify the debased language and images used to justify American practices and hypocrisy'.[22] But should not the first duty be to protect the innocent? Or to create new normative standards of behaviour by which American hypocrisy and double standards might be judged in a politically potent way? If critical theory depends upon exposing injustice and demanding a more moral practice, then what is the value of pre-emptively criticising practices justified in progressive terms as presumptively amoral or of ridiculing tentative moves to embrace such norms?

The sheer prevalence of hypocrisy and its centrality to international practice, as well as its potential utility for moral and normative activists, suggests the inadequacy of its exposure as the endpoint of political

---

[18] Kenneth Schultz, *Democracy and Coercive Diplomacy* (New York, NY: Cambridge University Press, 2001), 5.
[19] Andrew Kydd, 'Trust, Reassurance and Cooperation', *International Organization* 54 (2002), 325–358, quote at 327.
[20] Marc Lynch, 'Why Engage? The Logic of Communicative Engagement', *European Journal of International Relations* 8:2 (2002), 187–230; Hans Muller, 'Arguing, Bargaining, and All That: Communicative Action, Rationalist Theory, and the Logic of Appropriateness in International Relations', *European Journal of International Relations* 10:3 (2004), 395–435.
[21] Marc Lynch, 'Critical Theory, Dialogue, and Legitimacy'. In Jennifer Sterling-Folker (ed.), *Making Sense of IR Theory* (Boulder, CO: Lynne Rienner, 2005).
[22] Edward Said, 'The Treason of the Intellectuals', *Al-Ahram Weekly*, Issue no. 435 (June 1999), 24–30.

action.[23] Radical scepticism cripples any hope of progressive change. Against Chomsky, Jürgen Habermas saw the Kosovo intervention as holding genuine potential for 'the transformation of the "law of nations" into a law of world-citizens'.[24] While not blind to the potential dangers of a war, Habermas argued that against these risks must be set the vision of a new normative environment grounded in compulsory respect for human rights, backed by the restrained use of force subject to democratic and multilateral control. The aspiration for normative change means that, despite all scepticism and fear, 'confronted with crimes against humanity, the international community must be able to act'.[25]

Constructivism uniquely embraces hypocrisy as a principal mechanism for positive change in world politics. In the influential 'spiral model' of normative change, leaders 'adjust their behavior to the international human rights discourse without necessarily believing in the validity of the norms' but then find themselves trapped by their own rhetoric.[26] Constructivists often approvingly cite Jon Elster's 'civilizing force of hypocrisy' to suggest that the fear of public shaming leads actors to refrain from actions they would otherwise take, inducing more principled behaviour regardless of real beliefs.[27] Over time, insincere proponents of a moral stance may come to internalise the rhetoric, to believe what was once an affectation, with the 'mask' slowly becoming the 'face'. As Thomas Risse put it, 'when norm-violating governments find it necessary to make rhetorical concessions and cease denying the validity of human rights norms, a discursive opening is created for their critics to challenge them further'.[28] Sincerity is not the point, or even

---

[23] Jeffrey Isaac, 'Hannah Arendt on Human Rights and the Limits of Exposure, or Why Chomsky is Wrong About Kosovo', *Social Research* 69 (2002), 505–537.

[24] Jürgen Habermas, 'Bestiality and Humanity: A War on the Border Between Law and Morality'. In William Joseph Buckley (ed.), *Kosovo: Contending Voices on Balkan Interventions* (Grand Rapids, MI: Eerdmans Publishing, 2000), 306–316, quoted at 307.

[25] Jürgen Habermas, 'Letter to America', *The Nation* (2002).

[26] Thomas Risse, Stephen Ropp and Kathryn Sikkink (eds.), *The Power of Human Rights* (New York, NY: Cambridge University Press, 1999), 12 and 27.

[27] Jon Elster, 'The Market and the Forum'. In James Bohman and William Rehg (eds.), *Deliberative Democracy* (Cambridge, MA: MIT Press, 1997), 3–34; Jon Elster, 'Strategic Uses of Argument'. In Kenneth Arrow (ed.), *Barriers to Conflict* (New York, NY: W. W. Norton, 1995), 237–257.

[28] Thomas Risse, '"Let's Argue!" Communicative Action in World Politics', *International Organization* 54 (2000), 1–39, quote at 32.

necessarily desirable. What matters, for the constructivist agent, is to draw the targeted state into public declarations which in turn create strategic openings for pressure to act.

Why does hypocritical rhetoric have such power if everyone recognises it as such? One possible response, with apologies to *The X-Files*, is that people 'want to believe', a desire upon which liars can prey. A second possibility is simple utility: actors often share an interest in acting as if they believe each other in order to maintain the possibility of ongoing interaction and to avoid the costs of the change that would have to follow from admitting disagreement. Averting their eyes from obvious hypocrisy allows them to pretend to themselves and to others that the current situation remains tenable. But from a constructivist point of view, there is an even more consequential reason: eliciting moral rhetoric from powerful actors creates opportunities to then entrap them into living up to their rhetoric by public exposure and shaming. For this 'hypocrisy game', it is eminently rational for a moral activist to beg a great power to '*lie to me*'.

The constructivist causal mechanism between hypocrisy and change is 'a process of *argumentative "self-entrapment"* that starts as rhetorical action and strategic adaptation to external pressures but ends with argumentative behavior'.[29] Public compliance over an extended period of time can lead to the internalisation of the publicly avowed beliefs, changing the identity or sense of interests of the initially hypocritical actor. As Daniel Thomas describes the process, 'repressive states agree to be bound by human rights norms in the belief that they can gain international legitimacy without substantial compliance, and ... this "empty" commitment nonetheless promotes local, transnational, and interstate processes that undermine continued repression'.[30] Public posturing therefore can recast private preferences, as actors who employ rhetoric strategically find themselves constrained, self-entrapped or pressured to change.

Constructivist leveraging of hypocrisy depends on the existence of an audience which takes the moral positions seriously. The (insincere) utterances create a constituency of agents who then hold those actors

---

[29] Ibid. xx.
[30] Daniel C. Thomas, *The Helsinki Effect: International Norms, Human Rights, and the Demise of Communism* (Princeton, NJ: Princeton University Press, 2001), 3.

to their word, creating additional costs of political opposition that wouldn't have been there in the absence of such strategic morality. Such actions presuppose sources of political support or opposition that either themselves believe in the moral positions staked out, and will have very thick attachments to them (raising costs more than passive political opinion) or seize upon moral utterances to their strategic advantage (to force regimes to act in desired ways by making them look bad). One can only look bad and incur costs if some substantial audience believes one must be good or at least look good, and the thinner strategic demands of piety are less likely not to be seen for what they are, transparent attempts to score political points. For the audience to become a crucial participant in the joint legitimation processes, there must exist some critical, independent public sphere in which these audiences can make their voices heard and their political weight felt.

Hypocrisy can thus be leveraged into progressive change, by using the force of public exposure to bind states to their moral rhetoric, even if they employed it for nakedly strategic reasons.[31] This mechanism depends upon *publicity* for its potency. If – and only if – a public sphere exists which can make compelling demands upon states to redeem their rhetoric, normatively oriented critics can work to force great powers to live up to their strategically chosen rhetoric. Holding the powerful to their public commitments opens up possibilities for the weak to exercise power over the strong by shaming them with their own words. Of course, it may also only lead the powerful actors to offer more rhetoric in place of action: the attempt to coax an American humanitarian intervention in Darfur, which succeeded in getting the Bush administration to declare the horrors there a genocide but failed to get it to send any troops, offers a striking example.

The strategic intent behind this kind of moral argument conceals the most vulnerable point of the constructivist approach: if rhetoric is not converted into actual belief, internalised into a moral consensus, then agreement remains brittle. The pervasive expectation of hypocrisy can also blind actors to real issues. In the sanctions case, American officials were so convinced of the hypocrisy of its rivals – whether in Baghdad, Paris or New York – that they failed to appreciate the depth and sincerity

---

[31] Risse *et al.*, *The Power of Human Rights*.

of the growing moral outrage over the humanitarian cost of the sanctions until it was far too late.

Worse, the strategic use of moral hypocrisy renders a real moral consensus less likely in the long run. A wide range of theorists have noted the perverse dynamics of systems characterised by pervasive hypocrisy, described by Vaclav Havel as those where 'individuals need not believe all these mystifications, but they must behave as if they did ... they must live within a lie'.[32] In Havel's evocative words, 'because the regime is captive to its own lies, it must falsify everything'.[33] As James Scott puts it, 'forced compliance not only fails to produce attitudes that would sustain compliance in the absence of domination, but produces reactions against such attitudes ... Coercion can produce compliance, but it virtually inoculates ... against willing compliance'.[34] It is here that even the pragmatic embrace of hypocrisy as an effective means for moral change runs adrift: for all its short-term utility for moral agents, it ultimately corrupts the prospect of communicative action and strips away the foundations of legitimacy.

The sanctions on Iraq

The attempt to disarm Iraq involved the longest and most comprehensive multilateral sanctions regime in history, punctuated by threats of and actual use of military action.[35] This regime began with a high degree of normative consensus around the need to disarm Iraq and punish its deviant behaviour, but became open to argument as

---

[32] Vaclav Havel, *Open Letters* (New York, NY: Knopf, 1991), 136; Lisa Wedeen, *Ambiguities of Domination: Politics, Rhetoric, and Symbols in Contemporary Syria* (Chicago, IL: University of Chicago Press, 1999).
[33] Havel, *Open Letters*, 136.
[34] James C. Scott, *Domination and the Arts of Resistance* (New Haven, CT: Yale University Press, 1991), 109.
[35] Daniel Drezner, *The Sanctions Paradox: Economic Sanctions and International Relations* (Cambridge: Cambridge University Press, 1999); Robert Pape, 'Why Economic Sanctions do not Work', *International Security* 22:2 (1997); David Baldwin, 'The Sanctions Debate and the Logic of Choice', *International Security* 24:3 (2000); Lisa Martin, *Coercive Cooperation: Explaining Multilateral Economic Sanctions* (Princeton, NJ: Princeton University Press, 1992); Neta Crawford and Audie Klotz, *How Sanctions Work: Lessons from South Africa*, (New York, NY: St Martin's Press, 1999); Jean-Marc Blanchard and Norrin Ripsman, 'When do Economic Sanctions Work Best?', *Security Studies* 9:1/2 (1999/2000), 219–253.

humanitarian concerns and political frustration mounted. The political manipulation of the sanctions regime, along with the criminalising consequences so often associated with extended sanctions,[36] must be set alongside the very real relief which the Oil-for-Food Programme brought to a starving population. Similarly, the moral arguments over the sanctions cannot be reconciled without also dealing with the real strategic and military implications of the containment or rearmament of Iraq, or with the realities of a horribly tyrannical regime in Baghdad willing to exploit the suffering of its own people for political advantage.[37]

The Security Council imposed the sanctions after the Iraqi invasion of Kuwait, and the terms of their lifting were set by the ceasefire resolution after the war. Most observers expected them to be lifted shortly after the war, after Saddam fell from power. When he did not, the sanctions remained in place, seemingly perpetually. While the sanctions were supposed to generate popular opposition, this proved impossible in Saddam's tightly controlled regime. The sanctions tended to hit the weak and vulnerable much harder than they did Saddam's regime and his favoured constituencies. Indeed, the sanctions strengthened Saddam's domestic position by leaving his beleaguered population almost totally dependent on the state for survival. Iraq, like all polities under sanctions, adjusted creatively to the sanctions.[38] The sanctions created a system of artificial market conditions which allowed Saddam Hussein's regime to not only survive but to prosper from the concentration of legal and illegal economic activities in its own hands. At the same time, the sanctions caused tremendous disruption, poverty and misery among the Iraqi people. The combination of this great economic distress and the regime's ability to channel the impact of the sanctions actually strengthened the regime, making it less likely that any organised opposition would emerge.

---

[36] Peter Andreas, 'Criminalizing Consequences of Sanctions: Embargo Busting and its Legacy', *International Studies Quarterly* 49 (2005), 335–360.

[37] Sarah Graham-Brown, *Sanctioning Saddam: The Politics of Intervention in Iraq* (London: I. B. Tauris, 1999); Amatzia Baram, 'The Effect of Iraqi Sanctions: Statistical Pitfalls and Responsibility', *Middle East Journal* 54 (2000), 194–223; David Cortright, Alastair Millar and George Lopez, *Smart Sanctions: Restructuring UN Policy in Iraq* (South Bend, IN: Fourth Freedom Forum, 2002); 'Volcker Report'.

[38] David Rowe, *Manipulating the Market: Understanding Economic Sanctions, Institutional Change, and the Political Unity of White Rhodesia* (Ann Arbor, MI: University of Michigan Press, 2001).

The sanctions involved a comprehensive embargo on Iraqi exports and a complex system of controls of Iraqi imports. In principle, food and medicine were not covered by import restrictions, but all contracts were subject to review in the secretive and politicised UN's Sanctions Committee. The sheer magnitude of the task of monitoring and controlling the entry of goods into the country and their distribution created enormous inefficiencies. The oil embargo meant, furthermore, that the Iraqi government lacked the funds to purchase them prior to the passage of Resolution 986 (which passed in 1996 and came into effect in 1997). After that, pricing of the oil involved complex negotiations between the Iraqi government and the Sanctions Committee. The bureaucracy remained cumbersome and inefficient, with low levels of transparency and unclear standards (opening up all too predictable opportunities for corruption). The sheer difficulty of passing every transaction of a modern economy of twenty-two million people through an international bureaucracy guaranteed bottlenecks, delays, inefficiencies and pervasive corruption.[39] Finally, Sanctions Committee 'holds' (some $5 billion worth as of 2002, 98 percent of which were imposed by the United States) generated a ripple effect across sectors, complicating all planning efforts. In short, the sanctions regime made the Iraqi government a vital interlocutor in the distribution of humanitarian assistance, creating a range of troublesome interdependencies among the regime and the relief enterprise.

UN agencies were well aware of the humanitarian situation created by the sanctions.[40] As early as March 1991, Under-Secretary General Martti Ahtisaari reported that 'the recent conflict has wrought near-apocalyptic results upon the economic infrastructure'; a follow-up report by Sadruddin Aga Khan expanded upon these findings and urged massive humanitarian intervention. By 1993, disturbing reports began to filter out of NGOs and UN agencies about the impact of the sanctions on the Iraqi civilian population, including malnutrition and the near collapse of the public health system. By 1994, the UN's Food and Agriculture Organisation (FAO) was already warning of 'pre-famine conditions'. Reports by the FAO, the United Nations Children's Fund (UNICEF), the International Committee of the Red Cross, Save the Children and

[39] See 'Volcker Report' for details.
[40] Colin Rowat, 'UN Agency Reports on the Humanitarian Situation in Iraq'; www.cam.ac.uk/societies/casi; also see Graham-Brown, *Sanctioning Saddam*, for an outstanding review of these issues.

others painted an increasingly coherent picture of a humanitarian crisis which could not be dismissed as Iraqi propaganda.[41] A 1999 UNICEF report produced the first reliable evidence of escalating malnutrition, child mortality and morbidity, illness and the breakdown of the educational system.[42] International non-governmental organisation (INGO) and UN actors on the ground in Iraq were 'traumatized' by their direct experience with the humanitarian catastrophe related to sanctions.[43] Many grew morally troubled by what Dennis Halliday described as 'UN complicity in genocide'.[44]

It is crucial to see that this was not seen as evidence of policy failure by the United States or by most of the coalition supporting the sanctions, which did not understand the issue in moral terms: the entire point of the sanctions was to inflict pain on Iraq in order to force it to comply with the weapons inspections process. The human costs of the sanctions only became a policy issue after sanctions critics publicised the suffering of Iraqi civilians, forcing it onto the international agenda and demanding that the United Nations explain and defend its role in causing that suffering. These moral arguments helped to fundamentally reshape the norms governing sanctions over the next decade. In 1996, a UN review of sanctions called for measures to protect civilians from their effects, more sharply focused sanctions, regular monitoring of the humanitarian impact of the sanctions and greater expertise in the sanctions committees. Over the next five years, Secretary General Kofi Annan regularly focused on the impact of sanctions on civilians. In August 2000, Belgian law professor Marc Bossuyt stirred up a diplomatic storm with a report commissioned by the UN Human Rights Subcommission which attributed the humanitarian disaster in Iraq to the sanctions and called them 'unequivocally illegal'.[45]

The hypocrisy of almost every actor in the sanctions game was not simply a moral failure, or bad form; it was a key policy instrument.

---

[41] See various reports on http://www.reliefweb.int

[42] Michael Rubin, 'Sanctions on Iraq: A Valid Anti-American Grievance?', *Middle East Report on International Affairs* 5:4 (2001).

[43] Larry Minear *et al.*, *Toward More Humane and Effective Sanctions Management* (Watson Institute Occasional Papers 31, 1998), 9.

[44] See his interview in Anthony Arnove (ed.), *Iraq Under Siege: The Deadly Impact of Sanctions and War* (Cambridge, MA: South End Press, 2002).

[45] U.N. ECOSOC, Commission on Human Rights, its Commission on the Promotion and Protection of Human Rights: The Adverse Consequences of Economic Sanctions on the Enjoyment of Human Rights (Working Paper, Marc Bossoyt) ElCN.4/506.2/2000/33 (June 21, 2000).

France and Russia routinely accused the United States of hypocrisy for refusing to modify the sanctions in response to Iraqi concessions on weapons of mass destruction (WMD) inspections. Americans routinely blasted France and Russia for cloaking their venal financial interests in moral rhetoric. For its part, the anti-sanctions movement used the shaming power of publicity to try and force the United States and the United Kingdom to live up to their own moralising rhetoric with regard to Iraq.

The United States was the key actor in the sanctions regime, and therefore the prime target of allegations of hypocrisy, particularly since it cloaked its strategic goals in a moralising rhetoric. Challenges to the American moral stance came almost entirely from abroad, with domestic debate dominated by accusations of insufficient toughness towards Saddam. Still, the international criticism was important enough to compel the Clinton administration to present a detailed report on September 13, 1999, purporting to prove that 'the rulers in Baghdad – not the international community – are responsible for the problems, in particular the humanitarian deprivations, in Iraq'.[46] Five months later, a State Department presentation focused on 'the perfidy of the regime of Saddam Hussein . . . because Baghdad is again pushing the canard that sanctions rather than the misrule and the cynical manipulation of his own people that Saddam Hussein propagates are responsible for the suffering of the Iraqis'.[47] Still, American officials admit now that they lost the argument on sanctions and failed to effectively frame the issue.

The Clinton administration's public commitment to changing the Iraqi regime also played a decisive role in undermining confidence in its rhetoric.[48] Resolution 687, upon which the UN mandate rested, clearly stated that the sanctions would be lifted if Iraq complied with the disarmament provisions. By March 1997, under fierce domestic criticism, Clinton officials openly avowed that sanctions would not be lifted until Saddam Hussein was removed from power. Clinton's critics

---

[46] Jamie Rubin and Martin Indyk, 'Report on Saddam Hussein's Iraq', September, 13 1999; www.globalsecurity.org/wmd/library/news/iraq/1999/990913_indyk_rubin.htm.

[47] Jamie Rubin, Daily Press Briefing, February 29, 2000; http://secretary.state.gov/www/briefings/0002/000229db.html.

[48] David Malone, 'Iraq: No Easy Response to the Greatest Threat', *American Journal of International Law* 95 (2001), 235–245; Susan Wright, 'The Hijacking of UNSCOM', *Bulletin of the Atomic Scientists* 55 (1999), 3.

then demanded that he live up to the rhetoric.[49] American officials never understood the significance of this policy shift for its credibility among international audiences already expressing moral horror over the sanctions. The public discrepancy between the American position and the UN mandate made it easy for Iraq to divert attention from its own dishonesty. From the American perspective, the two were not incompatible: convinced that Iraq was cheating, the USA felt that anything was justified in the attempt to expose that cheating. But this left them insensitive to the impact of the inevitable exposure of their manipulations. As Scott Ritter, the former chief inspector for the United Nations Special Commission (UNSCOM), the agency mandated with inspecting Iraq's suspected non-conventional weapons programmes, complained, 'the problem with [American policy] is that we can't demand compliance with Security Council resolutions while simultaneously shunning the Security Council by pursuing a unilateral campaign to remove Saddam from power'.[50] French Foreign Minister Herbert Vedrine argued succinctly: 'we cannot have the same people telling us that not the slightest detail must be changed in the [Security Council] resolutions and also announcing or advocating a policy which has nothing to do with the same resolutions'.[51] Iraq had little difficulty presenting a case to the world that the United States would not take yes for an answer when American officials openly said as much.

In the UK, unlike the USA, major newspapers came out against the sanctions, Members of Parliament repeatedly raised the issue on the floor of the House of Commons, and major cultural figures took on the issue.[52] This domestic climate, along with Prime Minister Tony Blair's highly public invocation of an 'ethical foreign policy', created a unique set of opportunities for anti-sanctions activists. Blair's rhetorical entrapment helps to explain why the UK took such a leading role within the United Nations in seeking ways to maintain consensus, including Resolution 1284 (December 1999) and the 'smart sanctions' reforms.

[49] Benjamin Gilman, Chairman of the House International Relations Committee, quoted in John Goshto,'Envoys Sense Iraqi Edge on U.N.', the *Washington Post*, August 15, 1998, A16.
[50] Scott Ritter, 'Policies outlets,' *New York Times*, August 16, 1999.
[51] Dilip Hiro, *Neighbors, Not Friends* (New York, NY: Routledge Press, 2001), 155.
[52] Eric Herring, 'Between Iraq and a Hard Place: A Critique of the British Government's Case for UN Economic Sanctions', *Review of International Studies* 28 (2002), 39–56; personal interview Milan, Rai and in CASI Conference Report 2, November 2000.

The Iraqi regime, for its part, clearly understood the value of moral concerns for its strategy of getting the sanctions lifted, and made the moral delegitimation of the sanctions a central feature of its foreign policy throughout the 1990s.[53] Iraqi strategy was driven by both the attempt to have the sanctions lifted and by the opportunities created by the sanctions regime itself. Baghdad's complaints about American dishonesty were difficult to take, given the abundant evidence of its own deceit, while lamentations of civilian suffering by a regime responsible for slaughtering substantial portions of its own population rang hollow. It controlled the flow of information through its onerous system of media 'handlers' and careful presentation of evidence of suffering, and almost certainly manufactured statistics about the extent of the suffering – which ironically made it more difficult for honest anti-sanctions activists to be taken seriously. And it used the resources at its disposal – from lucrative oil vouchers to political support – to reward anti-sanctions campaigners.[54] In the end, however, Saddam's regime had little moral capital and could only win in these arguments by playing on the vulnerabilities in the positions of its opponents, by engaging in bribery or intimidation or by appealing to a common Arab or Muslim identity which could be posed as trumping any other strategic or moral considerations.

The campaign against the Iraqi sanctions used the constructivist strategy of leveraging the hypocritical moral rhetoric of the powerful to great effect. It scored great gains by exposing the hypocrisy of American and British moral rhetoric, by highlighting the very real humanitarian catastrophe in Iraq under sanctions and by using the power of publicity to rhetorically entrap the United States and the UK. Their own hypocrisy lay in the relative neglect of the realities of Saddam Hussein's regime, and of the strategic reality that their efforts – no matter how well intentioned – strengthened Saddam's hand. Their immensely powerful moral claim, that the international community should not be imposing massive humanitarian suffering on a captive population, was at least partly compromised by their relative blindness to the brutalities of Saddam's regime. For some, the blind spot rested on

---

[53] 'Duelfer Report'.
[54] Ibid. figure 18, chapter 2; Kevin M. Woods *et al.*, *The Iraqi Perspectives Report: Saddam's Senior Leadership on Operation Iraqi Freedom from the Official U.S. Joint Forces Command Report* (Annapolis, MD: Naval Institute Press, 2006), 28.

naivety, or on a moral urgency to respond in whatever way possible to the horrors they saw in the Iraqi civilian population. For some, motivations may well have been more venal.

For all of their good intentions, international delegations and media did serve the strategic propaganda purposes of the Iraqi government. There is no evidence that these groups had any impact on Iraqi decision making, or even tried to persuade the Iraqi government of the benefits of compliance with international norms and resolutions. They had no transnational contacts with Iraqi civil society or with the Iraqi regime which might have allowed them to convey useful information about shared ideas or norms – indeed, they might well have reassured the Iraqi government about opposition to the sanctions in the West and reinforced its strategy of resistance. Some anti-sanctions campaigners responded by admitting Saddam's poor record but placing it in the context of Arab and other authoritarian regimes supported by the USA and the UK. They also point to the double standards with regard to Israel, whose human rights record with regard to the Palestinians, illegal occupation of the West Bank and Gaza and nuclear weapons programme have never been met with the kinds of international sanctions to which Iraq has been subjected. Finally, anti-sanctions campaigners distinguish between the Iraqi regime and the Iraqi people, arguing that in a dictatorship such as Iraq's ordinary people cannot legitimately be punished for the leadership's foreign policy choices. None of these responses was fully satisfying, however, leaving them open to pointed attacks on their own moral authority.[55] After the fall of Baghdad, a series of investigations of the UN's Oil-for-Food Programme alleged institutional corruption and the complicity of a wide range of companies and individuals in profiteering from the sanctions regime.[56] It is clear that they took a serious toll on the overall legitimacy of the UN system.[57]

[55] This moral authority was particularly compromised when some prominent figures (such as the Marian Appeal's George Galloway) were accused of taking money from Saddam – an accusation which has never been proven, but which undoubtedly hurt the entire anti-sanctions movement by association.
[56] For an overview, see Kenneth Katzman, *Iraq: Oil-For-Food Program, Illicit Trade, and Investigations* (CRS Report for Congress, RL30472, March 21, 2005).
[57] Joy Gordon, 'Scandals of Oil for Food', *Middle East Report Online* July 19, 2004.

Oil-for-Food

The Oil-for-Food Programme demonstrates the mechanism of rhetorical entrapment, as the United States and United Kingdom took dramatic actions contrary to their expressed interests in order to restore a fraying normative consensus. The growing recognition of the humanitarian problems in Iraq had by 1995 begun to degrade support for the sanctions. As Russia and France seized on these problems to raise the possibility of lifting the sanctions, the United States was forced to engage in an argument about the normative and political foundations of the regime. While these states may well have raised the issue for rhetorical, self-interested reasons, the public recognition of Iraqi suffering inflicted by the sanctions significantly changed the strategic equation – at a time when few believed that Iraq had fully complied with the WMD inspections and disarmament process.

The United States and the United Kingdom designed what became Resolution 986 to blunt pressures to lift the sanctions, rather than to fully deal with the humanitarian problems they caused. It represented the minimum necessary to maintain the status quo of the sanctions while meeting the moral concerns of humanitarian activists. Indeed, most actors viewed the Oil-for-Food proposal as intended to derail the momentum to full lifting of sanctions, and the stringent conditions inserted by the United States as intended either to use Oil-for-Food to increase the pressure on Saddam Hussein's regime or else to force Iraq to reject the resolution and sacrifice its best rhetorical card. As Thomas Pickering later explained, 'there is no doubt that without the oil for food program ... the Iraqi government would continue to exploit the suffering of its people to force the international community to lift sanctions ... in a very real sense, the oil for food program is the key to sustaining the sanctions regime until Iraq complies with its obligations'.[58] The unanimous passage of the resolution allowed the USA and the UK to shift the burden of responsibility for the humanitarian problem onto Saddam Hussein's regime. On May 20, 1996 (after a defector had detailed the extent of Iraq's deceptions of the WMD inspection teams), Iraq concluded a Memorandum of Understanding

---

[58] Thomas Pickering, Undersecretary for Political Affairs, testimony before the Senate Foreign Relations Committee, May 21, 1998; personal interview with Pickering, 2000.

with the UN on the terms of the implementation of the Oil-for-Food Programme.[59]

When the United States trumpeted its humanitarian convictions, it was easy to write: 'is it plausible that Bill Clinton and Tony Blair, who are actively strangling the country, care about the fate of the children of Iraq?'[60] But where the moral purist might assail American or British hypocrisy, the constructivist would recognise the importance of the rhetoric and the attendant policy changes. However hypocritical, these great powers oversaw the creation of a programme which had a substantial effect in reversing a serious food crisis in Iraq, and affirmed a progressive new global norm. Sandy Berger's explanation that 'we have a moral duty to [feed the Iraqi people]' established an important rhetorical precedent and a moral commitment to which it could be held.[61] States which actually found strategic advantage in increasing the suffering of the Iraqi people (to build pressure for regime change) were forced to take a leading role in constructing a humanitarian programme designed to mitigate that suffering. The USA and the UK had accepted the reality of Iraq's humanitarian suffering, affirming the validity of the normative claim that such suffering was unacceptable, and had adjusted their strategic behaviour accordingly. This admission of the moral imperative to minimise human suffering under sanctions – rather than to intensify it in order to ratchet up pressure on the target state – became the basis of an important, progressive change in global norms.

The significance of lost moral consensus

The United States and its allies cared about these moral arguments because they mattered in concrete ways which constructivism is best placed to explain. This is not unusual in the context of multilateral sanctions. In contrast to rationalist theories of sanctions which focus on

---

[59] Memorandum of Understanding (May 20, 1996) between the Secretariat of the United Nations and the Government of Iraq on the Implementation of Security Council SCR 986; http://daccessdds.un.org/doc/UNDOC/GEN/N96/127/71/PDF/N9612771.pdf?OpenElement.

[60] Saad Hammoudi, member of the Iraqi National Assembly, quoted in *Mideast Mirror* 13, no. 238, December 9, 1999.

[61] Samuel Berger, National Security Adviser, remarks on Iraq, Stanford University, December 8, 1998; http://www.state.gov/www/regions/nea/981208_berger_ iraq.html.

the temptations of defection by self-interested actors, in cases such as South Africa 'international normative consensus resulted in most members voluntarily adopting a range of sanctions'.[62] In his analysis of the decade-long Libya sanctions, Ian Hurd describes strategies of moral argument and public perception management – as well as a pattern of declining compliance pegged to deteriorating normative consensus – which closely resembles the Iraqi case.[63] Kenneth Rodman, in his analysis of the COCOM pipeline case (Coordinating Committee for Multilateral Export Controls – a Cold War era American-led organisation to enforce an embargo on Western exports to the Soviet Bloc), similarly argues that states and corporate actors were more likely to comply with costly sanctions where they agreed with their ideological justification.[64]

The mechanism linking consensus and compliance lies at the level of individual calculation of self-interest.[65] If moral consensus is strong, actors will comply voluntarily because they agree with the reasons behind it. Viewed as something shameful, defections will be less likely, making enforcement much cheaper and less intrusive. A positive normative environment places a heavy burden on the would-be defector, since it has every reason to believe that other actors will frown upon – and punish – the defection. But if moral consensus fades, then actors are more likely to feel free to pursue their self-interest, putting the game back into the realm familiar to rationalist analysis. For self-interested actors, it no longer makes sense to forgo the economic gains to be found in defection if the sanctions serve no common purpose and there are no normative sanctions attached to violating the embargo. For moral actors, it became a matter of moral urgency to alleviate the suffering of the Iraqi people. A sanctions regime without normative legitimacy becomes costly to maintain and tends to generate resentment.[66]

---

[62] Audie Klotz, 'Norms and Sanctions: Lessons from the Socialization of South Africa', *Review of International Studies* 22 (1996), 173–190, quote at 173–174.

[63] Ian Hurd, 'The Strategic Use of Liberal Internationalism: Libya and the UN Sanctions, 1992–2003', *International Organization* 59 (2005), 495–526.

[64] Kenneth Rodman, *Sanctions at Bay? Hegemonic Decline, Multinational Corporations, and US Economic Sanctions Since the Pipeline* Case (Cambridge, MA: MIT Press, 1995), 107.

[65] Alastair Iain Johnston, 'Treating Institutions as Social Environments', *International Studies Quarterly* 45 (2002), 487–516.

[66] Ian Hurd, 'Legitimacy and Authority in International Politics', *International Organization* 53 (1999), 397–408 ; Checkel, 'Why Comply?'.

Trends in compliance with the Iraq sanctions clearly demonstrate that violations increased with public doubts about their moral validity. A strong initial consensus underlying the sanctions regime was manifested in high levels of compliance. The declining consensus was both moral and strategic. In addition to the moral qualms about humanitarian suffering discussed above, the Security Council was also wracked by persistent tension and crises over arms inspections and Iraqi disarmament. The formal consensus came under growing challenge beginning in 1997 until its dramatic collapse in December 1998, when the USA/UK failed to get a resolution in support of the 'Desert Fox' bombing campaign.

Even before the airstrikes ended, American and British diplomats had begun to speak about the road to rebuilding consensus. As a first step to clear the poisonous atmosphere in the Council, the Security Council agreed to move forward with a comprehensive review of the Iraq file. Led by Celso Amorim of Brazil, the review panel heard testimony from a wide range of relevant experts in both fields. Building on these panel reports, the UK took the lead, in close cooperation with the USA, in putting together a comprehensive resolution which would provide a road-map towards the lifting of sanctions while strongly reaffirming the demand for Iraqi compliance.[67] The negotiations went on for over eight months, and ultimately developed into one of the most complex Security Council resolutions in history. But in the end Resolution 1284 was passed over the abstention of four states (Russia, China, France and Malaysia).

Compliance evolved in clear response to the declining consensus. Through 1995 the majority of the work of the UN's Iraq Sanctions Committee involved requests by states for clarifications about whether a particular action would violate sanctions.[68] States wanted to comply, and publicly sought the advice of the committee on how to do so. As late as November 1997, a report by a London School of Economics survey group noted that as yet, there have been few attempts by UN member states to break the sanctions. *Compared to multilateral sanctions*

---

[67] This paragraph is based on personal interviews with a number of senior British and French officials dealing with the Iraq issue.

[68] Personal interviews with members of the British, French, Dutch, Portuguese and American representatives to the committee. Also see Paul Conlon, *United Nations Sanctions Management: A Case Study of the Iraq Sanctions Committee, 1990–1994* (Ardsley, NY: Transnational Publishers, 2000).

*against other states, the sanctions against Iraq stand out in their scope
and effectiveness.*[69]

By 1999 a dramatic increase in smuggling directly coincided with the
collapse of the UNSCOM programme and the escalating public criticism
of the American manipulation of the sanctions regime.[70] In April 2000,
the Canadian parliament called for the urgent de-linking of economic
from military sanctions and provision of humanitarian assistance; in June,
Italy's parliament approved a bill calling for lifting the sanctions on Iraq;
in July, Venezuela's President Hugo Chavez became the first elected head
of state to visit Baghdad since the sanctions were imposed; in August,
Indonesia's president called for a lifting of sanctions; in September and
October, over two dozen states sent flights carrying humanitarian goods
and politicians to Baghdad; in December, Ireland and Spain both sent
solidarity flights, while India very publicly explored the possibilities of
trade with Iraq. Criticisms and challenges to the Iraq sanctions came from
every continent and from a wide variety of international governmental
and non-governmental organisations. The annual Baghdad Trade Fair
attracted an ever-growing number of nationalities: in 1996, the first year,
sixteen countries participated; in 1997, twenty-six countries participated,
followed by thirty in 1998, thirty-six in 1999 and forty-five in 2000.
During an exceptional Security Council debate in 2000, a seemingly
endless succession of states criticised the legitimacy of the sanctions and
American sincerity in its stated rationales for maintaining them.[71] While
the United States vigorously defended the sanctions regime and placed the
blame on Saddam Hussein, virtually every state openly criticised what
was seen as a programme gone horribly awry.[72] By January 2001,
American officials warned that 'the longtime seepage in the UN-imposed
economic blockade of Iraq is threatening to become a flood'.[73]

---

[69] Peter Boone, Haris Gazdar and Athar Hussain, 'Sanctions Against Iraq: Costs
of Failure' (Report prepared by the Centre for Economic and Social Rights,
London School of Economics, November, 1997); emphasis in original.

[70] Roda Khalafi, 'Saddam Turns Up Pressure on U.N. Sanctions', *Financial Times*,
December 13, 2000, 12; *Los Angeles Times*, July 3, 2000; Barbara Crossette, 'Iran
Says It Seized Ship Smuggling Iraqi oil', *New York Times*, April 6, 2000, A12.

[71] UN Press Release SC/6833, March 24, 2000 and UN Press Release SC/6845,
April 17, 2000.

[72] Hasmy Agam, Ambassador of Malaysia, statement to Security Council,
March 24, 2000.

[73] Vivienne Ward, 'Iraqi Merchants Grow Resourceful in Skirting Sanctions',
Boston Globe, January 21, 2001, A4.

'Smart sanctions'

Comparing the Oil-for-Food negotiations with the 'smart sanctions' debates, carried out in a very different normative and strategic environment, is instructive. The smart sanctions debate explicitly began from an acceptance of the normative imperative of minimising humanitarian suffering, a norm to which even the United States and the United Kingdom now paid scrupulous rhetorical adherence (even if their actions still did not match their words). A transnational campaign against the sanctions played a far more active role in the smart sanctions debates of 1999–2002 than they had during the Oil-for-Food debates. The anti-sanctions network excelled at information politics, publicising and placing within a plausible narrative frame information produced by reputable NGOs and UN agencies about the objective humanitarian impact of the sanctions.[74] The network's success in forcing a public argument about the sanctions follows Risse's influential discussion of the logic of arguing: 'actors try to challenge the validity claims inherent in any causal or normative statement and to seek a communicative consensus about their understanding of a situation as well as justifications for the principles and norms guiding their actions'.[75]

Its strategy mirrored that of the landmines campaign, as they worked to change 'the debate from a political to a humanitarian issue, drawing media and public attention to the issue, and ultimately educating states about the limited military utility and dramatic negative humanitarian effects of landmines'.[76] Just as the landmines ban movement emphasised the lack of military utility of anti-personnel landmines, the anti-sanctions movement emphasised research and experience showing that sanctions did not 'work' in securing compliance or undermining the target regime. More broadly, it sought to humanise the issue and remove it from the realm of high strategy. The dominant frame reduced 'Iraq' to 'Saddam Hussein', casting it as a strategic problem of coercing a particularly unsympathetic individual while hiding the impact of the policy on Iraq's twenty-three million people. The anti-sanctions

---

[74] Richard Price, 'Transnational Civil Society and Advocacy in World Politics', *World Politics* 55:4 (2003), 589.

[75] Risse, '"Let's Argue!"', 7.

[76] Kenneth R. Rutherford, 'The Evolving Arms Control Agenda: Implications of the Role of NGOs in Banning Antipersonel Landmines', *World Politics* 53:1 (2000), 77.

campaign forced audiences to confront the human impact of the sanctions, which had generally been framed as simply a coercive tool to 'keep Saddam in his box'.

The campaign against sanctions on Iraq tapped into a larger international debate over the impact of UN sanctions prompted by some dozen sanctions packages imposed by the Security Council in the 1990s. As Cortright and Lopez put it, 'as the decade progressed, the increased visibility of suffering and death among Iraq children ... created a palpable sense of sanctions fatigue among Security Council members, generating caution about the implementation of new sanctions and outright condemnation of sanctions by some diplomats, scholars and activists'.[77] (Note that it is the *visibility* of suffering, not the suffering, itself, which is the causal factor.)

The anti-sanctions network operated at the international level, primarily around the United Nations, and in loosely knit networks sharing information across a wide range of national contexts.[78] Concerned experts recognised the need to produce reliable, credible information, and to offer viable alternatives such as targeted ('smarter') sanctions rather than simply criticising all sanctions. In the face of strategic logic, the technical and humanitarian experts realised that 'there may be a need then for more critical public campaigning to obtain reform of sanctions policies'.[79] This network included both 'inside' actors such as UN officials and 'outside' protest actors; such groups shared a concern for the humanitarian situation of civilians in states targeted by sanctions, and co-operated in disseminating information and political action, but they often differed seriously on crucial questions such as whether sanctions should be reformed or abandoned entirely. To combat their dismissal by government officials as 'well-meaning but ill-informed individuals', groups within the network produced detailed analyses of every aspect of the sanctions regime, condensed into sharply

[77] David Cortright and George Lopez, *The Sanctions Decade* (Boulder, CO: Westview Press, 2000), 2.
[78] Sidney Tarrow, 'Transnational Politics: Contentions and Institutions in International Politics', *Annual Review of Political Science* 4 (2001); Margaret Keck and Kathryn Sikkink, *Activists Beyond Borders: Advocacy Networks in International Politics* (Ithaca, NY: Cornell University Press, 1998).
[79] Koenrad Van Brabant, *Can Sanctions Be Smarter? The Current Debate* (London: Overseas Development Institute, report of a conference held December 16–17, 1998, published May 1999), 10.

focused talking points and distributed to relevant influential audiences. They made a point of studying the details of arcane UN programmes in order to be able to contest official discourse from a position of technical equality. This does not, of course, mean that they forswore the powerful moral and symbolic power of pictures of starving children. The moral claim of 'we should not be killing children' was powerful, but the complexity of the issue and the counter-frame blaming Saddam Hussein prevented the articulation of a single clear narrative assigning moral responsibility.[80]

The smart sanctions initiative came about as a response to the collapse of compliance with the sanctions. Washington had showed little interest in smart sanctions until consensus broke down and compliance plummeted, weakening the containment aspects of the sanctions. It was because of this shift in international opinion that the USA and the UK sought to rebuild support for the sanctions through the smart sanctions initiative of 2001.[81] When Colin Powell took over as US Secretary of State in February 2001, he brought with him a well-developed distaste for open-ended economic sanctions and a clear recognition that the existing sanctions were no longer viable.[82] Powell led a serious effort to negotiate a new regime of smart sanctions which would target the dramatically increased smuggling by removing restrictions on civilian items while tightening control over military use items through a more rigorous system of border inspections.

For the United States, smart sanctions was largely an exercise in perception management rather than a genuine problem-solving discourse. As Meghan O'Sullivan aptly summarised the prevailing sense inside Washington, 'despite substantial evidence to the contrary, Saddam Hussein has successfully convinced much of the world that the woeful humanitarian condition of Iraqi civilians is the result of sanctions, not of his own reluctance to ease their pain ... this widespread misperception of Western culpability for and indifference to the suffering of Iraqis ... has transformed sanctions fatigue into sanctions

---

[80] David Cortright, 'A fresh Look at Iraq Sanctions', *The Nation*, December 3, 2001, http://www.thenation.com/doc/20011203/cortright.

[81] Marc Lynch, 'Smart Sanctions: Rebuilding Consensus or Continuing Conflict?', *Middle East Report Online*, 2001.

[82] Richard Haass, Powell's new Director for Policy Planning, and his assistant Meghan O'Sullivan, had been in the forefront of developing new ideas for targeted economic sanctions at the Brookings Institution.

outrage'.[83] The problem in American eyes, then, was not the reality of Iraqi suffering but rather the supposed 'misperception' of American responsibility. The smart sanctions – like Oil-for-Food before them – were intended to rebuild international support and deflect moral criticism, while maintaining the core of the strategically valuable sanctions. But for all of the strategic intent, they powerfully reinforced the emerging new normative consensus governing international sanctions.

Smart sanctions divided the anti-sanctions movement. For those who saw the sanctions as an unconditional moral evil (or who saw America as irredeemable in its malevolence towards the Iraqi people), smart sanctions represented yet more hypocrisy – dressing up an immoral policy in new clothes. Hans van Sponeck, who resigned as director of the UN's humanitarian programme in protest, bluntly stated that 'instead of it being about saving children's lives, it's about saving face'.[84] For others, however, smart sanctions offered a set of practical tools which would enable the international community to live up to its rhetoric. These proposals would reconcile the strategic utility of sanctions with the newly accepted moral imperatives by finding ways to target the sanctions more directly at the regime while minimising their impact on Iraqi civilians. And they drew directly on the expertise and arguments generated by the 'insider' component of the anti-sanctions movement.

In principle, smart sanctions would work by restoring normative support through removing the humanitarian argument – or at least shifting the blame onto Saddam Hussein – without sacrificing the perceived need to maintain tight military controls. In practice, however, the proposal relied upon a high degree of co-operation from neighbouring states such as Jordan, Syria, the UAE and Turkey which had little interest in such increased demands. In the negotiations which followed, the USA and the UK won French and Chinese support, but could not persuade Russia to sign on and the proposal died. The ultimate failure of smart sanctions demonstrates the corrosive effects of pervasive hypocrisy. By 2001, distrust of the United States with regard to Iraq ran so deep that even a proposal which incorporated many elements of the sanctions critique could not regain normative support. And without

---

[83] Meghan O'Sullivan, 'Iraq: Time for a Modified Approach', *Brookings Institution Policy Brief #71*, February 2001, 1.

[84] Hans von Sponeck, 'Too much Collateral Damage: "Smart Sanctions" Hurt Innocent Iraqis', *Toronto Globe and Mail*, July 2, 2002, http://www.commondreams.org/views02/0702-03.htm.

such normative support, there was almost no reason to expect that the new regime would be effectively implemented.

The systemic crisis of legitimacy undermining the sanctions as a whole overwhelmed the pragmatic reforms which might have dealt with specific problems with the sanctions regime. While the smart sanctions proposals failed, two crucial points should not be neglected: the normative position that sanctions should be targeted to avoid excessively harming civilians had been firmly established even for the most enthusiastic supporters of the sanctions (the US and the UK); and practical policy instruments had been painstakingly developed which would in the future allow this normative consensus to be realised in practice.

Constructivism, Habermas and the possibility of consensus

Habermas offers an important warning for constructivists who see the hypocrisy game as a pragmatic way to mediate realist scepticism and moral progress. He considered the constructivist account of hypocrisy, 'concealing publicly indefensible interests behind pretended moral or ethical reasons necessitates self-bindings that either on the next occasion exposes a proponent as inconsistent or, in the interest of maintaining his credibility, lead to the inclusion of others' interests'.[85] Having summarised this logic, Habermas forcefully rejects it because communicative action requires 'the exclusion of deception and illusion ... participants have to mean what they say'.[86] 'Consensus' means more than a formal agreement which relies only upon the aggregation or the misrepresentation of preferences.[87] For consensus to carry a normatively binding force, public and private preferences must have been reconciled so that actors agree for the same reasons.[88] For Habermas, 'participants in argumentation must reach a rationally motivated

[85] Jürgen Habermas, *Between Facts and Norms* (Cambridge, MA: MIT Press, 1996), 340.
[86] Jürgen Habermas, 'From Kant's "Ideas" of Pure Reason to the "Idealizing" Presuppositions of Communicative Action'. In William Rehg and James Bohman (eds.), *Pluralism and the Pragmatic Turn* (Cambridge, MA: MIT Press, 2002), 11–40, quote at 34.
[87] Jürgen Habermas, *On the Pragmatics of Communication* (Cambridge, MA: MIT Press, 1998); also see Joseph Heath, *Communicative Action and Rational Choice* (Cambridge, MA: MIT Press, 2000).
[88] Habermas, *On the Pragmatics of Communication*, 84.

agreement, if at all, for the same reasons'.[89] His critical theory demands a move towards open communication, unmasking false consensus in order to allow the full expression of uncoerced and reasoned consensus.[90] Thomas Risse suggests that 'argumentative processes might well begin as purely rhetorical exchanges but often evolve toward true reasoning'.[91] But how can actors reach consensus – far less truth – through the unconstrained exchange of public argument if 'rhetoric ... is a form of deceit'?[92]

The public arguments over the sanctions demonstrate all too vividly how the pervasiveness of hypocrisy and deceit created a situation in which, as Hannah Arendt vividly put it, 'consistent lying ... pulls the ground from under our feet and provides no other ground on which to stand'.[93] Pervasive hypocrisy delegitimised all attempts at moral argument, helping to constitute the arena as a realist realm, in which states came to trust no one, persuasion was impossible, and states could do no better than to follow their own self-interest or moral imperatives as best they could.

The Iraq sanctions case illustrates powerfully how hypocrisy blocks the evolution of strategic agreement into communicative consensus. Accusations of moral hypocrisy tend to shut down reasoned argument – enraging the targets, endowing the accusers with a false sense of moral superiority and driving the audience into apathetic cynicism. For all the heated public controversy, there was very little real rational–critical debate about the sanctions. Moral argument in the case of the Iraq sanctions tended towards absolutes, with the two sides relentlessly defending incommensurable narratives rather than seeking to reconcile them into a consensus view.[94] For sanctions critic Anthony Arnove, the moral equation was clear: 'ordinary Iraqis are dying in numbers that defy comprehension, as a deliberate and predictable consequence of a policy designed to strangle the Iraqi economy'.[95] For then British Foreign Minister Jack Straw, the moral equation was equally

---

[89] Ibid 86; also see Habermas, *Between Facts and Norms*, 311.
[90] Robert O. Keohane, 'Governance in a Partially Globalized World', *American Political Science Review* 95 (2001), 1–13, quote at 2.
[91] Risse, '"Let's Argue!"' 9; Muller, 'Arguing, Bargaining and All That'; Lynch, 'Why Engage?'.
[92] Bailey, *The Prevalence of Deceit*, 29.
[93] Hannah Arendt, *Between Past and Future* (New York, NY: Viking Press, 1968), 258.
[94] Carne Ross, 'War Stories', *Financial Times*, January 28, 2005.
[95] Arnove, *Iraq Under Siege: The Deadly Impact of Sanctions and War*.

clear: 'It angers me when well-meaning people are taken in by these lies . . . The UN allows more than enough money for all the humanitarian goods the Iraqis need . . . It is the regime which refuses to use these funds to purchase food and medicine [because] it suits Saddam to make Iraqis suffer and starve'.[96] Such argument from moral absolute made a search for common ground difficult. Instead, as Ruth Grant puts it, 'the attempt to forge consensus will involve . . . pressure towards hypocrisy'.[97]

Years of systematic hypocrisy over the sanctions resulted, as Hannah Arendt foretold, in 'a peculiar kind of cynicism – an absolute refusal to believe in the truth of anything, no matter how well this truth may be established'.[98] By the late 1990s, literally nothing the United States said about Iraq could have any persuasive power with much of the world. On the other side, there was literally nothing that the Iraqi government could do which would convince the United States that it was sincere about complying with the disarmament resolutions.

Accusations and exposure of hypocrisy played key roles in shaping the political and moral arguments surrounding a decade of sanctions on Iraq. As concern about the impact of the sanctions mounted, actors increasingly resented the United States for its denial of the problem, its resistance to change and its increasingly blatant manipulation of the contract approval process for political ends. International consensus collapsed, leaving the United States with 'a strategy of domination based on compliance rather than legitimacy' – one which quickly proved unworkable and led inexorably to the 2003 American invasion of Iraq (which was in part justified by the collapse of the sanctions).[99]

The sanctions experience demonstrates both the strengths and the weaknesses of the constructivist approach to hypocrisy. The anti-sanctions network gained disproportionate influence with its moral argumentation, forcing the USA and the UK into a number of remark-able concessions (Oil-for-Food, smart sanctions) against their strategic preferences. These moral arguments set in place a clear normative consensus within the United Nations about what would be acceptable in future sanctions regimes. But these successes came at a heavy price.

[96] Jack Straw, 'Saddam Must Allow Weapons Inspectors Into Iraq or Suffer the Consequences', *The Times* (London), March 5, 2002.
[97] Ruth W. Grant, *Hypocrisy and Integrity: Machiavelli, Rousseau, and the Ethics of Politics* (Chicago, IL: University of Chicago Press, 1997), 54–55.
[98] Arendt, *Between Past and Future*, 257.
[99] Wedeen, *Ambiguities of Domination*, 6.

The United Nations is still struggling to repair the damage to its reputation done by a series of damning investigations of corruption in the Oil-for-Food Programme. Arab opponents of the sanctions, who prided themselves on their support for the suffering Iraqi people, were shocked to discover the depth of animosity towards them among ordinary Iraqis who considered them to have been supporting Saddam.[100] Finally, the United States has perhaps suffered most of all. The findings of recent global public opinion surveys amply convey the profound mistrust of the United States throughout much of the world, the outcome of these strategic practices and rejection of communicative engagement. The sanctions on Iraq formed one of the major planks in Osama bin Laden's campaign against America, and contributed immensely to solidifying Arab and Muslim beliefs in American hostility and dishonesty.

The global response to the American campaign for war against Iraq in 2002–2003, while beyond the scope of this chapter, powerfully demonstrates this corrosive power of hypocrisy. The world questioned American arguments for war in no small part because of the experience of the preceding decade. Deeply entrenched complaints about moving goalposts, indifference to Iraqi civilian casualties and unauthorised regime change preferences juxtaposed easily onto the new debates about war with Iraq. American inability to substantiate its claims about Iraqi weapons of mass destruction and ties to al-Qa'ida only fuelled this scepticism. And post-war revelations about the mendacity of Bush administration claims confirmed the worst criticisms from the earlier period. While hypocrisy alone cannot explain the outcome of these momentous political battles, it would be impossible to fully account for the global response to the American position without appreciating its corrosive effects.

[100] Lynch, *Voices of the New Arab Public*, chapter 6.

7 | *Paradoxes in humanitarian intervention*

MARTHA FINNEMORE

The rash of humanitarian interventions since the end of the Cold War has posed serious analytical problems for International Relations (IR) scholars. Traditional security scholars have struggled to understand the nature of 'humanitarianism' as an interest, often with the result that they simply discount it and emphasise other possible motivations for intervention. In these analyses, the intervention in Somalia is explained as an effort to export US values, intervention in Haiti was about controlling unwanted refugee flows, interventions in Bosnia and Kosovo are explained by the need to protect NATO's (North Atlantic Treaty Organization) credibility and maintain stability in Europe.[1] Humanitarianism was only window-dressing in every case. Constructivists, legal scholars and an increasing number of policy analysts have taken humanitarianism more seriously as a source of state action. They point to the increasingly dense network of human rights norms, law and transnational activist groups that all persuade (or coerce) policy makers and publics to support these interventions. The analytic problem for this group has been to understand why humanitarianism produces the sorts of actions it does in world politics and why its influence and effects seem so inconsistent and varied. Humanitarian concerns do not always produce interventions (as the Rwanda case makes painfully clear) nor do they produce interventions of the same kind.

Humanitarianism is not some single isolated impulse nor does it consistently produce identical effects. This seems obvious but analytically we have tended to treat norms and values like humanitarianism in isolation, trying to attach particular causal significance to each one

---

[1] Michael Mandelbaum, 'Foreign Policy as Social Work', *Foreign Affairs* 75:1 (1996), 16–32 at 17; Richard Haass, *Intervention: The Use of American Force in the Post-Cold War World* (Washington, DC: Carnegie Endowment for International Peace, 1994).

individually. This ignores the relationship *among* norms and the ways they interact. Norms never function in a vacuum; they are always part of some larger normative structure. To understand how norms work, we need to understand the complexity, contradictions and indeterminacy of the larger normative system in which political action takes place. Any policy decision of consequence is taken within a dense web of normative claims that often conflict with one another and create serious ethical dilemmas for decision makers. After all, if the prescriptions of norms and values were always clear or if they never conflicted with one another, we would not have to make any decisions; we would just follow the prescriptions. In this sense, normative conflict is what *creates* decisions since, absent conflicting normative claims, there would be nothing to decide.

Humanitarian intervention always occurs within an intricate structure of conflicting norms and values that determine whether and how it happens. Humanitarian intervention may be supported by powerful transnational human rights norms that have unprecedented power in contemporary politics. It may be undercut by geostrategic considerations rooted in the moral duties of politicians to protect their own state and citizens in uniform. It is often in tension with other values we hold dear, such as self-determination, and when coupled with military force, these tensions are greatly exacerbated. Waging war always involves widespread human rights violations, raising questions about whether humanitarian ends justify the suffering caused by military means. Humanitarianism, by itself, never provides a satisfactory explanation of an intervention, either analytically or morally. Only by examining the broader normative landscape in which it rests can we begin to understand the practice and ethics of humanitarian intervention.[2]

---

[2] Of course, one need not use constructivist analytics to find dilemmas in humanitarian intervention. See, for example, J. L. Holzgrefe and Robert O. Keohane (eds.), *Humanitarian Intervention: Ethical, Legal, and Political Dilemmas* (New York, NY: Cambridge University Press, 2003). Comparing those essays with this one illustrates the different things one 'sees' about humanitarian intervention with different theoretical glasses. For another collection, including some essays from a constructivist perspective, see Anthony F. Lang, Jr (ed.), *Just Intervention* (Washington, DC: Georgetown University Press, 2003). For a diverse array of perspectives that includes practitioners and engages many issues raised here, see Jonathan Moore (ed.), *Hard Choices: Moral Dilemmas in Humanitarian Intervention* (New York, NY: Rowman & Littlefield, 1998).

In what follows I examine the normative structure in which contemporary humanitarian interventions are embedded to make four arguments that bear on the themes of this volume. First, changes in normative structure have produced new patterns of humanitarian intervention. In an important sense, changing normative structure is what creates humanitarian crises. It defines who counts as 'human' and can make claims for protection. In the nineteenth century, humanitarian intervention was undertaken to protect white Christians only; by the twentieth and twenty-first centuries, most such interventions are undertaken to protect non-white, non-Christian people who previously would not have registered on the consciousness of potential interveners.[3] In addition, over the past 200 years and even in the past twenty-five years there has been a qualitative change in the kinds of expectations we as an international community have for government performance. We expect much more from governments than we ever have before, in terms of providing for citizens, guaranteeing their rights and protecting them from harm. Both of these changes shape our perceptions of what constitutes 'a humanitarian crisis'. Events that would have been regrettable or gone unnoticed twenty, fifty or one hundred years ago now constitute crises that provoke international debate and response, sometimes even military response.

Second, the normative structure and political rules we have to deal with these crises are often in tension or opposition in ways that make these conflicts particularly difficult to resolve. Some of these tensions are obvious, like the tension between intervention and self-determination. Others are less obvious but have powerful effects on our practical ability to achieve the kinds of solutions we say we want, and I discuss some of the operational implications of normative conflict on the ground. Third, changing normative structure shapes, not only our perception of crises, but our responses to these crises and the kinds of military action and post-conflict peace-building we undertake. We now offload much of the work in these crises onto international organisations, both intergovernmental and non-governmental organisations (IGOs and NGOs), without thinking much about the implications of this move. Among

---

[3] Martha Finnemore, 'Constructing Norms of Humanitarian Intervention'. In Peter J. Katzenstein (ed.), *The Culture of National Security: Norms and Identity in World Politics* (New York, NY: Columbia University Press, 1996), 153–185, and Matha Finnemore, *The Purpose of Intervention: Changing Beliefs about the Use of Force* (Ithaca, NY: Cornell University Press, 2003), chapter 3.

other things, this offloading implies changes in the way we constitute authority in global governance, but it also raises issues of accountability that we are only beginning to address.

In the final section I discuss some of the theoretical and ethical implications of these normative tensions in humanitarian intervention for constructivist scholars. Humanitarian crises pose genuine moral dilemmas. They often involve conflict among norms fundamental to international life – sovereignty, human rights and self-determination. These are not situations like some others discussed in this volume. Towns knows what a morally desirable outcome would be and wants to use her scholarship to help construct that solution. More facts, for example about the violent behaviour of Swedish men towards women, and new cultural frames, for example about gender equality in a multicultural setting, could create morally preferable outcomes. Similarly, Gurowitz knows what a morally better immigration policy would look like; it would be a policy that helped migrants and eliminated current policy confusion, and she sees constructivism as a tool to promote this policy. In many humanitarian crises, however, there simply *is* no good solution. Letting violence continue is clearly bad. Having an outside party impose a government that violates self-determination, is illegitimate or incompetent (or all three) is not so good either. These are often genuine moral dilemmas. The world is full of them and I discuss what constructivism can show us in these situations.

These are certainly not the only insights to be gained from an examination of the normative structure within which we do these interventions. I offer them only as examples of the many ways in which normative structures shape our perceptions of problems, structure the ranges of response we consider and limit the effectiveness of that response in our own normative terms. We tend to think of humanitarian interventions as having obvious material causes (e.g. lots of people dying). We also tend to think about the reasons solutions are difficult as primarily material (e.g. lack of troops on the ground, lack of relief supplies in the right place at the right time). In both cases, however, these material facts are related to human action through a complex normative structure that often provides conflicting interpretations of events and conflicting prescriptions for action. My goal is to understand some of these changing relationships in internationally held values and the impact they have on humanitarian intervention.

Creating humanity, creating crises

Humanitarian interventions occur in response to what now we call 'humanitarian crises', but who is 'human' worthy of protection, and what constitutes a 'crisis' requiring response are both matters of perception. Someone counts as 'human' in political and social life only if others recognise him or her as such. Something is a crisis only if it flies in the face of what we agree is acceptable. Thus, what constitutes a humanitarian crisis is always a function of the normative fabric of political life and standards of acceptable behaviour in the world.

One reason for the spate of humanitarian crises landing on the policy agenda in the 1990s was that these standards of acceptable behaviour had changed. Ethnic cleansing, genocide and mass killings of various kinds are hardly new in world politics, but they did not provoke the kinds of responses in earlier periods that we saw in the 1990s. Just a few decades ago a wide range of state-sponsored violence was tolerated that would now constitute major international crimes. People rarely applauded internal repression (or not publicly), but governments rarely intervened militarily if a state decided to kill, torture, relocate and dispossess its own citizens, and states did commit such abuses with some frequency.[4] The end of the Cold War may account for some of the change in responses but it certainly does not account for all of it. Fear of the Soviets was not blocking the US's ability to intervene in this hemisphere, yet large-scale massacres of indigenous peoples in Guatemala in the 1980s, and political 'disappearances' in Argentina and Chile during the 1970s did not provoke military intervention by Western governments.[5] People certainly noticed and made a fuss about

---

[4] Benjamin A. Valentino, *Final Solutions: Mass Killing and Genocide in the 20th Century* (Ithaca, NY: Cornell University Press, 2004); Samantha Power, '*A Problem from Hell*': *America and the Age of Genocide* (New York, NY: Perennial/HarperCollins, 2002).

[5] States did occasionally intervene for these reasons during the Cold War. The three cases are India's intervention in what is now Bangladesh in 1971, Tanzania's toppling of the Idi Amin regime in Uganda (1979) and Vietnam's intervention to overthrow Pol Pot in Cambodia (1979). For a fuller treatment see Nicholas Wheeler, *Saving Strangers: Humanitarian Intervention in International Society* (New York, NY: Oxford University Press, 2000), esp. chapters 2–4; and Finnemore, 'Constructing Norms of Humanitarian Intervention'. My point here is that the frequency with which mass killing is met with military intervention rose dramatically in the 1990s and the target state does not have to present additional security threats to the intervener to merit such attention.

these humanitarian abuses, but the willingness of governments to take costly political action in response to these abuses was minimal then. It is larger now. Spain's attempt to secure the extradition of Pinochet in the 1990s, and the widespread support for this in European legal and political circles, unthinkable twenty years ago, provides one indication of the changed normative climate. The increase in military interventions to prevent mass killings is another.

Who is 'human'?

The normative structure for humanitarian intervention is complex, but at least two prominent features have changed. First, who is 'human' and can legitimately claim protection has changed.[6] While there was humanitarian intervention in the nineteenth century, it was always undertaken by European powers to protect Christians, mostly against the crumbling Ottoman Empire. European powers did not intervene to protect non-Christians. Pogroms against Jews did not provoke intervention. Neither did Russian massacres of Turks in Central Asia in the 1860s. Neither did mass killings in China during the Taiping rebellion against the Manchus, mass killings by German colonial rule in Namibia or massacres of Native Americans in the United States. Certainly some Europeans recognised the victims in these atrocities as human but not all did and the degree of identification with these 'others' as fellow human beings was circumscribed.

Efforts by a large number of people around the world were required to universalise humanity and transform understandings of it in ways that would make contemporary humanitarian interventions conceivable, ergo possible. Two changes are of particular importance for the history of these interventions. One was the abolition of slavery and the slave trade. While human beings were legitimately and legally property, they were beyond the edge of humanity. Abolition made the humanity of these people harder to deny in formal, legal and political debates and with that status came certain, albeit minimal, privileges and protections.

The other process that institutionalised a new, more universal conception of humanity was decolonisation and the creation of sovereign

---

[6] This discussion draws on my earlier work in 'Constructing Norms of Humanitarian Intervention'. Citations to relevant historical material can be found there.

states and sovereign rights in the non-European world. The normative discourse surrounding colonisation involved bringing civilisation to savages and thus 'creating' humanity where it did not previously exist. Non-Europeans became human in European eyes by becoming Christian, by adopting European-style property rights and political arrangements, and entering into the European-based international economy. With decolonisation, this discourse changed. By the twentieth century, humanity was no longer something one could create by bringing savages to civilisation. Rather, humanity was understood to be inherent in individual human beings. It had become universalised and was not culturally dependent as it had been previously.

Neither change – abolition or decolonisation – was easy. Both were hard-fought by broad coalitions of slaves, former slaves, national liberation groups and their European sympathisers. But without the creation of this universalised understanding of humanity and codification of that understanding in formal international organisations like the United Nations (UN), the pattern of intervention we see in the late twentieth century would be hard to predict or explain.

Changed expectations for government performance

Also changed are internationally shared views about what governments owe their citizens. At a minimum, governments are expected to refrain from abuse; more generally, governments are expected to guarantee and provide a bundle of rights and services. This change in expectations, and concomitant rise in standards for government performance are clearly bound up in the rising power of human rights norms over the past several decades. The international human rights network has been hugely successful at mobilising publics and institutionalising standards for acceptable treatment of people in a wide range of states, especially powerful states, over the past thirty years.[7] It is easy to underestimate the effects of this change. Because there are still so many human rights violations going on all over the world, it is tempting to conclude that

---

[7] For a detailed examination of this process see Thomas Risse, Steven Ropp and Kathryn Sikkink, *The Power of Human Rights* (New York, NY: Cambridge University Press, 1999); Margaret Keck and Kathryn Sikkink, *Activists Beyond Borders* (Ithaca, NY: Cornell University Press, 1998), chapters. 1–3; Daniel Thomas, *The Helsinki Effect: International Norms, Human Rights, and the Demise of Communism* (Princeton, NJ: Princeton University Press, 2001).

respect for human rights must still be marginal in world politics. This mode of thinking misses crucial changes, however. While it is certainly true that there continue to be violations, the way people react to violations has changed markedly. The amount of mobilisation and pressure brought to bear on governments over human rights abuses is much greater than it was in the 1960s.[8]

The expansion and institutionalisation of human rights claims constitute a major qualitative change in the normative fabric of world politics. Specifically, human rights compromise basic features of state sovereignty since human rights are claims that states cannot do anything they want to their citizens, ergo they cannot have absolute control over what happens inside their borders. States cannot, for example, even do such basic things as keep political control or prevent secession by any means without paying some kind of political price. It is impossible to know how much these changes have dissuaded or deterred states from repressing citizens, since we cannot have information on non-events. What we can very clearly see, however, is an increased willingness of governments to create 'political prices' for human rights violations. This is true even against very large states now. European states, for example, have used the International Monetary Fund (IMF) to put pressure on Russia in response to its treatment of civilians in Chechnya. It is not simply the case that decision makers in these Western governments have become so high-minded and other-regarding in their views. Underpinning these and other protective actions by governments is strong pressure by the extraordinarily well-organised human rights networks that have sprung up since the 1970s.[9]

Rising standards of human rights respect are only part of a much larger package of changed expectations about governments, however. We expect states to do more than just refrain from torturing and killing citizens. We also now expect 'good governance' from states. What,

[8] Keck and Sikkink, *Activists Beyond Borders*, chapters 1–3; Thomas, *The Helsinki Effect*; Kathryn Sikkink, *Mixed Signals: U.S. Human Rights Policy and Latin America* (Ithaca, NY: Cornell University Press, 2004).
[9] Robert McElroy describes a variety of ways in which moral norms can influence the behaviour of governments. One is through internalisation of these norms by decision makers; another is through outside pressure by activists on decision makers. Both could be at work here; Robert W. McElroy, *Morality and American Foreign Policy* (Princeton, NJ: Princeton University Press, 1992). On activists, see Keck and Sikkink, *Activists Beyond Borders* and Thomas, *The Helsinki Effect*.

exactly, constitutes 'good governance' has been the subject of some debate, but the minimalist and most common usages focus on the requirement that government not be corrupt. Those demanding good governance also usually demand accountability, transparency, rule of law and participation of varying kinds and degrees. Good governance in this sense has become an important feature of a wide range of intergovernmental interactions and has become a major criterion for all kinds of development aid. The IMF and World Bank both now have extensive 'good governance' requirements and anti-corruption programmes, as do most bilateral aid programmes.[10] This is new. Corruption of the kind now being condemned, which usually involves use of public office for private gain, did not used to be an *international* issue. It might have been an issue in the domestic politics of some countries, sometimes an important one, but in many places practices now labelled as 'corrupt' were standard and normal for years. The wide-ranging attempt to impose this standard on all governments and public officials in all countries is unprecedented.[11]

Not being corrupt and providing some measure of transparency and accountability is only the new minimum among standards of performance for states, however. Increasingly, the standards are being pushed to include democracy and elections. In fact, the term 'good governance' is increasingly being defined to *include* democracy and elections. There is strong normative pressure on states to adhere to formal elements of democracy, such as having elections. The irony is that we apply this pressure even when we know that elections might actually promote instability in fragile states. In post-conflict states, elections are often divisive as candidates play the 'nationalist' or 'ethnic' card to rally

---

[10] Paul Wolfowitz, 'Good Governance and Development: A Time for Action', speech by Paul Wolfowitz, Jakarta, April 11, 2006, available at http://web. worldbank.org/WBSITE/EXTERNAL/EXTABOUTUS/ORGANIZATION/ EXTOFFICEPRESIDENT/0,,contentMDK:20883752~menuPK:64343258~ pagePK:51174171~piPK:64258873~theSitePK:1014541,00.html; World Bank, 'Helping Countries Combat Corruption: The Role of the World Bank' (The World Bank, PREM network, 1997); Thomas A. Wolf, Emine Gurgen, European II Department, 'Improving Governance and Fighting Corruption in the Baltic and CIS Countries: The Role of the IMF', IMF Working Paper WP/00/1, January 1, 2000.

[11] For a discussion of the ethical implications of this change see Mlada Bukovansky, 'The Moral Core of the International Anti-Corruption Regime', unpublished manuscript, Dartmouth College. For details about current anti-corruption efforts see the website of Transparency International at www.transparency.de.

support.[12] This is also a well-recognised problem in Africa where elections consistently tend to produce instability rather than alleviate it. In fact, a group of African NGOs and intellectuals have been trying to figure out a model of democracy that does not require elections for precisely this reason.[13]

Good governance standards and human rights standards are both examples of changed (and rising) _international_ standards for states' _internal_ behaviour. In both cases, matters that formerly lay within a state's sovereign control have become accepted topics of international scrutiny. As the scope of international scrutiny widens and standards rise, the level of performance required to be a state 'in good standing' in the international community has become higher now than ever before. Not surprisingly, many states do not meet these standards. When this happens, outside actors increasingly feel justified in intervening. Justifications are rooted in the fact that normative standards are being violated, and are buttressed by claims that these standards are widely held and often formally legitimised by international organizations (IOs). Because IOs are often the forum in which standards are set and legitimated, IOs are often given the task of intervening to uphold them. When corruption is the problem (a largely economic violation of normative standards), intervention is usually economic and economic actors such as the IMF and World Bank play a large role in policing this kind of performance. However, when state failures result in widespread violence, states, publics and IOs begin to call for forceful responses and, increasingly, those demands are met with force wielded by militaries who intervene in these states.

Normative tensions that make intervening difficult

What is new about humanitarian crises is not the fact of mass killing. What is new is the normative framework through which the world views these episodes. Rising expectations for government performance

---

[12] Roland Paris, _At War's End: Building Peace after Civil Conflict_ (New York, NY: Cambridge University Press, 2004); and Roland Paris, 'Peacebuilding and the Limits of International Liberalism', _International Security_ 22:2 (1997), 54–89.

[13] Personal communication, NGO staff member. For more on this irony see Michael N. Barnett and Martha Finnemore, 'The Politics, Power, and Pathologies of International Organizations', _International Organization_ 53:4 (1999), 699–732 at 720.

mean that mass killings are more likely to be understood as 'crises' – as violations of accepted standards of behaviour that require a response from outsiders. Also new is the normative framework that sets standards of behaviour for interveners. States cannot simply intervene in one of these crises in any way they please. There are well understood rules they must follow to make their intervention legitimate in the eyes of other states and mass publics, both abroad and at home. Those rules have changed by increments over the past twenty, fifty and one hundred years and now contain deep tensions that create serious ethical, political and logistical dilemmas for interveners. In this section I examine several of the most fundamental normative tensions facing interveners and show how these are not simply isolated matters for ethicists but filter down into the most basic operational details of military action. They shape our military responses to these humanitarian crises and make success elusive in our own normative terms, as I discuss below.

Perhaps the most powerful normative tension surrounding these actions is that between self-determination and humanitarian intervention. International legal scholars, among others, have written extensively about conflicts between such interventions and sovereignty norms, but sovereignty has hardly proved an insurmountable barrier to intervention and, in fact, has always been malleable and conditional in a host of ways.[14] Even among legal scholars, notions of sovereignty are coming under pressure to include understandings that would allow or even require intervention by outsiders in cases of humanitarian crisis and gross human rights abuse.[15] Underlying much of this malleability of sovereignty are two other sets of norms which I would argue are more basic and more powerful. One is human rights norms, discussed above. The other is self-determination norms, which have come to be intimately connected to human rights. In discussions about whether to intervene in humanitarian crises, sovereignty norms are almost always

---

[14] See Stephen D. Krasner, *Sovereignty: Organized Hypocrisy* (Princeton, NJ: Princeton University Press, 1999) and Sean D. Murphy, *Humanitarian Intervention: The United Nations in an Evolving World Order* (Philadelphia, PA: University of Pennsylvania Press, 1996).

[15] Fernando Tesón, *Humanitarian Intervention: An Inquiry into Law and Morality* (Dobbs Ferry, NY: Transnational Publishers, 1988); Francis M. Deng, *Sovereignty as Responsibility* (Washington, DC: The Brookings Institution, 1996). For a political scientist's analysis of legal change in this area see Theo Farrell, *Norms of War: Cultural Beliefs and Modern Conflict* (Boulder, CO: Lynne Rienner, 2005), chapter 5.

invoked by those resisting intervention and have become increasingly discredited by those advocating broader humanitarian action. Self-determination norms are more interesting and consequential precisely because even those who support broad and active policies of humanitarian action strongly support self-determination. In fact, humanitarian interventions are often done, in part, to promote self-determination of the victims.

Self-determination does not sit comfortably with humanitarian intervention. It is in tension with both words in that phrase: it is in tension with humanitarianism and it is in tension with intervention.

Self-determination vs. humanitarianism

When we intervene in humanitarian crises we want to save lives and stop violence which is often being perpetrated by officials of the government. At the same time, we refuse to simply overthrow governments and install new, more humane ones that will protect human rights and guarantee humane treatment of citizens. To do so would violate widely held norms about self-determination. The tension here lies in the fact that people (or at least some of them) often freely choose to 'determine' their fate using violence.

Self-determination, at bottom, may not be a very humane process. Certainly it has not been so historically. If one examines the ways in which states have 'determined' themselves in the past, they have killed a great many people in the process. The consolidation of the current array of states in Europe was an extremely bloody process that took several centuries. Self-determination in the United States only occurred through the ethnic cleansing of an entire continent of native peoples and an extremely bloody civil war.

The assumption that seems to underlie much of the humanitarian intervention since 1989 is that self-determination can and should only happen through enlightened discussion and the ballot box. Viewed from a liberal cosmopolitan ethical perspective, this may be progress. One would *like* to have peoples 'determine' themselves in this way rather than through violence, and raising the ethical bar for the self-determination process might be a good thing ethically. However this view may also be naive, at best, and hypocritical at worst. Citizens of the Western states who are pushing these norms and doing most of the intervening were not able to 'self-determine' without a great deal of violence, yet we now are expecting others to do so. Awareness of this fact often seems to be missing in discussions about how to approach these crises and the kinds of expectations we have of people suffering through them.

Does this apparent hypocrisy compromise international efforts to bring self-determination to the non-Western world through these interventions? Sikkink's discussions of consequentialism and 'comparison to the ideal', elsewhere in this volume, speak to some of these issues. The fact that the past behaviour of the messenger (Western interveners) does not fit the ideal self-determination process should not logically compromise the ethical value of the message (humane self-determination is desirable and good). However, Sikkink's concern with rigorous empirical evaluation of consequences as a component of ethical calculus means that interveners have a moral duty to be clear-eyed about the kinds of consequences that can reasonably be expected from different types of intervention. There may be situations where the consequences of intervention might be worse than the atrocities it seeks to stop. Certainly authors like Edward Luttwak believe this to be the case.[16] I suspect a more common problem is that potential interveners might know what actions might reasonably lead to better, if not perfect, outcomes than atrocity but cannot muster the political will to act. Assessments of the Rwandan genocide often make this case.[17] Alternatively, and perhaps related, potential interveners might find that assessing consequences of both intervention and non-intervention is extremely difficult, particularly in some of these very messy humanitarian crises. Inaction for several years in Bosnia was justified by worries about the consequences of intervention.[18] This would not obviate a moral duty to bring the best possible knowledge to bear in assessing consequences, but the best one might hope for is to be clear-eyed about the uncertainties. These are empirical debates about counterfactual consequences and whether

---

[16] Edward Luttwak, 'Give War a Chance', *Foreign Affairs* July/August 1999 and 'If Bosnians were Dolphins . . .', *Commentary* 96:4 (1993), 27–32; Richard Betts, 'The Delusion of Impartial Intervention'. In Chester Crocker, Fen Osler Hampson and Pamela Aall (eds.), *Turbulent Peace* (Washington, DC, U.S. Institute of Peace, 2001).

[17] Romeo Dallaire, *Shake Hands with the Devil* (New York, NY: Carroll & Graf 2004); Michael Barnett, *Eyewitness to a Genocide* (Ithaca, NY: Cornell University Press, 2002); Power, '*A Problem from Hell*'.

[18] I thank an anonymous reviewer for this point.

peaceful self-determination is (or was) possible in different situations; they are not ethical debates about whether self-determination is a good thing.

Self-determination vs. intervention

This tension is obvious. Citizens of the West pushing for intervention all profess great support for self-determination, but will go in with troops to change the self-determination process if they do not like either the process or the result. If the political process becomes violent (e.g. Somalia), the state becomes a candidate for outside intervention; if an elected government becomes violent, the state becomes a candidate for intervention (e.g. Serbia). This raises the question: if we force people to self-determine only by the processes and with the results we happen to like, are they really 'self-determining'? At a practical level, this raises questions about whether it is possible to force other states to be democratic and humane. At a more abstract level, it raises questions about whether states suffering such intervention are really self-determining.[19]

This normative tension between humanitarian intervention and self-determination creates a variety of political problems for policy makers and a host of operational dilemmas on the ground for militaries. The most important and most worrisome of these surround the problem of goals – what, exactly, are we intervening for in these crises? What outcome or end state do we want to achieve? One might think, in the abstract, that the logical outcome of a humanitarian intervention would be for the interveners to install a new humane government that does not abuse its citizens. In fact, something very like this was an option for interveners in the nineteenth century. When the French intervened in what is now Lebanon, then Syria under Ottoman rule, in 1860 they did exactly this. They stopped the killing, brokered new governing arrangements in consultation with other Europeans, put new people in charge and went home.[20] It is not clear that this kind of imposition of a new

---

[19] For an early argument about the widespread illusion of politically 'neutral' humanitarian intervention and its effects, see Walter Clarke and Jeffrey Herbst, 'Somalia and the Future of Humanitarian Intervention', *Foreign Affairs* 75:2 (1996), 70–85.

[20] A. L. Tiwabi, *A Modern History of Syria* (London: Macmillan, 1969), 131; William E. Echard, *Napoleon III and the Concert of Europe* (Baton Rouge, LA: Louisana State University Press, 1983), chapter 8; R. W. Seton-Watson, *Britain in*

government as a solution to mass killing is acceptable in contemporary politics. Increasingly, internationally shared notions about legitimate government are process-oriented. A legitimate government in contemporary politics is one in which the governed have somehow consented, and the most legitimate demonstration of consent is elections. It is not legitimate for interveners, even for the UN, to impose a particular solution, much less a specific government, on the target of a humanitarian intervention. The goal of these interventions is always some kind of a negotiated (i.e. consensual) settlement among the parties inside the target state.

A variety of practical and operational dilemmas flow from this valuation of political process (and settlement) over substantive outcomes. One is that interveners may find themselves intervening for a process that includes negotiated settlement and elections, which ultimately produces precisely the substantive outcomes they were intervening to avoid. This is what happened in Bosnia. The West intervened to prevent ethnic cleansing, but subsequent elections essentially ratified this result. Candidates who played ethnic and nationalist cards to rally voters were very successful in elections and garnered the lion's share of support.

Another consequence of this emphasis on negotiated settlement as a goal is that militaries on the ground find themselves fighting a war without enemies. Reflecting the larger political and social climate, military manuals on 'peace operations' now explicitly incorporate this process-oriented end state. In outlining these missions, the relevant army field manual says: '[T]he conflict, not the belligerent parties, is the enemy.' It goes on:

> As with any mission, commanders at all levels must have a common understanding of the end state and the conditions that constitute success prior to initiating operations. In peace operations, *settlement*, not victory, it the ultimate measure of success[21]

Europe, 1789–1914 (New York, NY: The Macmillan Company, 1937), 420–421.

[21] Both quotations from Department of the Army, *Field Manual 100-23: Peace Operations* (Washington, DC: Headquarters, Department of the Army, December 1994), v. Italics original. Department of the Army, *Field Manual 3-07.31: Multi-Service Tactics, Techniques, and Procedures for Conducting Peace Operations* (October 26, 2003) elaborates practical implications of many of these dilemmas, often with reference to recent operations experience.

Of course, force can facilitate settlement in a variety of ways (as the army field manual goes on to describe) but this notion that the goal is negotiated settlement creates practical dilemmas for military personnel using force in at least two important ways.

First, it requires a kind of impartiality and even-handedness that is complicated to execute in practice. Militaries are being asked to fight _for_ principles but not _against_ any bad guys in these situations. This differs from standard war fighting, where there are clearly enemies. It also differs from policing (another possible model of behaviour imposed on militaries in these situations) because there are no criminals one can round up and take to jail. The political end in these humanitarian interventions is neither victory (as in war fighting) nor justice (as it is in policing). The political end is some kind of reconciliation among people who are doing horrible things to each other. To achieve reconciliation, interveners have to treat all parties as if they were dealing in good faith (even when they are not) and treat them with a kind of even-handedness and impartiality. In the humanitarian intervention model of using force, you have to make peace with the criminals, not lock them up.[22]

How one implements this kind of impartiality on the ground is not clear and civilian decision makers are not always providing a lot of guidance to militaries on these questions. We as civilians are supposed to be controlling our militaries, which means providing guidance, but we have not thought through this problem politically or ethically. We want militaries to 'enforce peace' but at the same time we do not want them to mess up possibilities for a political settlement by making anyone mad. Situations such as the reluctance of NATO's IFOR troops to arrest war criminals in Bosnia, even though they intervened precisely to stop this kind of criminal behaviour, are one logical outcome of this. Such action is the product of this underlying tension between the need for political settlement and the 'enforcement' of law and justice.

A second consequence for militaries of having settlement, rather than victory, as a goal is that it makes it difficult or impossible to enter these operations with a clear 'exit strategy' already mapped out. Americans, perhaps because they have been scarred by the Vietnam experience,

---

[22] Eventually, some criminals may be named and efforts may be made to round them up, as in Bosnia or Rwanda, but this happens only much later, and very incompletely. It provides little guidance for initial interveners on the ground.

have been particularly fearful of military 'quagmires' and have put pressure on those proposing humanitarian interventions to demonstrate that US forces can get in and get out again in a tidy and timely fashion. Increasingly, it appears politically impossible to put US troops into a humanitarian crisis for assistance purposes without a clear plan for getting them out again. The problem is that, if the goal is settlement and reconciliation among the local belligerents, US commanders do not control that outcome; other people do. If you do not control achievement of the goal (settlement), it is difficult to plan for an exit after achieving it since you cannot know how long settlement will take or the terms on which it will be achieved. Often, the terms of settlement involve prolonged stays by intervening troops to guarantee the agreement and provide a secure environment in which reconciliation and rebuilding processes can begin. The more of these interventions we do, the more we are learning that the political requirements within intervening states for deploying troops in these crises (quick in, quick out, home by Christmas) run directly counter to some of the basic functional needs of achieving lasting settlement in the target states.

A third important operational norm that flows from this need for impartiality to achieve settlement but makes these interventions logistically difficult is multilateralism. As John Ruggie and his colleagues have noted, this is an extremely powerful norm in contemporary politics that permeates all kinds of political interaction. Particularly since the end of World War II, multilateralism has become essential to legitimate all kinds of decisions and exercises of authority in world politics.[23] Humanitarian interventions have been no exception. States very much want authorisation by some prominent international organisation condoning their intervention and, if possible, they want multilateral participation by other states in the enterprise. This has most often translated into intervention by an international organisation rather than by a state or states in their individual capacity. The UN has been the most frequent intervener in humanitarian disasters but well-publicised institutional weaknesses of that organisation have resulted in diversification of the organisations who intervene, rather than a move towards unilateralism. NATO intervened in Kosovo; the Economic Community of West African States Monitoring Group (ECOMOG) intervened in Liberia.

---

[23] John G. Ruggie (ed.), *Multilateralism Matters: Theory and Praxis of an Institutional Form* (New York, NY: Columbia University Press, 1993).

This kind of multilateralism did not used to be a requirement for legitimate humanitarian intervention. In the nineteenth century states could (and did) intervene unilaterally for humanitarian purposes. However, unilateral intervention for humanitarian purposes seems to have disappeared.[24]

While multilateralism makes humanitarian interventions easier politically, it does not obviously have that effect logistically. Multilateralism is not the same as 'burden-sharing' among states since multilateralism often creates more costs than it reduces. Coordinating with other militaries, particularly those outside of NATO where training and equipment is not up to a common high standard or may not be interoperable, is a nuisance and would not usually be the Pentagon's first choice.[25] But the reason to do these interventions multilaterally is not logistical, but political. While it may not make lots of logistical or tactical sense to have troops from a variety of different national armies mixed together in the intervening force, such multinational participation sends a powerful message of broad support for the operation that is essential to legitimating it both overseas and with civilian publics back home.[26]

The role played by international organisations[27]

The role of international organisations in legitimating and executing these humanitarian interventions is one clear change in the normative structure within which we do these operations, but the change in their role is much broader. After the intervention, when we have achieved some kind of settlement, it is international organisations who are given the lead roles in reconstructing these states and societies. It is the UN,

---

[24] See Finnemore, 'Constructing Norms of Humanitarian Intervention', for an extended discussion of this change.

[25] Interviews with Pentagon officials. *FM3-07.31* tactfully phrases this as follows: 'Most PO [peace operations] are multinational in character. This multinational aspect brings legitimacy to the operation. However, it also creates challenges as each nation brings with it individual perspectives and unique capabilities', I-2.

[26] For an analysis of these dynamics with particular attention to the 2003 Iraq conflict see Martha Finnemore, 'Fights about Rules: The Role of Efficacy and Power in Changing Multilateralism', *Review of International Studies* 31 (2005), 187–206.

[27] This section draws heavily on Michael Barnett and Martha Finnemore, *Rules for the World: International Organizations in Global Politics* (Ithaca, NY: Cornell University Press, 2004).

the Organisation for Security and Cooperation in Europe (OSCE), the World Bank and innumerable humanitarian assistance NGOs that implement the settlement agreement and make the myriad consequential decisions on the ground that will determine the fate of the people whom the interveners acted to save.[28] The reasons for this are worth exploring because they say something about the nature of authority in contemporary politics as well as the sources of legitimacy.

The role of IOs in legitimating and implementing these interventions is related to several characteristics of the kinds of process-oriented end states we now view as legitimate, discussed earlier. First, there is a perception that IOs will somehow be impartial, at least more impartial than any state, in the implementation of internationally legitimate processes for choosing new governments (like elections.) No one would even consider asking a national government to come in and run elections in Bosnia, Kosovo, Cambodia or East Timor. The only entities that have this kind of authority are international bodies. Related, there is a sense that IOs embody some kind of 'international will', international opinion or some generally accepted principles that are broader than the interests or views of any one state. This kind of representativeness adds to the credibility of these organisations in a world where consensual and participatory decision making are the most legitimate forms of decision making in political life. Finally, IOs are now able to lay claim to some amount of expertise in the business of reconstructing states and running elections. At a minimum, they have experience at it, which is often equated with expertise.

The fact that impartiality, expertise and a commitment to principles over particularistic interests contributes to authority and legitimacy is suggestive. It suggests that we are investing more authority internationally now in rational/legal bodies in much the same way Max Weber observed a century ago at the national level. International organisations are, after all, bureaucracies, and we are busily bureaucratising 'global governance' of all kinds, including humanitarian intervention, in much the way Prussia was bureaucratising domestic governance in the late nineteenth century. It is therefore worth entertaining the possibility that the reasons for this and the implications of this may be similar to the ones Weber identified.

---

[28] Current moves at the UN to institutionalise this function in a new Peacebuilding Commission underscore the growing importance and acceptance of this role.

Weber recognised that bureaucracies and organisations run on a very particular form of authority – rational/legal authority. It is a form of authority legitimated by both the impersonal rules through which it works (which we tend to see as fair and equal because they are impersonal) and by its reliance on deploying expertise and specialised knowledge to solve problems (which we tend to think must be more effective). It is a form of authority that modernity particularly values and views as legitimate and ethically 'good'. Certainly the general impersonal rules by which bureaucracies exercise their power are widely viewed as more legitimate and more authoritative than other sources of authority that have commanded respect in the past – dynastic affiliation, religion or even simply the will of Great Powers. In contrast to these, the rational/legal authority of IOs appears principled, impartial (ergo fair) and knowledgeable. These IOs, after all, are staffed by 'experts' in their areas of speciality who have clear, rational procedures for what they do (at least in theory).

This trend, whereby we create more organisations, treaties, regimes, international laws and other rational/legal authorities to govern international life, has broad implications for world politics. It means that in many contexts, international organisations like the UN and OSCE are more legitimate actors than individual states. States, after all, are generally understood to be safeguarding their own particularistic interests; indeed, state leaders have an ethical duty to safeguard their citizens. IOs, by contrast, are both products and producers of general, impersonal and international rules of accepted, civilised behaviour. They are created by treaties – generalised rational/legal rules – and (in theory) act according to those rules. As a consequence, IOs become uniquely legitimate actors in world politics. They can do things that individual states cannot legitimately do, for example reconstruct other states. If a state unilaterally were to go into a humanitarian crisis situation in another state and stop the killing, organise a new government and try to reconstruct that society by itself, these actions would be viewed as a form of colonialism and the government viewed as a puppet.[29] For this kind of reconstruction to be legitimate, it must be done by IOs.

As with other features of the normative landscape, however, this role for IOs is not without its problems. The same qualities that make IOs

---

[29] States do, of course, take this kind of action anyway at times. Other states may accept these actions as inevitable in certain situations, but will not accept them as legitimate. To the extent interveners value legitimacy, they will work through IOs.

authoritative and legitimate – their impersonal rules and their use of expertise – can also lead IOs to behave in self-defeating ways that undermine their overall missions. IOs can become so attached to their impersonal rules that the rules become ends in themselves, eclipsing the goals for which the rules were chosen in the first place. For example, IOs have clear rules for choosing new governments in reconstructing humanitarian crisis states: new governments must be the product of elections. IOs may be right that, in general, elections produce more stable and just governments, but in particular instances they can be destabilising. However, rules are rules, and IOs often proceed with elections even when they know that elections will be divisive and destabilising. Similarly, the Office of the United Nations High Commissioner for Refugees (UNHCR) has rules about how it treats refugees that lead it to provide aid to all-comers, regardless of their political opinions. These rules flow naturally from the humanitarian first principles which the organisation embodies but in practice may prove counterproductive. In Congo, for example, UNHCR found itself sheltering many of the same Hutu *interhamwe* militia members who had committed the genocide from which the refugees had fled. Further, the UNHCR found its camps being taken over by these militias who began to use them as bases for renewed anti-Tutsi attacks across the Rwandan border.

These dysfunctional tendencies in IOs may not be any worse than the flaws in other possible methods of accomplishing these reconstruction tasks. They may, in fact, be preferable. My point is only that we are offloading large pieces of these humanitarian operations onto international organisations without thinking through the adequacy of these entities for their assigned tasks. Some inadequacies are clear and have been widely discussed: IOs have insufficient resources and some, like the UN, were not designed for the kinds of military missions with which they have been charged in recent years. Other relevant features of these IOs have been less fully thought through. One such feature is the paradox that the same features that make bureaucracies effective and legitimate at performing complex social tasks (their rules and expertise) can also make them ineffective and dysfunctional. Another neglected feature of this relocation of authority to international bureaucracies is its consequences for accountability and representation. Max Weber understood very well that bureaucracy, for all its virtues, would also be unresponsive, repressive and unaccountable. What recourse, for example, do citizens in Bosnia or Kosovo have against the army of international civil servants and NGO staff who decide the outlines of their reconstructed polity? What methods do they have to demand accountability? As we expand the scope of authority for IOs, it is becoming clear that the 'democracy deficit' is not simply a problem for the European Union. The repeated demonstrations surrounding meetings of the World Trade Organisation (WTO), IMF, World Bank and G8 are evidence that this is a broad problem of global governance, and its impacts on people at the receiving end of humanitarian interventions require some extended consideration.

Moral dilemmas and constructivist analysis

It is hardly original to argue that humanitarian interventions are difficult to carry out. The question I have tried to engage is why, exactly, these operations are so difficult and why success is often elusive. They are not just difficult technically or logistically, although they may well be that. They are also difficult normatively in ways that only become apparent by taking normative structures seriously and analysing their effects.

Constructivist analysis cannot make moral conflict disappear but it does have important uses in these situations. One thing it can do is clarify, not just the norms in conflict, but *for whom* they are in conflict. It highlights the ethical referents of the analyst. The dilemmas I have sketched above are only dilemmas from a particular ethical perspective, one we might loosely call cosmopolitan or liberal. A realist might have a quite different normative orientation and assessment of these crises. Realists come in several varieties, but generally they would deny the existence of ethical duties across borders of the type entailed in cosmopolitan humanitarianism. They would be sceptical of any notion of universal human rights that required action on behalf of non-citizens. They also would not be terribly concerned about self-determination of foreign peoples. Realist ethics focus inward, on the national community. As George Kennan put it, 'The government is an agent, not a principal. Its primary obligation is to the *interests* of the national society it represents'.[30] Kennan goes on to voice scepticism about whether we can know what is right and moral for others, imposing our beliefs on

---

[30] George Kennan, 'Morality and Foreign Policy', *Foreign Affairs* 64:2 (1985/1986), 205–218 at 206, italics original. He is explicit a few lines down that these interests are primarily military security.

them. In the nasty arena of world politics, leaders do not have the luxury of worrying about other citizens in other states. Leaders' duties are to their citizens and their own political community. Meddling in the internal affairs of other states is a virtue only when it promotes one's own power and interests. Endangering or sacrificing one's own citizens to protect foreigners, particularly foreigners of no strategic value, is not only foolish but ethically dubious.[31] A realist would thus be much less troubled by the normative tensions described earlier. The fact that the world's contemporary normative structure is largely a liberal cosmopolitan one means she would have to formulate policies to serve her national interest within that structure of liberal social realities, but she would not lie awake at night worrying about dead and dying Bosnians, Rwandans or Sudanese, and she certainly would not worry about ensuring free elections and a democratic state for them at the cost of her own citizens' lives.

Another consequence of constructivist empirical analysis is to suggest a different view of history than that of the realists, one in which people play a role in making their own world and bear some responsibility for the world they make. Contrary to the realist view – that the basic dynamics of world politics are immutable and that our world is not different in essentials from that of the Athenians and Melians – constructivist analysis suggests that norms and norm structures *do* change and behaviour changes as a consequence. People's understandings of themselves, their relations to others, and of their desires, duties and interests change. World politics changes as a result. Empirical analysis of the history of humanitarian intervention makes this clear. Non-white, non-Christian people now can and do make claims on others for humanitarian assistance in a way unimaginable 100 or 200 years ago. Those claims are not always answered, as the Rwandans and Srebrenicans know well, but sometimes they are. Sometimes, indeed often, such claims mobilise transnational action through states, IGOs and NGOs on a global scale even when they do not produce military action. This is new. It is not part of some recurrent pattern of self-seeking power competition or some response to unfolding materialist

---

[31] For an extended discussion see Jack Donnelly, 'Twentieth-Century Realism'. In Terry Nardin and David R. Mapel (eds.), *Traditions in International Ethics* (New York, NY: Cambridge University Press, 1992), 85–111.

determinism (or, if it is, it is not clear how so). This is a change that arises from new social facts – new constructs of 'humanity', 'human rights' and 'responsibility to protect' – that are the products of human agency.

Third, a constructivist empirical analysis provides reasons to attend to the views of the weak, the marginalised, the 'done to' in world politics. Social facts like a universalised humanity, like human rights and responsibility to protect become powerful as they become broadly shared with deep conviction. As Sikkink points out in her chapter, one reason human rights norms are so powerful in contemporary life is that they are the product of negotiation among the world's states and have support among the world's peoples. These norms undergirding humanitarian intervention gain legitimacy among potential Western interveners and the publics in part because they have been supported by people all around the globe; they are not simply Western creations imposed on less powerful targets of intervention.

Constructivism's emphasis on such *inter*subjective understandings shifts our analytic focus in ethically important ways. Analytically, constructivist analysis creates space for, even demands, attention to the views of the many different actors involved in an intervention, since the legitimacy of an intervention, and to some extent its success, depends on the reactions of those upon whom intervention is visited. Views of the intervened upon, the 'done to', in these cases create political effects that analysts must study. The corollary of this view is that interveners must attend to the views of their targets if they are to formulate successful policies.

Assessing the views of target populations and, in particular, views of the marginalised in those places, is not always easy and not simply because of poor data. The intervened-upon often face their own normative dilemmas, as acute as any faced by interveners, and may be of mixed mind or split among themselves about the efficacy and ethics of foreign intervention. African National Congress support for sanctions against South Africa in the 1970s and 1980s was important in galvanising Western publics to pressure their governments, but different situations create different reactions. Lynch's discussion in this volume of reaction to sanctions against Iraq illustrates the opposite dynamics. Initial support for sanctions against Saddam among Arabs declined quickly as the human cost of sanctions was publicised in Arab media and elsewhere. As the extent of suffering caused by sanctions grew and became known outside Iraq, people's ethical calculus about whether the humanitarian costs were worth the benefits shifted, particularly in the Arab world.[32]

Views of target populations are also crucial to the success of post-intervention reconstruction efforts. No stable post-intervention politics are possible without some form of acceptance and local legitimacy for the regime interveners put in place. Emphasis in these operations on elections, 'ownership' of policies and programmes and local capacity-building are all practical effects of interveners' recognition that intersubjective understandings and normative judgements of the intervened-upon have powerful effects on the ground.

Finally, a constructivist analysis of these normative tensions does not lead us neatly to some blanket conclusion that, 'This should be our humanitarian intervention policy'. To the contrary, it shows why we should be suspicious of blanket prescriptions of this type. Formulating a general policy would require us to specify a priori which among several conflicting norms we will privilege regardless of circumstance or consequence, yet the ethics of these interventions depends very much on both.

Circumstances and context matter a great deal in deciding whether force is a moral response to humanitarian crisis. Attitudes of the victims, local politics in the target state, availability of willing interveners and motives of those interveners will all differ across cases and rightly should influence our judgements about whether intervention is desirable. Consequences, too, are integral to our moral judgements of these interventions. Violent intervention is a means, not an end. Whether humanitarian intervention is a good thing depends critically on whether it achieves, or can reasonably be expected to achieve, the moral goals proponents set for it and at what price. Again, this will vary. In some cases, there might be a straightforward military strategy that one could reasonably expect will save many lives at the cost of few. In other cases, applying standard ethical rules about inflicting harm proportional to good achieved might yield a much less certain result.

This crucial role of context and consequences means that judgements about the morality of humanitarian intervention cannot be left only to philosophers. Assessing context and consequences requires detailed knowledge of particular conflicts in particular parts of the world and

---

[32] See also Marc Lynch, *Voices of the New Arab Public: Iraq, al-Jazeera, and Middle East Politics Today* (New York, NY: Columbia University Press, 2006).

particular militaries that might intervene. Is intervention in Darfur a good thing? It depends in no small part on who intervenes with what military capacity, exactly what they would do and how locals might reasonably be expected to react. Ethical judgement about specific cases thus requires research and knowledge. It requires the best possible information and analysis about likely consequences of our actions.

The very mixed consequences of military intervention as a tool of human rights enforcement have been the subject of some soul-searching among humanitarians in recent years. Failures to act in Srebrenica and Rwanda and the resulting atrocities there persuaded many that military action was an essential tool for protection.[33] Subsequent interventions in Kosovo and Timor were hardly unmitigated successes, however. Kosovo raised big questions about which military means should be used. Charges that NATO forces did know or should have known that bombing would escalate ethnic cleansing were made loudly as were complaints about civilian casualties resulting from NATO's targeting civilian infrastructure it deemed important for Milosevic's political and military control.[34] Both Kosovo and Timor also raise questions about whether military means can create any kind of self-sustaining and self-determining polity. As Anne Orford points out, there is a powerful sense in which these interventions, even multilateral ones, have an 'imperial', even 'colonial' character that quashes the savagery of non-Western others (often ignoring roles played by the West in creating local tensions) and reconstructs target communities according to their preferred liberal capitalist model.[35] Humanitarian intentions do not, by themselves, make interventions moral. Knowledge of foreseeable consequences, shaped in part by learning from experience, must also play a role.

These changes – expanding humanity, giving voice to the targets of intervention, paying serious attention to likely consequences – would all

---

[33] For a history of this shift, see David Chandler, *From Kosovo to Kabul: Human Rights and International Intervention* (London: Pluto Press, 2002); Thomas Weiss, 'Principles, Politics, and Humanitarian Action', *Ethics and International Affairs* 13 (1999), 1–22.

[34] See for example Noam Chomsky, *Rogue States: The Rule of Force in World Affairs* (Cambridge, MA: South End Press, 2000), esp. chapter 3, and Edward Said, 'Protecting the Kosovars' at www.zmag.org/ZMag/saidkosovar.htm. For a very different analysis see Wheeler, *Saving Strangers*, esp chapter 8.

[35] Anne Orford, *Reading Humanitarian Intervention: Human Rights and the Use of Force in International Law* (Cambridge: Cambridge University Press, 2003).

constitute something like moral progress in the view of many liberal cosmopolitans but one important lesson of this constructivist analytic exercise is to show that progress does not make dilemmas go away. Rather (and perhaps ironically), moral change, even moral progress, can create new dilemmas. We might think it 'progress' that people can now appeal for humanitarian intervention who previously were not even considered human, but more appeals for intervention are what create many of the paradoxes and dilemmas discussed above. Morally, most of us would not want to go back; ignoring genocides and atrocities would be moral regress. But the fact that we now have to think about these events and that our standards for successful outcomes are high (including both peace and democracy) means that we face new problems. Morally, this is what my grandmother might have called 'a fancy problem'; we agonise about these problems (to intervene or not, whether humanitarian ends justify violent means, what would constitute a moral and feasible outcome) but at least we now live in a world where such problems are entertained and choices about them are consciously made.

As the foregoing has shown, tensions in the normative structure surrounding humanitarian interventions are a large part of what makes them so difficult, operationally. It makes it difficult to craft politically acceptable solutions that will achieve the ends intended. In moral terms, however, these interventions may be difficult for the 'right' reasons. At the risk of some simplification, I suspect we are finding these operations difficult in part because we are demanding better (in ethical terms) policy solutions than we ever have before. Features of these interventions that plague us now were simply not matters of great concern to policy makers or publics fifty or one hundred years ago. In earlier eras, peace simply got imposed, repression was part of that process, and if a lot of locals got killed during these interventions, that was an unfortunate but necessary part of political life. Many of the paradoxes and tensions I have outlined here come about precisely because people are not willing to settle for this kind of solution any more. Interveners cannot simply impose a peace of their choosing; some kind of consent is required. International law now demands due process and other legal protections for perpetrators of genocide and ethnic cleansing.

Current efforts to deal with these humanitarian crises according to these more demanding ethical criteria may fail. Western interveners may get frustrated and simply stop intervening to help in these situations. But before we turn our backs, we should consider that part of the reason we are finding these situations so difficult is that we have raised the bar for ourselves and are holding ourselves to more demanding criteria than we ever have before. This strikes me as a reason to continue struggling with these contradictions and to be a bit more patient as we work towards solutions for these crises.

8 | Inevitable inequalities? Approaching gender equality and multiculturalism

ANN TOWNS

Introduction

Through the identification of previously understudied dynamics and mechanisms of change, constructivist analyses can provide new leverage on ethical dilemmas as well as distinctive guides for action. Drawing on the constructivist strand within International Relations (IR) concerned with identity/difference, I try to demonstrate that its (1) focus on self/othering practices, (2) deconstruction of taken-for-granted binaries and (3) demonstration of alternative, feasible interpretations of a problematic all have crucial ethical implications. Although there is no distinctive constructivist set of ethics as such, constructivism is nonetheless central to ethical action since it provides a unique understanding of how the world operates. This, in turn, opens new possibilities for thinking about ethical dilemmas and shows distinctive venues for action. Constructivist scholarship, like the study of international relations in general, is unavoidably normative.

The empirical focus of this chapter is the presumed contradiction between multiculturalism and gender equality, a contradiction which has become a topic of debate concurrent with a rising tide of international migration. The alleged contradiction between multiculturalism and gender equality presents an ethical dilemma for those committed to equality, as there is an apparent trade-off between gender equality and the equal worth of the value systems of different cultural groups. Assertions that the empowerment of women is uniquely and closely tied to Western values and beliefs have indeed become remarkably prevalent. As an illustration, Susan Okin argues that multiculturalism in Western countries is detrimental to women, since it is non-Western cultural traditions that presumably support male violence against women, female genital mutilation, rape and other deplorable practices. As a number of IR scholars have noted, cross-border movements of peoples have challenged established definitions of national identity.[1] In this chapter, I use the case of Sweden – often identified as the international vanguard of gender equality – as one arena where a national self is elaborated and defined in contrast with foreign/minority others.[2] In a discussion about the Swedish political left, prominent Swedish political scientist Bo Rothstein echoes Okin and sums up the dilemma well in contending that the left

> wants two things which cannot be realized simultaneously: gender equality and multiculturalism. Multiculturalism means that people's cultures [*folkliga kulturer*] should be considered of equal worth, none should be upheld or receive special support by the political system, especially not Western culture. According to the left, there are no particularly good values in, for instance, the Nordic or Western culture which should be promoted. Instead, all cultures have intrinsic value and should be equally affirmed.
>
> But sometimes this doesn't quite work ... in reality, what hides behind the calls for cultural recognition by very many different ethnic groups is severe, hopeless, cruel and inhuman oppression of women. In Sweden, this has affected a large number of young women of immigrant background.[3]

If we accept these terms of debate, there appears to be a direct conflict between gender equality and multiculturalism. The empowerment of women seems to necessitate the stigmatisation and degradation – even extinction – of non-Western cultures and the advancement of Western values. As Okin contends, non-Western women might 'be much better off if the culture into which they were born were either to be extinct or, preferably, to be encouraged to alter itself so as to reinforce the equality

---

[1] E.g. Francis Fukuyama, 'Identity and Migration', *Prospect* 131 (2007); Rey Koslowski (ed.), *International Migration and the Globalization of Domestic Politics* (New York, NY: Routledge, 2005); Ole Waever, Barry Buzan, Morten Kelstip and Pierre Lemiare (eds.), *Identity, Migration and the New Security Agenda in Europe* (London: Pinter Publishers, 1994).

[2] I would like to thank the Swedish Institute for International Affairs and the European Commission for the generous support that made this research possible. I am also indebted to the participants in the book project, and to the participants in the International Relations Colloquium of Göteborg University, Sweden, for providing helpful suggestions.

[3] Bo Rothstein, 'Multikulturellt kvinnoförtryck', *Göteborgs-Posten*, March 6, 2004, 2.

of women'.[4] For a constructivist who adopts equality as a starting premise, defining increases in equality as progress, what would be the ethical response to this dilemma of choosing between multiculturalism and gender equality?

Constructivism clearly does not provide a guide for prioritising among abstract principles, so there is little assistance in this regard. The approach simply cannot help us decide which of the two equality principles is more essential: gender equality or multiculturalism. Instead, among constructivists concerned with identity/difference, one first response might be the claim that *any* seemingly progressive development towards equality has an underbelly, since any attempt of embracing and validating practices as 'equal' provides standards for inequality by separating out and denigrating 'unequal' others. It is only to be expected that gender equality struggles have exclusionary effects, some constructivists may contend, since such consequences are an aspect of the Othering practices inherent in identity-formation. Even standards for identifying equality conditions have the effect of stigmatising and denigrating some actors as inferior, generating a hierarchy in the very attempts to overcome inequality.

I use the case of Sweden partly to make the argument that the discourse on gender equality of the past decade has become constitutive of ethnic difference and inequality in Sweden, defining gender equality as 'Swedish culture' and setting it apart from 'immigrant/non-Western culture', which is presumably patriarchal and dangerous to women. The chapter thus draws on IR scholarship on identity/difference, scholarship which has analysed international politics as the production of inside/outside boundaries.[5] An identity, such as the Swedish national identity with which this chapter is concerned, is a relational concept which

---

[4] Susan Moller Okin, *Is Multiculturalism Bad for Women?* (Princeton, NJ: Princeton University Press, 1999), 22–23.

[5] E.g. David Campbell, *Writing Security: United States Foreign Policy and the Politics of Identity* (Minneapolis, MN: University of Minnesota Press, second edition, 1998); Roxanne Doty, *Imperial Encounters: The Politics of Representation in North–South Relations* (Minneapolis, MN: University of Minnesota Press, 1996); Naeem Inayatullah and David L. Blaney, 'Knowing Encounters: Beyond Parochialism in International Relations Theory'. In Yosef Lapid and Friedrich Kratochwil (eds.), *The Return of Culture and Identity in IR Theory* (Boulder, CO: Lynne Rienner Publishers, 1996), 65–84; Jennifer Milliken, 'Intervention and Identity: Reconstructing the West in Korea'. In Jutta Weldes, Mark Laffey, Hugh Gusterson and Raymond Duvall (eds.), *Cultures of Insecurity: States, Communities, and the Production of Danger* (Minneapolis, MN: University of Minnesota Press, 1999), 91–118; Iver B. Neumann, *Russia and the*

denotes the social meanings and practices through which a community becomes distinctively recognisable or known as such. It is only through contrast and differentiation from that which is unlike that the like can be identified and known as such. IR scholars have pointed to the ways in which international migrants may unsettle the imagined boundaries of national identity by crossing state borders.[6] Indeed, international migrants often become conceived as the Other within, a cross-border challenge to the coherence of the national community presumed to form the foundation of the nation-state.

There is a reluctance in previous IR literature on self/other processes of differentiation to expressly address the ethical implications of such work. It is possible to read an ethical stance into this strand of scholarship, however, which points to the futility of moral quests for equality or community. With this chapter, I want to emphasise that the identification and analysis of the denigrating effects of how gender equality has become approached should not, as a next logical step, *necessarily* lead a constructivist to reject gender equality struggles as futile and simply productive of new forms of inequality. Another option is to start from where we are, with the practical existence of an ethical standard, as Richard Price discusses in the introductory chapter to this volume. We may then explore, reveal and provide alternatives to the problems that inhere in the way gender equality and multiculturalism are presently approached.

In my case, this entails accepting as a premise that gender-based murder, physical violence, rape and sexual assault are reprehensible acts. I thus confine the discussion of gender equality to these violent practices. As a first step, I demonstrate the perilous Othering effects of

Idea of Europe: A Study in Identity and International Relations (London: Routledge, 1996); Iver B. Neumann, 'Self and Other in International Relations', *European Journal of International Relations* 2:2 (1996), 139–74; Iver B. Neumann, 'European Identity, EU Expansion, and the Integration/Exclusion Nexus', *Alternatives* 23:3 (1998), 397–416; Iver B. Neumann, *Uses of the Other: 'The East' in European Identity Formation* (Minneapolis, MN: University of Minnesota Press, 1999); Bahar Rumelili, 'Liminality and Perpetuation of Conflicts: Turkish–Greek Relations in the Context of Community-Building by the EU', *European Journal of International Relations* 9:2 (2003), 213–248; Ann Towns, 'Paradoxes of (In)Equality: Something is Rotten in the Gender Equal State of Sweden', *Cooperation and Conflict* 37:2 (2002), 157–179; Weldes *et al.*, *Cultures of Insecurity*; Jutta Weldes, 'The Cultural Production of Crises: U.S. Identity and Missiles in Cuba'. In Weldes *et al.*, *Cultures of Insecurity*, 35–62.
[6] E.g. Waever *et al.*, *Identity, Migration and the New Security Agenda in Europe*; Campbell, *Writing Security*; Towns, 'Paradoxes of (In)Equality'.

how these ills are conceptualised and combated in order to argue that if equality is a criterion to assess moral progress, then these exclusionary effects need to be incorporated in the moral calculus guiding action. If one insists on pointing to 'immigrant culture' as a culprit for male abuse of women, then the implications of stigmatising immigrants need to be carefully considered and weighed. One needs to be able to ethically justify and take responsibility for, rather than plead ignorance of, the deleterious effects of approaching gender equality in such a way.

The deconstruction of widely taken-for-granted binaries provides a second constructivist way to approach the ethical problem presented by the alleged conflict between gender equality and multiculturalism. A second step in an analysis that begins with 'where we are' involves putting in question the feasibility of interpreting a problem a certain way, revealing the unexamined assumptions that underlie predominant approaches to a problem. My chapter attempts to show that the widely accepted distinction between 'Swedish' and 'immigrant' cultures, as two groups of people with mutually exclusive and internally consistent sets of gender values, is untenable. Neither label does what it sets out to do: delineate two categories of people that exhibit distinctive views on gender equality. The chapter brings to the fore the problematic presumptions that have to be accepted in order to claim that there is a conflict between values held by Swedes and immigrants around gender equality.

My argument is not simply that the Swedish/immigrant binary is based on stereotypes rather than well-grounded evidence, however. The argument reaches further than that. The very distinction between 'Swedes' and 'immigrants' is difficult to maintain – it is far from clear who is a Swede and who is an immigrant, as will be elaborated in the chapter. Since the distinction is so difficult to make, there *are* no two given categories whose cultures can be said to align in favour of or against gender equality. If no clear line can be drawn between Swedes and immigrants so that we can classify people, it becomes impossible to assess and compare the gender values and practices of each group. The risk is that gender equality itself becomes a criterion for classification: by embracing gender equality, a person becomes identified as Swedish. Gender-equality-as-Swedish-culture then becomes true by definition, an unfalsifiable truth claim.

Revelations about what appears as given can provide 'freedom from unacknowledged constraints', as Richard Ashley and many others have argued.[7] And the deconstruction of the Swede/immigrant binary should provide release from the equality conundrum as posited by Rothstein and others. If this chapter is successful, it should become clear that the presumed contradiction between multiculturalism and gender equality in Sweden is a product of a problematic conceptualisation of culture and cultural groups. It should become clear that there is no necessary trade-off between multiculturalism and gender equality as conceptualised in Sweden. A constructivist analysis can thus resolve an ethical dilemma by casting it in a different light, showing that it may not be an ethical dilemma at all.

This leads to the third and final contribution of constructivist analyses – showing alternatives, other possible and feasible ways of conceptualising a problematic. In her contribution to this volume, Kathryn Sikkink underscores the importance of being inspirational and of not simply pointing to the problems in the present order of things. Being inspirational in terms of setting out plausible alternatives has not been central to constructivist analyses concerned with identity/difference, which have tended to leave such alternatives implicit. Because of space constraints, this chapter stops short of developing anything near a substitute approach to understanding rape, male violence against women and male murder of female partners. It nevertheless provides some – hopefully inspirational – sketches of alternatives in several ways. The chapter begins by showing how immigration and gender equality were conceptualised in Sweden before the culturalist framework became predominant in the 1990s. Additional alternative interpretations will then be introduced as points of comparison to the present view of culture and gender equality throughout the chapter. In the conclusion, I provide some brief additional suggestions of how one may think about the role of culture in male abuse of women.

The three present tasks – the demonstration of Self/Othering practices, the deconstruction of the Swede/immigrant binary and the presentation of alternative, feasible interpretations – are interwoven in the chapter, which is divided into three sections. The first provides a brief background elaboration on ethnicity in Sweden and a note on methodology. The second section provides an empirical analysis of the discourse of gender equality and immigration in Sweden, showing the shifts between the

---

[7] Richard Ashley, 'Political Realism and Human Interests', *International Studies Quarterly* 25 (1981), 227.

1970s and the present understanding of gender equality as values and practices that set apart Swedes from others. The chapter concludes with a discussion of the perils of the present culturalist approach to gender equality and sketches some alternatives.

Immigrants and Swedes as technical and ethnic categories

For a reader who is not familiar with the politics of immigration and multiculturalism in Sweden, a brief background discussion is in place. The understanding of what immigrants *are* and their place in the ethnic landscape in Sweden is quite distinct from societies such as the United States. Prior awareness of a few important points will ease the subsequent reading.

Technical immigrants ≠ ethnic immigrants. A first, important point to note is that actual, technical immigration to Sweden is only loosely related to becoming identified as an 'immigrant' in public policy, the media and other public fora. Around 12 percent of the population in Sweden is foreign-born and has technically immigrated to Sweden, one of the highest ratios in Europe.[8] If we expand the technical definition of immigrants to include people who have at least one parent who has immigrated to Sweden – a group referred to as 'second generation immigrants' or Swedes with an 'immigrant background' in official statistics – then the present ratio of immigrants in Sweden is around 26 percent.[9] In the technical sense, between 12 and 26 percent of the Swedish population is classified as first or second generation immigrant.

Being an immigrant does not simply refer to having immigrated to Sweden, however, it also carries ethno-national meaning, indicating whether a person has adopted 'Swedish' values and habits and speaks Swedish properly. Immigrants in this ethnic sense is a broad label for 'people who do not have Swedish identity', in the words of a former Minister of Immigration.[10] In contrast with the United States, where

[8] SCB – Statistiska Centralbyrån, *Tabeller över Sveriges befolkning 2004* [Tables on the Swedish Population 2004] (Örebro: SCB, 2005), 165.
[9] Marie Demker and Cecilia Malmström, *Ingenmansland? Svensk immigrationspolitik i utrikespolitisk belysning* (Lund: Studentlitteratur, 1999), 116.
[10] Former Minister of Immigration Maj-Lis Lööw, as quoted in *Svenska Dagbladet*, 'Staten vill diskriminera svenskar och invandrare', March 28, 1996.

one can simultaneously identify as American and of immigrant background, Swedes and immigrants are primarily understood as mutually
exclusive categories. These are not seen as compatible, in other words,
and it is difficult for a person to be identified as both Swedish and of
some sort of immigrant background. What is more, immigrants and
Swedes have become the most important ethnic classifications in public
policy and the media.

The technical classification as an immigrant is only loosely related
to becoming identified as an immigrant in the ethnic sense. Many, many
people who have immigrated or whose parents immigrated to Sweden
never become identified as immigrants in the ethnic sense. And many
people who were born in Sweden and have no experience of living in
another country are nonetheless labelled immigrant and thus non-
Swedish.

Although the differentiation of Swedes and immigrants in the ethnic
sense is the subject of the subsequent analysis, an additional point is
worthy of mention. It is important not to presume an equation between
'race' and immigrant standing in Sweden, assuming ethnic immigrants
to be non-whites in the US sense of the term. The differentiation
between Swedes and immigrants does not primarily rest on certain
physical features or skin colour. While physical features are not entirely
unimportant, being an immigrant is not a proxy or euphemism for being
non-white in Sweden. As an example, many of the large groups of
immigrants from Finland and the former Yugoslavia have been constituted as 'immigrants' in the ethnic sense (whereas those from Norway
and Denmark have generally not). Having internalised 'Swedish
values', behaving in 'Swedish' ways and speaking Swedish with no
trace of a foreign accent are much more important markers of being
an ethnic immigrant than are physical features.

The determination of who is a Swede and an immigrant in the non-
technical, ethnic sense is a complicated, fluid and contextual process.
There are simply no clear and firm criteria of differentiation that
hold across context. It is telling that many individuals are expressly
unsure about whether they identify as Swedish, and they may do so
under some circumstances and not others. What is more, ethnic fluidity
has been a conscious if contradictory political strategy since the mid-
1970s, when the government officially declared Sweden to be a multicultural society in which technical immigrants were promised the
opportunity to choose the extent to which they adopt a Swedish

cultural identity.[11] Public registration of ethnic identity – even if based on self-labelling as in the USA – has not been used in Sweden since World War II. Recent suggestions to create ethnic data have met massive resistance. Given the fluidity of the distinction and the reluctance to document ethnic identification, there is simply no data available that sorts ethnic Swedes from ethnic immigrants, even in terms of basic numbers. The resulting difficulty of making general, well-founded claims about ethnic Swedes and immigrants should be obvious.

That said, differentiations between Swedes and immigrants are nonetheless constantly made and do have effects. And as the standards of differentiation shift, so does the classification. The focus of this chapter is the view that gender values and practices – culture – is characteristic of 'Swedes' and 'immigrants' as two distinctive cultural groups. While predominant, this view has certainly not lacked contestation. It is this predominant approach that is the subject of the chapter, however, which means that the challenges and objections are largely left out of the analysis.

This chapter looks at the shifting representations of 'Swedes' and 'immigrants' through the lens of gender equality primarily in the main daily newspapers. For the examination of press representations, I used the index *Svenska Tidningsartiklar* [*Swedish Newspaper Articles*] from 1975 to the present, which lists titles and a summary of the contents of articles in the major newspapers. For the periods when there was a drastic increase in articles on the gender oppression of 'immigrant' women, I used the University of Göteborg library for a close textual reading of nearly one hundred relevant articles.

---

[11] In the mid-1960s, the term 'immigrant' officially replaced the former 'foreigner'. In the mid-1970s, public policy was elaborated for 'immigrants' and 'minorities' under a common label: 'immigrants and minorities'. The 'immigrants and minorities' policy thus combined 'minorities' (identified as Jews, gypsies, Saamis, Estonians, Tornedal Finns and a few other groups whose history in Sweden was as long as that of non-'minorities') with people who had recently immigrated to Sweden and their offspring for an unspecified number of generations. The assumption was that all 'immigrants' would eventually become 'minorities', an assumption with very little support in the long history of immigration to Sweden. In the mid-1980s, authorities realised that 'immigrants' did not fit the international 'minority' definition, and once again the two categories were separated. In the early 1990s, it was suggested that 'immigrant' encompass persons who were of non-EC citizenship and who had lived in Sweden less than five years. The definition was, then, in essence the same as the 'foreigner' of the 1960s, as one cannot be naturalised in less than five years.

Gender equality and the differentiation between Swedes and immigrants

The understandings of what it means to be 'Swedish' and 'immigrant' have changed significantly during the post-World War II period. These changes are not the given result of migration patterns and the meeting of peoples with set characteristics. Instead, the criteria for differentiating between Swedes and immigrants have altered through much more complicated processes. As we will see below, it was not until the 1990s that culture in general, and gender equality values and practices in particular, came to be seen as primary distinguishing principles between Swedes and immigrants.

Throughout the twentieth century and contrary to popular belief, a fairly steady stream of people of non-Swedish citizenship has immigrated to Sweden. In the years immediately after the war, 122,000 Nordic refugees, 45,000 Germans and 30,000 people from the Baltic region came to Sweden, though some of them did not remain permanently. Immigration has since ebbed and flowed, with 1970 and 1994 the years of largest immigration since the immediate post-war period.[12] Neither academia nor the press paid much attention to the issue, although occasional articles appeared, many of which pointed to Finnish immigrants in particular as a social hygiene hazard.

1960s–1980s: immigrants and Swedes through work

From the 1960s to the mid-1980s, the Swedish social and public landscape was dominated by a largely Marxian ontology (with Social Democratic modifications) that centred on work, class conflict and economic inequalities. This world view provided a particular lens from which to make sense of Swedish society, its actors and the processes productive of social outcomes. This lens helped interpret and give meaning to the large groups of people who immigrated from Yugoslavia, Italy, Turkey and Greece during the late 1950s and early 1960s, the thousands of Polish Jews, Hungarians and Czechs as well as Portuguese, Spaniards and Greeks who fled authoritarianism to Sweden during the same period, and to the increase in non-European immigration of refugees that began in the mid-1970s. A large number of people representing a wide

---

[12] Demker and Malmström, *Ingenmansland?*.

span of nationalities, religious affiliations, political ideologies, sexual orientations, educational levels, ages and so on, in addition to unique life histories, immigrated to Sweden between the 1960s and late 1980s. The problems and well-being of immigrants and Swedes were nonetheless fitted into a single framework of work and the economy. Immigrants were discussed primarily as labour, and the media representations centred on the risks of immigrants ending up at the bottom of Swedish class society.[13] Class struggle and production, not culture, were understood as the driving forces of the social world.

Through these lenses, it was difficult to see either gender or women in arenas other than work. Although violence against women was prevalent in practice throughout Swedish society, as Lindvert argues, these lenses discouraged the identification of violence against women as a public problem.[14] Instead, discussions of gender equality in the 1960s and 1970s were largely centred on integrating women into the paid labour market. Public daycare, employment in the public sector and paid parental leave were understood as central components for increasing the status of women, Swedes and immigrants alike.

Gender equality in general, and violence against women in particular, was thus still not something presented as distinguishing Swede from immigrant. It is important to make note of this fact, since much of the gender-related public policy which is now upheld as distinctively Swedish was in place or under construction during this period. In fact, until the late 1970s, the discussions of immigrants continued to pay virtually no attention to women. Instead, immigrants in these accounts often seem to have *men* as a referent, with the immigrant problematic defined thereafter. Although employment was seen as central to integration and a successful life, work was also presumed to be the source of many of the integration problems of immigrants: culture shocks, discrimination and so on. With women immigrants less exposed to paid work, they were presumably also sheltered from these problems.

[13] David Schwarz, *Svenska minoriteter. En handbok som kartlägger invandringspolitiken och befolkningsminoriteternas ställning inom det svenska samhället* (Stockholm: Adlus/Bonniers, 1971); Billy Ehn, 'Kamouflerad försvenskning'. In B. Ehn, Jonas Frykman and Orvar Löfgren (eds.), *Försvenskningen av Sverige: Det nationellas förvandlingar* (Stockholm: Natur och Kultur, 1993), 259.
[14] Jessica Lindvert, 'A World Apart: Swedish and Australian Gender Equality Policy', *Nora: Nordic Journal of Women's Studies* 10:2 (2002), 99–107.

By the mid-1980s, political refugees emerged as the primary group of technical immigrants to Sweden. Nearly thirty thousand Iranians and tens of thousands of Iraqis (many of them Kurds) as well as thousands of Somalis, Ethiopians, Vietnamese and Latin Americans immigrated to Sweden in the 1980s.[15] At this time, gender oppression was still not often associated with the culture of immigrants, nor was gender equality predominantly presented as a specifically Swedish characteristic. In fact, gender equality was sometimes represented as a *threat* to the continuity of Swedish culture rather than a part of it, as women's entrance into the paid labour market was thought to have wide-reaching cultural consequences.[16]

During the 1980s, researchers and the media took a growing interest in the position of immigrant women as workers.[17] The immigrant worker thus ceased to be male by default. A number of reports centred on the risks of immigrant women being squeezed out of the labour market as a result of changes in production processes,[18] and on the risks of occupational injuries associated with their monotonous and physically stressful job situations.[19] The framework for understanding the well-being of immigrant women (and men) was thus still largely that of capitalist production and the labour market.

Mid-1990s–present: immigrants and Swedes through culture

'Yesterday another immigrant woman was murdered – for cultural reasons.'[20]

---

[15] Demker and Malmström, *Ingenmansland?*, 48.
[16] See e.g. Errand Bergman and Bo Swedin, *Solidaritet och konflikt: etniska relationer i Sverige* (Stockholm: Carlssons, 1986), 82.
[17] E.g. Margareta Matocic, 'Arbetets värde för jugoslaviska kvinnor inom kommunal- och fabriksarbetarförbundets avtalsområde', *De invandrade kvinnornas situation i arbetslivet*, Report no. 5/86 (Stockholm: Jämfo/DEIFO, 1986).
[18] E.g. Karen Davies and Johanna Esseveld, *Att hoppa hage i den svenska arbetsmarknaden: en studie av arbetslösa fabrikskvinnor* (Stockholm: Rabén och Sjögren, 1988); DEIFO, *Invandrarnas situation i Arbetslivet*, Report no. 9. Commission for Immigrant Research, Ministry of Labour (Stockholm: DEIFO, 1987); Wuokko Knocke, *Invandrade kvinnor i lönearbete och fack* (Stockholm: Arbetslivscentrum, 1986).
[19] E.g. Christina Jonung, *Report to the OECD on the Integration of Migrant Women into the Labour Market*, Commission for Immigration Research, (Stockholm: EIFO, 1982).
[20] *Aftonbladet*, February 10, 1997.

During the 1990s, in line with international developments, the ontology which presented class conflict and work as a foundation for approaching the world was thoroughly challenged in a number of ways in Sweden. Following the broader cultural turn internationally, the conception of Sweden as multicultural and of Swedes as 'a culture' had a major breakthrough.

The scale and implications of this transformation are rather extraordinary. Throughout most of the post-war period in Sweden, sharing a national culture had rarely and only peripherally been understood as a factor that distinguished Swedes from others.[21] In fact, it was widely accepted that being Swedish largely rested on a rejection of nationalism and patriotism – speaking of values and practices as specifically 'Swedish' and thus superior would paradoxically negate a person's Swedishness. Now, however, 'culture' and 'cultural difference' entered the discussions of immigrants and Swedes alongside production and work.[22]

The mid-1990s saw a second crucial development in the Swedish social landscape: gender equality became expressly and strongly associated with Sweden and Swedish values. As such, gender equality became a framework for classifying people as 'Swedes' and 'immigrants'. It is beyond the scope of this chapter to discuss how this came about at length.[23] The crucial point is that the identification of gender equality as a set of specifically Swedish values was not an effect given simply by immigration itself. Instead, a complex series of international and domestic events led up to this association. For instance, the United Nations and the Inter-Parliamentary Union both pronounced Sweden to be the world's most gender equal country in 1995. This received an enormous amount of attention in Sweden and touched off a series of articles with headlines such as 'Sweden got Prize in Gender Equality', 'Sweden a Champion on Gender Equality' and 'Sweden Best at Electoral Gender Equality'.[24]

Sweden's entry into the European Union is another important factor, as this generated a host of comparative studies and newspaper articles

[21] E.g. Ehn, 'Kamouflerad försvenskning', 259.
[22] E.g. Demker and Malmström , *Ingenmansland?*, 106; Aleksandra Ålund and Carl-Ulrik Schierup, *Paradoxes of Multiculturalism: Essays on Swedish Society* (Aldershot: Avebury, 1991).
[23] For a lengthier discussion, see Towns, 'Paradoxes of (In)Equality'.
[24] *Svenska Dagbladet*, September 8, 1995; *Dagens Nyheter*, September 8, 1995; *Svenska Dagbladet*, August 28, 1995.

on the status of women in Europe and Sweden between 1990 and 1995. In the steady stream of writing on how Europe looks to Sweden for gender equality that has developed since 1995, the reader can learn that 'Europe's women get advice in Sweden', 'The gender equal Swedish model – with extensive parental leave and public daycare – is exported to the EU' and 'Sweden is host for conference on gender equality'.[25] By ambiguously referring to both the Swedish state and Swedish values, such proclamations about Sweden have helped identify gender equality as a trait distinctive of Swedish culture.

The new cultural framework and the connection of gender equality with Swedish culture have created the ability to distinguish between and see 'immigrants' and 'Swedes' differently than previously possible. This development took place simultaneously with another surge in immigration in the early 1990s. Immigration from the former Yugoslavia increased dramatically as a result of the war, and former Yugoslavians came to constitute by far the largest group of immigrants of the 1980s and 1990s. Immigration from Iran, Iraq and the Horn of Africa continued as well, as did immigration from the Nordic countries, Europe and the rest of the world.

The connection of gender equality with Swedish culture has had the effect of sorting immigrant from Swedish women and approaching the oppression of immigrant women as distinctively rooted in the presumably different cultural values of their male partners and relatives. Headlines such as 'Oppression of Women as Culture' and 'A Cultural Question that is Abused' abounded in the late 1990s.[26] With the new cultural framework, journalists could now see patterns of behaviour where they may not have appeared previously. For instance, in the beginning of 1997, a mass of articles appeared in all the major papers, connecting a series of cases of male murder or of violence against female family members through 'immigrant culture'. The murder of an 'Iraqi' (sometimes confused with 'Iranian') girl in Umeå by her brother and cousin could now be connected with the murder of a 'Lebanese' woman by her ex-husband in Malmö. Murders and beatings of women by 'Kurds', 'Croatians', 'Kosovo-Albanians', 'Turks', 'Bosnians', 'Lebanese' and other men were connected as 'immigrant' and separated from violence at the hands of Swedish men.

---

[25] *Göteborgsposten*, May 5, 2000; *Dagens Nyheter*, January 23, 2001; *Göteborgsposten*, January 31, 1999.
[26] *Svenska Dagbladet*, February 27, 1997; *Arbetet Nyheterna*, February 11, 1997.

Similar causal narratives were reproduced and circulated in all the main papers: immigrant women were the victims of a 'clash of cultures', in which they sought the freedom that a Swedish lifestyle affords. The violence, in these accounts, constitutes 'retaliations against immigrant women who break family norms' and who attempt to 'live like Swedish girls, in other words, go to clubs and dance with unknown men'.[27]

It is important to note that the cultural divide that has become operative in Sweden cannot be equated with the alleged clash of values between the West and Islam. Instead, the interpretive framework combines this division with a distinction between the Protestant North and Catholic South, to produce a world in which only the 'culture' of Northern Protestant Europe is safe for women. The patriarchal culture of 'the Mediterranean countries, Northern Africa and the Middle East', rather than religion, is upheld as an explanation of gender-based violence.[28] As one article explains:

> the clan and tribe-world exists in many south European countries, especially around the Mediterranean. In southern Italy, southern Spain, Greece and North Africa, among other areas, the family is the most important thing of all. The man decides, and his authority is strongly associated with the women of the family. If they are seen as too sexually liberated, the man loses his status, and the man, or the men, must take action to defend the family's honour.[29]

The claims about immigrant culture and violence against women were legitimated in a particular way. Rather than the usual string of experts on violence used in the media – such as social workers, psychologists and the police – immigrants as such are used as informants to provide insights into the patriarchal culture presumed to shape their behaviour. Media reports became filled with explanations by the offenders themselves, with justifications such as 'she didn't follow an Arabic pattern of life' by a man who murdered his ex-wife, or 'you have to be a Muslim to

---

[27] *Svenska Dagbladet*, 'Patriarkat styr repressalier' [Patriarchy Controls Reprisals], February 8, 1997; *Svenska Dagbladet*, 'Hovrätt fastställde dom i syskondrama' [Court Establishes Verdict in Sibling Drama], April 26, 1997.

[28] E.g. *Aftonbladet*, 'Ett rykte kan leda till hedersmord' [A Rumour Can Lead to Honour Murder], January 22, 2002.

[29] *Arbetet Nyheterna*, 'En kulturell fråga som missbrukas' [An Abused Cultural Question], February 11, 1997. See also *Göteborgsposten*, February 16, 1998.

know why you do a thing like this'.[30] Through anthropological attempts
to find evidence and learn about the non-Swedish patriarchal culture that
prompts such crimes, reports from high schools and neighbourhoods rich
in immigrants appeared. As a typical example, *Arbetet Nyheterna* discusses a visit to Rosengård, an immigrant neighbourhood in Malmö:[31]

> **Women squashed in clash of cultures**
> – *In our culture boys have greater freedom, say immigrant girls
> at the Rosengård School.*
> Last Monday a Turkish woman was seriously stabbed by her own
> brother. She had brought disgrace upon her family by going to a
> dance club.
> Barely a month ago a woman was killed by her brother and cousin
> in Umeå.
> The meeting between the values of two cultures can be problematic.
> Not the least for the young immigrant girls who are often torn
> between the stringent rules of the family and the pull from the freer
> lifestyle of Western culture . . .
> Hebah Achichk [15 years old] has to be home at 9 p.m. If she wants
> to be out longer, she must be accompanied by her older brother. If a
> friend of the family saw her drinking alcohol it would burden her for
> the rest of her life. Pop music and clothes are easier, but Hebah is not
> allowed to wear skirts that are too short.
> – 'At the same time, I'm thankful to my parents for letting me do
> half of what Swedish girls do. They want me to have an education and
> do not wish for me to stay at home doing the dishes.'

With foreign patriarchal culture as the explanatory framework, it is
clear that *any* immigrant man becomes a potential perpetrator and all
immigrant women their possible victims:

> Incidents like those in Stockholm and Umeå could just as well happen
> in Rosengård, the youths think.

Initially, immigrant women were pointed to as the primary victims
of the non-Swedish patriarchal culture of violence. Soon, the view

---

[30] *Svenska Dagbladet*, 'Nytt mord på invandrarkvinna', February 10, 1997;
Aftonbladet, 'Fick inte följa islams tradition – slog ihjäl hustrun', February 11,
1997; *Göteborgsposten*, 'Brodern åtalad', February 5, 1997.
[31] *Arbetet Nyheterna*, January 9, 1997.

developed that gender violence by immigrants also constituted a rejection of and frontal attack on 'Swedish culture', personified by Swedish women. Whereas the violence against immigrant women who became too Swedish represents an indirect rejection of Swedish culture, 'immigrants' are now portrayed as actively seeking out Swedish women to take vengeance on a society that has failed them. This behaviour, and the rejection of gender equality that underlies it, has become presented as reversed racism and Swedish-hate (*svenskhat*). *Dagens Nyheter* (February 18, 2000) talks to four young Swedish and immigrant women:

All four notice the reversed racism, the racism that leads to some immigrants viewing Swedes as lesser beings.

– 'F***ing svenne [*approx. "Swedie"*], that's what they say,' Jessica says.

The article then equates calling a person a 'Swedie' with calling a person a 'nigger':

That's the equivalence of blatte [*approx. 'nigger'*]. And it is Swedish girls that are affected the most. Because they are whores as well. Svenne-whores . . .

By the early 2000s, immigrants were no longer seen as wholly determined by their 'culture of origin' but were also thought to be strongly shaped by social segregation in Sweden. The immigrant status of eight boys who gang-raped a Swedish 14-year-old girl in Rissne outside of Stockholm made great headlines in February of 2000, generating a host of articles on the attitude of immigrant men towards Swedish women. The view that immigrant men – pained by the indignities suffered in Swedish society and driven by patriarchal cultures – vented their frustrations on Swedish women produced headlines such as 'Girls Become Objects of Revenge' (*Dagens Nyheter* March 3, 2000) and 'They Despise Swedish Women' (*Dagens Nyheter* February 18, 2000).[32]

As before, immigrants were used as informant experts of the culture and life situation that prompted their actions. *Dagens Nyheter* (February 12, 2000) talks to a group of four 'immigrant' boys, representing people of Southern European and Middle Eastern origin:

---

[32] To be sure, these dominant representations were contested by less prominent accounts in which 'immigrants' and 'Swedes' were not dichotomised and in which common causes of gang rape were discussed (such as the role of pornography, group pressure and the failure of adults to intervene).

'It Can Happen To the Nicest Guy.'
– 'Now all immigrant guys will be labelled as f***ing *svartskallar* [people with black hair] that rape Swedish girls,' says Ali. His family comes from Turkey and lives in Rinkeby outside of Stockholm ...
– 'Now the racists will have something new to invoke,' he says. 'They have already been here, hollering about all the immigrants who want to rape Swedish women and who ought to be thrown out. So you have to have brothers and friends that help you fight if someone starts mouthing off to you.'
– 'Rinkeby had just started to get a good reputation,' Richard says. 'But now they talk a bunch of crap about all of us immigrants that live here.'

The difficult and exposed life situation of immigrants in segregated immigrant neighbourhoods, including the threat of racist violence, is presented as background knowledge for understanding why immigrants are hostile to Swedish women. Social segregation, like patriarchal culture, is presented as strongly determining of the behaviour of immigrant men.

None of the four think the rape was planned.
– 'It probably just happened,' Richard says. 'It can happen to the nicest guy, that he participates in a gang-rape.'

The last sentence – 'it can happen to the nicest guy' – which becomes the headline and thesis argument of this article like several others, is highly revealing and worthy of some reflection. In addition to being a threat to immigrant women, it now becomes clear that *any* immigrant, even the nicest among them, is a potential rapist of Swedish women.
To develop this point, the article demonstrates the immigrant boys' denigrating views of Swedish women:

It is a major crime to rape a woman, the four decide.
– 'But it is not as wrong to rape a Swedish girl as raping an Arabic girl,' Hamid says. 'The Swedish girl gets lots of help afterwards, and she has probably already f***ed. But the Arab girl will have trouble with her family. For her it is a big shame to be raped. It is important that she remains a virgin until she gets married.'
The other three sit silent. Nobody says that it is just as horrible for all women to be raped.

In case the message of the article was not already clear, the main thesis is then spelled out:

> **It was no coincidence** that it was a Swedish girl that was raped in Rissne – that is very clear from the conversation with Ali, Hamid, Abdallah and Richard. All four in some way look down on Swedish girls and claim that this attitude is common among young men with parents who have immigrated to Sweden . . .
>
> – 'It is much too easy to get a Swedish whore . . . no, girl, I mean,' Hamid says and his choice of words makes him crack an embarrassed grin . . . 'Many immigrant guys are with Swedish girls when they are teenagers. But then when they get married they take a real woman from their own culture who hasn't been with a guy. That's what I'll do. I don't have much respect for Swedish women. You can say that they are f***ed to shreds.'

The way in which the gang rape in Rissne was approached by the Swedish government is also instructive. It was *the Minister of Youth and Integration*, then Ulrica Messing of the Social Democrats, who intervened, and not the Minister of Gender Equality. Messing produced a debate article in response to the Rissne rape, entitled 'The Swedish-Hate Must Be Countered', presenting the gang rape as a problem of patriarchal immigrant views and a rejection of Swedish culture:

> The reports from Rissne had placed in focus a serious attitude question that we have not had the courage to debate earlier. It is the gravely prejudiced and sometimes aggressively hostile attitudes that can be found among some youths with a foreign background against native-born Swedes and against Swedish culture.[33]

As reversed racism, patriarchal immigrant culture no longer becomes a problem that primarily victimises immigrant or Swedish women. Instead, immigrant culture becomes an assault on Swedish culture itself. This has stimulated a number of media responses from well-known people who have not previously expressed much public interest in male violence against women. For instance, widely read popular historian Herman Lindqvist has argued that 'the murders and gross violations of young immigrant women in Sweden are more than a tragedy for those involved', continuing that 'Swedish society has to

[33] *Aftonbladet*, February 25, 2000.

make demands on those who want to live in our country... those that despise and reject Swedish culture and Swedish customs should not reside in Sweden'.[34]

This idea, that immigrant patriarchal culture presents an affront to the Swedish nation, has also generated an interest in male violence against women among extremist xenophobic forces. The two largest Nazi organisations in Sweden, *Nationalsocialistisk front* (National Socialist Front) and *Svenska Motståndsrörelsen* (The Swedish Resistance Movement) now both mobilise around gang rape, rape and violence against women, presenting these ills as a result of immigration. As one example among many, *Svenska Motståndsrörelsen* passed out fliers in Stockholm in response to an assault rape committed in October of 2005, 'to make clear that it was racial strangers [*rasfrämlingar*] who had committed the crime'.[35] Their adjacent report of the activities, published in the magazine *Nationellt Motstånd* (National Resistance), encourages demonstration that 'our young girls and women are not prey to those who do not even fulfil the basic requirements of civilisation. One's whole essence screams for an opportunity to show them! Anything but direct action is meaningless.'[36]

Feasible conceptualisation?

It should be clear from the previous discussion that gender equality has become strongly associated with Sweden and Swedish culture, distinguished from a patriarchal culture which predisposes immigrants to rape, abuse and sometimes murder women. At this juncture, I will provide a brief reflection on the unexamined assumptions that underlie this approach to the problem. What does one have to presume and accept in order for this understanding to make sense?

There are two primary if often implicit sets of empirical claims made among those that point to immigrant culture as a source of male violence against women. Both contain underlying assumptions needed for the cultural framework to make sense. The first is that immigrant men are much more prone to rape, physically abuse and murder women than are Swedish men. The second is that immigrant abuses of women

---

[34] *Aftonbladet*, February 15, 1997.
[35] Magnus Söderman, 'Motståndsrörelsen agerar mot våldtäkt', *Nationellt Motstånd*, October 25, 2005; www.patriot.nu/artikel.asp?artikelID=333.
[36] Ibid.

have entirely different causes than does Swedish violence. I will investigate each of these claims in turn.

Given the predominance of the first idea, that immigrant men are
more prone to rape and abuse women, the evidence is surprisingly scant
and shaky. A major problem is obviously the lack of stable categories in
Sweden – if there is no consensus and constancy in terms of who is an
'immigrant' and who is a 'Swede', it becomes impossible to compare
with any certainty the frequency of rape and male violence against
women between the two groups. There is simply no such data. This
alone makes any assertions about immigrants and Swedes, in the ethnic
sense, puzzling. Accepting this claim is largely a leap of faith.

There is some data on technical immigrants and Swedes, however.
The Swedish National Council on Crime Prevention has assembled data
of male violence against women in intimate relations (wife, girlfriend
or ex) reported to the police for the year 1998. This data compares
adult Swedes (born in Sweden to two Swedish-born parents) with
foreign-born immigrants and second generation immigrants (at least
one foreign-born parent).

The total annual number of cases of male abuse of women in intimate
relationships is estimated to be around 40,000 (only 20–25 percent of
which is actually reported to the police).[37] Second generation immigrants are only slightly overrepresented among the perpetrators compared with their ratio in the population as a whole (12 percent of
perpetrators, 9 percent of population). However, foreign-born residents
were overrepresented among male abusers of women in intimate relations, constituting 25 percent of the perpetrators while making up
11 percent of the general population in 1998. Technical Swedes,
in turn, made up 63 percent of the perpetrators while constituting
80 percent of the general adult population.[38]

So what can we learn from this data? One obvious mistake which
appears often to be made in the debate is to claim that at least 25 percent
of foreign-born men engage in physical abuse of their partners. Based on
the Council numbers, around 1.1 percent of foreign-born males physically battered a woman in 1998 (compared with 0.4 percent of

---

[37] 2001 numbers. Nilsson, for the Swedish National Council on Crime Prevention
(2002), 22.
[38] Swedish National Council on Crime Prevention, *Våld mot kvinnor i nära
relationer. En kartläggning.* Rapport (2002), 33.

technically Swedish men); 98.9 percent of foreign-born males did not. Rape and murder are even less frequent than battery.

Is the fact that 1.1 percent of foreign-born males batter women, compared with 0.4 percent of technically Swedish men, supportive of the claim that 'immigrant culture' predisposes men for violence whereas 'Swedish culture' does not? One way to answer this question may be a comparison with how other groups created in the statistics have been treated. The Council shows the overrepresentation of unemployed men among batterers to be much greater than that of foreign-born men: 43 percent of the perpetrators were unemployed, compared with 17 percent of the general population (26 percentage points of over-representation for the unemployed, compared with 14 percentage points for the foreign-born). Yet such statistics have not generated a series of articles with headlines such as 'another woman murdered due to unemployment' or any governmental initiatives specifically directed at unemployed men to stop the violence. One implication for ethical practice, then, would be for scholarly work, media, public advocacy and public policy to frame the same issues of violence towards women in Sweden not in such terms that involve a significant moral cost in terms of immigration policy and damaging cultural contestations, but rather one that could address two problems simultaneously – unemployment and violence against women – rather than creating another problem in the process. It is hoped that this chapter can con-tribute to just such a productive opening.

The reluctance to generalise about men as a group might be even more instructive. According to Council statistics, men carry out 94 percent of lethal violence, 88 percent of violent crime and almost 100 percent of the rapes in Sweden.[39] These are rather high levels of overrepresentation for a group that makes up slightly less than half of the population. Some Swedish feminists have contended that gender culture, specifically the norms, values and practices of masculinity, are to blame for much general violence as well as for rape and violence against women. The response to this suggestion has been aggressive, to say the least. A brief illustration through one reaction from Bo Rothstein, the political science professor cited in the introduction, should suffice to make the point. He rejects claims that 'male violence

---

[39] Swedish National Council on Crime Prevention, *Brottsutvecklingen i Sverige 2001–2003*. BRÅ rapport (2004), 32.

against women is not something deviant but a normal behavior of men' as 'totally unscientific ... Qualified research shows clearly that this is not the case, that men who abuse women clearly deviate in terms of mental illness and other aspects ... Is it legitimate to spread insulting prejudices about and negatively stereotype men as a group in the name of feminism?'[40]

One should of course ask precisely the same question about the use of statistics on immigrant men. Is it legitimate to spread insulting prejudices about and negatively stereotype foreign-born men as a group based on statistics such as that showing 1.1 percent of the group having battered a female partner? I, for one, would minimally argue for consistency: if it is illegitimate for one group, it must be so for another.

Rape, physical abuse and murder of women constitute a serious problem in Swedish society. Council estimates suggest that around 25,200 cases of violence against women are at the hands of a Swedish man, 4,800 cases have a Swedish-born perpetrator with at least one foreign parent, and 10,000 cases have a foreign-born perpetrator. The problem clearly cannot simply or even primarily be attributed to immigrants. But could it be that the *causes* of male violence against women are nevertheless different among Swedes and immigrants? This takes us to the second empirical claim that has to be accepted in order for the cultural explanatory framework to be feasible: immigrants are driven by their culture to violence, whereas Swedish men abuse women in spite of their culture.

For this conceptualisation to make sense, 'culture' has to be understood in a structurally holist manner, as a consistent set of values and habits that define and distinguish 'cultural groups' from one another. Cultural groups are thus made to be internally homogeneous, with each member socialised by the same values and habits. Patriarchal norms, values and habits must be presumed to form a joint culture of the Mediterranean–Middle Eastern–North African peoples, constituting one common socialising force that moulds all of its individual members. Swedish culture is likewise made to be a homogeneous set of norms, values and habits that do not socialise its individual members to physically abuse women.

[40] Bo Rothstein, 'Männen diskrimeras av urartad feminism', *Dagens Nyheter*, March 6, 2005.

'Culture' must not only be seen as internally consistent but also as relatively stable and tied to a physical space for these accounts to make sense. Culture thus becomes an inheritance from a cultural place of origin. Patriarchal culture is then made to be shared baggage that immigrants bring with them to Sweden, baggage which then continues to determine their behaviour, generation after generation. Until freed through successful adoption of so-called Swedish values, all 'immigrants' can thus be understood as carriers of a culture that predisposes them for rape, spouse abuse and murder.

Is this a feasible conceptualisation of culture? Critics contend that culture so conceived has become almost equivalent to ideas about biological race – cultural classifications have taken the place of the racial categories central to racial biology. And culture conceived this way becomes almost as static and inescapably determining of the individual as biology within eugenics.[41]

Even if one finds the conceptual association with racial biology reprehensive, aren't these representations nevertheless empirically sound? A number of feminist scholars – Chandra Mohanty and Uma Narayan among them – have shown what Narayan calls the 'dangerous lacks of detail' in claims such as those about the alleged Mediterranean– Middle Eastern–North African patriarchal culture.[42] The region is afforded no internal complexity, as if there were no internal variations and contradictions in the values and practices of the residents. Hundreds of millions of individuals are presumed to share a common patriarchal culture, conceived as a uniting force despite variations in class, form and level of education, family situation, drug and alcohol consumption, religious practice, sexual orientation, physical abilities and so on and so forth. The patriarchal features of this 'culture' furthermore appear to be almost entirely insulated from change. The claims in

---

[41] E.g. James M. Blaut, 'The theory of cultural racism', *Antipode* 24:4 (1992); Etienne Balibar and Immanuel Wallerstein, *Ras, Nation, Klass-mångtydiga identiteter* (Göteborg: Daidalos, 2002); Katarina Mattsson and Mekonnen Tesfahuney, 'Rasism i vardagen'. In Ingemar Lindberg and Magnus Dahlstedt (eds.), *Det slutna folkhemmet: om etniska klyftor och blågul självbild* (Stockholm: Agora, 2002), 28–41.

[42] Uma Narayan, *Dislocating Cultures: Identities, Traditions and Third World Feminism* (New York/London: Routledge, 1997), 49. See also Chandra Talpade Mohanty, '"Under Western Eyes: Feminist Scholarship and Colonial Discourses', *Feminist Review* 30 (1988), 61–88.

Sweden that point to a largely monolithic patriarchal culture of origin do not even attempt to grapple with these complexities and variations. Instead, it is simply alleged that the Mediterranean–Middle Eastern–North African region is a place 'where "time stands still" and "one culture rules all"', to borrow Narayan's words.

The cultural framework also rests on an understanding of 'Swedish' men who rape, beat or murder women as individual exceptions to a monolithic Swedish culture which discourages such behaviour. Alcoholism, economic problems and mental illness are generally held forth as explanations for Swedish cases.[43] This presumes an equally questionable view of 'Swedish culture' as separable from other cultures, as internally consistent, free of contradictions and without variation. This also presumes as invalid much careful research carried out by feminist scholars. This research generally does not make claims about or assume a monolithic Swedish patriarchal culture that exerts the same influence on all Swedish men. Instead, the scholarship wrestles with variations and inconsistencies to show precisely the complex nature of how norms and values in Sweden help produce rape and male violence against women.[44]

In order for the cultural framework to make sense and be feasible, one has to accept different explanations for the same practices among Swedes and immigrants. And for this to be viable, it is not sufficient to simply ignore all the potential explanatory factors that would connect 'immigrant' gender violence with that of 'Swedes'. Some evidence must be presented that shows immigrants to be affected primarily or exclusively by their allegedly monolithic culture of origin, evidence which rules out the importance of unemployment, psychological problems, exposure to pornography and other hostile portrayals of women, abuse of drugs and alcohol, a family history of violence, or – unthinkable thought – the exposure to patriarchal ideas and values in Sweden that cannot be attributed to the culture of origin. Likewise, turning to 'Swedish' violence, evidence must be presented to counter the

[43] Paulina De los Reyes and Irene Molina, 'Kön, klass och ras/etnicitet: en nödvändig trilogi för den feministiska forskningen', *Sofia* 1 (2000), 6.
[44] E.g. the findings of Stina Jeffner, *Liksom våldtäkt, typ . . . Om ungdomars förståelse av våldtäkt* (Stockholm: Utbildningsförlaget Brevskolan, 1998) and Katarina Wennstam, *En riktig våldtäktsman. En bok om samhällets syn på våldtäkt* (Stockholm: Albert Bonniers Förlag, 2004).

findings of Swedish feminists about the importance of patriarchal norms, values and practices in accounting for rape and battery.

One of the main difficulties for critics of the cultural framework is that the attribution of gender equality to Swedish culture has become a truism rather than a stereotype. By engaging in gender equality practices, a person can become seen as successfully integrated into Swedish culture. The 98.1 percent of foreign-born men who do not batter their partners do not necessarily present a challenge to the cultural framework, since their non-violence can be interpreted as an indication of the curing effects of Swedish values. The tens of thousands of men who do rape or batter women in Sweden each year do not necessarily challenge the framework either. They can easily be excluded from Swedish culture – such a person can be labelled either an 'immigrant' with foreign values, or an alcoholic or mentally ill, in the case of Swedes where no foreign heritage can be identified. Any simple empirical challenge to the association of gender equality with Swedish culture can thus successfully be met. And any empirical challenge to the association of immigrants with the oppression of women can likewise be met.

Conclusion

It should be clear that gender equality and multiculturalism are widely considered to be incompatible ideals in Sweden. Gender equality has become closely associated with Swedish culture, differentiated from what is presumed to be patriarchal immigrant cultures. Non-Swedish culture has thus become viewed with suspicion, as values and habits that oppress and degrade women. Initially, in the mid-1990s, the well-being of immigrant women was at the centre of the debate. Increasingly, however, Swedish women were also seen as victims of immigrant men. It is interesting to note that by the very end of the 1990s, what had originally emerged as a concern about immigrant women was no longer so clearly about women at all. Women often merely became the site on which competing views of culture and multiculturalism were debated and negotiated.

A first task of this chapter was to suggest that developments in Sweden should give us pause, as the meanings and practices of gender equality have become fraught with a series of deleterious effects that should be included in the moral deliberation. The conceptualisation and subsequent attempted elimination of one form of oppression, that of women, has helped first define and then stigmatise the entire category of 'immigrants', including 'immigrant' women. There is no doubt that this has fuelled xenophobia in Sweden, including neo-fascist movements which now use gender equality as a recruitment tool. The insistence that gender equality is an exclusively Swedish or (north) Western cultural trait also undermines gender equality work within communities and movements organised around a non-Swedish cultural identity.

As Kathryn Sikkink underscores in her chapter in this volume, judgement about what is possible and ethical must rest on sound social science (obviously always a matter of sound interpretation and bound up with ontological assumptions). Had the culturalist conception been a proper approach to the problem, the denigration of 'immigrant culture' might be justifiable. However, the conceptual and empirical foundations for this approach are so poorly supported that it seems unfeasible – upon closer reflection – to insist on a cultural divide around the question of rape and violence against women. And because of the poor analytical basis, the culturalist framework has additional deleterious effects whenever turned into public policy.

The second task of this chapter was to deconstruct the taken-for-granted binary distinction between Swedes and immigrants, a distinction which is central to the way in which multiculturalism and gender equality have become seen as incompatible ideals that pose an ethical dilemma. The chapter started by arguing that the very distinction is difficult to maintain, in the ethnic sense of the terms. Whereas it is possible to identify people who have or have not immigrated to Sweden, no clear line can be drawn between 'Swedes' and 'immigrants' as cultural categories. There is no convincing evidence that either label delineates two mutually exclusive groups, each with internally consistent gender values and practices. 'Immigrant culture' is simply not a good or adequate proxy for patriarchal values and practices in Sweden.

If one finds it feasible to reject the claims about a distinctive 'Swedish culture' that can be clearly differentiated from immigrant cultures around rape and violence, then there is no necessary trade-off between gender equality and multiculturalism as conceived in the debate. Indeed, the key to gender equality does not have to be found in culture conceptualised this way. Another option is to identify values and practices that help produce rape and violence, in all their complexity and variability among contexts and social situations. These are the values that need to be 'extinct or, preferably, to be encouraged to alter [themselves] so as to reinforce the equality of women'.[45] This is clearly a more demanding task, since it does not allow for falling back on familiar categories and comfortable hierarchies. Much feminist scholarship is already engaged in analysing the many distinctive and complex ways in which women become subjected to violence and rape, however, and thus provides rich insights for those interested in leaving the deceptive culturalist framework behind.

[45] Okin, *Is Multiculturalism Bad for Women?*, 22–23.

9 | Interstate community-building and the identity/difference predicament

BAHAR RUMELILI

What do constructivist theory and the experiences of international institutions tell us about what kinds of community to build and how to build communities in international relations? Recently, the constructivist scholarship in international relations (IR) has invested a significant deal of theoretical and empirical attention in security communities and processes of interstate community-building.[1] The very fact that certain states have transcended the realist world of power politics to conduct their relations on the basis of mutual trust and identification has been taken as solid evidence that progress is possible in international relations. In normative terms, interstate community-building has been considered a positive development in two respects. First of all, it has been widely believed that community relations based on mutual trust and identification consolidate a condition of stable peace, where states come to neither expect nor prepare for war against each other. Secondly, interstate communities in the context of membered institutions serve as fruitful grounds for the consolidation and outward diffusion of international norms, specifically through the imposition of membership conditionality. Constructivist scholars have pointed to various examples of interstate communities, both within and outside

---

[1] E.g. Emanuel Adler and Michael Barnett (eds.), *Security Communities* (Cambridge: Cambridge University Press, 1998); Bruce Cronin, 'From Balance to Community: Transnational Identity and Political Integration', *Security Studies* 8:2/3 (1999), 270–301; Bruce Cronin, *Community Under Anarchy* (New York, NY: Columbia University Press, 1999); Colin H. Kahl, 'Constructing a Separate Peace: Constructivism, Collective Liberal Identity, and Democratic Peace', *Security Studies* 8:2/3 (1999), 94–144; Janice Bially-Mattern, 'Taking Identity Seriously', *Cooperation and Conflict* 35:3 (2000), 299–308; Michael. C. Williams, 'The Discipline of Democratic Peace: Kant, Liberalism and the Social Construction of Security Communities', *European Journal of International Relations* 7:4 (2001), 525–553; L. Nathan 'Domestic Instability and Security Communities', *European Journal of International Relations* 12:2 (2006), 275–299.

Union (EU), the Association of South East Asian Nations (ASEAN), the
Organisation for Security and Cooperation in Europe, the US–Canadian
relationship, the US–Israeli relationship and the group of democratic
states writ large.[2]

Unlike previous studies on international communities,[3] constructivist
scholars have relied on 'collective identity' as the central variable in
explaining the formation and consolidation of such interstate communities. They have argued that in communities, states come to positively
identify with each other, such that they see each other as 'part of self'
rather than as 'other'. However, while employing the concept of 'collective identity', constructivist scholars have not always attended to its
manifold normative implications. In fact, as this chapter will contend,
the focus on the concept of identity has uncovered new normative
challenges about how to build interstate communities and what kinds
of communities to build. These challenges arise from the intricate
relationship that identity has with difference, from the dependence of
identity on the production of difference with 'others'. Granted this
dependence, can (we) build interstate communities that avoid the discrimination and exclusion of outsider states? Or should we? Should
interstate communities replicate the exclusivity of nation-state communities in order to achieve a similar degree of integrity and cohesion? Or
should they aspire to a post-national, post-Westphalian form in order to
escape the replication of the conflictual history of nation-states among
interstate communities? How can such a form be achieved in practice?
Does differentiation – on which identity depends – necessarily entail
'othering', a term which is indiscriminately used in the literature to

---

[2] See Ole Waever, 'Insecurity, Security, and Asecurity in the West European Non-
war Community'. In Adler and Barnett, *Security Communities*, 69–118; Amitav
Acharya, *Constructing a Security Community in Southeast Asia: ASEAN and the
Problem of Regional Order* (London and New York: Routledge, 2001); Emanuel
Adler, 'Seeds of Peaceful Change: The OSCE's Security Community-building
Model', in Adler and Barnett, *Security Communities*, 119–160; Sean M. Shore,
'No Fences Make Good Neighbors: The Development of the US–Canadian
Security Community, 1871–1940'. In Adler and Barnett, *Security Communities*,
333–367; Kahl, 'Constructing a Separate Peace'.
[3] E.g. K. Deutsch, S. Burrell, R. Kahn, M. Lee, M. Lichterman, R. Lindgren,
F. Loewenheim and R. van Wagenen, *Political Community and the North Atlantic
Area: International Organization in the Light of Historical Experience* (Princeton,
NJ: Princeton University Press, 1957).

denote a wide spectrum of self/other relations that include discrimination, denigration, exclusion and violence? What sort of a relation with the outside world would ensure that the external relations of these communities are not conflict-producing? What sort of a relation with the outside world would ensure the more effective expansion of community norms? Should moral equality be the guiding normative principle in the relations between these communities and the outsider states? Or is some degree of moral hierarchy necessary for the consolidation and diffusion of community norms?

This chapter will discuss how such normative dilemmas and challenges that arise from the intricate relationship between identity and difference have been dealt with both in the constructivist literature and by community-building international institutions. The first section of the chapter will discuss the ongoing debates in the constructivist literature on the relationship between identity and difference. It will propose some alternative ethical criteria on the basis of which self/other relations may be evaluated. The second section will compare how two community-building institutions, the European Union and the Association of South East Asian Nations, have faced the identity/difference predicament in their external relations and evaluate their policies on the basis of the proposed ethical criteria.

Identity and difference: an ongoing debate in constructivist IR theory

The literature in IR has not fully attended to the intricate relationship between the construction of collective identity and the production of difference. In fact, the literature has taken two divergent paths on this issue.[4] Broadly speaking, constructivist scholars of a more liberal persuasion have downplayed the dependence of identity on difference and sought to explain the construction of collective identity within (security) communities solely through processes that are endogenous to the community.[5] This has promoted an understanding of community formation

---

[4] Bahar Rumelili, 'Constructing Identity and Relating to Difference: Understanding the EU's Mode of Differentiation', *Review of International Studies* 30 (2004), 27–47.

[5] For example, in Emanuel Adler and Michael Barnett's analysis, exogenous conditions only figure as precipitating conditions for the development of a security community, for example 'an external threat [can] cause states to form alliances',

as a self-generated and self-sustained process that is not dependent on others in order to be. For example, a democratic community would be constructed as states that share norms about popular sovereignty, universal suffrage and limited mandate who come to identify with each other and develop a sense of 'collective self'. Scholars who designate themselves as post-structuralist or critical constructivist, on the other hand, have underscored the ontological dependence of identity on difference and focused on how the construction of any collective identity inevitably entails the exclusion, discrimination and 'othering' of those constituted to be different. Therefore, 'collective identity is a relation between two human collectives; that is, it always resides in the nexus between the collective self and its others, and not in the self seen in isolation'.[6] For post-structuralist/critical constructivist scholars, democracy, as an identity category, requires the existence of non-democracy. Consequently, in forming a community, democratic, norm-abiding states need non-democratic and norm-violating states, and in fact produce them as such through dominant discourses and representations.

More recently, some constructivist scholars have begun to take more nuanced positions on the relationship between identity and difference. In these more nuanced arguments, the debate has been transformed from one about the role of difference in identity formation into two new debates: one is about the role of the 'constitutive outside' in the formation of collective identity, and another is about whether differentiation from others necessarily entails othering in the negative sense. This section will discuss these two debates in turn and argue that in order to provide a guide for ethical action, constructivist scholars working on the identity/difference problematique should concentrate their empirical research on the following: first, rather than downplaying the role of the 'constitutive outside' in the formation of collective identity, constructivist research should highlight the conflicts and struggles over the construction of the boundaries of identities. Second, it should concentrate on the identification of different forms of othering, normative

but the factors conducive to and necessary for the formation of a collective identity are totally endogenous to the community; Emanuel Adler and Michael Barnett, 'A Framework for the Study of Security Communities'. In Adler and Barnett, *Security Communities*, 38.

[6] Iver B. Neumann, 'European Identity, EU Expansion, and the Integration/Exclusion Nexus', *Alternatives* 23:3 (1998), 397–416.

evaluation of what constitutes good as opposed to bad othering, and empirical studies of the conditions under which different forms of othering come into being in different contexts.

Identity and its constitutive outside

More and more constructivist scholars recognise that construction of identity requires practices of differentiation, while arguing that these practices can and do take place endogenously within the community, not requiring an 'outside' for the constitution of the community. Alexander Wendt, for example, has distinguished between pre-social (corporate) and social identities of states and argued that corporate identities are 'constituted by self-organizing homeostatic structures', and as such are 'constitutionally exogenous to Otherness'.[7] According to Wendt, 'if a process is self-organizing, then there is no particular Other to which the Self is related'.[8] In addition, Wendt has argued that some state identities, such as democratic, are type identities that involve minimal interaction with 'others' (only in the constitution of 'member-ship rules'), and represent characteristics that are 'intrinsic to the actors', such that 'a state can be democratic all by itself'.[9] Only 'role' identities, such as enemy, friend or rival, are relational and require the existence of an 'other' state.[10]

Other constructivist scholars have distinguished between self-reflexive differentiation practices that take a past condition of the self as their reference point, and outward-oriented differentiation practices that are based on the denigration of external actors. Ole Waever, for example, has argued that 'despite the wish of various post-structuralists and critical theorists to catch the EU and the West "othering" various neighbors,

---

[7] Alexander Wendt, *Social Theory of International Politics* (Cambridge: Cambridge University Press, 1999), 224–225.

[8] Ibid. 225.   [9] Ibid. 226.

[10] In a later article I think Wendt diverges from his earlier account by developing an argument about the need for mutual recognition between individuals and groups; see Alexander Wendt, 'Why a World State is Inevitable', *European Journal of International Relations* 9:4 (2003), 491–542. This need for recognition shows that no actor can possess 'an identity all by itself' (cf. Wendt, *Social Theory*, 226). However, it is necessary to note that mutual recognition takes place between two priorly constituted identities and in that regard is different from the mutual constitution of identities between self and other; see Rumelili, 'Constructing Identity and Relating to Difference'.

the dominant trend in European security rhetoric is that the other is Europe's own past (fragmentation)'.[11] Similarly, Thomas Diez has argued that in contrast to '[O]therings between geographically defined entities [that] tend to be more exclusive and antagonistic toward out-groups', the European Union 'has opened up the possibility of the construction of a political identity through a less exclusionary practice of temporal difference'.[12]

Entering the debate from a more philosophical angle, Arash Abizadeh has argued that collective identity is different from individual identity in that it does not require an external other; the recognition required by a collective identity can come solely from its own constituent parts, that is, the individuals who make up the collectivity.[13] Through this argument, Abizadeh seeks to refute the widespread particularist thesis that human collectives are necessarily bounded and demonstrate that a cosmopolitan political order based on solidarity with humanity as a whole is possible.

In effect, these arguments only amount to a more sophisticated restatement of the earlier liberal constructivist accounts that view community formation as a self-generated, self-sustained process. In these accounts, outsiders are absent; they enter the picture only when they intend to adopt this previously formed collective identity in whose constitution they took no part.[14] I would argue that such refuting of the role of the constitutive outside in identity formation leads constructivists down the dangerous path of essentialising collective identities and thereby undermining their very own constructivist premises. The arguments that are used to 'absent' the outsiders in identity formation, such as corporate identity and reflexive, inward-oriented differentiation, inevitably presuppose pre-given collectivities, with pre-given boundaries and uncontested histories. Wendt's layered identity conception where corporate identities, defined as 'bodies and territory', are

[11] Waever, 'Insecurity', 100.
[12] Thomas Diez, 'Europe's Others and the Return of Geopolitics', *Cambridge Review of International Affairs* 17:2 (2004), 320.
[13] Arash Abizadeh, 'Does Collective Identity Presuppose an Other? On the Alleged Incoherence of Global Solidarity', *American Political Science Review* 99:1 (2005), 45–60.
[14] Wendt, *Social Theory*, 341; Frank Schimmelfennig, 'International Socialization in the New Europe: Rational Action in an Institutional Environment', *European Journal of International Relations* 6:1 (2000), 109–139.

'constitutionally exogenous to Otherness' indicates that he has in mind collectivities with somehow pre-given and fixed boundaries and membership. Any ambiguity, controversy or political struggle regarding who belongs and what is included is theoretically ruled out because the settlement of such questions would inevitably entail practices of differentiation and inclusion/exclusion with respect to outsiders.

Similarly, I would argue that the notion of a European identity that solely takes its own past as its other inevitably presupposes a pre-given past that a pre-given European collectivity shares. Only when we assume that the questions of boundaries and membership are permanently settled can we talk about a collectivity having a shared past that it can take as a reference point in the construction of its identity. This is in contrast to those who see temporal othering as a characteristic of a post-sovereign and post-modern Europe that refuses to fix its identity and membership.[15] However, even though Diez argues that temporal othering requires a much 'looser definition' of self, he also observes that the European Union increasingly resorted to geographical otherings after the 1990s, when the enlargement question became more prominent.[16] To me, this indicates that whether temporal or geographical otherings will dominate is not a question solely of whether European identity is endogenously loosely or strictly defined, but also a matter of how this European identity is constituted by outsiders. When the European identity and its boundaries are recognised and not contested by outsiders, it may be possible to reproduce the European identity solely or predominantly through temporal othering. However, when the European identity and its boundaries are effectively contested by outsiders, it becomes increasingly necessary to re-assert and re-claim this identity through geopolitical otherings.

The normative implications of essentialising identities are much too serious to ignore, especially in the post 9/11 environment, where essentialised differences are widely posited as a cause for conflict. Disregarding the role of the constitutive outside would reify the constructions of the 'West' or of the 'democratic community of states', without calling into question how the 'existence' of such collectivities is bound up with the construction of certain 'outsiders' as non-West or non-democratic. For constructivism to raise a critical voice when those 'outsiders' are further constructed as objects of war, it needs to be able

[15] Waever, 'Insecurity'; Diez, 'Europe's Others'.   [16] Diez, 'Europe's Others', 321.

to question their constitution as 'objects' with those identities, and to moreover recognise the complicity of the self in the construction of those very 'others'. In fact, it is the non-essentialist conception of identity that gives constructivism much of its critical edge, currently. In that sense, the practices of external differentiation that are necessarily implicated in community-building are not a price to be paid for progress but an essential mechanism that guarantees the ever-contested nature of identities in international relations.

In addition to essentialising identities, isolating international communities from their constitutive outside(s) brackets important struggles and conflicts over boundaries and membership. It silences the relations of power and domination in the interaction of security communities with outsiders, by reducing it to a voluntaristic process where outsiders fulfil certain conditions and the community institution admits those states that validate its identity. Such an understanding disregards the authority of the community institution to define and shape the dominant discourses that ascribe identity and difference, its power to include and exclude and thereby bestow or inflict on the outsider states both the material and the symbolic benefits and costs of inclusion and exclusion, its ability to construct the outsiders as morally inferior and as potentially threatening, and thereby authorise certain forms of behaviour towards them.

It may be argued that when the international collectivity is set at the global level[17] as in the cosmopolitan approach to international relations, these negative implications of essentialising identities disappear. After all, essentialising humanity as an entity would only be at the expense of non-humans. What such an argument overlooks, however, is the process of arriving at such a global community. At present, there is not a sufficient normative basis at the global level to constitute a community. When analysts and commentators talk about the 'international community', they actually have in mind a subglobal community that shares – mostly liberal – norms. Therefore, the expansion of the subglobal 'international community' to the global level necessitates the transfer of norms from certain states (or actors) to others through the differentiation – at least initially – of certain actors as 'norm-violators', and their – albeit temporary – exclusion. In other words, even when the ultimate community is imagined to be at the global level, the process of

---

[17] Abizadeh, 'Collective Identity'.

arriving at such a community requires practices of external differentiation and exclusion.

The normative implications of the claim that identity is complicit in the production of others as different are profound. It means that the moral responsibility for being different does not fall squarely on the other; the self is simultaneously responsible for perceiving and representing the other's differences in a certain way. Most liberal constructivist scholars would find this claim to be disturbing and morally objectionable. For liberal constructivists, differences do exist and are not (at least entirely) produced as such. There are states that routinely torture their citizens, and those that forbid such practice; there are countries that deny their female citizens the most basic human rights, and those that do not. Such differences are real and carry profound consequences for individuals. The articulation and criticism of these differences in others constitute a moral duty for the self, rather than making the self complicit in the production of difference.

However, the end result of denying the complicity of self in the production of others is often the essentialisation of others' differences. Liberal constructivists assume that difference, as a factor in international relations, can be eradicated through the progressive expansion of communities. If, however, identity depends on difference, there will always be others who are perceived to be and represented as different, even though in objective terms, they may not be that different. The complicity argument underlines the role of perceptions and representations in the production of difference in international relations. If this complicity is not recognised, then the produced differences can too easily be cast as innate features of others.

In addition, recognising the self's complicity in the production of others as different does not necessarily lead us to a moral relativism where we are unable to distinguish 'when [that] other is morally reprehensible and not deserving of such moral consideration'.[18] Depending on how the differences of others are perceived and represented by the self, it may still be possible to fulfil one's moral responsibility to the other and still defend certain norms and values as good. Finding a balance between these two moral imperatives has led some constructivist scholars to the argument that it is necessary to distinguish between 'good' and 'bad' forms of othering.

[18] Richard Price, 'Introduction', this volume, 47.

Forms of othering

As has been stated before, othering is a term that is indiscriminately used in the literature to denote a wide spectrum of self/other relations that include discrimination, denigration, exclusion or violence.[19] Earlier, post-structuralist scholars such as David Campbell underscored how the necessity to secure identities generates a relationship of othering between the self and its constitutive others, without distinguishing between different forms of othering. Campbell, for example, focused on how the constitution of state identities in relation to difference produces foreign policy practices that are dependent on discourses of fear and danger and that construct the external realm as inferior and threatening.[20] Moreover, Campbell has argued that in the performance of state identities, 'the potential for the transformation of difference into otherness'[21] is almost always realised because the nationalist imaginary 'demands a violent relationship with the other'.[22]

While Campbell's link between performance of identity and othering generated a wide range of critical studies that exposed such practices in the foreign policies of various states,[23] it offered no prescriptions about how such practices can be avoided or at least their negative implications ameliorated. As a result, such studies failed to fully realise their critical potential. As Diez aptly puts it, 'a critical theory addressing the problem of identity/difference depends on the possibility of different kinds of difference: more or less exclusive, antagonistic, and violent ones. If there were no such possibility, the theory would become fatalistic and would no longer be critical.'[24] Along similar lines, in an earlier study, I argued that the ontological dependence of identity on difference does not necessitate a behavioural relationship of 'othering' between self and other,[25] restrictively defined in this case as the securitisation of the

---

[19] As a concept, Othering is in general construed and will be used in this chapter in the negative sense, even though self/other relations can and do include relations of love and admiration.

[20] David Campbell, *Writing Security* (Minneapolis, MN: University of Minnesota Press, 1992).

[21] Ibid. 78.   [22] Ibid. 13.

[23] For example, Jutta Weldes, Mark Laffey, Hugh Gusterson and Raymond Duvall (eds.), *Cultures of Insecurity* (Minneapolis, MN: University of Minnesota Press, 1999).

[24] Diez, 'Europe's Others', 322.   [25] Rumelili, 'Identity, Difference, and the EU'.

other, i.e. the perception and representation of the other as a threat to one's identity.

Although there is a general notion in the literature that some forms of othering are preferable to others, scholars do not often specify the forms of othering they talk about or the normative basis they base their judgements of preferability on.[26] Therefore, in the absence of an existing discussion on what would constitute good as opposed to bad othering, in the remainder of this chapter I would like to advance some propositions.

One possibility is to base the ethical criterion on the behaviours towards the other that are made possible by the widespread representations of the other. For example, it may be argued that forms of othering that do not legitimise violence towards the other are ethically permissible. In stipulating this criterion, there may be disagreement about how violence should be defined, whether it should be limited to physical violence or defined more broadly to include relations of exclusion, discrimination and domination. Another ethical criterion could be whether or not representations of the other produce conflict with the other. In any case, forms of othering constitute only the conditions of possibility for such behavioural outcomes, which come into being through interaction with other factors. It may be that representations that are very negative do not produce conflict with the other (as they may be internalised by the other as in the master–slave relationship) or do not legitimise violence towards the other (as they may be overridden by other norms that prohibit such violence). For example, even though popular representations of Turks living in Germany are often very negative, these do not translate into political action in the form of their expulsion.

Another possibility is to base the ethical criterion on the substantive, emotive or normative content of the representations. Othering may involve securitisation, denigration, exoticisation, eroticisation or

---

[26] As a first step in this direction, Thomas Diez identifies four strategies of Othering: representing the other as an existential threat, representing the other as inferior, representing the other as violating universal principles, and representing the other simply as different. He also argues that representing the other simply as different, while also not innocent, is preferable to the other three; see Thomas Diez, 'Constructing the Self and Changing Others: Reconsidering "Normative Power Europe"', *Millennium* 33:3 (2005), 628.

negation of the other.[27] One may advance an ethical criterion where certain representational practices constitute forms of 'bad' othering regardless of their behavioural implications or effects on the other. For example, one may stipulate that representational practices that fall short of casting the other as a moral equal are not ethically permissible, even when practices such as denigration may allow co-operation with the other or induce positive change in the other. This is the ethical position advocated by post-structuralist scholars such as David Campbell: 'The radical interdependence of being that flows from our responsibility to the other ... give[s] rise to a different figuration of politics, one in which its purpose is the struggle for – or on behalf of – alterity, and not a struggle to efface, erase, or eradicate alterity.'[28]

A third possibility is to base the ethical criterion on the effects that othering has on the other. It may be argued that certain forms of othering are 'good' because they induce positive change in the other. For example, 'shaming', which is a positively discussed strategy in the constructivist literature on normative change, is a form of othering. Shaming involves the casting of the other as morally inferior in a public forum, and is generally more effective if the other is represented as violating universal principles. However, under certain conditions, shaming and other related representational practices can and do become counterproductive. Representing the other as morally inferior, for example, may lead certain actors to develop a defensive reaction where they reject the construction of their identity as such. The non-recognition of their identity as a moral equal (or for that matter as morally superior) may lead them to even develop a violent reaction.

A final possibility for an ethical yardstick is to distinguish between different identities and their modes of othering. In the literature, it is frequently argued that the nation-state is prone to 'violent forms of Othering' while other, post-modern entities, such as the European

[27] David Spurr, *Rhetoric of Empire: Colonial Discourse in Journalism, Travel Writing and Imperial Administration* (Durham, NC: Duke University Press, 1993).

[28] David Campbell, 'The Deterritorialization of Responsibility: Levinas, Derrida, and Ethics after the End of Philosophy'. In David Campbell and Michael J. Shapiro (eds.), *Moral Spaces: Rethinking Ethics and World Politics* (Minneapolis, MN: University of Minnesota Press, 1999), 50.

Union, may not be so.[29] Similarly, Abizadeh argues that modes of identity constitution that are 'open to cosmopolitan solidarity', such as the constitution of European identity by reference to values such as human rights and democracy, entail 'good' forms of othering.[30] In this chapter, I refer to such universalist identities as inclusive identities. According to such arguments, interstate communities with inclusive identities and fluid boundaries, arguably like the European Union, would represent good forms of othering because they would allow for the eventual inclusion of the other.

I argue, however, that it is hard to reach a moral judgement about the preferability of inclusive or exclusive identities. Inclusive identities, such as a democratic identity, construct the other as less than self, and allow the possibility that the other may become like self. In that sense, they construct a temporary difference and fluid borders with their others. Yet at the same time, inclusive identities necessarily embody a hierarchy; in constructing the other as less than self, they construct the other as inferior. Inclusive identities are secured by others who aspire to, and eventually succeed in, becoming like self. Therefore, inclusive identities seek to shape, induce, convert, discipline, and if all else fails force the other into becoming like self. In other words, inclusive identities can and do legitimise violence towards the other, the legitimisation of the recent US war on Iraq in the name of regime change being a prominent example.

On the other hand, exclusive identities, such as ethnic, cultural or civilisational identities, entail the construction of the other as non-self; they construct a permanent difference and strict boundaries with their others. In contrast to inclusive identities, exclusive identities may or may not embody a moral hierarchy. Exclusive identities, that construct others as their moral equals, allow for separate co-existence between different identities. However, exclusive identities that construct their others as morally inferior legitimise violence. And, while inclusive identities at worst seek to force the other into change, exclusive identities can go as far as legitimising the annihilation of the other. Many sorts of ethnic, racial and xenophobic violence are made possible through exclusionary othering.

---

[29] John G. Ruggie, 'Territoriality and Beyond: Problematizing Modernity in International Relations', *International Organization* 47:1 (1993), 139–174; Diez, 'Europe's Others'.
[30] Abizadeh, 'Collective Identity', 58.

Community-building in practice

As pointed out by Price, an important contribution of constructivism to normative theory is to bridge the normative–empirical gap; to analyse the 'plausibility' of the 'empirical claims implicit in ethical theorizing'.[31] In that spirit, in this section, I proceed to the analysis of the actual community-building practices of two interstate communities, the European Union and the Association of South East Asian Nations.[32] In this comparative analysis, my objective is two-fold. The first is to demonstrate that the identities of these communities are by no means pre-given, nor are they self-generated and self-sustained. These identities are being continuously re-negotiated and re-produced through interaction with various 'outsider' states. Secondly, I seek to evaluate their modes of identity constitution and othering on the basis of the four possible ethical criteria that I have identified. Does it produce conflict with or legitimise violence towards the other? Does it induce positive change towards the other? Do the dominant representations of the other establish an ethical relation with the other (in terms of the content of representations)? Does the nature of collective identity allow for an ethical relation with the other?

In terms of their institutional structures and the collective identities they profess to uphold, the EU and ASEAN are widely different from each other. The EU is a supranational organisation that aims at economic and political integration, while ASEAN is a less formally institutionalised framework of intergovernmental co-operation. Yet, particularly in terms of the last criterion, the cases of the EU and ASEAN provide a useful comparison because they represent varying degrees of inclusivity–exclusivity in terms of the nature of their collective identities. While the EU has promoted a partly inclusive/partly exclusive collective identity combining universalist norms of democracy and free market with a notion of 'Europeanness', ASEAN has endorsed a predominantly exclusive collective identity based on shared beliefs about regional norms and boundaries. As a result of this difference in collective identities, the EU and ASEAN have faced different limitations

---

[31] Price, 'Introduction', 17.

[32] I am not claiming that these cases are representative of the entire range of community-building initiatives. They represent cases of community-building at the regional level in the context of membered institutions.

and implications of the identity/difference predicament and developed different policy responses.

The EU

As a community-building institution, the EU has promoted a collective identity that is partly inclusive and partly exclusive in nature. This duality is apparent in any statement of EU 'community' identity, most importantly in the Treaty on European Union, which states in Article 49 that 'any European country which respects the principles set out in Article 6(1) – liberty, democracy, respect for human rights and fundamental freedoms, and the rule of law – may apply to become a member of the European Union'.[33] Among the identity criteria listed in this statement, being European (i.e. being geographically situated in Europe) is bounded and exclusive, and thus embodies a conception of difference that is based on inherent characteristics, and not acquirable by others. The other identity criteria, respecting the principles of liberty, democracy, human rights, fundamental freedoms and the rule of law, are, on the other hand, inclusive and universal in aspiration, and, in principle, acquirable by any other state.

Neither aspect of this European identity is pre-given, nor solely self-generated. Instead, the constitution of both aspects has been possible by differentiating Europe from its 'outside'. In defining the exclusive aspects of the European identity, that is in geographically demarcating Europe, the EU has been productive of inherent differences with outsiders. Because only European states can become members of the European 'community,' questions of where Europe begins and ends have been fundamental to constructing a European collective identity.[34] However, these questions have never had definitive answers: Europe is merely a geographical construct, with no natural or pre-given boundaries; the geographical parameters of Europe have not only shifted throughout the centuries but also within the short history of the EU as well. In objecting to Britain's membership in the EEC, de Gaulle had argued that the 'maritime' Britain was inherently different from

---

[33] 'Treaty on European Union (consolidated text)', *Official Journal of the European Communities*, C325, December, 24 2002.
[34] Neumann, 'European Identity'; M. Anderson, 'European Frontiers at the End of the Twentieth Century'. In M. Anderson and E. Bort (eds.), *The Frontiers of Europe* (London: Pinter, 1998), 1–10.

268 Moral Limit and Possibility in World Politics

'continental' Europe.[35] When Morocco applied for membership in the EEC in 1987, it was told that membership was open to Europeans only, and that Morocco is not part of geographical Europe.[36] Opponents to Turkey's membership in the EU argue that its history and culture make it inherently non-European.

On the other hand, in defining the inclusive aspects of European identity around the principles of liberty, democracy, respect for human rights and fundamental freedoms and rule of law, the EU has constructed outsider states to be different in terms of acquirable characteristics. The 1993 Copenhagen Council has delineated the conditions that the candidate states had to satisfy for EU membership: stable institutions guaranteeing democracy, the rule of law, human rights and respect for and protection of minorities; a functioning market economy, and the ability to take on the obligations of membership, namely the *acquis communautaire*. Through the interim status of candidacy in its enlargement policy, the EU monitors the degree of fulfilment of these conditions and evaluates eligibility for membership accordingly.

The co-existence of inclusive and exclusive identity criteria in Europe's collective identity has led the EU to develop two forms of othering in relation to various states on the European periphery. With regard to certain states, such as those in Central and Eastern Europe, the EU has predominantly invoked the inclusive aspects of its collective identity, constructed their differences on the basis of acquirable characteristics, and associated with them. By making the fulfilment of the Copenhagen criteria a condition for their membership, the EU constructed a space of superior/inferior in relation to Central and Eastern Europe, where it claimed the superior identity of having stable and mature democratic and capitalist institutions and the authority to evaluate and monitor the Central and Eastern European societies' progress towards these ideals. For analytical convenience, I refer to this form of self/other interaction as inclusionary othering. On the other hand, with respect to the states south of the Mediterranean, such as Morocco, the EU invoked mostly the exclusive aspects of its identity, constructed their identities as inherently non-European, and dissociated from them.

---

[35] Charles de Gaulle, Press Conference in the Elysée Palace, January 14, 1963, quoted in D. de Giustino, D., *A Reader in European Integration* (New York, NY: Longman, 1996).
[36] 'Brussels Rejects Rabat's Bid to Join EEC', *The Guardian*, July 21, 1987.

Although the EU has developed some level of close institutional relations with these states, these arrangements have always carefully precluded the possibility of membership. I refer to this form of self/other
interaction as exclusionary othering. Some other states, such as Turkey,
have been put in a 'liminal' position, where they have been the target of
both inclusionary and exclusionary othering practices. Unlike Morocco
or the Central and Eastern European societies, Turkey is differentiated
from Europe on the basis of both inherent and acquired characteristics.
In the context of these competing discourses, the EU has kept a fluctuat-
ing social distance towards Turkey, alternating between inclusionary and
exclusionary steps. Since 1999, the EU has adopted a more inclusionary
discourse towards Turkey, first by granting Turkey EU candidacy status,
and later by commencing negotiations for Turkey's accession.

If we are to evaluate the EU's othering practices on the basis of the
four ethical criteria that I have proposed in the previous section, the
picture is mixed. On the one hand, in certain cases of conflicts between
member and non-member states, the EU's practices of exclusionary
othering have helped legitimise the community member's violence
towards the outsider states. The end result has been the exacerbation
of these existing conflicts. Greek–Turkish relations until 1999 is a case
in point. In a cross-examination, the constitutive and reproductive
effects of the EU discourse on the representations of the 'other' in the
two countries are very apparent.[37] At various crisis points, the EU's
representations of Turkey as non-European have lent validity and
legitimacy to Greek representations of Turkey as different and as a
threat. In addition, they have justified the expectation that Turkey
would engage in aggressive (i.e. non-European) forms of foreign policy
behaviour. Moroccan–Spanish relations are another example. The EU
representations of Morocco as non-European legitimised and validated
the construction of Morocco as different and threatening in Spain. This
can be clearly seen in how the 2002 Perejil crisis was represented as a
conflict between a European self and a non-European other in Spain,
rather than as an incident between any two neighbours.[38] In addition,
the construction of Morocco as non-European has helped justify Spain's

[37] Bahar Rumelili, 'Liminality and the Perpetuation of Conflicts: Turkish–Greek
Relations in the Context of Community-Building by the EU', *European Journal
of International Relations* 9:2 (2003), 27–47.
[38] Bahar Rumelili, 'Conflict, Identity, and the Inclusion/Exclusion Nexus: EU
Border Conflicts and the Conditions for their Transformation', paper presented

digression from EU norms in 'resolving' the crisis with military force. The construction of the event as the 'invasion of European territory by a non-European state' domestically justified the Spanish operation and muted international criticism.

In contrast to these two cases, the EU's practices of inclusionary othering towards Poland have helped alleviate the potential sources of dispute in Polish–German relations after the reunification of Germany. The construction of Poland as a 'part of Europe' delegitimised the discourses of difference and threat that may possibly have been employed against Poland in Germany to stir up the Oder–Neisse dispute and seek revision of the border. Instead, the mutual recognition of each other's identity as 'European', facilitated by the EU discourse, created the normative and ideational basis for deepening co-operation.[39] Similarly, Greek–Turkish relations improved after 1999, as the EU adopted a more inclusionary discourse towards Turkey by declaring Turkey to be a candidate. The prospect of Turkey's inclusion in the EU facilitated a foreign policy re-thinking on Greece's part, such that encouraging Turkey's Europeanisation came to be seen as a way to manage the bilateral conflicts. In Turkey, it has fostered an awareness that EU membership would necessitate a totally transformed relationship with Greece.[40]

In terms of their effects on the other, a similar distinction between practices of inclusionary and exclusionary othering is in order. The EU's practices of inclusionary othering have promoted a lot of positive (from the EU's perspective) changes in the candidate countries, in terms of their transition to democracy and market economy. The positive effect of inclusionary othering does not solely stem from the inducement provided by the membership carrot. The construction of the candidate countries as 'potential' Europeans has also had an 'enabling impact'[41] and facilitated the internalisation of EU norms. On the other hand, the EU's ability to promote positive change in its periphery has been limited

at the American Political Science Association Annual Meeting, Philadelphia, 2003.

[39] Ibid.

[40] Rumelili, 'Identity, Difference, and the EU'; Bahar Rumelili, 'Transforming Conflicts on EU Borders: The Case of Greek–Turkish Relations', *Journal of Common Market Studies* 45:1 (2007), 105–126.

[41] Thomas Diez, Stephan Stetter and Matthias Albert, 'The European Union and Border Conflicts: The Transformative Impact of Association', *International Organization* 60:3 (2006), 563–593.

to the countries it has offered a membership perspective to. The EU has not been able to instigate significant changes in the countries that it constructed as non-European. First of all, the EU's expectations of progress in democracy and human rights from those states were remarkably lower. For example, the 1995 Barcelona Declaration, which started the Euro-Mediterranean (Euromed) Programme for the EU's co-operation with North Africa and the Middle East, recognised 'the right of each of [the partners] to choose and freely develop its own political, socio-economic and judicial systems'.[42] Similarly, the country that is constructed as an 'outsider' has less material and symbolic incentives to identify with European norms. As Said Haddadi notes in the case of Euromed co-operation, reform depends on the country's will to democratise, and the EU's approach can be exploited by less open governments and might lead to further suppression of freedoms.[43]

The history of the reform process in Turkey clearly illustrates how practices of inclusionary and exclusionary othering produce differential effects. The EU's potential impact on Turkey was caught in a vicious circle while the EU's exclusionary discourse dominated. Even though Turkey always expressed a strong desire for membership, it lagged behind in fulfilling the Copenhagen criteria. Questions raised about the Europeanness of Turkey were widely perceived in Turkey as evidence of Europe's reluctance to accept Turkey as a member, of the double standards the Union applied, and even of an inherent historical animosity. This allowed those in the elite who had no interest in change to fend off legitimate criticisms of its shortcomings in human rights and democracy. It also tied the hands of reformers. Deficiencies in human rights and democracy continued, in turn reinforcing doubts in the EU about Turkey's identity and credentials.[44]

The EU's 1999 decision to grant candidacy status to Turkey has largely broken this vicious circle. The EU's inclusionary discourse that constructed Turkey as a potential European discredited the perceptions of European double standards and conspiracy. It enabled the reformers to legitimise the necessary legal and policy changes in the name of validating Turkey's European identity. As a result, since 1999, many

---

[42] Said Haddadi, 'The EMP and Morocco: Diverging Political Agendas?', *Mediterranean Politics* 8:2/3 (2003), 80.
[43] Ibid.
[44] Thomas Diez and Bahar Rumelili, 'Open the Door', *The World Today* (Aug./Sept. 2004), 18–19.

changes that have previously been regarded as impossible, such as curtailing the role of the military, lifting capital punishment, allowing TV and radio broadcasts in languages other than Turkish and accepting a UN-sponsored reunification plan for Cyprus, have been enacted. Although problems in the implementation of certain reforms remain, there has emerged a strong domestic constituency that uses the prospect of EU membership to push for further reforms.[45]

In terms of the content of representations, the EU discourse constructs a moral hierarchy of superior/inferior both with the states it constructs as potential-European and those it constructs as absolutely non-European. In other words, the Central and Eastern European states were inferior (prior to enlargement) because they are less-European, and North African countries are inferior because they are non-European. Space considerations do not allow me to give detailed examples of such representations, but empirical studies that have analysed the EU discourse have all highlighted this space of superior/inferior.[46] Shaped by a Euro-centric ideology, the EU discourse represents the EU as a model to its periphery and to the rest of the world.

The EU policy makers and analysts have been attentive to the charges that the EU is discriminatory and exclusionary in its enlargement policy and external relations. However, the EU has so far not been able to develop a policy response that will enable it to develop constructive relations with the states in its near-abroad and diffuse its norms without committing to the costly, and institutionally unmanageable, project of an 'ever-expanding' Union. Following the conclusion of the 2004 enlargement, the need to develop such a policy has become even more urgent. One policy response has been to finance and support cross-border co-operation between bordering regions in member and non-member states so as to alleviate the costs of and concerns about exclusion.[47]

[45] Ibid.
[46] Iver B. Neumann, *Uses of the Other: The East in European Identity Formation* (Minneapolis, MN: University of Minnesota Press, 1999); Iver B. Neumann and Jennifer M. Welsh, 'The Other in European Self-Definition: An Addendum to the Literature on International Society', *Review of International Studies* 17:4 (1991), 327–348; Michelle Pace, 'The Euro-Mediterranean Partnership and the Common Mediterranean Strategy? European Union Policy from a Discursive Perspective', *Geopolitics* 9:2 (2004), 292–309.
[47] Thomas Christiansen, Fabio Petito and Ben Tonra, 'Fuzzy Politics around Fuzzy Borders: The European Union's Near-Abroad', *Cooperation and Conflict* 35 (2000), 389–415.

Another policy option that has not been officially articulated but nevertheless put into de facto implementation is the diversification of membership alternatives. In addition to the fact that some EU member states have voluntarily opted out of the Eurozone and the Schengen area, the ten new member states have been admitted in 2004 with a temporary (up to seven years) moratorium on the free movement of people. The European Council has inserted a clause in Turkey's Negotiations Framework Document that such derogations may be permanent in Turkey's case. This diversification of membership alternatives has been so far undertaken on an ad hoc basis, when necessary to secure agreement within the EU. However, if such measures are mutually accepted, and not solely directed at controversial cases, such as Turkey, they may serve to blur the lines of inclusion/ exclusion around the EU.

Finally, the EU has adopted a variety of institutional arrangements for co-operation with outsider states, including the Euromed Programme with North Africa and the Middle East, and Partnership and Co-operation Agreements with former Soviet Republics in the Caucasus and Central Asia. Recently, these institutional arrangements have been integrated into the European Neighbourhood Policy (ENP).[48] However, these institutional arrangements, while furthering contact and co-operation, all serve to produce the boundary between the European 'selves' and non-European 'others' and foreclose its future contestation. In addition, the EU's external relations are predicated on security concerns broadly defined, and serve to construct the non-EU space as a source of instability, poverty, crime and illegal immigration.[49] Therefore, these institutional arrangements serve to heighten, rather than remedy, the sense of exclusion and discrimination of outsider states.

ASEAN

Compared to the EU, ASEAN represents an alternative form of community-building in international relations. While the EU has promoted a partly inclusive/partly exclusive collective identity, the collective

[48] Karen E. Smith, 'The Outsiders: The European Neighborhood Policy', *International Affairs* 81:4 (2005), 757–773.
[49] Pace, 'The Euro-Mediterranean Partnership'.

identity promoted by ASEAN has been predominantly exclusive. Two factors contribute to the exclusiveness of Southeast Asian collective identity. The first is the shared beliefs about the certainty of regional boundaries. The 1967 Bangkok Declaration that founded the Association of South East Asian Nations stated that 'the Association is open for participation to all States in the South-East Asian Region subscribing to the aforementioned aims, principles and purposes'.[50] Even though the Declaration did not explicitly define Southeast Asia's geographical limits, there was considerable certainty among ASEAN member states about where the region's ultimate boundaries lay.

This certainty was reflected in the intentional building of institutional relations with the states of the region, even when the possibility of their membership seemed distant. Burma (now Myanmar) and Cambodia were initially asked to join, but declined on the basis that ASEAN's perceived pro-US sympathies were incompatible with their declared neutrality.[51] The Treaty of Amity and Cooperation – the Bali Treaty of 1976 – was opened to accession by states outside of Southeast Asia, pending the consent of all states in Southeast Asia. In this document, the definition of Southeast Asia explicitly included Cambodia, Laos, Burma and Vietnam even though they were not members of ASEAN then.[52] The goal of One Southeast Asia was deemed accomplished with the membership of Vietnam in 1995, Laos and Myanmar in 1997 and Cambodia in 1998. As Severino, the Secretary-General of ASEAN, stated at the time: 'Southeast Asia has fulfilled the destiny set for it by geography'.[53]

The second factor that has contributed to the exclusiveness of Southeast Asian collective identity has been the fact that community norms and principles, such as non-interference and consensual decision making, have not had a universalising aspiration. Instead, ASEAN has underlined the cultural specificity of the community norms and values, and their appropriateness for Southeast Asia's political and historical

---

[50] 'Bangkok Declaration', August 8, 1967; www.aseansec.org/1212.htm.
[51] Jeannie Henderson, *Reassessing ASEAN*, Adelphi Paper 238 (Oxford: Oxford University Press, 1999).
[52] R. Amer, 'Conflict Management and Constructive Engagement in ASEAN's Expansion', *Third World Quarterly* 20:5 (1999), 1031–1048.
[53] Rodolfo C. Severino, 'Diversity and Convergence in Southeast Asia', keynote address, the Ninth Annual Conference of the Harvard Project for Asian and International Relations, Beijing, August 28, 2000; www.aseansec.org/3217.htm

circumstances. The region's historical narrative stresses how the political, economic and cultural ties among the peoples of Southeast Asia were severed through colonial designs, but then rebuilt through ASEAN.[54] National sovereignty and the principle of non-interference are seen as essential to 'protect the small and the weak from domination by the powerful'.[55] In addition, the community's procedural norms of consensual decision making and settling differences through consultation have been presented as a uniquely 'ASEAN way' to co-operation. Setting formal institutions and dispute settlement procedures are dismissed as 'Western' ways that presume the pre-existence of an adversarial relationship between states. The ASEAN community has explicitly distinguished itself from Europe, stating that unlike the European Union, 'it does not mean to transform itself into a political union under any form of central supranational authority' nor has it 'assigned itself the mission of converting its members to a uniform political set-up'.[56]

After the Asian economic crisis, the norm of non-interference has become increasingly questioned, with internal critics arguing that had ASEAN not been so tightly bound by it, it could have issued timely warnings to Thailand about its worsening condition. ASEAN took a first step in this direction by establishing a regional financial and macroeconomic surveillance process, known as the ASEAN Surveillance Process. While Acharya argues that this indicates a trend towards the increasing 'intrusiveness' of ASEAN regionalism, he also notes that ASEAN proved resistant to the inclusion of political issues (such as Myanmar's human rights record) or to the institutionalisation of the Surveillance Process into a Surveillance Mechanism.[57]

The shared beliefs about the certainty of regional boundaries among ASEAN members have not obviated the need to produce a sense of difference with outside states in order to maintain the boundary and the

[54] Ibid.

[55] Rodolfo C. Severino, 'Sovereignty, Intervention and the ASEAN Way', address at the ASEAN Scholars Roundtable, Singapore, July 3, 2000; www.aseansec.org/3221.htm.

[56] 'Overview –The Association of Southeast Asian Nations'; http://www.aseansec.org/64.htm.

[57] Amitav Acharya, 'Regionalism and the Emerging World Order: Sovereignty, Autonomy, Identity'. In Shaun Breslin, Christopher W. Hughes, Nicola Phillips and Ben Rosamond (eds.), *New Regionalisms in the Global Political Economy* (London: Routledge, 2002), 29.

sense of collective identity. Neither have these boundaries been free of contention, as evident when states outside these boundaries have either applied for or implied interest in membership. For example, in 1996 Papua New Guinea proposed that it should be made a 'permanent associate member' of ASEAN. Although Papua New Guinea had observer status since 1976 and had acceded to the Treaty of Amity and Cooperation in 1987, these arrangements were not intended to lead Papua New Guinea into ASEAN membership. Thus, its request for permanent associate membership received a lukewarm reception.[58]

Australia's efforts to redefine itself as a member of the Asian region in the 1980s and 1990s have also contested the exclusive definition of ASEAN identity.[59] While Australia's efforts have intensified the institutional relations between ASEAN and Australia, they have also increased the necessity to (re)articulate the differences that separate Australia from Southeast Asia. In the course of their relations with Australia, ASEAN states have continued with their exclusive conception of the Southeast Asian region, and view Asia Pacific Economic Cooperation (APEC) and co-operation with Australia as institutional co-operation between two distinct regions. Despite Australia's efforts at redefining its identity as a member of the region, ASEAN has explicitly dismissed the possibility of Australian membership in ASEAN (Australia has not sought membership). In the eyes of at least several Southeast Asian states, Australia cannot co-operate in the ASEAN way because it lacks 'Asian'ness. As Malaysia's Mohammed Mahathir stated bluntly, 'calling Australia an Asian country has no meaning whatsoever'.[60] In addition, Australia is not included in the Asia–Europe (ASEM) meetings, despite its overt request to be, the proposals for an ASEAN Free Trade Area (AFTA), and the ASEAN Plus Three Process.

Thus, ASEAN's interactions with its 'constitutive outside' are predominantly characterised by exclusionary othering. If we evaluate ASEAN's othering practices on the basis of the four proposed ethical criteria, we see that ASEAN's rigid boundaries have not necessarily

[58] Henderson, Reassessing ASEAN, 82.
[59] J. Wiseman, Global Nation? Australia and the Politics of Globalization (Cambridge: Cambridge University Press, 1998); G. Smith, D. Cox and S. Burchill, Australia and the World (Oxford: Oxford University Press, 1996); R. A. Higgott and K. R. Nossal, 'Australia and the Search for a Security Community in the 1990s'. In Adler and Barnett, Security Communities, 265–294.
[60] Higgott and Nossal, 'Australia', 283.

promoted conflict nor legitimised violence towards outsider states. ASEAN has even contributed to the management of some conflicts beyond its boundaries, such as the Chinese claim to exclusive sovereignty over the South China Sea as a 'lost' Chinese territory, which conflicted with the Malaysian claim to the Spratly Islands and the Philippine claim zone of Kalayaan. In February 1992, China passed a controversial territorial law, which effectively converted the South China Sea area to Chinese internal waters and imposed a series of limitations on navigation. In July 1992, ASEAN issued its Declaration on the South China Sea, which indicated ASEAN's desire to negotiate a code of conduct with the Chinese over the issue. Tensions further escalated in the region after February 1995, when China occupied the Mischief or Panganiban Reef in the Philippine claim area. This occupation further unified the ASEAN states – both claimant and non-claimant – around the issue.[61] While initially resisting multilateral involvement in the issue, China eventually signed a declaration on conduct for the South China Sea with ASEAN in November 2002. This marked the first time that China accepted a multilateral agreement over the issue.

On the other hand, ASEAN has not been able to positively influence the bilateral relations between Australia and Indonesia, which have historically been volatile and prone to quick escalation of tensions. These tensions escalated to new heights especially during the 1999 East Timor conflict. Despite Australia's history of involvement in regional organisations, Australia's leadership of the peace-keeping force International Force for East Timor (INTERFET) – which had significant ASEAN participation – caused deep resentment. In Indonesia, the peace-keeping operation was perceived as Western imperialist interference and was imputed with ulterior motives. Arguing that Australia's leadership reflects a failure to take into account Indonesian sensitivities, the Indonesian daily *Kompas* surmised that 'who knows whether, with such an approach, the West wants to apply a Balkanization policy in Southeast Asia'. Upon the arrival of Australian troops in East Timor, Indonesia tore apart the 1995 security agreement with Australia, indicating a major setback in relations.

As to be expected, ASEAN's mode of exclusionary othering has not induced normative change in outsider states. In contrast to Europe, the

---

[61] Leszek Buszynski, 'ASEAN, the Declaration on Conduct, and the South China Sea', *Contemporary Southeast Asia*, 25:3 (2003), 343–362.

expansion of ASEAN did not impose any requirements on prospective members or involve an interim status of candidacy during which the prospective members' suitability for community norms and procedures would be monitored and evaluated. Instead, 'the expansion of ASEAN involved the extension of the ASEAN way'.[62] For example, in the context of persistent political repression in Myanmar, the norm of non-interference formed the basis of ASEAN's engagement with Myanmar and its determination to admit Myanmar into ASEAN. In ASEAN's view, political repression in Myanmar could not be used to justify the exclusion of Myanmar since such a move would constitute interference in internal affairs. ASEAN put forth the concept of 'constructive engagement' to explain its response to the Myanmar situation. As explained by an Indonesian foreign policy official, this meant that ASEAN is telling the Myanmar regime to change 'very quietly, in a Southeast Asian manner, without any fanfare, without any public statements' which would 'embarrass and isolate them'.[63]

In terms of the content of the representations, the moral space of superior/inferior is less prominent in ASEAN's discourse, compared to that of the EU. This is mostly because ASEAN norms do not have a universalistic aspiration and are constructed as culturally specific to Southeast Asia. When this cultural specificity is not recognised and Southeast Asian societies and governments become the target of Western criticisms, the moral space becomes more prominent. The most negative representations are often directed at the 'West', mainly Europe, the USA and Australia. Southeast Asian leaders frequently depict Western criticisms and intrusions as 'imperialistic', 'arrogant' and downright 'rude'.

Promoting an exclusive identity has not kept ASEAN away from entering into various forms of flexible and overlapping institutional arrangements with outsider states. These arrangements include the Post-Ministerial Conferences, the ASEAN Regional Forum, APEC and the ASEAN Plus Three Process.[64] Because ASEAN promotes an

---

[62] Acharya, 'Regionalism', 27.
[63] Acharya, *Constructing a Security Community in Southeast Asia*, 110.
[64] The Post-Ministerial Conferences provide a forum for consultation with non-ASEAN dialogue partners, which are Australia, Canada, the European Union, Japan, New Zealand, the United States, China, South Korea, Russia, India and the UN Development Programme. In addition to these partners, the ASEAN Regional Forum also includes Mongolia, Papua New Guinea and North Korea as

exclusive identity, these arrangements between ASEAN and non-ASEAN countries are based on a shared understanding of ASEAN's firm boundaries. Therefore unlike the EU, these arrangements do not need to reproduce the boundary by constructing the non-ASEAN countries as a source of instability and threat, and marking their exclusion.

What kinds of community to build?

Identity-based groupings in international relations carry with them many normative dilemmas that result from the dependence of identity on difference. If this dependence is not carefully managed, these groupings may promote conflict with outsiders, while purportedly stabilising peace within. This chapter introduced these dilemmas that accompany community-building, and discussed how the constructivist literature approaches questions of identity/difference. It proposed alternative ethical criteria according to which self/other relations may be evaluated, and evaluated the community-building practices of the EU and ASEAN according to these criteria.

The analysis undertaken in this chapter shows that the answer to the question of what kinds of community to build depends on the ethical principles that we are advocating. For example, if we are foremost interested in normative change and progress in world politics, then communities with inclusive identities that engage in inclusionary othering are preferable. Interstate communities, such as the EU, which allow for the potential inclusion of others if they fulfil certain normative conditions, often successfully diffuse out community norms. On the other hand, such an effect is absent in exclusive communities such as ASEAN, where membership is based on inherent characteristics, rather than the fulfilment of certain conditions. However, if we are foremost interested not in normative change, but in building an equitable relationship with the other, exclusive communities that do not seek to convert the other but accept its differences may potentially be better. While a moral space of superior/inferior was prominent in ASEAN's interaction with Australia, it was not that prominent in case of other outsider countries. And finally, if our utmost ethical criterion is avoiding conflict with and securitisation of the other, inclusionary othering

observers. The ASEAN Plus Three Process promotes institutionalised co-operation with China, Japan and South Korea.

fares better; however, exclusionary othering practices can be successful under certain conditions. In the case of the EU, inclusionary othering has helped mitigate conflicts on the borders of the EU, while exclusionary othering helped aggravate them. Yet in case of ASEAN, we see that exclusionary othering has not necessarily promoted conflict with out-sider states except in the case of Australia. The primary reason why exclusionary othering promoted conflict and constructed a moral space of superior/inferior in the case of Australia is because Australia sought to contest the exclusive definition of ASEAN identity.

The experiences of two regional community-building institutions analysed in this chapter suggest that their identity relations with out-sider states are very much shaped by the nature of their collective identities. Although they represent alternative forms of collective iden-tity, neither has been able to avoid the discrimination and exclusion of (certain) outsiders. Thus, we can conclude that neither has advanced to a post-territorial logic. However, both institutions have been careful to adopt policies that can possibly mitigate the potentially adverse implications of such exclusion. In case of the EU, this has taken the form of cross-border co-operation programmes and institutionalised co-operation with outsider states. ASEAN has also adopted various forms of flexible and overlapping co-operation arrangements with out-sider states. Needless to say, the conclusions of this chapter derive from the analysis of two regional communities, and the analysis of other community-building processes, perhaps less institutionalised ones such as the community of democratic states, may necessitate a further qualifi-cation of arguments.

10 | Progress with a price

RICHARD PRICE

What to do when faced with moral dilemmas in world politics such as the putative trade-offs between amnesties and criminal tribunals, humanitarian intervention and self-determination, the vexing conundrums presented by immigration or the exclusionary identity dynamics involved in expanding peaceful communities? Are policies which fall short of desirable ethical objectives ideals nonetheless justifiable, including practices of evident hypocrisy? How do we really know we have reached an ethical limit, or fallen short in ways that deserve the withholding of moral praise? This volume has sought to shed light on such questions, on the premise that research programmes which have shown how moral norms arise and have an impact on world politics ought to be well placed to help us answer the ethical question of 'what to do'. We have sought here to leverage the constructivist agenda of theorising and empirically explaining how moral norms matter towards the normative project of identifying plausible moral alternatives to deal with global challenges. We explicitly recognise that constructivism is but one possible path to take to do so, and enjoin others for their contributions in thinking further through the relationship between the empirical and the normative. This volume offers its contributions in the spirit of fruitfulness and in the hope of inviting other theoretical approaches in International Relations and other disciplines such as philosophy to draw upon and critique and build upon these efforts, and ultimately to engage with practitioners in dealing with the central challenges of contemporary global politics which unavoidably have ethics at their core.

Constructed contexts

One of the chief injunctions of this volume is that context matters in ethical problems in world politics. And the authors here share a particular understanding of that context and its manifold implications for

281

ethics. The context within which agents think and act is socially constructed, as are the very ethical positions practitioners or analysts bring to bear in even identifying a situation as a moral problem or dilemma in the first place. As Martha Finnemore observes, this constructivist ontology requires an analysis of the 'ways in which normative structures shape our perceptions of problems, structure the ranges of response we consider, and limit the effectiveness of that response in our own normative terms' (p. 200). The implications of this are several and important.

One implication is that the contributors of this volume are generally suspicious of the holy grail of one-size-fits-all ethical formulas of the type of utilitarianism or Kantian deontology as sufficient to resolve tough ethical dilemmas. This does not mean such approaches are not enormously important – far from it, as such venerable traditions deeply inform the perspectives taken here, such as Kathryn Sikkink's argument against torture or Marc Lynch's arguments weighing the pros and cons of sanctions.[1] But it does mean that judgements as to the ultimate suitability of their application in many cases rest on the kinds of empirical and often grubby diplomatic or operational details that are typically not the greatest value-added of more philosophical approaches to ethics where the formulation of principles of as generalisable applicability as possible is generally privileged, a point developed systematically in Christian Reus-Smit's chapter. As Finnemore has underscored, even if (virtually) everyone in the international community agrees humanitarian intervention would be ethically desirable in the case of Darfur, assuming that it is simply wrong for, say, any particular country like Canada to have failed to have taken enough initiative to successfully secure the Security Council authorisation elides seriously grappling with the difficult social fact that virtually no state's people seem ready to offer their lives enough for the kinds of necessary combat operations for such an intervention. Or as Lynch is at pains to point out, those who advocated an end to sanctions against Iraq as unethical rarely paid

---

[1] There are thus no pretensions to be reinventing the ethical wheels here, since any consequentialist ethic, such as utilitarianism, implies an empirical assessment of outcomes. Moreover, as Henry Shue counselled me some time ago, rare indeed is the deontological formulation that in fact ignores empirical consequences altogether: 'thou shalt not kill' could also be expressed as 'stop at the consequence of killing'. The hoped-for contribution of this volume, rather, is adding to our stock of empirical and theoretical considerations to consider in dealing with ethical challenges in world politics.

adequate attention to the complexities of how their position was ruthlessly manipulated by a murderous dictator.

But if to no small extent the answer to the ethical question of 'what to do' is 'it depends' – on the details of possibility and limit in a given case – this volume obviously doesn't rest with that conclusion, which could be taken to be as trite in its unhelpfulness as it is profoundly true. Rather, the book seeks to make contributions regarding just what it is upon which ethically defensible action depends exactly, when the deductive integrity of eminently necessary ethical guideposts of general moral rules frays under the strain of concrete application. A chief contribution here is the identification of different sources and types of moral dilemmas, which carry different implications for moral limit and possibility. There are clashes between ethics and interests, and there are conflicts between moral norms. Some of the latter do appear to be genuine conflicts for which there is no good solution, but many upon close analysis reveal themselves not to be immutable dilemmas but rather predicated upon (1) social constructions amenable to change or (2) ethical positions underpinned by unwarranted empirical suppositions.

To begin with the first of these, some dilemmas arise because of conflicts between ethics and the political realities of (even socially constructed) interests and practices 'on the ground', a dichotomy constructivists mostly tend to resist insofar as the latter are often understood to encompass 'material realities'. But very real tensions crystallise in examples such as the incompatible pulls of multilateralism for the legitimacy of international interventions with the brute fact that such operations tend to be much more inefficient than unilateral action, often to the point of frustrating the goals of such action if not preventing it altogether, particularly in the operational details on the ground as Finnemore is at pains to underscore. Or the fact that physically opening borders for the benefits of increased trade and the erasing of borders with communications carries with it the social reality of increasing the prospects of travelling to other countries and the physical reality of increased attempts at cross-border movement of peoples, as Amy Gurowitz shows.

Still, some of these tensions only produce moral dilemmas from and for a particular ethical perspective – as Finnemore highlights (p. 201), the dilemma between self-determination and humanitarian intervention is only felt by practitioners or observers of a cosmopolitan bent: 'what constitutes a humanitarian crisis is always a function of the normative fabric of political life and standards of acceptable behaviour in the world'. Similarly, the dilemmas Gurowitz wrestles with between a commitment to democracy and a humanitarian approach to immigration often embraced more by elites than democratic societies at large would not trouble a communitarian let alone a sceptic, nor one not committed to democratic decision making where policy ought to reflect the will of the people. In that sense, morality or moralities produce their own dilemmas for those faced with decisions to act or justify, and sometimes themselves 'make success elusive in our own normative terms', to cite Finnemore (p. 207). This is due to the conflicting demands of ethics at a given time and place. But also, recognition that humanity's own ethical standards will change over time and across cultural, political, social and legal space means that moral dilemmas will never disappear, and moral satiation will always be elusive, since moral victories also tend to serve to raise the bar of ethical standard. In so doing, examples of moral progress may in fact widen the gap between predominant practice and moral aspiration in world politics and make morality seem even more elusive as subsequent practice fails to live up to what may be something of a temporary moral highpoint. But we ought not lose sight of the fact that this is progress defined in a humanitarian sense. As Lynch argues, moral progress was had in the Iraq sanctions episode even given the tragedies involved, insofar as it is extremely unlikely the world will ever see again such comprehensive multilateral sanctions that harm civilians in such devastating ways.

All this presupposes specification of what constitutes progress, which the authors in this book articulate unambiguously. This project analyses moral challenges that present themselves as dilemmas not just for the author or a given practitioner, but dilemmas as broader social realities with global import. That is, dilemmas arise not only from the tensions between operational practice and moral aspirations, nor just for a particular agent from conflicting moral demands on an individual, but as larger international social realities arising from the incompatibility between moralities as widely shared, intersubjective social structures in world politics: self-determination and sovereignty of indigenous peoples; the self-determination of norms of democratic politics and the closed doors of such polities towards immigrants; self-determination and humanitarian intervention. At one level, this means that, as Finnemore states:

To understand how norms work, we need to understand the complexity, contradictions and indeterminacy of the larger normative system in which political action takes place. Any policy decision of consequence is taken within a dense web of normative claims that often conflict with one another and create serious ethical dilemmas for decision makers. After all, if the prescriptions of norms and values were always clear or if they never conflicted with one another, we would not have to make any decisions; we would just follow the prescriptions. In this sense, normative conflict is what *creates* decisions since, absent conflicting normative claims, there would be nothing to decide (p. 198).

Further, the discovery in analysing the spread of international moral norms that – even given the vagaries of interpretation and contestation – many moral impulses are widely shared and not simply the pretensions of the powerful, makes the ethical problems that much more acute as global dilemmas. That is, where painful trade-offs are understood and experienced by intervener and intervened; by jurist, victim and diplomatic peacemaker; by politicians representing a democratic jurisdiction and balancing aspirations for immigrants or the spread of peaceful transnational security communities – all with implications for practice around the world as national standards inform international ones. These shared ethical norms can be of a procedural kind, as per the important research of Risse, Lynch, Müller and others which enjoins researchers to find examples of genuine truth seeking and consensus in global politics as opposed to relations of bargaining or coercion as a path to co-operation and justice. But does the discovery of such empirical processes in fact deliver the ethical? Risse asks exactly the right question which issues from the International Relations empirical application of a Habermasian dialogic ethic: 'Does establishing a reasoned consensus about the situation on the ground and/or the norms guiding the interaction make for a "better" outcome?'[2] Further engagement with Risse's answer to this question will be enjoined later in this chapter. For the present discussion it will do to note that contributors to this project suggest that an agreed process of dialogue in which all have a stake is far from the only viable path to justice (which isn't to say it isn't often preferable to the alternatives such as coercion). As Finnemore

---

[2] Thomas Risse, '"Let's Argue!" Communicative Action in World Politics', *International Organization* 54 (2000), 20.

notes with cases such as Bosnia in mind: 'To achieve reconciliation, interveners have to treat all parties as if they were dealing in good faith (even when they are not) and treat them with a kind of even-handedness and impartiality.' The problem is that 'interveners may find themselves intervening for a process that includes negotiated settlement and elections, which ultimately produces precisely the substantive outcomes they were intervening to avoid' (pp. 211, 212).

Still, in concert with the Habermasian project, Finnemore emphasises an important ethical implication of taking seriously all contributors to the construction of intersubjective moral standards and the requirements of legitimacy:

> a constructivist empirical analysis provides reasons to attend to the views of the weak, the marginalised, the 'done to' in world politics . . . Constructivism's emphasis on such *inter*subjective understandings shifts our analytic focus in ethically important ways. Analytically, constructivist analysis creates space for, even demands, attention to the views of the many different actors involved in an intervention, since the legitimacy of an intervention and, to some extent its success, depends on the reactions of those upon whom intervention is visited. Views of the intervened upon, the 'done to', in these cases create political effects that analysts must study. The corollary of this view is that interveners must attend to the views of their targets if they are to formulate successful policies. (p. 220)

Thus, one implication of the intimate relation between the empirical and the ethical introduced in the introductory chapter is that a satisfactory ethic can only at its peril attempt to ignore the relation between the actor and acted upon, or, ethically even better (if not realised in so many situations), the relations of agents genuinely acting with one another in solidarity. Further, it underscores the difficulties in one-sided monological attempts to think through moral dilemmas without enjoining the moral dilemmas faced by the weak, the disinherited, the 'acted upon' and how they conjoin with those of the powerful, the wealthy, the interveners. Thus from Jonathan Havercroft's chapter we are enjoined to recognise that indigenous peoples are presented with their own dilemmas: what are the appropriate solutions to resolve obstacles to self-determination in a world of sovereign states that cannot be wished away? Is negotiation with settler governments little better than co-optation? Is some form of reparations the appropriate way to frame these issues, are more aggressive forms of protest acceptable within indigenous traditions? Indeed, turning the dilemmas of recognition another degree inward to the constitution of marginalised peoples themselves, who is to be recognised as indigenous in the first place, given all the complications involved therein?

These considerations by themselves do not indubitably promise to resolve all dilemmas any more than a utilitarian proposal of the adding up of satisfactions might, particularly given the views of those contesting such practices (the Serbs in Kosovo, for example). But it is to point out the great moral weight of situations where the victims, the repressed, enjoin with the international community in rightful action, such as in the call of the African National Congress for sanctions against the apartheid government of South Africa. And such considerations are built into the ontological position of constructivism which regards social legitimacy as an indispensable ingredient for communities that are to balance the demands of stability and justice.

The ethics of constructivism

Nonetheless, for some of these kinds of dilemmas, there are in fact, as Finnemore resigns, *no good solution* in the offing, in the sense of a response that can attend satisfactorily to one or the other cherished value without significant sacrifice of another. Indeed, that is what makes such situations dilemmas. It is important to acknowledge that even as constructivists embrace an ontology that posits real possibilities of change in world politics, there are situations even from this perspective, and additionally and particularly from this perspective which takes morality as social structure seriously, that cannot be changed willy-nilly by those charged with the realities of political decision making or judgement. Sometimes something of moral value cannot be realised and has to be sacrificed in a situation of acting or deciding, that is, of choice. But if some of the situations in one respect share an affinity with the tragic realist vision of politics, where this volume differs at least from contemporary realism is not assigning the unrealisability of inter-national moral goods such as those of the cosmopolitan kind as the unchanging lot of humanity or as primarily the causes rather than solutions to repetitively dire problems. Progress in such terms can be and has been had, even if in achieving it new problems and conflicts in resolving them are defined by the inherent restructuring of moral standards of possibility and impossibility that moral change itself makes possible. But this form of ever-present moral conflict denies the presumption of realism that moral improvement in world politics can be presumptively dismissed as ethically dangerous and ontologically implausible, as a project that 'sounds nice but regrettably is not the world we live in'.

This ethical position draws upon a second analytical strength of constructivism's emphasis on the socially constructed nature of context, which lies in demonstrating different configurations of political space across time and cultures, such that some ways of being are made possible, improbable or even ruled out of the conceptual universe. Ann Towns demonstrates this technique expertly in her chapter, skilfully relativising contemporary debates in Sweden which pit immigration against culture and gender equality by showing how in the past immigrants were discussed primarily as labour, and gender equality was not something presented as distinguishing Swede from immigrant. 'In fact, gender equality was sometimes represented as a *threat* to the continuity of Swedish culture rather than a part of it.' The conclusion then is that 'the identification of gender equality as a set of specifically Swedish values was not an effect given simply by immigration itself', and this powerful empirical device disarms the ethical position which would justify the exclusion of immigrants as a necessary bargain in the name of progress in gender equality. Progress (as in gender relations) is possible, drawing upon and furthering international human rights standards, though even such progress may not be laudable if bought at the price of regress in other dimensions and in ways that need not have happened or at least need not be perpetuated once we become aware of their effects through analyses such as these.

Problems even of the most wrenching kinds are sometimes addressed in ways such that the label of progress is reasonably assigned, though this is not to say that victory is had in some unidirectional or irreversible way. At a minimum, this volume emphasises that even successes in addressing moral dilemmas, indeed by virtue of that very success, breed new moral contexts which thus challenge humanity with novel moral dilemmas. Material factors do so too; advances in communications technology and the ability to transport goods and people quickly across the globe are a crucially important enabling factor for even considering humanitarian rescue in ways that were literally not possible in epochs past. Thus, it might be preciously small consolation indeed for those torn by the agony of contemporary dilemmas that their very wrenching with such dilemmas may indicate from a historical perspective an improvement of humanity's lot. For example, the agony of 500 persons killed by NATO's war against the former Yugoslavia in 1998 may pale with the scale of its antecedents, though it is not inappropriate to remind ourselves of the infinitely greater inhumanity with which such developments have too routinely been dealt. Nor to stop and reflect upon the sense in which current indignation at some facets of the contemporary treatment of immigrants is a moral luxury in the narrow sense of comparing problems today to previous eras even in the same country when millions were summarily deported or worse, something for which Gurowitz judges that the world's largest immigrant target state today no longer has the stomach.

Thinking through the relation of constructivism to realism on the question of ethics raises the question of the ethics of constructivism more generally. Quite to the contrary from the conservative critique that constructivism is biased towards the study of 'good' norms that 'worked', the opposite challenge could also be marshalled: does constructivism entail a political or ethical position at all? It has frequently been contended that constructivism is an approach, a method, an ontology or a social theory, but that it is not a substantive political theory or theory of international relations as such. This position implies the understanding that constructivism is best understood as not itself constituting a normative theory, that it is politically neutral concerning the outcomes of political life (conflictual versus co-operative, for example) and agnostic on ethical questions such as the priority of individual or community.[3] Is this the case, and what are the implications for thinking about the potential contributions of constructivism for normative theorising in world politics?

On the one hand, this view of constructivism's alleged agnosticism helps explain the varieties of constructivism and how constructivism has lent itself to being harnessed to numerous more obviously substantive theories, some with no small differences between them. Thus we have so-called conventional and critical or Marxian constructivisms, 'thick' and 'thin' constructivisms, modernist, post-modernist and holist constructivisms, feminist and post-colonial constructivisms, and so on. While it may be the case that to this point in the English-speaking

---

[3] Emanuel Adler, *Communitarian International Relations* (New York, NY: Routledge, 2005), 13.

academy of International Relations, a predominantly liberal cast has characterised constructivist scholarship, on this reading there is nothing to preclude realist or other illiberal constructivisms.[4]

At the same time, the historicist underpinnings of constructivism would seem to make its proponents hard pressed to maintain a strong view of its alleged neutrality, given the premise that all theories as cultural artefacts embody a perspective from somewhere and for something as put famously by Robert Cox, among others. And indeed, the analytic of constructivism does seem to foreclose key contentions of some political theories. This is particularly the case with materialist theories, which would locate all the explanatory leverage we need in the likes of military or economic power or in unalterable givens of nature. Furthermore, constructivism's emphasis on the possibilities of social and political change that are not confined to the realm of the domestic polity does seem to preclude conservative international political theories which as a matter of presumption discount the possibility of moral change across borders as enough of an anomaly that initiatives to those ends can be reliably dismissed as 'unrealistic'. Indeed, Sikkink turns realist charges of idealism upon their head in the case of criminal tribunals, demonstrating that the negative effects attributed to them by sceptics often don't stand up to empirical demonstration, at least not yet enough to justify their ethical dismissal, and that one would ignore the pervasive realities of international justice mechanisms at one's peril.

This volume has identified dilemmas that arise mostly for those from a cosmopolitan perspective, though its authors are self-conscious in doing so, and analyse issues that aren't just dilemmas for them but that engage issues international in scope through the spread of cosmopolitan sensibilities in national and international contexts. To be sure, all constructivist ethics need not be cosmopolitan, though constructivism does provide powerful grounds for cosmopolitan normative theories. Here it is instructive to visit a third kind of dilemma which is the subject of focused concentration in this volume, namely those that arise between moralities as social structures that are amenable to more ready dissection which paves the way for quite plausible political alternatives for change. Many of these are the product of a diagnosis which takes seriously social processes missed by alternative theoretical perspectives

---

[4] See J. Samuel Barkin, 'Realist Constructivism', *The International Studies Review* 5:3 (2003), 325–342.

such as materialist or rationalist approaches, which thus run the danger of the wrong prescription. Wendt is right to underscore that the claim that a phenomenon (like the structures of world politics) is a social construction does not mean it is easy to change; indeed, if they were that easy to change sceptics might be right in disregarding them as epiphenomenal to other mechanisms of social and political life. But calling something a social construction does entail that it is possible to change, as opposed to supposedly immutable realities such as biological givens of human nature.[5] Those who do not take morality seriously offer little in the way of serious diagnosis of just how morality operates; critical theorists who do take the ethical dimensions of political life seriously have too often failed to provide plausible alternatives to processes such as othering and their injustices that are seemingly inherent in identity politics. This volume has sought among other things to fill in precisely these gaps, and as such lies somewhere between realism and the most utopian poles of critical theory.

Illustrating the possibilities of genuine progressive change, Towns in her analysis of the politics of gender equality and immigration in Sweden nonetheless brilliantly cracks open the taken-for-granted assumptions in a political discourse which pits immigration policies as a trade-off against progress in the status of women. She demonstrates that this putative dilemma is itself a social construction that, once exposed, opens up ready paths to more progressive policies that do not have to come at the price of unduly exclusionary immigration policies. In such cases, constructivists address in an important respect the criticism that constructivism has mostly been liberal in the sense of identifying 'good' liberal norms that 'worked', since these chapters identify sources of injustice that themselves become visible from a constructivist perspective, and indeed from social practices that have been subject to celebration as prime examples of erstwhile moral progress, such as the liberal democratic peace or security communities.

Pulling back from a generation of critical identity politics literature which seemed to leave us with a pessimistic appraisal of the pervasiveness and indeed inevitability of 'othering' in identity politics, Bahar Rumelili

---

[5] Noting of course that biological phenomena are subject to no small change, even in relatively short terms for certain species, though typically meaningfully major changes in human biology manifest themselves over time horizons much more vast to be of consequence for the immediacy of resolving ethical dilemmas.

shines in demonstrating how the very kind of community-building practices that have decisively attenuated historical animosities between traditional great power combatants in world politics have at the same time
produced their own exclusionary and sometimes conflict-producing
dynamics with those outside those communities. Here too we have a
conflict that arises from the progressive social processes taken seriously by constructivists – community-producing processes of identity
formation – but whose conflict-producing consequences have gone
overlooked by the recent generation of scholarship on security communities and social structures of amity in world politics. While critical
theorists have indeed noted those tendencies in their insistence of
identity as a process of othering, they have neither posited plausible
alternative strategies, nor dissected adequately whether different kinds
of othering can be identified with different ethical implications. This
task Rumelili takes to heart in identifying four different criteria by
which to assess community-building practices, all of which need not
entail equally undesirable forms of exclusion. Thus she puts on the
agenda of politicians forging closer ties with other communities the
demand to consider the following implications of the discourses of
identity and difference involved in such projects (p. 266):

> Does it produce conflict with or legitimise violence towards the other?
> Does it induce positive change towards the other? Do the dominant
> representations of the other establish an ethical relation with the
> other (in terms of the content of representations)? Does the nature
> of collective identity allow for an ethical relation with the other?

Havercroft similarly demonstrates that the usual antipathy of sovereignty and self-determination that has rendered stillborn the efforts
towards the latter for indigenous peoples in a world of states misrep-
resents how many indigenous peoples themselves understand self-
determination, and obscures that no small common ground exists in
the politics of consent. Gurowitz, while taking seriously the political–
economic pressures underpinning the immigration situation, is nonetheless able to make plain that '*If* we as a society have constructed the
undocumented migrant as a criminal, we, it seems, are faced with two
choices: we can let them dissolve into society or we can arrest or deport
them. As long as they are constituted as illegal and criminal, we cannot
easily acknowledge the critical role that they play in the economy
nor our role in bringing them here' (p. 159). Decriminalising the

very immigration that is in fact actively solicited by the American political economy, in short, would dissolve what for many is the under-standable red line of law (immigration reform as 'rewarding criminals') that lies behind moral opposition to compromises that would mean-ingfully improve the situation of immigrants. And recognising the social production of the immigrant as criminal and the complicity of the target state in fostering immigration is the first step.

With this self-consciousness of the cultural relativity of the analysts' own ethics as well as that of the social structures governing the situation being studied, just how far can one go then in delimiting what is deemed ethically possible at a given juncture? Indeed does positing any limits for ethical possibility make sense? Gurowitz navigates skilfully between contemporary political economic realities forging debates on immigra-tion in the USA, namely, that 'the USA has a structural demand for low-wage migrant labour – much of it undocumented and much of it Mexican'. Further ethical critique would deconstruct that political–economic structure and seek to change it, including by a more just global trading regime, not to mention a just global immigration regime. These, while not championed by Gurowitz in her chapter, are neither necessarily precluded by the advocacy of the more immediate policies favoured by Gurowitz to provide humanitarian improvement of the situation. Indeed until such larger international structures producing the movements of peoples are in fact favourably altered, she does point the way to forms of action that could claim to make a difference, as opposed to falling short of much more ambitious comparisons to the ideal which, until their realisation, do amount to failure. The critical position would counter that such reformist gestures simply facilitate the perpetuation of systems that are fundamentally unjust and that call for more revolutionary action. This is not an unreasonable position, partic-ularly on constructivists' own terms, insofar as scholars documenting change and processes like learning in world politics have often empha-sised the crucial importance of a 'crisis' as a catalyst for major shifts. The ethical prescription that would follow is to foment the conditions for crisis rather than abate them. The position forwarded here is that if one weighs demonstrable human gains against the failures of an ideal, let alone making things worse in the hopes of more fundamental change arising from the purposeful generation of a crisis, then those gains come out pretty well, especially if they cannot be demonstrably shown to render impossible or even more unlikely further progress towards more fundamental change. And this constructivism is particularly well positioned to do. This involves delicate trade-offs. Lynch in his analysis warns when the techniques favoured by constructivists as mechanisms of strategic moral action threaten to undermine their own grounds. Rhetorical entrapment, moral exhortation, shaming and exposure, and the like all offer real power and tactical benefits, but 'if rhetoric is not converted into actual belief, internalised into a moral consensus, then agreement remains brittle'.

The resulting ethical stance would not be critical of but rather open to efforts to reach even farther for the ideal, as Sikkink underscores even as she delicately dissects the immobilising potential of such idealism as a form of criticism. At the same time this stance would approach exasperation when such a disposition is not reciprocated; that is, when criticisms from that ideal point of view target (to the point of dismissing) the smaller victories along the way that do effect meaningful change in real human lives if not whole systems, a tact which fosters a deep cynicism that undercuts moral action.[6] This is particularly so since constructivist scholarship's major contribution has been to demonstrate how sometimes initially small developments open wedges to wider change, from genealogical studies of unintended consequences of shifts in language[7] to the ultimate boomerang effects of small rhetorical concessions to human rights activists. Who, really, would have thought that the Helsinki accords, routinely disparaged in the 1970s as an inconsequential sell-out, would prove to have sowed the seeds for revolutionary peaceful change in the Soviet bloc?[8] Who a few years (let alone weeks) before its occurrence in 1998 would have really thought that the idea of Britain arresting Augusto Pinochet for his role in torture in Chile was anything but the highest flight of fancy? It is in a similar vein that Havercroft points out the potentially salutary effects of anchoring indigenous self-determination claims in a United Nations declaration, namely, that 'watering down the right to self-determination may serve as a strategic stepping-stone for greater protection of indigenous rights under international law in the long term'.

[6] See Patricia Owens, 'Hannah Arendt and the Problem of War, Hypocrisy and Wars on Hypocrisy', paper presented at American Political Science Association Annual Meeting, Philadelphia, September 2, 2006.
[7] Richard Price, *The Chemical Weapons Taboo* (Ithaca, NY: Cornell University Press, 1997).
[8] See Daniel Thomas, *The Helsinki Effect: International Norms, Human Rights, and the Demise of Communism* (Princeton, NJ: Princeton University Press, 2001).

Going even further into a type of ethical dilemma that can be shown empirically to be less or different than it is often made out to be, Sikkink shows how the putative dilemma between the supposed conflict-dampening benefits of amnesties for those who engineer atrocities and the justice of criminal tribunals evaporates upon recognition of the social reality of advances in international criminal law and institutions. That is, it is the holding out of the promise of amnesties, and not the promise of justice including through criminal tribunals, which is shown to be the more idealistic position. The social reality of contemporary political life is the utter frailty of such amnesties in the face of the onslaught of domestic and international political practice and legal norms and institutions like universal jurisdiction which combine to render the longevity of such promises dubious. This is a stunning reversal of the usual invocation of reality of the sort 'torture is here to stay so let's figure out how to live with it'. This isn't to confuse the efficacy of such criminalisation processes for eliminating conflict with their mere existence, but since Sikkink demonstrates that the claim that denials of amnesties and tribunals for atrocities do make conflicts worse is in fact not (yet) empirically sustainable, then the empirical fact that such amnesties rarely last shifts the terms of ethical debate substantially. Similarly, it is in Lynch's study that the difference between a realist ethic of politics as the sceptical art of the possible and that of constructivism is exposed. For the realist, hypocrisy is so endemic that to fail to simply expect and embrace it as the rule and act accordingly is to commit oneself to folly, whereas the constructivist analysis presented here suggests reasons for not making such an early commitment since there is structural space for progressive detours through these minefields. To fail to recognise this exposes one to the costs of illegitimacy to which the extreme sceptical position is ill-equipped to respond, and which so frustrated the George W. Bush administration's ability to achieve its ambitious goals due to its tone-deafness to legitimacy as reality.

Still, it is crucial to note that the ultimate ethical position developed here is contingent, and open to empirical challenge: if in fact tribunals are more decisively shown to make things worse than plausible and actually existing alternatives as opposed to implicit comparisons to counterfactual ideals, then Sikkink is prepared to revise her moral support for such tribunals. This is a most important point for this project, and it is the ethical corollary of the explanatory agnosticism of coming down where the evidence lies, which for many constructivists has translated into a rigorous and self-reflexive working methodology of carefully weighing alternative accounts against one another. This contingency, doubled by the potential social malleability of our world in which sometimes anything does seem to be possible, ought to make us modest in our claims, and underscore the necessary humility in our ethics whether as practitioners or especially as observers.

Humility comes also from the proposition that moral progress almost invariably results not in simple resolution but rather comes at the price of creating new moral dilemmas. It comes further still from recognising that the very processes diagnosed and implicitly heralded as avenues of moral progress in one context may have very different effects in another. Thus, the shaming techniques identified as so important for progress in human rights and other issues pushed by transnational advocacy networks, and advocated by Havercroft as a potentially powerful resource for indigenous peoples, are shown by Rumelili to be regarded as inappropriate and likely to engender backlash in an ASEAN context which trumpets an 'Asian way' of consensus building and quiet diplomacy as opposed to confrontation. Lynch underscores that a prescriptive implication of constructivism is for moral entrepreneurs to positively beg decision makers – 'Lie to me!' (so I can entrap you in your rhetoric) – though only to a point as will be seen in the next section. The political prescriptions pointed to by the explanatory findings of constructivism thus are not necessarily unproblematically translated into universal global ethical counsel, but must be handled with care.

Even more, humility is engendered by recognition that the standards we may uphold now, we ourselves as individuals or as communities would have run afoul of in the past. As Finnemore rightly points out, 'citizens of the Western states who are pushing these norms and doing most of the intervening were not able to "self-determine" without a great deal of violence, yet we now are expecting others to do so', rarely reflecting upon 'what if' such standards had been applied to their own civil wars or the colonising of indigenous peoples as Havercroft reminds us. And yet, for all these reasons for humility in our ethics, constructivism at the same time gives us additional rigorous grounds to judge and act.

The ethics of hypocrisy

These considerations bring us to the issue of hypocrisy that in the introduction was flagged for particular attention in the contributors' analyses.

At a minimum, this volume highlights that there would seem to be a significant ethical difference between hypocrisy which is practised as a temporary way station in difficult circumstances on the road to making things better, and which is accompanied by efforts to achieve just that, and hypocrisy meant to obstruct such developments in favour of more venal objectives. As Lynch argues, hypocrisy figures importantly in constructivist accounts as a mechanism on the road to compliance with norms, such as the literature that stresses the impact of holding governments to account if they rhetorically profess adherence to human rights norms.[9] Yet if hypocrisy is pervasive and particularly if it is propagated by the powerful, it may well not just undermine the perceived integrity of the particular actors, but erode the belief in and commitment to norms, and indeed the social function of legitimacy more generally, which is required for hypocrisy's applauded piggy-back effects.

In this way, forms of hypocritical political practice can be revealed as important social mechanisms aligned with Wendt's account of the tipping points that mark transitions from Hobbesian to Lockean or Kantian cultures of anarchy. Just as a cultural shift can be said to transpire when an attribute (of friend, rival or enemy) comes to be seen as a property of the system itself as opposed to merely a property of a particular agent, so too can hypocrisy be seen as an attribute of a particular agent or, more damaging to international morality more generally, of the system itself.[10] Thus, endemic hypocrisy, particularly by the powerful given their more pervasive influence in world affairs, would undercut the agency of ethical activism more generally, and indeed threaten to evacuate its power altogether, thus deflecting boomerangs and other mechanisms of change whether it be by corporations, states or members of transnational civil society.

The result for normative theory is a more nuanced approach than regarding all hypocrisies as created equal. Those practices which seek to ameliorate the moral dimensions of a dilemma that are sacrificed for others are very different from those which sacrifice such moral goods for instrumental objectives and cynically manipulate them as a diversion from the latter. Thus, defending the intervention in Kosovo despite

[9] Thomas, *The Helsinki Effect*; Thomas Risse, Stephen Roppe and Kathryn Sikkink, *The Power of Human Rights: International Norms and Domestic Change* (Cambridge: Cambridge University Press, 1999).
[10] Alexander Wendt, *Social Theory of International Politics* (Cambridge: Cambridge University Press, 2000), 264.

its violation of the international law of war is a more tolerable form of hypocrisy if accompanied by rigorous efforts to repair and alter the fabric of international law torn in the process in order to accommodate such situations in the future (as Canada is arguably doing in pushing the Responsibility to Protect agenda), rather than being caught in the mire of having to defend its opposite in the absence of such practice, as confronted some states opposed to the US-led attack against Iraq in 2003. Hypocrisy, in short, creates its own moral imperatives for decision makers and those who judge which themselves serve to raise the bar; failure to reach for that bar engenders cynicism, which in turn undercuts the ground for even genuine subsequent moral action.

Havercroft's analysis shows that members of settler states and their governments with liberal values as well as international organisations, which might otherwise champion such norms as self-determination, human rights and diversity, find themselves caught in accusations of hypocrisy, not willing to apply those norms fully to indigenous peoples if it presages cessation from sovereign states or other deleterious potential implications. What could we thus expect but that such a situation would engender cynicism, suspicion and other roadblocks to a mutually satisfactory solution to dilemmas of indigenous self-determination in a world of sovereign territorial states? That said, the identification of hypocrisy itself is not enough. This hypocrisy is useful in identifying a moral limit (that it is wrong to exclude one category of peoples from a right that all other types of peoples already enjoy under international law). But still, hypocrisy is not particularly effective at getting states to change their behaviour, as it has been in other cases that constructivists have analysed. This is because the long history of relations between indigenous peoples and settler societies has been one in which settler societies have repeatedly not recognised indigenous peoples through the hypocritical application of norms. This underscores the general point about the potential gap between the ethics of critical theory and the ontological/explanatory contributions of constructivism flagged in the introduction, that 'expecting effects from revealing the inconsistencies between the rhetorical and practical would imply that the global structures of power are erected on different principles than they really are'.[11]

---

[11] Radmila Nakarada, 'The Uncertain Reach of Critical Theory'. In Paul Wapner and Lester Edwin J. Ruiz (eds.), *Principled World Politics: The Challenge of Normative International Relations* (Lanham, MD: Rowman and Littlefield, 2000), 68.

An interesting issue to emerge from the analyses of hypocrisy in this volume concerns the trade-offs involved in the explicitness of political practice and judgement and their justifications. Thinking through the desirability of the kinds of international truth-seeking dialogues he and others have sought to empirically investigate, Risse has plausibly argued that:

> the more an issue is subject to public scrutiny, the more likely it becomes that materially less privileged actors have access to the discourse and that their arguments carry the day and convince an audience. Moreover, actors who can legitimately claim authoritative knowledge or moral authority (or both) should be more able to convince a skeptical public audience than actors who are suspected of promoting 'private' interests. The moral power and authority of many NGOs seems to be directly related to this feature of public discourses.[12]

So far, so good. But this position assumes that the publics of a democracy will generally be morally right in their positions, or that democracy as a value is cherished as such a pinnacle of justice such that what a fully democratic process decides is just. While many of the contributors to this volume have themselves documented just those processes which underpin Risse's supposition, the analyses of this volume interestingly challenge blanket positive appraisals of necessarily moral goods flowing from democratisation, deliberation and civil society. There is plenty of evidence to show that an increased role of civil society does produce morally desirable change, to be sure, but the analysis of hypocrisy raises interesting challenges that it always be so.

At times, one implication of the analyses here is that the scholarly (analytical) or political (democratic) demand for transparency can run afoul of other championed moral values. The tension most evident in cases considered in this volume arises from democratic demands of accountability, transparency and societal deliberation with other ethical goods. In a recent survey only one country among nine surveyed registered a positive view of immigrants, and scholars of immigration routinely document very unfavourable public opinion towards immigrants.[13] In short, if most of the target countries of immigration in the

---

[12] Risse, '"Let's Argue!"', 22.
[13] Associated Press/IPSOS Poll, 'Reactions to Immigration in Leading Nations'; www.ipsos-na.com/news/pressrelease.cfm?id=2253.

world were perfectly democratic on the issue of immigration, they would in all likelihood have at the very best significantly more restrictive immigration policies than many currently have in place. Political elites in at least some target countries of immigration, however, have been able to design and implement at various times policies which are not particularly responsive to at least this one important gauge of democratic process, namely responding to public opinion.

The injunction for practitioners in such positions is typically to be called on the carpet to explicitly defend their positions, with howls of protest of hypocrisy. But is it obvious that an immigration policy is undesirable which according to the letter of the law appears rather restrictive, perhaps as a deterrent to what would politically be received as an overwhelming numbers of immigrants, but is in practice applied more leniently? What if this produces the humanitarian benefit of permitting more willing immigrants to move to the place of their wishes than would be the case with a policy applied strictly? Or a policy which openly and honestly advertised the more lax practice lest it incur the moral liability of putting up a hypocritical front, but in the end likely invites rapid collapse due to domestic backlash to significant increases in immigration (which scholars have well documented)? Hypocrisy more in the sense of 'not saying one thing and doing it' than 'saying one thing and doing another' can be a virtue as Gurowitz among others shows, though again ultimately an ethical assessment depends upon further actions taken to address the source of the hypocrisy.

The point is that at a glance many people, especially those arguing from a more cosmopolitan standpoint with regard to immigration policy, are in favour of both the democratic process and progressive policies toward immigration, while it is not at all clear how compatible those are. In this sense, and as I will argue below, hypocritical policies may be preferential, from a humanitarian or cosmopolitan standpoint, to policies that force a choice in one direction or another, almost certainly to the detriment of the economy, or migrants or both.

This case further intrigues in the sense that Gurowitz charts an uncomfortable dilemma that many – theorists and politicians alike – might want to put aside or wish would go away. Civil society groups here have taken on a characteristic role of exposing hypocrisy, yet some prominent ones have done so with an agenda far from the cosmopolitan ends often chartered to date by constructivist IR scholars. The Minuteman Project is a group that claims to be 'doing the jobs that

Congress won't do' and that calls for 'national awareness to the decades-long careless disregard of effective U.S. immigration law enforcement'.[14] Rather than leaving us with this dilemma by exposing the hypocrisy of immigration policy, however, Gurowitz proposes as an ethical way forward decriminalising the very forms of immigration that are tolerated and encouraged by the American political economy, which in turn would dissolve the need for such hypocrisy in the longer run and thus vitiate its corrosive effects.

If there are sometimes arguments then for not being explicit about the justifications for one's policies, Sikkink on the other hand provides powerful arguments for being explicit – namely the deficits brought about by the *implicit* counterfactuals that often underlie what she dissects as implausible ethical positions. In the case of torture, she points out that there is no dilemma if one simply always sides on the deontological 'no torture' side of the argument. But there is the interesting dilemma for scholars of whether to 'even go there' in the sense of debating torture, as that risks giving more legitimacy to the other side than one may feel is warranted. Sikkink makes the politically important argument, and choice, that not doing so leaves the empirical arguments that are necessary to justify torture to those advocating torture. Her analysis of the relation of the empirical to the ethical in this crucial case, and in particular the role of rigorous social science in ethics, is exemplary:

> When 'evidence' is produced for torture's effectiveness, it is almost always provided by a person who has carried out torture or authorised it. In other words, since torture is a crime, the 'evidence' for the effectiveness of torture is provided by the person who has committed the crime of torture. Such a person has a strong self-interest in convincing themselves and the audience of the necessity of torture. If they wish to live with themselves and justify their behaviour to others, they must convince all of us that torture was effective. So, we have a counterfactual situation, where the evidence we are using to weigh whether or not torture was effective is being provided by someone who has committed a crime and has strong legal and psychological reasons for justifying it. No serious researcher would accept evidence in these circumstances. (p. 102)

---

[14] Minuteman Project; www.minutemanproject.com/default.asp?contentID=2.

Beyond the intrinsic power of her case against torture, her technique of dissecting the pathologies of the counterfactuals that underpin ethical argument provides one way, perhaps, of attempting to get back to an ethical taken-for-granted after it ruptures, a subject for much further scholarly attention.

Second, Sikkink shows that if comparisons to the ideal should be made explicit in judgements of political practice to avoid unfair condemnation, this could at once disarm critics of erstwhile progressive practice but at other times expose progressive policies as untenable in certain political circumstances. This brings us to a key axis motivating this volume: upon what basis does one castigate or praise a development as complicity in the injustice of the status quo or as moral progress? Some formulations of the critical argument seem to presume that progress in 'problem-solving' necessarily precludes more critical interventions in world politics, to use Cox's famous terms. Thus, for example, adjustments to alleviate crises within capitalism such as social assistance programmes do not really contribute to justice in a meaningful way since they actually serve as means to keep capitalism afloat, a system which is to be regarded as fundamentally unjust. The implication of the earlier argument in this chapter is that the burden upon such critical arguments is in fact to show that less than revolutionary progressive developments do in fact preclude the possibility of more fundamental justice being attained, not to mention that such fundamental change is a politically responsible possibility or that smaller progress renders such fundamental justice impossible. If, on the other hand, 'problem-solving' kinds of interventions do in fact render more fundamental justice more difficult, then they may well be legitimately subject to condemnation. Given the ethical position of critical theorists, and the ontological position of constructivism, it is difficult to imagine making such cases of impossibility, though the chapters in this volume demonstrate what such claims might look like.

Lynch makes a signal contribution on this issue in his chapter by positing how certain forms of hypocrisy are in fact not worth the short-term gains insofar as they threaten to undercut the possibility of moral practice more generally. He puts the point forcefully in arguing that

hypocritical moral argument over time devastates the credibility of all moral argument, and erodes the legitimacy of almost all major actors and institutions. The expectation of hypocrisy renders meaningful dialogue nearly impossible, stripping away even the possibility of a normative consensus. The potentially beneficial contribution to moral progress offered by the leveraging of hypocrisy must therefore be weighed against the degenerative potential of a systemic loss of legitimacy. (p. 168)

The delicate line here lies in judgements on what the scope for fundamental change is in world politics. In the desuetude of great power war, the abolition of the slave trade, avoidance of the use of some of the most inhumane implements of war such as landmines, nuclear, biological or chemical weapons, the rise of humanitarian interventions, and the protections realised of various human rights standards, constructivists have shown developments that, from the perspective of the Ancient Greeks or Romans, the great empires of Asia, the absolutist monarchs of Europe, and so on would surely seem revolutionary indeed, even if they are not always held to be so by all of our contemporaries.

This volume, in building upon the constructivist agenda, thus makes a claim that evidence of progressive moral change in world politics lies in the very raising of our ethical expectations which themselves can be demonstrated over time. These novel moral contexts themselves are constitutive of the critical position which in turn challenges the very ground upon which it exists, creating the conditions for its own ever-present elusiveness, and without whose force many of the novel moral dilemmas that vex our world would not exist. Critical theory despite its oft-scathingly sceptical scalpel is thus indispensable for moral progress, and on this score its scepticism can be different from a realist scepticism of morality bred of a denial of meaningful possibilities of historical change in the human condition.

All this is, it must be said, highly qualified by such woeful evidence that in so many other and basic dimensions of world politics things are no better if not worse. Yet the findings of this volume tell us that, armed with the historical sense characteristic of the constructivist tracking of moral change, the outrage in some circles at the killing of some 500 civilians in the NATO intervention in Kosovo in 1998 is at once itself a constitutive moral good for that which is to come if at the same time agonising to those who made the difficult choice of waging war with its attendant destructiveness to save even more lives in peril.

The critical conscience in application shares here in certain respects an affinity with the powerful Hobbesian insight of realism that it is relative gains that matter so often in human affairs. As so much of the time it does. But the very grounds upon which those assessments of relative gain and loss are made can and do shift, including at times and in some places to the betterment of humanity. And awareness of the relativity of the very grounds upon which moral assessment is possible in contemporary political life enjoins us to approaching criticism with a healthy generosity for those in positions to make choices whose ultimate impact we may only be able to assess in a historical sense, but for whom constructivism in the present can provide additional grounds for moral choice.

Index

Abizadeh, Arash, 258, 265
agency, 41, 49
agonism, 121–3
Ahtisaari, Martti, 178
Alfred, Taiaiake, 129, 132
amnesties, 30, 45, 94, 95, 295
anarchy, 31, 297
Anaya, James, 113, 128
Andreas, Peter, 34, 145
Angell, Norman, 59
Annan, Kofi, 165, 179
Arendt, Hannah, 194, 195
Aron, Raymond, 58
Association of South East Asian Nations
    (ASEAN), 273–9
    and Australia, 277
    and China, 277
    and identity, 266, 275, 276, 277–80
    and Indonesia, 277
    and Myanmar, 278
    norms, 274–5, 278, 296
    Treaty of Amity and Cooperation,
        274, 276
atrocities, 206, 222–3

Barnett, Michael, 42
Bass, Gary, 105
Beitz, Charles, 16, 65
Belkin, Aaron, 98, 104
Berger, Sandy, 185
Bolton, John, 24
Booth Walling, Carrie, 93, 94, 95, 107
Bosnia, 15, 46, 209, 211, 212, 286
Bossuyt, Marc, 179
Bush Administration, 24, 98, 99–101,
    175, 196

Cairns, Alan, 114
Campbell, David, 46–9, 262, 264

Carens, Joseph, 147–53, 154, 161–2
Carr, E. H., 53–6, 57
Chomsky, Noam, 28
civil wars, 95
Clinton Administration, 144, 180–1
Cochran, Molly, 65
communicative action, 12, 176, 193
community-building, interstate
    and democracy, 256, 259, 266, 267
    and identity, 254–61, 266, 267, 279,
        280, 292
consequentialism, 96–8, 209, 221
    and causal argument, 102
    and counterfactuals, 97–8, 107, 111
    see also counterfactuals
    and human rights trials, 85, 93, 97–8
    and torture, 98, 102
    rule-consequentialism, 91–2
    vs. principle-based arguments, 85–7, 91,
        95, 96, 98, 103
constitutive norms see norms, constitutive
constitutive theory, 13, 14, 16, 122, 123
constructivism, 197, 289, 290
    and community-building, 254–61, 279
    and consequentialism, 86, 93, 96, 97
    and counterfactuals, 18, 29, 68, 108,
        109, 110, 295, 301
    and empirical research, 13, 17–18, 23,
        219–20, 283, 286
    and ethical reasoning see ethical
        reasoning and constructivism
    and humanitarian intervention, 220–1
    and hypocrisy, 25, 29–31, 78, 167, 176,
        295, 302
    and normative theory see normative
        theory. and constructivism
    and political crisis, 50–2
    and rationalism, 20–1, 23, 25, 43, 172
    and recognition, 115–17

305

Cambridge Studies in International Relations